Handbook of Polyester Drug Delivery Systems

Handbook of Polyester Drug Delivery Systems

Editor

Jakub Sarto

scitus
academics

Handbook of Polyester Drug Delivery Systems
Edited by **Jakub Sarto**

ISBN: 978-1-68117-692-5
Library of Congress Control Number: 2016958859

SCITUS Academics LLC,
616, Corporate Way, Suite 2, 4766,
Valley Cottage, NY 10989

www.scitusacademics.com

Printed in United States of America on Acid Free Paper

Preface

Polymers that can degrade into biologically compatible components under physiologic conditions are advantageous for the preparation of drug delivery systems (DDS). The use of biodegradable polymers precludes the need for retrieval at the conclusion of the dosing regimen, thereby avoiding the potential complications associated with the use of non-degradable systems. Homopoly - mers and copolymers, obtained from glycolide, lactide and⍰⍰ -caprolactone and trimethylene carbonate (TMC), are the most commonly considered drug delivery vehicles. However, there are still few implantable drug delivery systems obtained from biodegradable polymers.

Attachment of drugs to high molecular weight polymers can significantly improve both tumor targeting and therapeutic efficacy due to the enhanced permeability and retention effect observed in tumor tissue. However, the commercial availability of well-defined water-soluble polymeric systems with narrow polydispersities that are biocompatible, nontoxic, and nonimmunogenic is rather limited. Even with the progress of novel materials, polyesters still endure at the controls of drug delivery technologies.

Handbook of Polyester Drug Delivery Systems provides comprehensive information of polyester drug delivery systems that covers a wide-ranging of materials design, manufacturing techniques, and applications.

Polyglycolide (PGA) was one of the first biodegradable synthetic polymers investigated for biomedical applications and was synthesized for the first time in 1954. In the beginning, it was not considered for biomedical applications because of its thermal and hydrolytic instability. However, the ability to degrade inside the human body became a great advantage.

Table of Contents

Chapter 1

Polymers in Drug Delivery

Apurva Srivastava, Tejaswita Yadav, Soumya Sharma, Anjali Nayak, Akanksha Kumari, Nidhi Mishra*

*Apurva Srivastava, Tejaswita Yadav, Soumya Sharma, Anjali Nayak, Akanksha Kumari, Nidhi Mishra**

Department of Applied Science, Indian Institute of Information Technology, Deoghat, Jhalwa, Allahabad, India

ABSTRACT

Polymers are being used extensively in drug delivery due to their surface and bulk properties. They are being used in drug formulations and in drug delivery devices. These drug delivery devices may be in the form of implants for controlled drug delivery. Polymers used in colloidal drug carrier systems, consisting of small particles, show great advantage in drug delivery systems because of optimized drug loading and releasing property. Polymeric nano particulate systems are available in wide variety and have established chemistry. Non toxic, biodegradable and biocompatible polymers are available. Some nano particulate polymeric systems possess ability to cross blood brain barrier. They offer protection against chemical degradation. Smart polymers are responsive to atmospheric stimulus like change in temperature; pressure, pH etc. thus are extremely beneficial for targeted drug delivery. Some polymeric systems conjugated with antibodies/specific biomarkers help in detecting molecular targets specifically in cancers. Surface coating with thiolated PEG, Silica-PEG improves water solubility and photo stability. Surface modification of drug carriers e.g. attachment with PEG or dextran to the lipid bilayer increases their blood circulation time. Polymer drug conjugates such as Zoladex, Lupron Depot, On Caspar PEG intron are used in treatment of prostate cancer and lymphoblastic leukemia. Polymeric Drug Delivery systems are being utilized for controlled drug delivery assuring patient compliance.

Keywords: Polymeric Drug Delivery, Biocompatible Polymers, Smart Polymers, Polymeric Implants, Polymeric Drug Formulations

1. INTRODUCTION

Polymers have become an integral part of drug delivery systems due to their improved pharmacokinetic properties. They have better circulation time than conventional small drug molecules thus target tissue more specifically. Tremendous use of polymers has been witnessed in the area of polymer therapeutics and Nano medicines [1] . Polymers in reservoir based drug delivery systems have shown immense progress in the form of hydrogels and liposomes. Diffusion based drug delivery systems (as shown in Figure 1) and solvent activated drug delivery systems are the other areas being explored for utilizing the polymers [1] . In diffusion based drug delivery systems drug is dissolved in a non-swell able system or a fully swollen matrix which do not decompose during their activation time. Solvent activated systems like hydrogels swell and release the drug when exposed to aqueous environment; this mechanism is depicted in Figure 2. They are hydrophilic in nature [2] . Biocompatible polymers offer a safe passage for drug delivery due to their well engineered molecular architecture according to the transitions in the underlying mechanisms of the biological process. Biodegradable polymers break due to cleavage of covalent bonds between them and bio erodible polymers bring about erosion of the polymer due to dissolution of linking chains without bringing about any change in chemical structure of the molecule [2] . Various drug release mechanisms can be studied comparatively in Figure 3. Polymers serving as drug carrier should be water soluble, nontoxic and non-immunogenic. They work passively in minimizing drug degradation and improving circulation time. Another important issue is the safe excretion of the drug [1] . If the polymer is non- degradable it should be ensured that it is not accumulated within the body and if it is degradable the broken components should be such that they lie below renal threshold level, non toxic and should not produce any immune response [1] . Polymers mimicking biological systems respond to external stimulus such change in pH or temperature and as a result their properties such as solubility, hydrophobic/ hydrophilic balance, release of biomolecule (drug molecule) and conformation are altered [1] .

Various Polymers Used in Drug Delivery

PLGA

In past two decades poly lactic-co-glycolic acid (PLGA) has been among the most attractive polymeric candidates used to fabricate devices for drug delivery and tissue engineering applications. PLGA is biocompatible and biodegradable, exhibits a wide range of erosion times, has tunable mechanical properties.

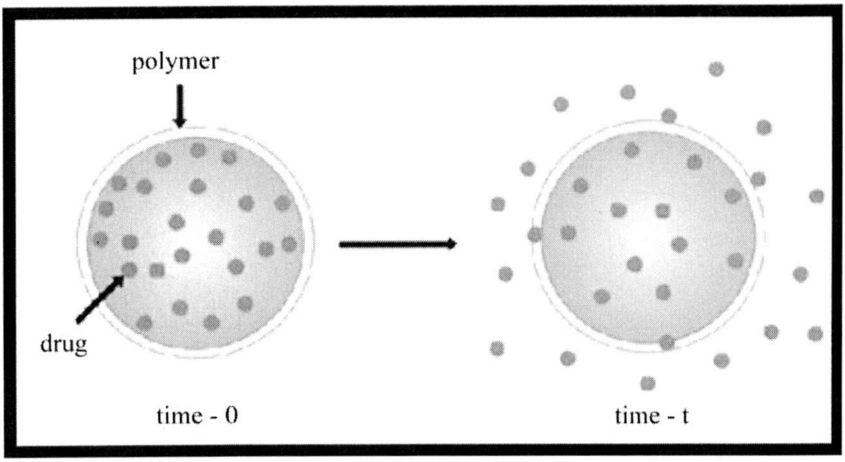

Figure 1. Diffusion based drug delivery system [6] .

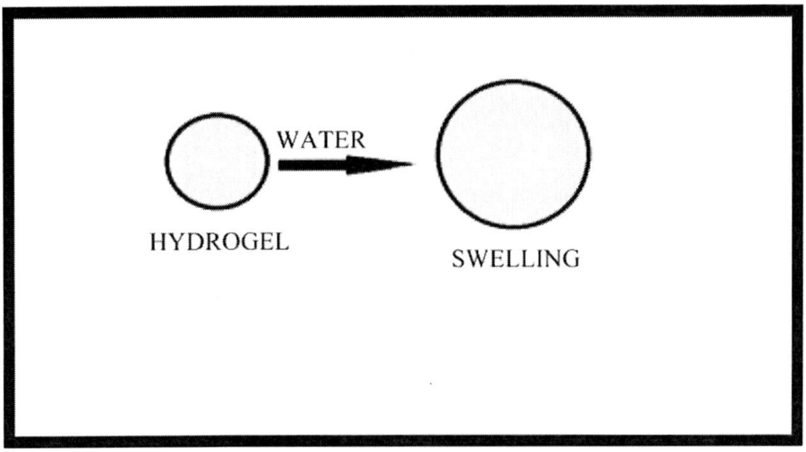

Figure 2. Hydrogel based drug delivery system.

Polyglycolic acid (PGA) is a biodegradable, thermoplastic polymer and the simplest linear, aliphatic polyester. It can be prepared starting from glycolic acid by means of polycondensation or ring-opening polymerization. PGA has been known since 1954 as a tough fiber-forming polymer.

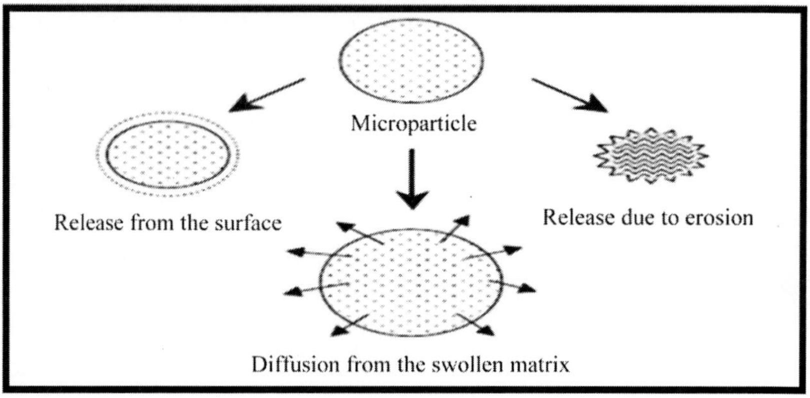

Figure 3. Various drug release mechanisms [5] .

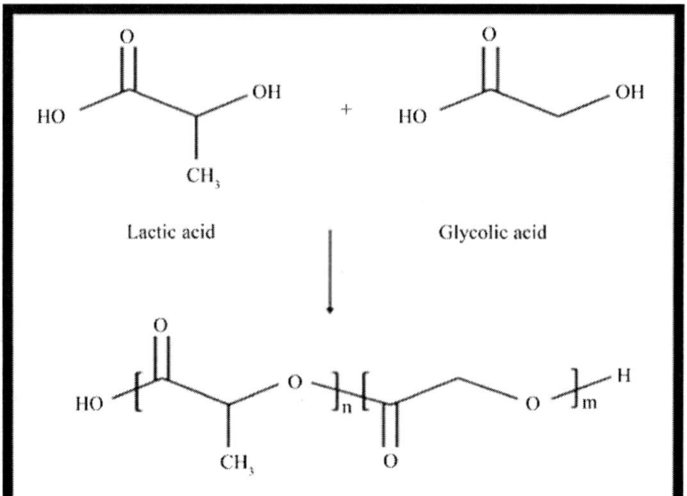

PGA(poly glycolic acid)

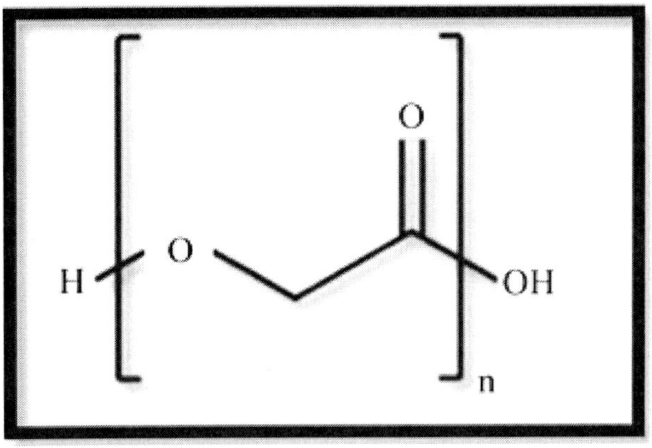

PGA(poly glycolic acid)

Poly-l-glutamic acid

Polyglutamic acid (PGA) is a polymer of the amino acid glutamic acid (GA). Gamma PGA is formed by bacterial fermentation.

Gamma PGA has a wide number of potential uses ranging from food and medicine to water treatment. It is widely being used as a drug delivery system in cancer treatment.

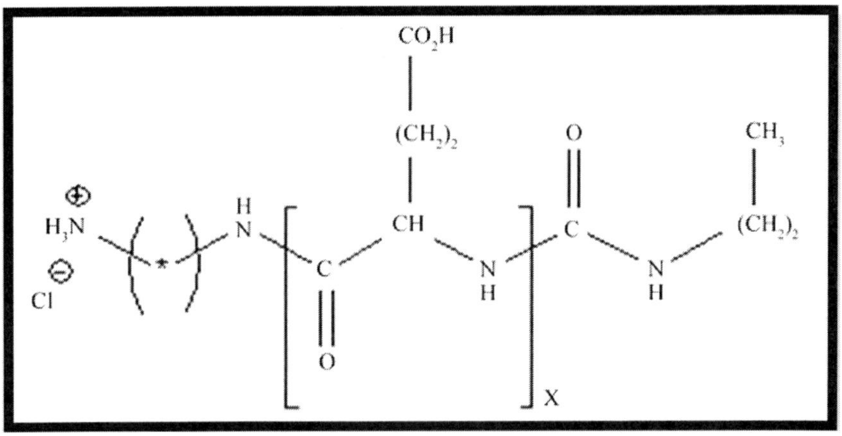

Poly-l-glutamic acid

Polylactic acid

It is a biodegradable thermoplastic aliphatic polyester derived from renewable resources, such as co r n starch (in the United States and Canada), tapioca roots, chips or starch (mostly in Asia), or sugarcane (in the rest of the world).

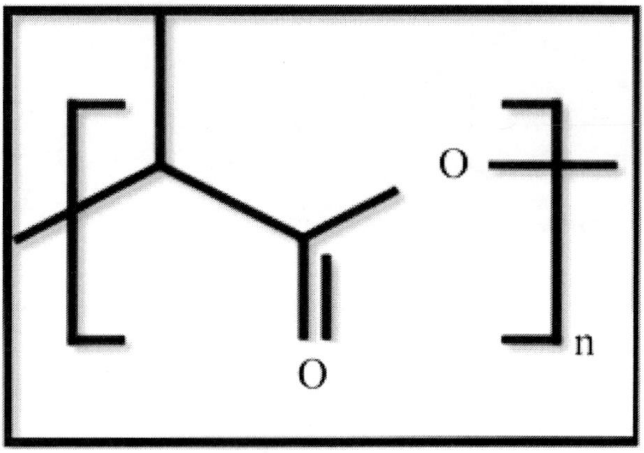

Poly lactic acid

PNIPAAm [Poly(N-isopropylacrylamide)]

It is a temperature responsive polymer that was first synthesized in the 1950s.It can be synthesized from N-isopropylacrylamide which is commercially available. It is synthesized via free radical polymerization and is readily functionalized making it useful in a variety of applications.

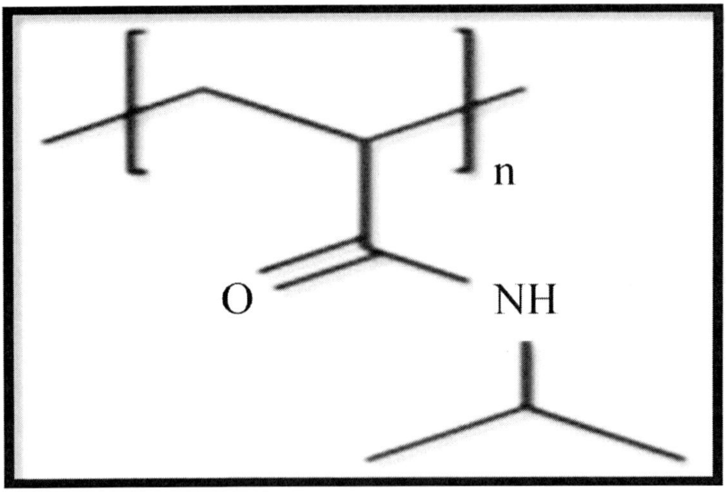

PNIPAAm [Poly(N-isopropylacrylamide)]

pHEMA[Poly 2-hydroxyethyl methacrylate]

It is a polymer that forms a hydrogel in water. Poly (hydroxyethyl methacrylate). It was invented by Drahoslav Lim and Otto Wichterle for biological use. Together they succeeded in preparing a cross-linking gel which absorbed up to 40% of water, exhibited suitable mechanical properties and was transparent. They patented this material in 1953.

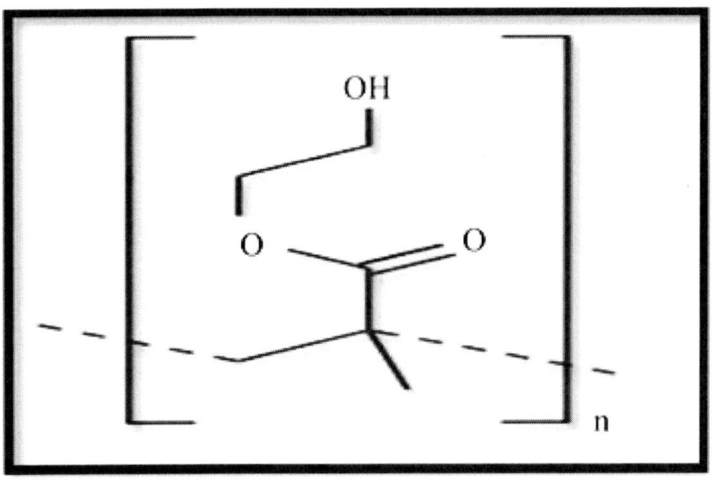

pHEMA[Poly 2-hydroxyethyl methacrylate]

PPy [Polypyrrole]

It is a type of organic polymer formed by polymerization of pyrrole. Polypyrroles are conductin polymers, related members being polythiophene, polyaniline, and polyacetylene. The Nobel Prize in Chemistry was awarded in 2000 for work on conductive polymers including polypyrrole. The first examples of polypyrroles were reported in 1963 by Weiss and coworkers.

PPy [Polypyrrole]

PAMAM [Poly (amidoamine)]

It is a class of dendrimer which is made of repetitively branched subunits of amide and amine functionality. PAMAM dendrimers, sometimes referred to by the trade name Starburst, have been extensively studied since their synthesis in 1985, and represent the most well-characterized dendrimer family as well as the first to be commercialized. Like other dendrimers, PAMAMs have a sphere-like shape overall, and are typified by an internal molecular architecture consisting of tree-like branching, with each outward "layer", or generation, containing exponentially more branching points

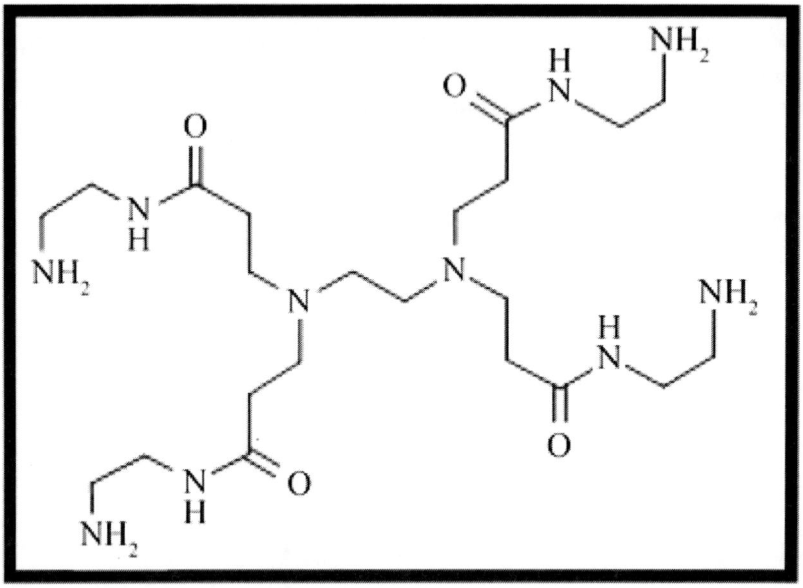

PAMAM [Poly (amidoamine)]

DEXTRAN

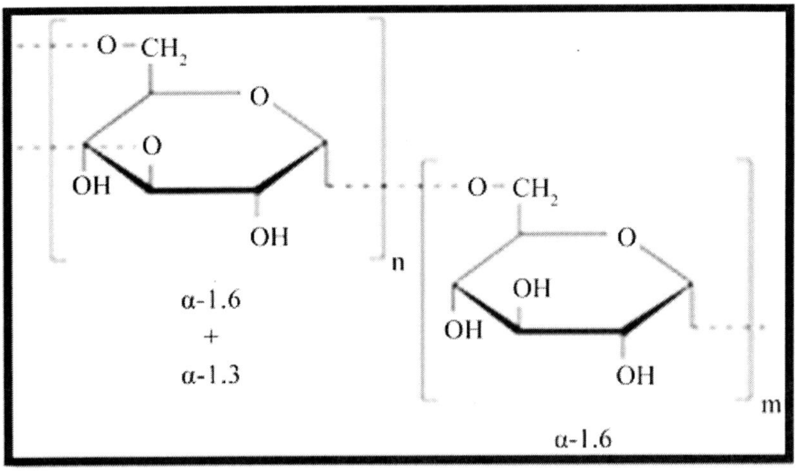

DEXTRAN

STRUCTURE: Dextran is can be defined by Leuconostoc mesenteroides (lactic-acid bacteria with the help of which dextran is synthesized using sucrose) which contains a glucan which is (16)-linked and has side chains that are attached to the backbone of 3-positions of glucose units. The straight chain consists of α-1,6 glycosidiclinkages between the molecules of glucose. The branching starts from α-1,3 linkages [1] .

DISCOVERY HISTORY—Allene Jeanes was a scientist at the USA's Northern Regional Research Lab in 1940. One day a company of soft drinks sent them one sample of their product which became thick and sticky. It was found out that this stickiness was due to the presence of a bacterium that converted the sugar present in the soda to dextran. This bacteria was assumed to have come from the dental plaque of one of the workers at the factory. The scientist then discovered that bacterium can be grown in the lab in a sugar solution which will make lots of dextran. This was then purified, dried and sent to korea which helped the soldiers to survive and helped them to heal.

2. CONVENTIONAL USE OF POLYMERS IN DRUG DELIVERY

Conventional drug delivery systems use doses of drugs in form of capsules, tablets which are formed by compression, coating and encapsulation of bioactive drug molecules [2] . Polymers play a versatile role in such conventional formulations; they serve as binding agents in capsules, film coating agents in tablets and viscosity enhancers in emulsions and suspensions. Some of the polymers given along with bioactive drug molecules include cellulose derivatives, poly (N-vinyl pyrrolidone) and poly (ethylene glycol) PEG.

3. SMART POLYMERS

Smart polymers are those which exhibit change depending upon the change in environmental conditions. In medicine stimuli responsive polymers show the change in their properties in response to the change in biological conditions [7] . The various stimuli may be temperature, pressure, pH, electric field, magnetic field, light, change in concentration, ionic strength, redox potential etc. [1] . Responses to such stimuli include dissolution, precipitation, swelling, change in conformation, and change in hydrophobic and hydrophilic properties. There is change in pH along the GI tract which is considered during design of oral drug delivery systems [8] . The cancerous tissue and swelled tissue show a drastic variation in pH. Polymer bound drugs are released in such tissues due to deprotonation/protonation of complex polymer structure under the conditions of altered pH. Poly (methacrylic acid) jointure with PEG, referred to as P (MAA-g-EG) has been used for oral protein delivery [3] . Similarly temperature responsive polymers bring about change in hydrophilicity/hydrophobicity of polymers enhancing their membrane permeation. PNIPAAm, is a thermoresponsive polymer and it is being thoroughly studied for its ability to undergo a negative temperature-dependent phase transition. Below its lower critical solution temperature , PNIPAAm exists as a hydrophilic coil, whereas above the LCST, PNIPAAm chains convert sharply into a hydrophobic globule [3] . This volume phase transition arises from the hydrophilic/hydrophobic balance of polymer chains, which is modulated by formation and disruption of electrostatic and hydrophobic interactions both within and among the molecules. Alteration in polymer properties can be used to:

- Adhere to the cell surface
- Break down cellular membrane and
- Release biologically active compound.

Stimuli responsive polymers can be broadly categorized into micelles, polyplexes and polymer drug conjugates.

4. POLYMERS IN NOVEL DRUG DELIVERY SYSTEMS

Chemical engineers, pharmacologists and scientists are using polymers for developing controlled drug release systems and sustained release formulations [3] . Novel drug delivery systems include micelles, dendrimers, liposomes, polymeric nanoparticles, cell ghosts, microcapsules and lipoproteins. Recent advancements in polymer based encapsulations and controlled drug release systems help in regulating drug administration by preventing under or overdosing [2] . These advanced systems play a promising role in improving bioavailability, minimizing side effects and other types of inconveniences caused to the patients. Studies need to be performed in the areas of surface and bulk properties of polymers as these properties govern their utilization various applications. Role of polymers in drug delivery will grow steeply in future to handle various unsolved issues. These issues may include site specific drug delivery in subcellular organelles, harnessing chemical, physical and biological properties efficiently to optimize drug administrations. Nano composites have shown to penetrate deep blood brain barriers [2] .

Through this paper we emphasize on the role of polymers in existing and novel drug delivery systems both as formulations and in devices, their advantages and limitations.

Advantages:

1. Polymers used in colloidal drug carrier systems, consisting of small particles, show great advantage in drug delivery systems because of optimized drug loading and releasing property [1] .

2. A polymer (natural or synthetic) is aggregated with a drug in controlled drug delivery and hence it gives a effective and controlled dose of dug avoiding overdose [1] .

3. The degradable polymers are ruptured into biologically suitable molecules that are assimilated and discarded from the body through normal route.

4. Reservoir based polymers is advantageous in various ways like it increase the solubility of incompetently soluble drugs and it lowers the antagonistic side effects of drugs [2] .

5. Magneto-optical polymer coated and targeted nanoparticles are multimodal (optical and MRI detection) while Quantum Dots are only optically detectable.

6. Some Quantum dots contain Cd which is known to be toxic to humans. Magneto/optical nanoparticles whether polymer coated or targeted

are composed of iron oxides/polymers which are known to be safe, therefore have great future.

7. Dextrans is the common polymer used for coating of iron oxide (plasma expander and affinity for iron) and are used for treatment of iron anaemias since 1960 and is still in operation.

8. In controlled release, some of the polymers like polyurethanes for elasticity, polysiloxanes for insulating ability are used for their intended non-biological physical properties.

9. Current polymers like Poly 2-hydroxy ethyl methacrylate, polyvinyl alcohol, Polyethylene glycol are used because of their inert characteristics and also they are free of leachable impurities [3] .

10. In Biodegradable polymers, the system is biocompatible and it will not show dose leaving behind at any time and the polymer will keep its properties until after exhaustion of the drug.

11. In hydrogels like drug delivery systems, the properties of polymer materials like PEG,(the easy polymer used to design hydrogels), can be managed to enhance features like size of the pore, which is used to manage rate of diffusion of the conveyer drugs. PEGylation was considered to minister many diseases like hepatits B and C, neutropaenia connected with cancer chemotherapy (PEG-GCSF) 28 and various types of cancers [PEG] glutaminase merged with a glutamine anti-metabolite 6-diazo-5-oxo-norleucine (DON].

12. Polymers span from their use as films or binders covering agents in tablets to flow managing agent in liquids or emulsions for improving drug security and to alter the delivering characteristics. Micelles due to its smaller size have a small circulation time in the body. Hence, it results in an advantage of entering in the tumour cells easily, because of the EPR effect.

13. Large importance of polymers in drug delivery has been noticed because they give a distinctive property which so far is not achieved by any of the materials [4] .

14. Polymers are preferable in the fact that they habitually show a pharmacokinetic profile as contrast to small-scale molecule drug with lengthy circulation time and they also have the ability for tissue targeting.

15. Gold nanoparticles are easy to prepare, good capability of co existence, and their capacity to attach with other biomolecules without changing their properties.

16. Biggest benefit of utilizing polymers in drug delivery is their control (manipulation) on their properties (e.g. linkers and molecular weight) to modify to the need of drug delivery systems.

17. Difficulties and challenges

18. Difficult to scale the process up and production in high amounts is expensive as microspheres are batch operations inherently [9] .

19. It is possible to reproduce the distribution of size of the microsphere particles but the result is not uniform generally and the standard deviation that we get is equal to half of the average size. This is quite common. The distribution of the size should be as narrow as possible since the rate at which the drug will be released as well as syringability depends on the size of the sphere directly.

20. With the presence of organic solvents and aqueous-organic interfaces on drugs that are encapsulated leads to adverse effects like eliminating the bioactivity of microspheres.

21. It is not an easy task to remove the organic solvents totally as mostly they are toxic and there should be a regulation on the concentration of residual solvents in the microsphere.

22. A crucial limitation in the development of biodegradable polymer microspheres for controlled-release drug delivery applications is the difficulty of specifically designing systems that exhibit precisely controlled release rates.

23. Core-shell microparticles are significantly more difficult to manufacture than solid microspheres.

24. Handling and fabricating the microspehre's architecture is not easy as its shell and core must be immiscible.

25. Hydrogels have an ability to rapidly swell with water which may lead to faster release of the loaded drug than desired followed by the degradation of the polymer [10] . There is a period of release of hours to days for hydrophilic drugs that are delivered usinghydrogel systems and it is considered to be much lesser than hydrophobic polymers based delivery systems like microspheres or nanospheres.

26. There is a probability of controllable drug administration through the electrical stimulation of conducting polymers. One of the examples of such a polymer is polyprrole (Ppy) [11] . But they are not used generally as they have limitations related to the choice of dopant and molecular weight of the delivered drug.

27. A hindrance to oral administration of some classes of drugs, mainly peptides and proteins is caused due to hepatic first-pass metabolism [12] and degradation by enzymes within the gastrointestinal tract.

28. There are limitations of the mucosal surface for drug delivery as well. The first limitation being the low flux associated with mucosal delivery and the second as well as a major limitation of the trans mucosal route of administration is at the site of absorption due to lack of dosage form retention.

29. The conventional chemotherapeutic agents (using Nano scale polymers as carriers) that we are aware of work by destroying the cells that rapidly divide. This leads to the damage of normal healthy cells that divide rapidly such as cells in the macrophages, bone marrow, digestive tract, and hair follicles due to chemotherapy.

30. There are some side effects in many chemotherapeutic agents that includes mucositis (lining of the digestive tract affected by inflammation), loss of hair (alopecia), myelosuppression (white blood cells production is reduced leading to immunosuppression),dysfunction of the organ, and even anemia or thrombocytopenia [13] . These side effects lead to some difficulties like they impose dose reduction, treatment delay, or the given therapy is not continuous.

31. The cell division may be efficiently stopped near the center in solid tumor cells because of which chemotherapeutic agents become insensitive to chemotherapy.

32. Most of the times chemotherapeutic agents cannot penetrate and reach the core of solid tumors because of which they fail to kill the cancerous cells.

33. Most of the traditional chemotherapeutic agents often get excreted from the circulation being engulfed by macrophages and therefore they remain in the circulation for a very short time and cannot interact with the cancerous cells that lead to ineffectiveness of the chemotherapy.

34. Collagen has a limitation that it causes immunogenic responses in some patients therefore is not fit for use. It has a variant, atelocollagen. Atelocollagen preparation involves removal of the telopeptide from collagen. It has also been used for decrease in the potential immunogenicity. Collagen also has a poor mechanical strength and it cannot easily develop reproducible release rates [14] .

35. Gelatin is cross-linked with glutaraldehyde while preparing the drug delivery system. This binds to and inactivates some protein drugs.

5. DRUG DELIVERY DEVICES-REQUIREMENTS OF POLYMERS IN DRUG DELIVERY SYSTEM

5.1. Dendrimers

Dendrimers are hyperbranched, monodisperse (uniform size particles in a dispersed phase), 3-D molecules of size 1 - 100 nm macromolecules. They solubilize by accommodating both hydrophobic and hydrophilic drugs. They consist of 3 structural components,

1. Central core (multifunctional)
2. Branched units
3. Surface groups

They are being used in the delivery of drugs and in other therapeutic agents at the specific sites. Drug can be encapsulated in the interior of the dendrimers (Figure 4) or can be adsorbed on and conjugated to the surface groups [2] . Sialylated dendrimers are inhibitors of the haemagglutinin of human erythrocytes by influenza viruses [2] .

The dendrimers are water soluble and on hydrolysis releases free 5FU. Such dendrimers are very useful carriers for anti-tumour drugs [2] . Dendrimers also act as carriers (vectors), in gene therapy [26] . PANAM (polyamidoamine) dendrimers are also being used as carrier of genetic material. The amino groups at the dendrimer end react with phosphate groups of nucleic acids and form transfection complexes. For preserving the activity of DNA during dehydration, the transfection complexes are encapsulated in hydrophilic polymer, and then they are deposited on or sandwiched between fast degradation rate functional polymer films to mediate gene transfection [2] .

5.2. Polymeric-Nano Particulate Systems

On the basis of method of preparation these can be Nanocapsules or Nanospheres.

Microspheres and microcapsules

Micro/Nano spheres are matrix system in which the drug is dispersed within the polymer throughout the body of particle. Micro/Nano capsules are vesicular systems in which cavity contains drug (oily/aqueous core) and is surrounded by a single ultrathin membrane of polymer (reservoir systems for controlled release of drug) as depicted in Figure 5.

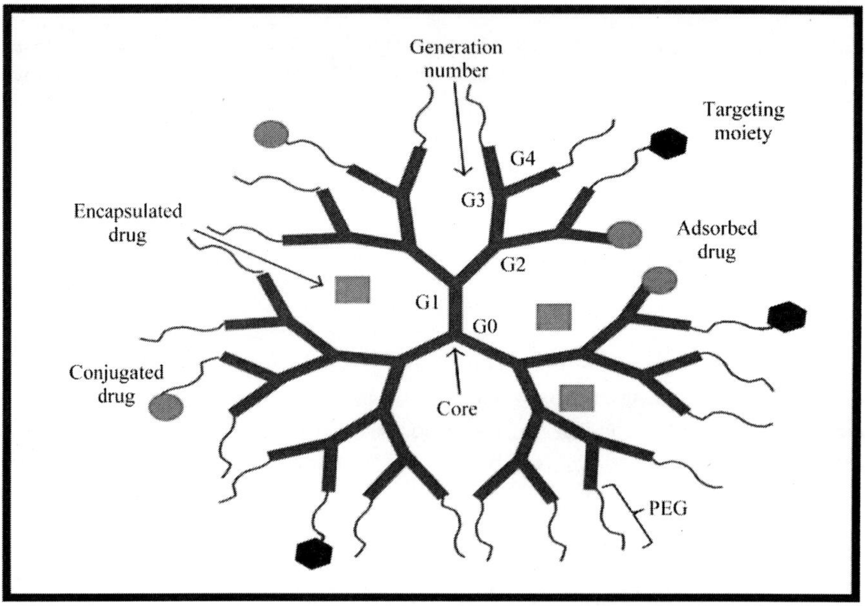

Figure 4. Simultaneous delivery of hydrophilic and hydrophobic drugs by encapsulation within hydrophobic cavities inside branching clefts, adsorption to the surface (ionic interaction) or direct covalent conjugation with functional groups on the surface [15] .

Drugs are released from the micro/nanosphere and micro/nanocapsule by diffusion through the polymer or by degradation of the polymer. Micro/nanospheres and micro/nanocapsules can be injected or taken orally. Lupron Depot is an injectable microsphere which is made up of lactic acid-glycolic acid copolymer and leuprolide acetate and entraps LHRH in order to treat prostate cancer [2] .

5.3. Hydrogel System

Hydrogels are cross-linked networks of water-soluble polymers and are three dimensional. Hydrogels can be made both from natural and synthetic polymers. They are highly absorbent. Biodegradable hydrogels are being used as carriers for controlled drug delivery because of their inertness for many drugs and their biocompatibility. Hydrogels have very high porosity due to which the release rate of drug crucially depends upon the diffusion coefficient of the drug molecules. The tailoring of porosity of hydrogel can be done by controlling the level of cross-linking, which in turn affect the rate of delivery of the entrapped drug particles. The ability of hydrogels to rapidly swell in aqueous medium, promote the rate of release of the entrapped drug and degradation of the polymer [2] . Drug delivery through hydrogels is explained in Figure 6.

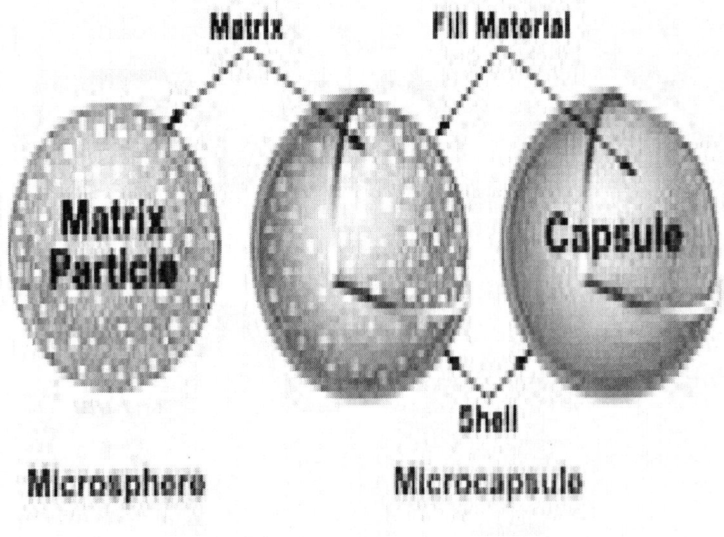

Figure 5. Microsphere and microcapsule [16] .

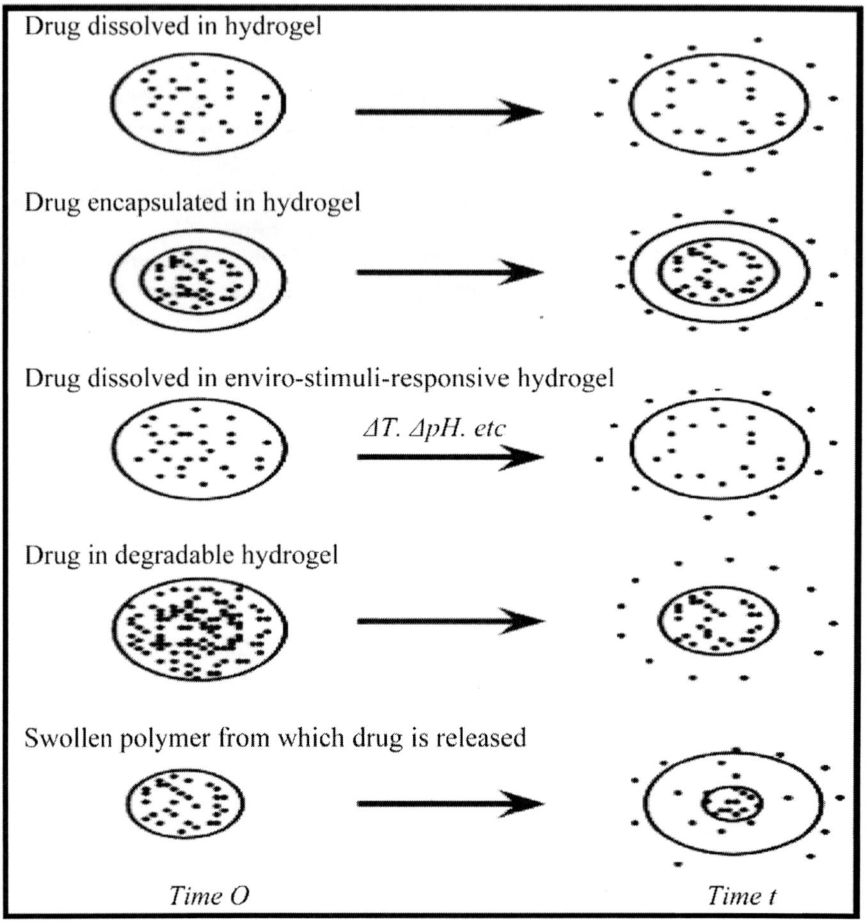

Figure 6. Hydrogel [17] .

5.4. Solid Lipid Nanoparticles

Solid lipid nanoparticles are carrier system in which melted lipid is dispersed in an aqueous surfactant by micro emulsification or high pressure homogenization. They are stable colloidal system with solid hydrophobic core. The core contains the dispersed or dissolved drugs. Surface coating with hydrophilic polymers like Polyethylene glycol (PEG) minimizes their uptake by liver and enhances bioavailability. It entraps both hydrophilic and lipophilic drugs. Solid lipids nanoparticles containing ibuprofen have been blended into dextran hydrogels are suitable for oral formulations.

5.5. Magnetic Nanoparticles (MNPS)

Drugs are bound with magnetic nanoparticles e.g. oxidized iron or magnetite (dextran coated) and are injected into blood stream. A high power magnetic field is generated outside the bodies which pull these drugs out of suspension and deliver the drug to a localized disease site. Coating these with dextran or PEG makes them stable water dispersible system.

5.6. Polymeric Micelles (PMS)

Polymeric micelles have a core shell structure formed by spontaneous self-assembly of individual amphiphilic di/tri block co-polymers (shown in Figure 7). They have both hydrophilic and hydrophobic regions which is good for drugs with poor solubility. Core is formed by hydrophobic block polymer blocks (poly-(propene glycol), poly-(caprolactone) etc.) and shell is made up of hydroplilic polymer (PEG).

5.7. Liposomes

Liposomes are vesicles composed of phospholipids and cholesterol. They are amphiphilic. The internal aqueous core is suited for delivery of hydrophilic drugs and the phospholipid bilayer encapsulates hydrophobic drugs. The modification of surface by attaching dextran or PEG to the phospholipid bilayer increases their circulation time in blood.

5.8. Implants

In most of the implants (a drug delivery system), a permeable polymeric membrane surrounds the core of solid drugs. The implants can be modified into different shapes, such as films, pellets, plugs, rods and discs [2] . The implants can be classified as non-biodegradable and biodegradable implants, depending on the polymer used. The polymers mostly used in the non-biodegradable implants include polyvinyl alcohol (PVA), silicone and ethylene vinyl acetate (EVA). Silicone can be customized to be both a permeable or impermeable layer depending on the grade and thickness of silicone used. Biodegradable systems can be made either by natural polymers (e.g. albumin, gelatin and collagen) or by synthetic polymers, such as Polylactic acid, olyglycolic acid and polylactic-co-glycolic acid (PLGA) copolymer [2] . In biodegradable implants, drug release occurs during polymer degradation. Implants approved by the FDA for eye: Retisert, Vitrasert, and Ozurdex [2] . Retisert, is an intraocular implant for the treatment of noninfectious uveitis that contains fluocinolone acetonide (FA). It is composed of an FA tablet containing PVA, magnesium stearate and microcrystalline cellulose. Vitrasert, is an intraocular implant that contains ganciclovir surrounded by PVA/EVA. It release drug in controlled fashion and is used to treat cytomegalovirus (CMV) retinitis. Ozurdex, is a biodegradable sustained release intravitreal implant that delivers dexamethasone to the vitreous humor and retina in order to treat macular edema and noninfectious posterior uveitis.

6. APPLICATION SCOPES OF POLYMERS IN DRUG DELIVEY SYSTEM

Polymers are playing important role in pharmaceuticals. They are used as binders in tablet, increases solubility of poorly soluble drugs, used as film coatings on drugs to disguise their taste and enhances their stability etc. Some polymers which are used in drugs are discussed below.

6.1. Biodegradable Polymers

Biodegradable polymers have either hydrolytically or proteolytically labile bond in their backbone to make it chemically degradable [18] . At present two types of biodegradable polymers exists: natural polymers and syn- thetic polymers. Collagen and gelatin are two natural biodegradable polymers that are mostly used in drugs [19] .

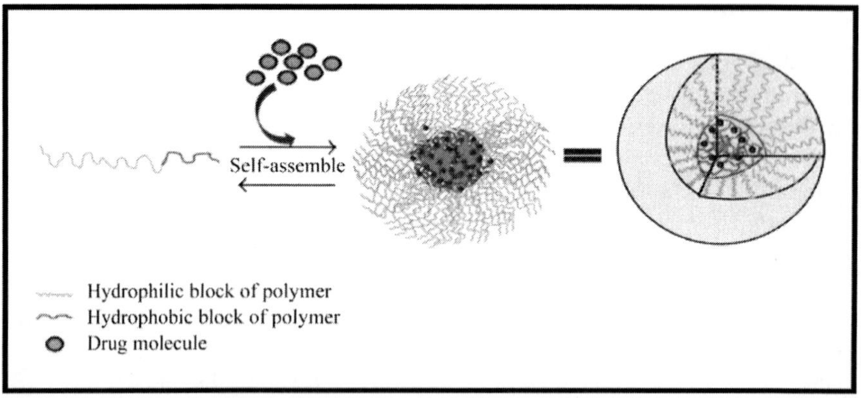

Figure 7. Drug loading of PMs by self-assembly of amphiphilic block copolymers in aque- ous solution [25] .

Collagens are biocompatible, non-toxic, can be easily isolated and purified in large quantities. Gelatin is a thermoreversible polymer [19] . Gelatin is easily available, have low antigen profile and have low binding affinity to drug molecules. All these properties make it suitable for drug delivery. Gelatin is cross-linked with glutaraldehyde to prepare it for drug delivery system. Synthetic biodegradable polymers are also present that include PLA, PLGA, PGA, poly(phosphazenes), poly(caprolactone), poly(anhydride), poly(phosphoesters), poly(cyanoacry- lates), poly(acrylic acid), poly(amides), poly(ortho esters), polyethylene glycol, and polyvinyl alcohol and poly (isobutylcynoacrylate), poly(ethylene oxide), and poly(paradioxane). Among these, PLGA, the copolymer of PLA and PGA are mostly used polymers in drug delivery [18] [23] . Large numbers of biodegradable synthetic polymers rely on the hydrolytic cleavage of ester bonds [18] .

- Polyethylene glycol: Polyethylene glycol is a hydrophilic polymer. Some features like low toxicity, lack of immunogenicity, antigenicity and excellent biocompatibility make it preffered polymer [18] . Its hydrophilic nature provides the protection to protein from any immune response.

- Polyesters: They have esters bond in the main chain [19] . Due to their biocompatible and biodegradable feature, PLA, PGA and their copolymer PLGA and poly (caprolactone) have been extensively used.

- Polyanhydrides: Polyanhydrides are biocompatible and bioabsorbable materials. They can be easily removed from the body because they can be degraded into their diacid counter parts in vivo [19] .

- Polyamides: They contain the repeated unit of amide group and are hydrophilic in nature. Due to the presence of amide groups and hydrogen bonds, they have good mechanical properties and show high polar behaviour [19] . They are used to deliver low molecular weight drugs.

- Polyorthoesters: A number of studies have been done on the use of polyorthoesters as encapsulating material for various drugs.

- Polyaprolctone: PCL have been taken into consideration to be used as implantable biomaterial because it has ester linkage that can be hydrolysed in physiological conditions. It can also be used for preparation of long term implantable devices because it degrades very slowly.

6.2. Non-Biodegradable Polymers

Non-biodegradable polymers are commonly used in diffusion-controlled system [20] . Due to non biodegradable polymers, there is no initial burst release in diffusion-controlled systems. The permeability and thickness of the polymer, the solubility and the release area of the drug determines the release kinetics of the drug form the diffusion controlled system. Silicone, cross-linked Polyvinyl Alcohol, and Ethyl Vinyl Acetate are mostly used in drug formulations. Silicones are used as permeable or impermeable material. The permeability or the impermeability of the silicone material is decided by the thickness and the grade used. EVA is impermeable to many drugs, thus, commonly used as a membrane to surround the drug core. There is reduction in the release area due to EVA membrane, thus reduces the drug release rate. PVA is used as controlled elution membrane in the release area because they are permeable to various lipophilic drugs. Alteration in the thickness layer helps in achieving the desired release kinetics.

6.3. Smart Polymers

They are high performance polymers which change according to the environment they are residing in. Even a small change in the environment can bring large changes in the polymer's properties. They can change the conformation, adhesiveness and water retention properties in response to pH change. They are used for production of hydrogels and other materials. These properties of smart polymers make them suitable for utilization in drug formulations. Some smart polymer are formed by the cross linking of the pH sensitive smart polymeric chains. The polymer composition, the nature of the ionizable groups, the hydrophilicity of the polymer backbone and the cross linking density decide the behaviour of the smart polymers. The cross linking density affects the permeability of the solute inversely, the higher the cross linking density, the lower the permeability [27] . Alginate gel beads are co-precipitated with a biologically active agent to form a sustained release gels. This gives the advantage of high loading of drugs while achieving better protein stability. LCST is a polymer, which have been tested in controlling drug delivery matrices. Copolymerisation of the NIPAAm with alkyl methacrylates maintains the temperature sensitivity because it increases its mechanical strength. There is reduction in the transportation of the bioactive molecules out of the polymers by surrounding the LCST with a thick layer of poly NIPAAm polymer [27] .

6.4. Gels

These are hydrophilic polymers and have linear structures used in topical drug delivery. Linear structure is formed by covalent bonding between monomer units such as amides, ester, orthoesters, and glycosidic bonds [19] . Topical polymers are mostly prepared by organic polymers such as carbomers [21] . They are prepared by natural or synthetic polymers. Polymers which are used in its preparation include the natural gums tragacanth, pectin, agar, alginic acid and carrageenan; semi synthetic materials such as hydroxyethyl cellulose, methylcellulose, carboxymethyl cellulose and hydroxypropylmethyl cellulose; and the synthetic polymer, carbopol [21] .

6.5. Polymers in Mucoadhesive Delivery

For developing the liquid ocular delivery system, the hydrophilic polymers should be used because they can be used as viscosity modifying or enhancing agent. Polysaccharides are frequently used in the ocular mucoadhesive delivery system. Its derivatives are hyaluronic acid, methyl cellulose, hydroxypropyl methylcellulose, gellan gum, chitosan, xanthan gum, carrageenan and guargum. Chitosan is a polysaccharide polymer. Its biodegradable, low toxic and biocompatible properties make it suitable for use in drug formulations [19] . Some other used non- ionic polymers for mucoadhesive properties are poloxamer, polyvinylpyrrolidone and polyvinyl alcohol [22] .

6.6. Polymer Drug Conjugate Used for Cancer Treatment

There is a physiological labile bond between the drug and the polymer. Paclitaxil [poly(L-glutamic acid)] is used as a chemotherapeutic agent to treat ovarian, breast and lung cancer. It has been studied in phase III trials. It has an ester linkage between its 2'hydroxyl group and the carboxylic acid of poly(L-glutamic acid) [19] . PEG and PAMAM are covalently conjugated with a chemotherapeutic drug Paclitaxil to increase its efficiency as an anticancer drug delivery system. Both increase its solubility. After an in-vitro study on human ovarian cancer cell it was found that PEG based conjugate reduced the activity of the paclitaxil by 25-fold and the PAMAM-G4 dendrimer increases its efficiency by more than 10 times [18] . 5-flourouracil drug causes cell death. Nagarwal et al. Synthesized an encapsulating agent nanospheres of PLA polymer for 5-flurouracil [18] .

7. CONCLUSION

Polymers are quite advantageous in drug delivery. This leads to enhanced drug delivery with better pharmacokinetics handling all safety parameters. Mechanism and time taken for drug delivery system for a particular tissue or cellular compartment still needs to be studied. In order to design the most suitable polymer therapeutic many queries including gene delivery p need to be answered as well. This leads to the synthesis of the smart polymer. In targeted drug delivery systems the site of action should be clearly known.

Biocompatible polymers provide better control over the toxicity of the samples; this leads to more reliable drug delivery and ensures patient's safety. Novel strategies like dendrimer synthesis and controlled polymerisation techniques are now well established. Development of therapeutics at nano level with novel improved features utilizing polymeric materials to address unresolved medical needs and to enable the application of personalized medicine is still required. Currently, the main goals in this field are to enable and support further research efforts towards translatable and competitive product development. With this as a goal, the rapid and successful translation of emerging polymeric drug delivery systems in the future can be derived by interdisciplinary and open-minded approach.

REFERENCES

1. Schmaljohann, D. (2006) Thermo and pH Responsive Polymers in Drug Delivery. Advanced Drug Delivery Reviews, 58, 1655-1670.

2. Liechty, W.B., et al. (2010) Polymers for Drug Delivery Systems. Annual Review of Chemical and Biomolecular Engineering, 1, 149-173.

3. Pallerlaand, S. and Prabhakar, B. (2013) Review on Polymers in Drug Delivery. American Journal of Pharmtech Research, 3, 901-917.

4. Biomaterials Tutorial. http://www.sigmaaldrich.com/material science/biomaterials/tutorial.html

5. Jawahar, N. and Meyyanathan, S.N. (2012) Polymeric Nanoparticles for Drug Delivery and Targeting: A Comprehensive Review. International Journal of Health and Allied Sciences, 1, 217-223.

6. Shaik, M.R., Korsapati, M. and Panati, D. (2012) Polymers in Controlled Drug Delivery Systems. International Journal of Pharma Sciences, 2, 112-116.

7. Yang, W. and Pierstorff, E. (2012) Reservoir Based Polymer Drug Delivery Systems. Journal of Laboratory Automation, 17, 50-58.

8. Srikanth, P., Raju, N., Raja, S.W. and Raj, S.B. (2013) A Review on Oral Controlled Drug Delivery. International Journal of Advanced Pharmaceutics, 3, 51-58.

9. Kim, K.K. and Pack, D.W. (2006) Microspheres for Drug Delivery. 19-50.

10. Hoare, T.R. and Kohane, D.S. (2008) Hydrogels in Drug Delivery: Progress and Challenges. Polymer, 49, 1993-2007.

11. George, P.M., LaVan, D.A., Burdick, J.A., Chen, C.-Y., Liang, E. and Langer, R. (2006) Electrically Controlled Drug Delivery from Biotin-Doped Conductive Polypyrrole. Advanced Materials, 18, 577-581.

12. Patel, V.F., Liu, F. and Brown, M.B. (2011) Advances in Oral Transmucosal Drug Delivery. Journal of Controlled Release, 153, 106-116.

13. Sutradhar, K.B. and Amin, M.L. (2014) Nanotechnology in Cancer Drug Delivery and Selective Targeting. ISRN Nanotechnology, 2014, Article ID: 939378.

14. Park, J.-H., Allen, M.G. and Prausnitz, M.R. (2005) Biodegradable Polymers Microneedles: Fabrication, Mechanics and Transdermal Drug Delivery. Journal of Controlled Release, 104, 51-66.

15. Lee, J.H. and Nan, A. (2012) Combination Drug Delivery Approaches in Metastatic Breast Cancer. Journal of Drug Delivery, 2012, Article ID: 915375.

16. Shanmugam, S., Reddy, J.S. and Vetrichelvan, T. Formulation and in Vitro Evaluation of 5-Fluorouracil Microcapsules by Using Different Methods of Micro Encapsulation. http://www.pharmatutor.org/articles/formulation-invitro-evaluation-5-fluorouracil-microcapsules-different-methods-microencapsulation

17. Peter, G., Emmanuelle, R. and Daniel, S. (2012) Hydrophilic Polymer Networks with Environmental Sensitivity (New Nani Formulations). http://www.flintbox.com/public/project/19743

18. Liechty, W.B., Kryscio, D.R., Slaughter, B.V. and Peppas, N.A. (2010) Polymers for Drug Delivery Systems. Annual Review of Chemical and Biomolecular Engineering, 1, 149-173.

19. Vilar, G., Tulla-Puche, J. and Albericio, F. (2012) Polymers and Drug Delivery Systems. Current Drug Delivery, 9, 367-394.

20. Yang, W.-W. and Pierstorff, E. (2012) Reservoir-Based Polymer Drug Delivery Systems. Journal of Laboratory Automation, 17, 50-58.

21. Bhowmik, D., Gopinath, H., Kumar, B.P., Duraivel, S. and Sampath Kumar, K.P. (2012) Recent Advances in Novel Topical Drug Delivery System. The Pharma Innovation, 1, 12-31.

22. Yousef, J. and Sanaz, H. (2012) Novel Drug Delivery Systems for Modulation of Gastrointestinal Transit Time. In: Sezer, A.D., Ed., Recent Advances in Novel Drug Carrier Systems, InTech Publisher, Rijeka.

23. Martinho, N., Damgé, C. and Reis, C.P. (2011) Recent Advances in Drug Delivery Systems. Journal of Biomaterials and Nanobiotechnology, 2, 510-526.

24. Ahmed, E.M. (2013) Hydrogel: Preparation, Characterization, and Applications: A Review. Journal of Advanced Research, 6, 105-121.

25. Xu, W., Ling, P.X., and Zhang, T.M. (2013) Polymeric Micelles, a Promising Drug Delivery System to Enhance Bioavailability of Poorly Water-Soluble Drugs. Journal of Drug Delivery, 2013, Article ID: 340315.

26. Madaan, K., Kumar, S., Poonia, N., Lather, V. and Pandita, D. (2014) Dendrimers in Drug Delivery and Targeting: Drug-Dendrimer Interactions and Toxicity Issues. Journal of Pharmacy and Bioallied Sciences, 6, 139-150.

27. Mahajan, A. and Aggarwal, G. (2011) Smart Polymers: Innovations in Novel Drug Delivery. International Journal of Drug Development & Research, 3, 16-30.

Chapter 2

Polyester Dendrimers: Smart Carriers for Drug Delivery

Jean-d'Amour K. Twibanire [1,2,*] and T. Bruce Grindley [1,*]

[1]*Department of Chemistry, Dalhousie University, 6274 Coburg Road, P.O. Box 15000, Halifax, NS B3H 4R2, Canada*

[2]*CanAm Bioresearch Inc., Winnipeg, MB R3T 0P4, Canada*

ABSTRACT

Polyester dendrimers have been shown to be outstanding candidates for biomedical applications. Compared to traditional polymeric drug vehicles, these biodegradable dendrimers show excellent advantages especially as drug delivery systems because they are non-toxic. Here, advances on polyester dendrimers as smart carriers for drug delivery applications have been surveyed. Both covalent and non-covalent incorporation of drugs are discussed.

Keywords: polyester dendrimers; biocompatibility; drug delivery; smart carriers; drug delivery pathways; polymersomes

1. INTRODUCTION

The concept of using high molecular weight polymeric systems as potential drug delivery systems was initially introduced by Ringsdorf [1,2] and Kopeček [3,4]. In chemotherapy, the use of high molecular weight systems results in enhanced targeting of tumor tissue and improved efficiency of the treatment [5,6,7], an effect explained in part by the enhanced permeability and retention (EPR) phenomenon observed in tumor tissues [8,9,10]. The EPR effect is the property by which certain sizes of molecules such as liposomes and macromolecular drugs tend to accumulate in tumor tissues much more than they do in normal tissues [8,9,10,11]. A good drug molecule must selectively target and bind the receptor microenvironment to ultimately elicit an appropriate biological response. A large number of newly developed drug molecules however, are rejected by the pharmaceutical industry and will never benefit a patient because of poor bioavailability caused by low water solubility and/or poor cell membrane permeability. In addition, a good number of launched drugs exhibit suboptimal performance for the same reasons. Consequently, efficient ways of enhancing bioavailability and biocompatibility of new drugs are of particular interest. Dendrimers offer a particularly attractive alternative as drug delivery systems as they offer a high drug-loading capacity either by encapsulation or conjugation [12,13,14,15]. Encapsulation and conjugation of drugs with dendrimers have shown immense utility for delivery of hydrophobic drugs (enhancing solubility) [16,17], labile drugs (sheltering from harsh surroundings), and small molecule drugs (avoiding fast elimination and exposure to healthy tissues). Interest in the use of dendrimers for drug delivery and medicinal applications has mushroomed in the last few years [18,19,20,21,22,23,24,25,26,27,28,29,30,31,32,33,34,35,36,37,38,39,40,41,42,43,44,45,46,47,48,49] and numerous reviews have appeared on dendrimers in drug delivery and biomedical applications [50,51,52,53,54,55].

Certain unique dendritic features clearly set these compounds apart as special and optimum nanoscale carriers in medical applications. These unique features include polyvalency, high degree of branching, high solubility, globular architecture and most importantly, their well-defined architectures (monodispersity) which translate into a more consistent well-defined polymer that brings better reproducibility of results. The success of dendritic nanoparticles for drug delivery applications largely depends on the ability of scientists to design smart carriers with the ability to overcome drug leakage, immunogenicity, cytotoxicity, reticuloendothelial system uptake, and hemolytic toxicity among other shortcomings. One strategy to overcome these shortcomings is to use polyester dendrimers which have been shown to be non-toxic and biocompatible [19,56,57,58,59,60]. By attaching a drug to a suitable carrier, it is possible to enhance its aqueous solubility, increase its circulation half-life, target certain tissues, improve drug transit across biological barriers, and slow drug metabolism [61,62,63,64,65,66]. Optimization of these features to maximize drug bioavailability to diseased tissues while minimizing drug exposure to healthy tissues, results in improved therapeutic efficacy.

Polyester dendrimers have been shown to be associated with various novel applications and are particularly promising as drug carriers. The use of biodegradable dendrimers emerged as a strategy to produce desirable large molecular weight carriers that achieve high accumulation and retention in diseased tissues, but allow rapid and safe elimination of non-toxic dendrimer fragments into the urine.

2. DENDRIMERS AND COMMON DRUG DELIVERY PATHWAYS

2.1. Oral Drug Delivery

Amongst the many routes for drug delivery, the oral route is preferred [18,67,68,69,70], probably because of patience preference. For many existing and new drugs such as therapeutic peptides, peptidomimetics, oligonucleotides and others, oral bioavailability is in many cases below acceptable levels. To overcome this problem and to guarantee a sufficient high oral uptake, the use of efficient oral drug delivery systems is important. Transport of a dendrimer through the epithelial layer of the gastrointestinal tract depends upon the dendrimer's characteristics. Housing a drug inside a soluble dendrimer host not only solubilizes it but also allows it to bypass using a transporter protein for movement from the intestinal tract into the blood. Often drugs are not compatible with use of the protein transporter system that is designed to pass nutrients. The oral route using dendrimers looks very promising especially with anticancer and antihypertensive drugs [23,71,72,73,74,75].

2.2. Transdermal Drug Delivery

The human skin is a readily accessible surface for drug delivery. Transdermal drug delivery can be used as an alternative route of administration to accommodate patients who cannot tolerate oral dosage forms. It is also of great advantage in patients who are nauseated or unconscious. Drugs that cause gastrointestinal upset can be good candidates for transdermal delivery because this method avoids direct effects on internal organs such as the stomach and intestine. In addition, drugs that are degraded by the enzymes and acids in the gastrointestinal system may also be good targets. However, many new drugs are hydrophobic causing low water-solubility that results in insufficient levels of drug delivered into cells. Water soluble and biocompatible dendritic species are known to improve drug solubility and plasma circulation time via transdermal formulations and to deliver drugs quickly and effectively [72,76,77,78,79,80,81]. In this regard, dendrimers have been shown to be useful as transdermal drug delivery systems for various types of medications [77,80,81], including anticancer, antiviral, nonsteroidal anti-inflammatory and antihypertensive drugs.

2.3. Ocular Drug Delivery

Ocular drug delivery has been a major challenge to pharmacologists and drug delivery researchers due to the eye's unique anatomy and physiology [82]. The most common route of administration for the treatment of various ocular diseases is the topical application of drugs to the eye. Because of drainage of the excess fluid via the nasolacrimal duct and elimination by tear turnover, the intraocular bioavailability of topically administered drugs is poor. Research advances have shown that the use of drug delivery systems such dendrimers can help to overcome the many disadvantages and complications associated with ocular drug delivery [83,84].

2.4. Drug Delivery by Injection

Drug administration by injection encompasses intramuscular (IM), intravenous (IV), and subcutaneous (SC) drug administrations. Medication delivered via injection often acts rapidly and has essentially high bioavailability. Injections are useful for drugs that are poorly absorbed or ineffective when given orally. Injection is also an excellent way to administer drugs to patients who are nauseated or unconscious. However, because the drug is delivered to the site of action extremely rapidly with IV injection, there is a risk of overdose if the dose has been calculated incorrectly, and there is an increased risk of side effects if the drug is administered too rapidly. Numerous reports of IV administered dendrimer-drug complexes have appeared [85,86,87,88,89]. For example, 2'-(benzo[1,2-c] 1,2,5-oxadiazol-5(6)-yl(N_1-oxide) methylidene)-1-methoxy methane hydrazide presents antichagasic activity but has low water solubility. Guest–host interactions with a dendrimer result in good drug solubilization. These interactions can be controlled by varying the solution pH, allowing drug deliverance [85].

3. COVALENT AND NON-COVALENT DENDRIMER-DRUG SYSTEMS

Polymer therapeutics includes polymeric drugs, polymer-drug conjugates, polymer-protein conjugates, polymer-DNA complexes, and polymeric micelles to which drugs are covalently linked and/or physically entrapped

[90,91,92,93,94,95]. Conventionally, nanoscale therapeutics is derived from polymer-drug conjugates, in which a drug is covalently bound through cleavable linkages such as the pH sensitive *cis*-aconityl, hydrazine, and acetal linkages [56,90,91,92,93,94,95,96,97,98]. On the other hand, supramolecular drug delivery systems based on block copolymer micelles or dendritic systems have shown great promise and utility for tumor targeting and drug delivery [8,19,99,100,101,102,103]. Both covalent and non-covalent systems can utilize the enhanced permeability and retention (EPR) phenomenon [9,10,11]. Major disadvantages of drug delivery systems based on non-covalent entrapment of drugs into core-shell architectures are the lack of kinetic stability of polymer micelles that are susceptible to infinite dilution arising from their administration and poor drug loading capacity. Nevertheless, reports of simple yet effective and versatile approaches that employ non-covalent interactions for mediating the formation of macromolecular assemblies to encapsulate, transport, and release therapeutic agents have appeared [104,105,106,107,108].

To achieve positive results in the encapsulation and release of a guest drug, suitable dendrimer-guest partners must be carefully selected. For example, the complexation of opposite charged PEG block copolymers with cationic amino methacrylates or anionic styrene sulfonates has been explored [109]. Polymer-drug partners with specific acid-base interactions between hydrophobic drug molecules (R_1–COOH) and polymer segments (NH_2–R_2) improved the drug loading capacity [110]. Hydrogen bonding formation between the guest drug and the host polymer has also been explored [111,112,113,114,115,116].

Another innovative way to deliver a drug conjugated to or adhering to a dendrimer is to further conjugate the dendrimer to aptamers [117,118,119,120]. The aptamers can be selected to bind to specific cell types, such as cancer or other disease cells with different cell-surface biomarkers. For example, carboxy-coated PAMAM dendrimers were conjugated to amino groups of the aptamers by forming activated esters from the carboxy groups [117,118,121]. Such an approach could easily be adapted to carboxy-coated polyester dendrimers that would have the advantage of having low toxicity and biocompatibility associated with polyester dendrimers.

4. POLYESTER DENDRIMERS

4.1. Attractive Features of Polyester Dendrimers for Drug Delivery Applications

Improving the therapeutic index of drugs is a major incentive for innovation in many therapeutic areas such as cancer, inflammatory and other infectious diseases like HIV. Polyester dendrimers constitute an attractive class of compounds because they are biodegradable and biocompatible [61]. In addition, whenever they have been tested, they have been found to have low toxicity [56,122,123], unlike other dendrimers [124]; this is extremely important if these molecules are to be used as frameworks for drug delivery and other biological applications in biological systems. Like other dendrimers in general, polyester dendrimers have interior void spaces which may be used to encapsulate small molecule drugs, metals, or imaging moieties. Not only does encapsulation increase the half-life of the drug due to controlled release, it also reduces the drug toxicity due to lessened drug exposure to healthy tissues en route to the receptor microenvironment or diseased tissues. Because a prolonged therapeutic level can be achieved due to a sustained drug release [125], the frequency of dosing can be reduced which would in turn contribute to improved compliance by the patient. The surface hydroxyl groups of polyester dendrimers are responsible for their high solubility and miscibility and for their high reactivity. These highly reactive surfaces can be modified to optimize bio-distribution, receptor mediated targeting, and/ or controlled release of encapsulated active moieties or attached drugs [57]. In addition, polyester dendrimers have labile ester functionalities which are steadily hydrolyzed *in vivo* to release entrapped or covalently attached drugs. Higher generation polyester dendrimers can easily be prepared with facile synthesis of other dendrimers and a variety of methods have been reported for ester bond formation [126,127,128,129,130,131,132,133,134,135]. The synthesis of polyester dendrimers in general [135] and those derived from bis-2,2-hydroxymethylpropanoic acid (bis-HMPA) in particular [58] have been reviewed. A recent attractive strategy is the use of uronium-based coupling agents, TBTU [136], TATU [137], and COMU [138] to promote ester bond formation between carboxylic acid dendrons and polyalcoholic cores [139]. This regioselective esterification of primary hydroxyls in the presence of non-protected secondary or tertiary hydroxyls (Grindley-Twibanire esterification) is efficient for the *O*-6 acylation on carbohydrates and it has recently been applied in the divergent construction of a second-generation mixed polyester dendrimer [139], the preparation of Lyme disease glycolipid antigens [140], and the direct synthesis of maradolipids and other trehalose 6-monoesters and 6,6′-diesters [141]. The reduction in synthetic steps means less cost for the final product and in addition, the elimination of protection/deprotection steps leads to minimized chemical wastes, which is important as we move towards a greener chemistry and a greener world.

4.2. Advances in Polyester Dendrimers for Drug Delivery Applications

Fréchet and coworkers have contributed tremendously to the area of polyester dendrimers [56,57,96,97,126,142,143,144,145,146,147]. In early 2000, this group prepared and evaluated various dendritic architectures composed of a polyester dendritic scaffold based on the monomer unit bis-HMPA for their suitability as drug carriers both*in vitro* and *in vivo* [63]. The systems were found to be water soluble and nontoxic. In addition, the potent anticancer drug, doxorubicin (DOX), was covalently bound via a hydrazine linkage to a high molecular weight 3-arm poly(ethylene oxide)-dendrimer hybrid as shown in Figure 1. The highly potent anticancer agent doxorubicin is a fluorescent compound, and this provides a convenient analytical tool for monitoring the biodistribution of the polymer-DOX conjugate. The polymer-DOX conjugate showed no significant accumulation in any vital organ including the liver, heart, and lungs. This is a significantly different distribution pattern than is observed for the free drug, which partitions into a variety of organs such as the liver and heart [148].

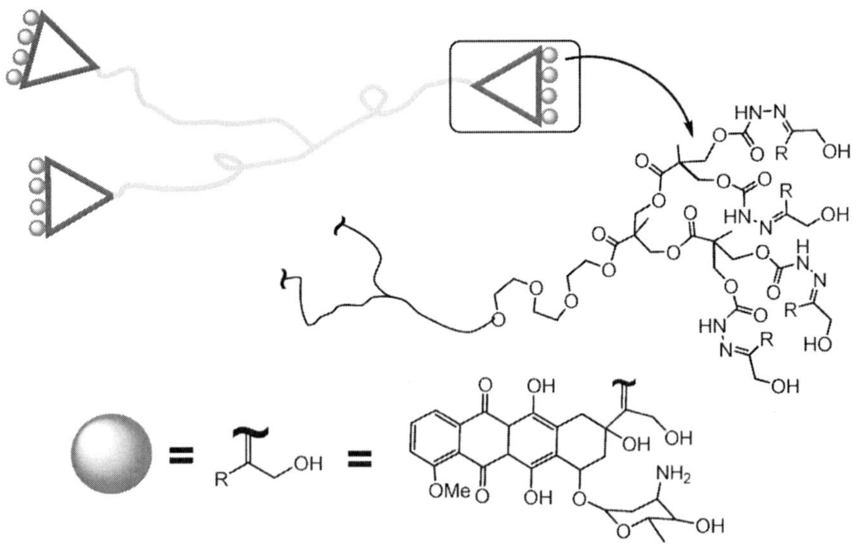

Figure 1. Doxorubicin-functionalized model polyester dendrimer for therapeutic studies.

The polymer-DOX conjugate had a circulation half-life of 72 min, which is significantly longer than the half-life of the free doxorubicin (~8 min). This is an indication that the dendritic form of the carrier favourably enhanced the pharmacokinetics and the biodistribution of the drug. The results of the cytotoxicity of drug-polymer conjugate *in vitro*suggested that polyester dendrimer-based systems do not exhibit a significant toxic effect and the drug release rates from the hydrazine linker encouraged further evaluation of the model compound as a polymeric drug carrier. *In vitro* evaluation of the conjugate was performed in various cancer cell lines to compare the cytotoxic activity of the bound drug in relation to the free drug. The three cell lines examined exhibited a range of sensitivity to the free doxorubicin, from 0.025 μg/mL for B16F10 to 0.62 μg/mL for the MDA-MB-435 cell lines. In all three cell lines examined, the free drug was considerably more potent than the drug-polymer conjugate; 6-fold in the B16F10 cells, 50-fold in the MDA-MB-231, and 9-fold in the MDA-MB-435 cells. In summary, the dendrimer-DOX system shows no accumulation in any vital organ examined, including the liver, heart, and lungs. The results suggest that this polyester dendritic backbone is a highly water soluble, nontoxic, and biocompatible polymer [63].

After contradictory reports [63,149], the hydrolysis kinetics of low molecular weight and polymeric doxorubicin hydrazone carboxylates were reinvestigated [150]. It is now believed that DOX toxicity was likely not observed due to the specific linkage to DOX, which allowed intramolecular cyclization to produce an inactive version of DOX [150].

The system evaluated here had a molecular weight of 22,550 g/mol prior to functionalization. To further increase the circulation half-life to effectively exploit the EPR phenomenon [8,9,10], higher molecular weight systems were prepared and evaluated [13,56]. The biological evaluation of a library of eight polyester dendrimer-poly(ethylene oxide) (PEO) bow-tie hybrids of the form shown in Figure 2 was described [56]. Evaluated polymers were designed to include a range of MWs (from 20,000 to 160,000) and architectures with the number of PEO arms ranging from two to eight. For these bow-tie dendrimers, the number of PEO arms can be adjusted to provide polymers of different architectures by using dendrons of different generations. By tuning the combination of the number of PEO arms and their length, a variety of MWs can be prepared. Accordingly, a small library of eight polymers was prepared where the PEO functionalized dendron was varied from the first to the third generation (two to eight arms). PEO arms with MWs of 5000–20,000 were used to prepare polymers with MWs ranging from 20,000 to 160,000 since one goal here was to prepare long-circulating drug carriers.

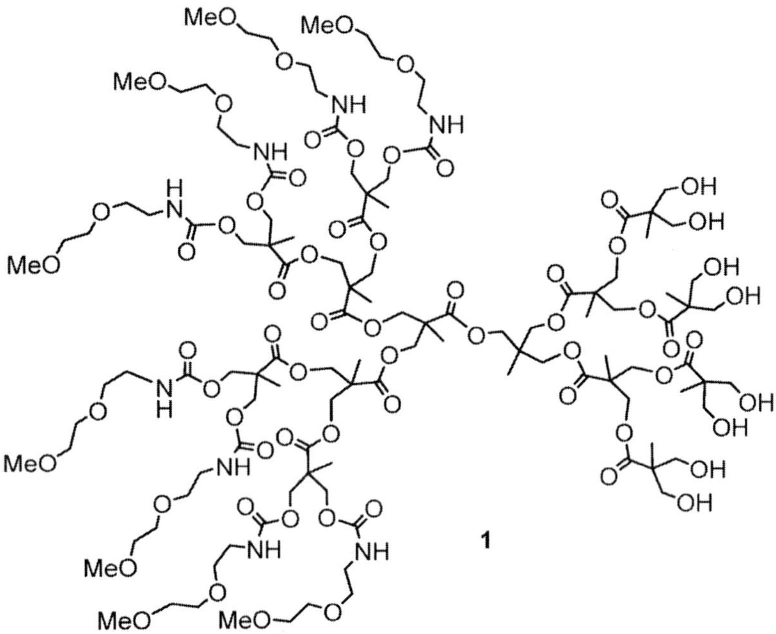

1

Figure 2. Fréchet's polyester dendrimer-[poly(ethylene oxide)]. A "Bow-tie" type dendrimer.

In order to track the polymers *in vivo*, some dendrimer hydroxyl groups of each bow-tie polymer were statistically converted to tyramine carbamates as shown in Scheme 1, by activation of the polymers with a limited amount of 4-nitrophenyl chloroformate, followed by excess tyramine [56]. After investigating the *in vitro* cytotoxicity of the polymers, the *in vitro* biodegradability, the biodistribution, and the biodistribution in tumored mice, the following observations and conclusions were made. *In vitro* experiments revealed that the polymers were nontoxic to cells and were degraded to lower MW species at pH 7.4 and pH 5.0. Biodistribution studies with ^{125}I-radiolabeled polymers showed that all carriers with MWs of 40,000 and greater had plasma circulation times in excess of 24 h, while those with lower MWs were cleared more rapidly with significant quantities excreted in the urine. Comparison of the renal clearances for the four-arm *versus* eight-arm polymers indicated that the more branched polymers were excreted more slowly into the urine, a result attributed to their decreased flexibility. Polymers with "two arms" which have essentially linear architectures were rapidly taken up by the liver. The biodistribution results of two long-circulating high MW polymers in mice bearing subcutaneous B16F10 tumors indicated high levels of tumor accumulation.

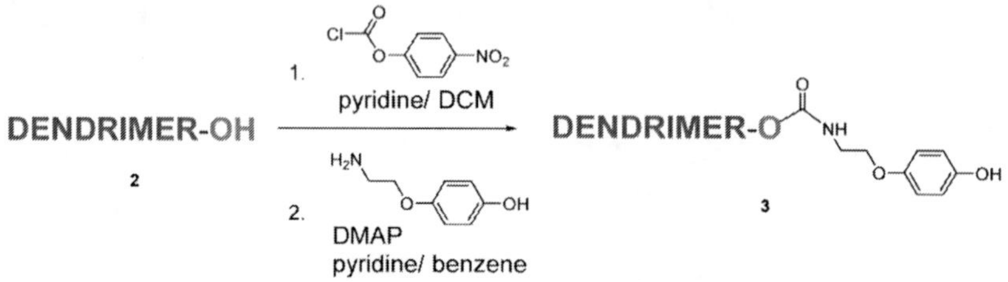

Scheme 1. Functionalzation of bow-tie dendrimers for biodistribution studies.

Overall, the attractive features of this type of branched carriers including degradability, lack of toxicity, long circulation half-lives, and high levels of tumor accumulation make them very promising for therapeutic applications [56]. In addition, because a long blood circulation time is a prerequisite for tumor targeting using the EPR effect [9,151], it is evident that bow ties with molecular masses >40 kDa are acceptable candidates for passive tumor targeting. Accordingly, this type of systems was further evaluated (in mice with cancerous tumors) as drug delivery systems with the highly potent doxorubicin as the attached drug [57].

For this therapeutic study in mice with cancerous tumors, a [G-3]-$(PEO_{5k})_8$-[G-4]-$(OH)_{16}$ bow tie with a molecular mass of 45 kDa was used because it is more branched and contains less PEO per dendron than the other prepared bow ties [57]. Highly branched bow ties exhibit good steric protection of their payloads, whereas bow ties containing just enough PEO to prevent renal clearance have higher theoretical drug-loading capacities [56,57]. In order to achieve a drug loading comparable to polymers or liposomes that have been previously used to deliver DOX (≈10 wt%) [152,153], the bow tie with 16 hydroxyl groups provided a sufficient drug payload given that the yield of the hydrazone formation with polyester dendrimers is roughly 50% [13,63]. The attachment of doxorubicin via pH-sensitive hydrazone linkages is shown in Scheme 2 [57,63].

Several detailed experiments were conducted on the dendrimer-DOX conjugate including cytotoxicity in cell culture, biodistribution in tumor-implanted mice, and chemotherapy experiments on C-26 colon carcinoma [57]. This tumor model was chosen because it represents a challenging cancer cell line that is relatively sensitive to free DOX in cell culture but not*in vivo*, a finding that has been attributed to the inability of the drug to attain sufficient intra-tumor concentrations [154]. Additionally, a positive control experiment (using Doxil) was also conducted in order to evaluate the effectiveness of dendrimer-DOX in comparison to the FDA-approved doxorubicin carrier Doxil.

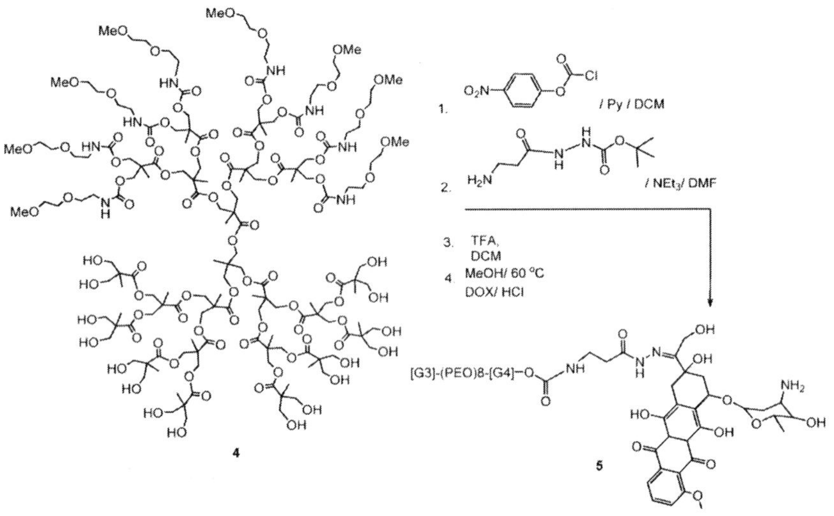

Scheme 2. Functionalization of bow-tie dendrimers for therapeutic studies.

In summary the antitumor effect of doxorubicin (DOX) conjugated to a biodegradable dendrimer was evaluated in mice bearing C-26 colon carcinomas. A bow tie biodegradable polyester dendrimer containing 8–10 wt% DOX was prepared. The design of the dendrimer carrier optimized blood circulation time through size and molecular architecture, drug loading through multiple attachment sites, solubility through PEGylation, and drug release through the use of pH-sensitive hydrazone linkages. In culture, dendrimer-DOX was >10 times less toxic than free DOX toward C-26 colon carcinoma cells after exposure for 72 h. Upon *in vivo* administration to mice bearing cancerous cells, dendrimer-DOX was eliminated from the serum with a half-life of 16 h, and its tumor uptake was nine fold higher than *in vivo* administered free DOX at 48 h. In addition, a single *in vivo* injection of dendrimer-DOX at 20 mg/kg DOX equivalents 8 days after tumor implantation caused complete tumor regression and 100% survival of the mice over the 60 days experiment. No cures were achieved in tumor implanted mice treated with free DOX at its maximum tolerated dose (6 mg/kg), drug-free dendrimer, or dendrimer-DOX in which the DOX was attached by means of a stable carbamate bond. The antitumor effect of dendrimer-DOX is similar to that of an equimolar dose of liposomal DOX (Doxil). There is no doubt that the remarkable antitumor activity of dendrimer-DOX results from the ability of the dendrimer to favorably enhance the pharmacokinetics profiles of attached doxorubicin.

In another study, Namazi and Adeli reported the synthesis and controlled release of biocompatible prodrugs of β-cyclodextrin linked with PEG-containing Ibuprofen or Indomethacin [155]. The same group also prepared citric acid–polyethylene glycol-citric acid (CPEGC) triblock dendrimers as biocompatible compounds up to the third generation, and investigated them as potential drug-delivery systems [156,157]. The preparation of a second-generation dendrimer of this type is shown in Scheme 3. Here, the encapsulation and the controlled release of anti-inflammatory drugs 5-aminosalisylic acid, mefenamic acid, and diclofenac were investigated [157]. Citric acid and poly(ethyleneglycol) (PEG) were selected because of their good water solubility, low toxicity and biocompatibility and these moieties are widely accepted for use in drug formulations. A series of complexes/drugs from the synthesized dendrimers were prepared. It is worthy pointing out that the isolated water-soluble dendrimers were capable of binding and solubilizing non-polar hydrophobic molecules.

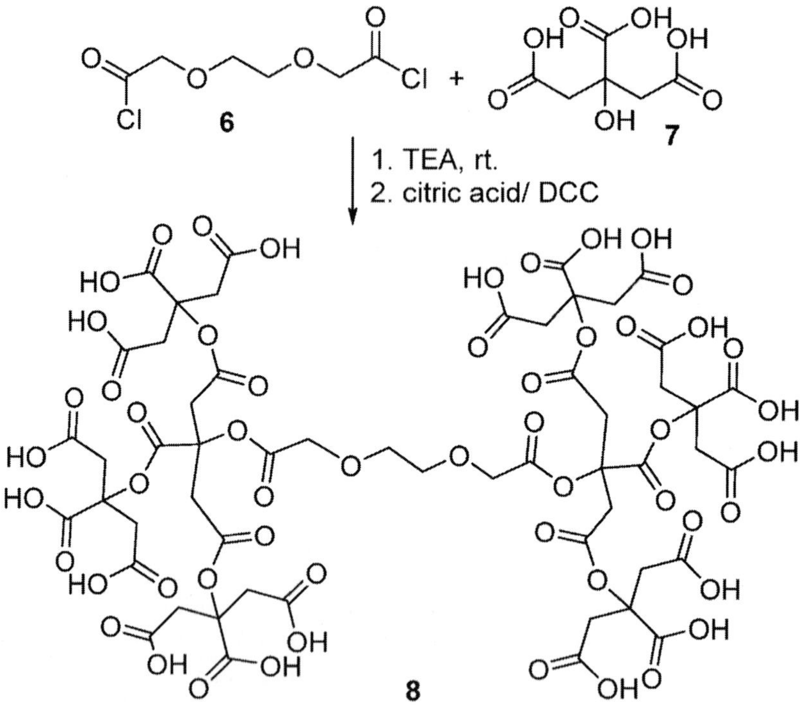

Scheme 3. Synthesis of second-generation dendrimer for drug delivery studies [155,156,157].

During controlled release investigation, it was noticed that in all cases after approximately 350 min, the release of drugs from the complexes was approximately completed and was changed to a very slow rate [157]. The ability of this type of non-toxic dendrimer to enhance pharmacokinetic profiles of encapsulated drugs is evidence that these dendrimer-drug complexes could be considered as potential drug-delivery systems. This system is a promising polymeric backbone for use as scaffolds in the development of well-defined polymeric drug carriers.

To date clinical experience with neutron capture therapy (NCT) is with the non-radioactive isotope boron-10 (BNCT). The use of other non-radioactive isotopes such as gadolinium has been limited, and to date, it has not been used clinically. BNCT has been evaluated clinically as an alternative to conventional radiation therapy for the treatment of malignant brain tumors and recurrent head and neck cancers [158,159,160,161]. Consequently, efficient methods for the delivery of boron-10 to biological tissues have been the subject of longstanding research. However, an obstacle to mainstream application of BNCT for cancer treatment has been the selective delivery of adequate boron concentrations to target tissues [162]. To address this problem, high boron content species such as polyhedral borane clusters, closo-$[B_{10}H_{10}]^{2-}$, closo-$[B_{12}H_{12}]^{2-}$, and the isoelectronic icosahedral family of carboranes, closo-$C_2B_{10}H_{12}$, have attracted significant attention [158]. With this in mind, Adronov and coworkers prepared aliphatic polyester dendrimers based on bis-HMPA that incorporate an easily controllable number of carboranes within the interior of the dendritic structure [163]. Newkome and coworkers had previously reported the production of water-soluble carborane-functionalized dendrimers, involving the reaction of alkyne moieties with decaborane to form ortho-carborane cages within the interior of cascade macromolecules [164]. Here [163], It was critical to develop a bifunctional carborane synthon that matches the dual functionality of the bis-HMPA monomer, allowing it to be inserted within the dendrimer synthesis at any generation using traditional esterification reactions. This flexibility in the position of carborane insertion provided control over the boron concentration within a specific dendrimer target compound. Scheme 4 illustrates this synthetic strategy.

Upon peripheral deprotection to liberate a polyhydroxylated dendrimer exterior, the resulting structures exhibited aqueous solubility as long as a minimum of eight hydroxyl groups per carborane were present. More importantly, irradiation of these materials with thermal neutrons resulted in emission of gamma radiation that is indicative of boron neutron capture events occurring within the carborane-containing dendrimers, indicating that these structures should serve as potential BNCT agents.

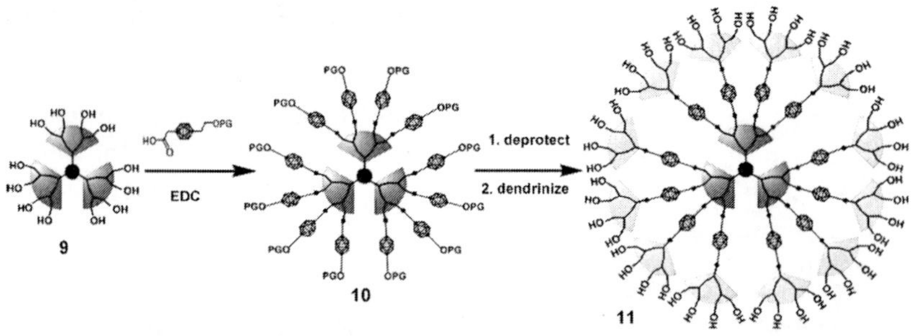

Scheme 4. The strategy for incorporation of a carborane synthon into the polyester dendrimer [163].

A higher percentage of anticancer pharmaceuticals currently in use are natural products and natural product analogues [165,166]. Among others, two water soluble analogues of the alkaloid camptothecin are increasingly in clinical use [167,168,169,170]. Like many other pharmaceutical drug candidates, camptothecins have suboptimal properties mostly caused by their low water solubility and this resulted in their failure in early clinical trials [167]. Researchers have continued to modify camptothecin analogues in an attempt to circumvent poor water solubility while retaining anticancer potency. However, dose-limiting side effects caused by the water-solubilizing functionalities include severe to life-threatening diarrhea and myelosuppression [171,172]. Consequently, smart delivery vehicles for camptothecins that can reduce side effects while enhancing potency are of particular interest [23,74,173,174,175]. The work of Grinstaff and coworkers using polyester dendrimers represents an interesting example [101]. Here, a biocompatible polyester dendrimer made up of the natural metabolites, glycerol and succinic acid, was prepared for the encapsulation of the antitumor camptothecins (10-hydroxycamptothecin (10HCPT) and 7-butyl-10-aminocamptothecin (BACPT)). Figure 3 illustrates an example of this type of polyester dendrimer and the encapsulation of 10-hydroxycamptothecin in the dendritic interior [101]. Cytotoxicity studies of the dendrimer-drug complex toward four different human cancer cell lines, human breast adenocarcinoma (MCF-7), colorectal adenocarcinoma (HT-29), non–small cell lung carcinoma (NCI-H460), and glioblastoma (SF-268), were performed. The results with 10HCPT in HT-29 cells indicated that the dendrimer-10HCPT assembly had a 3.5-fold increase in potency relative to DMSO-dissolved 10HCPT and a 4.1-fold increase in comparison to DMSO-dissolved 10HCPT stock with subsequent dilutions made in water.

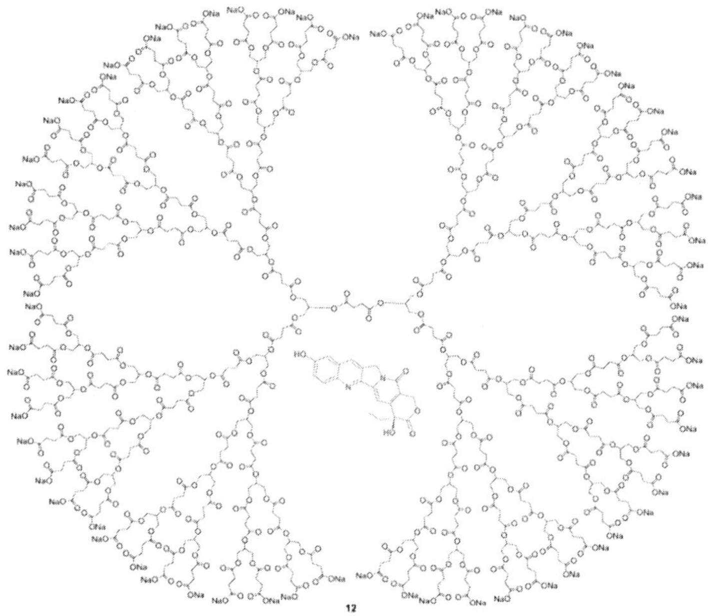

12

Figure 3. Encapsulation of antitumor camptothecin [101].

To determine whether the increase in anticancer activity conferred by dendrimer-encapsulated 10HCPT was observed with other cell lines, 10HCPT dissolved in DMSO and the dendrimer-encapsulated 10HCPT formulations were compared in a diverse human cancer cell panel consisting of the MCF-7 human breast adenocarcinoma, the NCIH460 human large cell lung carcinoma, and the SF-268 human astrocytoma. Interestingly, the dendrimer-encapsulated 10HCPT exhibited an improved degree of potency relative to the DMSO-dissolved drug in each cell line. Specifically, the IC_{50} values for the DMSO-dissolved 10HCPT compared with the dendrimer-encapsulated 10HCPT was reduced from 72.0 to 10.1 nmol/L for the MCF-7-treated cells, from 32.4 to 16.7 nmol/L for the NCI-460-treated cells, and from 13.1 to 4.6 nmol/L for the SF-268-treated cells.

The more hydrophobic camptothecin analogue, BACPT, which possesses a 10-fold greater cytotoxic activity in most tumor cell lines when compared to 10HCPT, was also examined. The dendrimer encapsulation process allowed an enhanced aqueous solubility to the BACPT of 440 μmol/L. HCPT). Even though the dendrimer encapsulation afforded no improvement on the cytotoxicity toward HT-29 cells relative to DMSO-dissolved drug, the dendrimer-encapsulated BACPT exhibited an improved degree of potency relative to the DMSO-dissolved agent in each of the other cell lines.

Comparing the DMSO-dissolved BACPT to the dendrimer-encapsulated BACPT, the IC_{50} values were reduced from 26.7 to 8.3 nmol/L for the MCF-7-treated cells, from 1.2 to 0.6 nmol/L for the NCI-H460-treated cells, and from 6.6 to 1.2 nmol/L for the SF-268-treated cells. The results in this work [101] strongly suggest that these types of polyester dendrimers may be of significant utility in improving the aqueous solubility of other camptothecin analogues as well as other hydrophobic drugs with suboptimal pharmacokinetics.

The discovery and development of new and potent drugs is a time-consuming and costly process. It may take up to 15 years to develop a new drug, mostly because of lengthy clinical trials [176]. A more economical and viable strategy is to devise effective delivery systems for drugs that have failed to provide optimum therapeutic benefit since controlled release of a drug at a specific target can significantly improve the effectiveness of a drug and thereby increase the therapeutic benefit [177]. With this in mind, Hildgen and coworkers synthesized novel polyester-*co*-polyether (PEPE) dendrimers having a hydrophilic core [102]. The core was synthesized using the biocompatible moieties, butanetetracarboxylic acid and aspartic acid, and the dendrons were derived from PEG, dihydroxybenzoic acid or gallic acid, and PEG monomethacrylate. Dendrimers were then obtained by coupling the dendrons to the core [102].

A second generation dendrimer of this type is shown in Figure 4. This type of dendrimer demonstrated good ability to encapsulate the guest molecule with loadings of 15.80 and 6.47% w/w for rhodamine and β-carotene respectively. The release of the encapsulated compounds was found to be slow and sustained, suggesting that these dendrimers can serve as potential drug delivery systems [102].

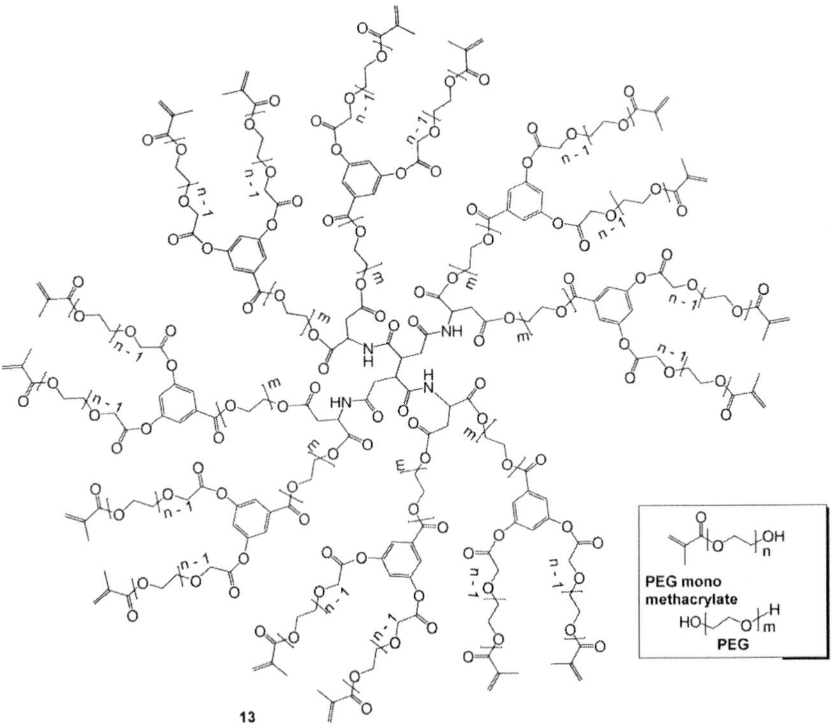

13

Figure 4. A novel second-generation dendrimer with a hydrophilic interior [102]. The letters m and n indicate the number of ethylene glycol repeats.

Around the same time, the same authors investigated the influence of molecular architecture of PEPE dendrimers on the encapsulation and release of methotrexate [178]. In this study, effects of alterations in the chemical structure of PEPE dendrimers on the encapsulation and release of methotrexate was investigated. A series of PEPE dendrimers of different architecture were synthesized [178]. The biocompatibility of this type of dendrimers was evaluated *in vitro* by assessing their cytotoxicity on RAW 264.7 cells using the lactate dehydrogenase assay. Dendrimers caused no cell death even at a concentration of 250 mg/mL, suggesting that they are acceptable for pharmaceutical applications. They also showed good capacity to encapsulate methotrexate, with loading as high as 24.5% w/w. Increasing in the number of branches and the size of internal voids were shown to enhance the encapsulation. On the other hand, the absence of aromatic rings as branching units drastically reduced the loading capacity. Using spectroscopic studies, it was illustrated that physical entrapment, weak hydrogen bonding and hydrophobic interactions were the mechanisms of encapsulation. The release of methotrexate included a burst release in the first 6 h followed by a slower release over a period of 50 or 168 h. Increasing the number of branches decreased the initial burst release and in contrast, the absence of aromatic rings in the dendritic structure resulted in a very rapid release [178]. Thus, this new macromolecular system exhibits promising characteristics for the development of new polymeric drug carriers.

The transformation of linear polymers into dendronized polymers is another avenue of polymer synthesis that has received attention. When monodisperse dendrons are attached to a linear polymer backbone, the resulting dendronized polymers have new properties and new potential applications, resulting from the almost dendritic nature of the new system. In this regard, Fréchet, Szoka and coworkers [179] synthesized rigid-rod dendronized linear polymers consisting of a poly(4-hydroxystyrene) backbone and fourth generation polyester dendrons [179]. Figure 5 shows a schematic representation for this type of dendronized polymers. Both *in vitro* and *in vivo* evaluations of the polymers were then carried out to determine their suitability as drug delivery vehicles. Cytotoxicity assays indicated that these polymers are well tolerated by cells *in vitro*. Detailed biodistribution studies of the polymers in both non-tumored and tumored mice revealed that as for random coil linear polymers, renal clearance was a function of polymer size [179]. High accumulation in organs of the reticuloendothelial system was exhibited by a dendronized polymer with a very high molecular weight (Mn = 1740 kDa), but was not as significant for smaller polymers with Mn = 67 kDa and Mn = 251 kDa. Even though polymers with degradable backbones are more suited to prevent long-term accumulation [180], these highly functionalizable, nontoxic, dendronized polymers represent a promising new scaffold for polymeric systems with pharmacokinetic properties appropriate for use as drug carriers.

Paclitaxel is a mitotic inhibitor used in cancer chemotherapy which has shown substantial clinical efficacy for various cancer types including ovarian, breast, colon, head and neck, and non-small cell lung cancers [181,182]. Due to its poor solubility however, paclitaxel is usually formulated as a 1:1 mixture of Cremophor EL and ethanol, which is diluted in normal saline or dextrose solution to a final paclitaxel concentration of 5% for administration [182]. This formulation has severe side effects caused by its Cremophor EL and the organic solvent [183,184]. Consequently, several attempts have been made to increase the poor paclitaxel solubility (0.3 mg/mL) using various formulations or prodrug conjugates [185,186,187,188,189,190,191,192,193]. Kontoyianni, Sideratou and coworkers [194] successfully functionalized commercially available hyperbranched aliphatic polyester Boltorn H40 [63,195,196] with PEG chains to afford a novel water-soluble BH40-PEG polymer exhibiting unimolecular micellar properties appropriate for application as a drug delivery system

[194]. After paclitaxel was encapsulated, the solubility of the anticancer drug was enhanced by a factor of 35, 110, 230, and 355 in aqueous solutions of BH40-PEG with concentrations of 10, 30, 60, and 90 mg/mL, respectively. After an initial slow release during the first 100 minutes, more than 50% of the drug was released at a steady rate that is desirable in controlled release systems and release was almost complete within 10 h. The toxicity of BH40-PEG was assessed *in vitro*with A549 human lung carcinoma cells and found to be nontoxic for 3 h incubation up to a 1.75 mg/mL concentration. The anticancer drug was also found to efficiently internalize in cells, primarily in the absence of foetal bovine serum, while confocal microscopy revealed the preferential localization of the drug compound in cell nuclei [194]. This is another example of how polyester based macromolecules can enhance the pharmacokinetic profiles of attached or encapsulated drugs.

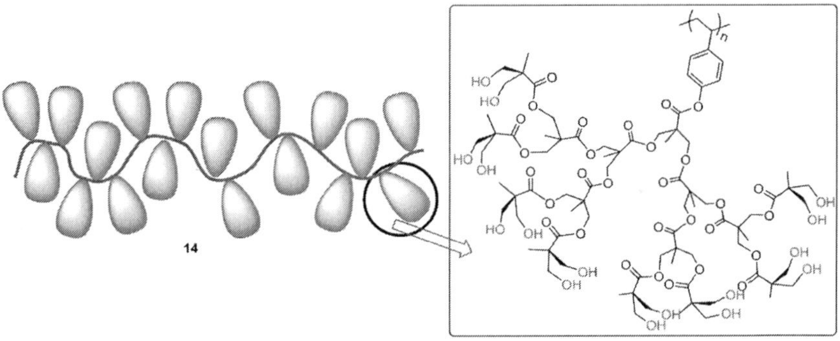

Figure 5. A representation of a dendronized linear polymer and the structure of fourth-generation dendronized poly(4-hydroxystyrene) [179].

Other recent attempts to improve paclitaxel pharmacokinetic profiles include the work of Kissel and coworkers [197]. The authors aimed to formulate nanoparticles from three different hyperbranched polymers, namely unmodified dendritic polyester (Boltorn H40), a lipophilic, fatty acid modified dendritic polymer (Boltorn U3000), and an amphiphilic dendritic polymer (Boltorn W3000) (see Figure 6) for drug delivery of paclitaxel and to investigate their properties. Boltorn series hyperbranched aliphatic polyesters have great potential for applications in the biomedical field [198] due to their low toxicity, immunogenicity [56], and biodegradability [63]. Here [197], a solvent displacement method allowed preparation of nanoparticles from all three hyperbranched polymers. The lipophilic Boltorn U3000 formed the biggest nanoparticles while the amphiphilic Boltorn W3000 formed the smallest ones. Degradation profiles were investigated by short time pH-stat titration. Boltorn H40 showed a faster degradation rate than the fatty acid containing polymers. For Boltorn H40, degradation rate was also investigated in longer term mass loss studies resulting in 30% degradation during 3 weeks. Cytotoxicity studies for the nanoparticles revealed low cytotoxicity for all three polymers. All three types of nanoparticles were then loaded with paclitaxel and their release profiles were studied. Sizes and zeta potentials remained stable after loading and did not change significantly. Boltorn U3000 and W3000 represent interesting candidates for drug delivery application due to their high loading efficiency.

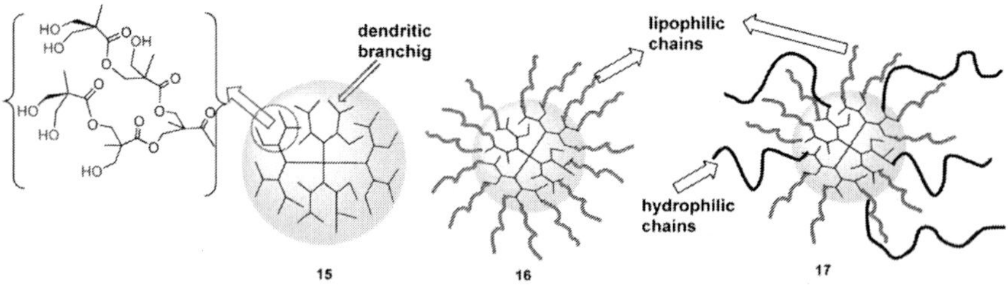

Figure 6. Schematic illustration of the Boltorn series: (**15**) Boltorn H40; (**16**) Boltorn U3000; and (**17**) Boltorn W3000 [197].

The work of Wang and Xu [199] also illustrates the potential of Boltorn series hyperbranched aliphatic polyesters as drug delivery systems. Here, a commercially available dendrimer-like hyperbranched polymer was used as a starting material in the development of a facile synthetic route for the construction of a folic acid-based multivalent targeted drug delivery system [199]. In this system, fluorescein was incorporated to act as the imaging reagent, folic acid as the targeting reagent, and methotrexate as the chemotherapeutic reagent. This method used the unpaired hydroxyls on the Boltorn dendrimer to conjugate with fluorescein, thereby making good use of the defect in the polyester. Folic acid, methotrexate, and fluorescein were all successfully attached to the polyester as illustrated in Figure 7. Even though the application of this multivalent targeted drug delivery system in clinical drugs was not reported, this system exemplifies a potentially inexpensive and well-defined multivalent targeted drug delivery carrier [199].

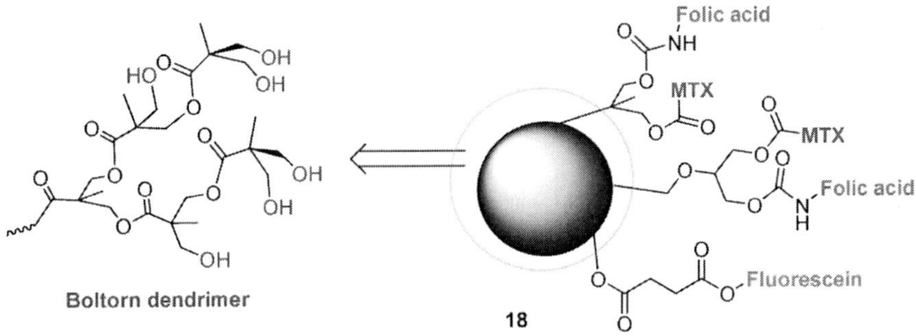

Figure 7. The synthesis of the folic acid-based targeted drug delivery system [199].

Recently, Nyström and coworkers modified Boltorn H30 and H40 using an average of 5 PEG chains prior to the encapsulation of DOX for delivery to breast cancer cells [200]. DOX-loaded H30-PEG10k nanoparticles exhibited controlled release over longer periods of time and flow cytometry and confocal scanning laser microscopy studies indicated that the cancer cells could internalize the DOX-loaded H30-PEG10k nanoparticles. This contributed to the sustained drug release, and induced more apoptosis than free DOX. These findings are further indications that Boltorn based nanoparticles may offer an alternative strategy for delivering drugs to cancer cells.

The various types of delivery vehicles studied to date, including linear polymers, micellar assemblies, liposomes, and polymersomes, do not possess all the desired design features [201] one would want in an efficient drug carrier. Features such as a long blood circulation time, high tumor accumulation, high drug loading capacity, low toxicity, low polydispersity index, and simple preparation are necessary for a suitable drug carrier. Considering the above criteria, PEGylated dendrimers constitute an attractive option, because their size and degree of branching can be precisely controlled and they possess multiple functional appendages for the attachment of both drugs and solubilizing groups.

To minimize the hydrolytic susceptibility of the ester bond during synthesis of drug conjugates, Fréchet, Szoka and coworkers reported an elegant synthesis that combines the biocompatibility of bis-HMPA dendrimers with the robustness of polyamide dendrimers, yielding a hybrid scaffold capable of translation into clinical studies [98]. A drug loaded PEGylated ester-amide dendrimer is shown in Figure 8. The biodistribution of the ester-amide dendrimer was determined in C26 tumored female Balb/C mice. Mice were injected with 8 mg Dox eq/kg, formulated as Doxil or compound **19**. After 48 h, Dox had significantly accumulated within the tumor compared to insignificant amount in vital organs. This observation is important because lowering Dox accumulation in the vital organs is important for reducing toxicity, while uptake by tumor tissue must be maintained to promote treatment efficacy.

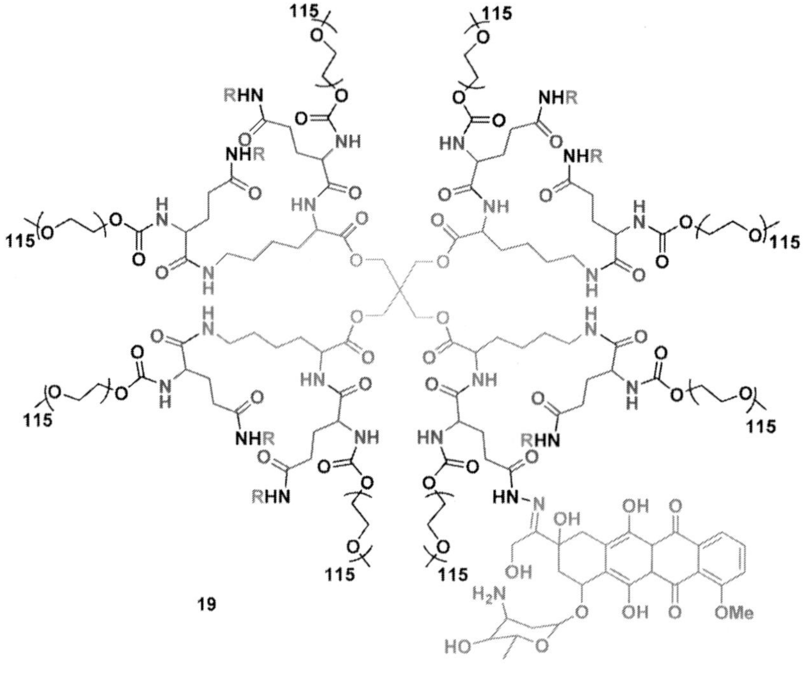

19

Figure 8. A drug (DOX) loaded PEGylated ester-amide dendrimer [98].

For therapeutic studies, a dose-response experiment was performed in C26 tumored Balb/C mice, and four treatment groups were investigated, Doxil (20 mg Dox/kg) and compound **19** (10, 15, and 20 mg Dox/kg). Dose-dependent survival was observed and all three groups treated with loaded PEGylated ester-amide dendrimer **19** showed significant tumor growth delay and prolonged survival. Mice treated with compound **19** at 20 mg Dox/kg had 9 out of 10 mice tumor free at the end of 60 days. The results in this study and earlier studies [57] confirm that Dox-loaded PEGylated dendrimer carriers are as effective as Doxil against the C26 tumor model.

In another recent study, Malkoch, Fadeel and coworkers elegantly evaluated the biocompatibility of a library of aliphatic polyester dendrimers based on bis-HMPA [59]. In addition, dendrimers with two different chemical surfaces (neutral with hydroxyl end group and anionic with carboxylic end group) and dendrons corresponding to the structural fragments of the dendrimers were also evaluated. Commercially available PAMAM dendrimers with cationic (amine) or neutral (hydroxyl) end groups were also included for comparison. *In vitro* studies were conducted in human cervical cancer and acute monocytic leukemia cells differentiated into macrophage-like cells as well as in primary human monocyte-derived macrophages. The entire hydroxyl functional bis-HMPA dendrimer library demonstrated excellent biocompatibility, whereas the cationic, but not the neutral PAMAM exerted dose-dependent cytotoxicity in cell lines and primary macrophages. Studies to evaluate material stability as a function of pH, temperature, and time, demonstrated that the stability of the 4th generation hydroxyl functional bis-HMPA dendrimer increased at acidic pH. This is further indication that bis-HMPA polyester dendrimers are degradable and non-cytotoxic.

Polymeric micelles can be formed in solution only above the critical micelle concentration. However, micelles formed from amphiphilic block copolymers have attracted attention in drug delivery because of their ability to decrease unwanted side effects, prolong the circulation time, and reduce uptake by the reticuloendothelial system (RES) [202,203,204,205]. On the other hand, micelles injected into the body are usually subjected to severe dilution and this normally leads to their dissociation and a rapid release of physically encapsulated drugs. Consequently, their effectiveness in drug delivery and their *in vivo* application are considerably reduced [206]. The use of amphiphilic polymeric unimolecular micelles can help to eliminate problems associated with the dissociation and the large sizes of polymeric micelles. Dendrimer-like star polymers composed of a hydrophobic star polymer core and a hydrophilic dendron shell, have a potential to deliver drugs more effectively via appropriate structure-tuning. Wang and coworkers synthesized well-defined folate-functionalized dendrimer-like star polymers, by combining living ring-opening polymerization (ROP) of L-lactide and dendrimer synthesis [207,208]. Here [207,208], a poly(L-lactide) star polymer was selected as the hydrophobic core and non-toxic biodegradable dendrons based on bis-HMPA were used as the shell [208,209]. Surface functionalization using carboxylic acid groups allowed further conjugation with PEG oligomers for water solubility enhancement. These dendrimer-like star polymer nanoparticles were then functionalized further with folic acid because it is known that folic acid is non-immunogenic and has a strong binding affinity to the folate receptors, which are overexpressed on the surface of many human tumor cells [210,211,212]. Scheme 5 shows the functionalization of this type of dendrimer-like star polymers using folic acid and the fluorescent probe, Hilyte488. Hilyte488 was attached to the G1-g3-FA conjugate to form G1-g3-FA-Hiyte488. UV–vis spectroscopy was employed to determine the number of Hilyte488 units incorporated per G1-g3-FA. *In vitro* results showed that FA-functionalized and anticancer drug-loaded degradable dendrimer-like star polymer (DLSP) could specifically target and kill human KB cells [209].

This folate-functionalized degradable amphiphilic dendrimer-like star polymer (FA-DLSP) hybrid formed unimolecular micelles in the aqueous solution with a mean particle size of about 15 nm as determined by dynamic light scattering and transmission electron microscopy. To study the feasibility of the dendrimer-like micelles as potential nanocarriers for targeted drug delivery, the anticancer agent DOX was encapsulated in the hydrophobic core, and the loading content was determined by UV/VIS analysis to be 4% by weight. The DOX loaded dendrimer-like micelles demonstrated a sustained release of DOX due to the hydrophobic interaction between the polymer core and the drug molecules [207]. The hydrolytic degradation *in vitro* was monitored by weight loss and proton nuclear magnetic resonance spectroscopy to gain insight into the degradation mechanism of the micelles. It was found that the degradation was pH-dependent and started from the hydrophilic shell and moved gradually to the hydrophobic core. Flow cytometry and confocal microscope studies revealed that the cellular binding of the FA-DLSP hybrid against human KB cells with overexpressed folate-receptors was about twice that of the neat DLSP (without FA). The *in vitro* cellular cytotoxicity indicated that the FA-DLSP micelles (without DOX) had good biocompatibility with human KB cells, whereas DOX loaded micelles exhibited a similar degree of cytotoxicity against human KB cells as that of free DOX. These results clearly show that this type of dendrimer-like unimolecular micelles are a promising nanosize anticancer drug delivery system with excellent targeting properties [207].

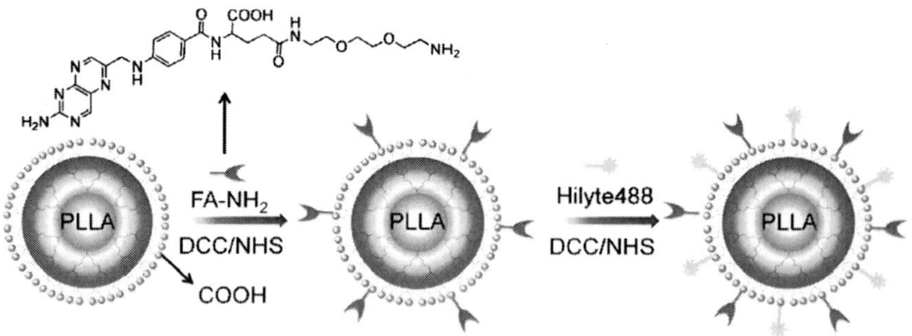

G1-g3-(COOH)$_{144}$ **20** G1-g3-FA **21** G1-g3-FA-Hilyte488 **22**

Scheme 5. Functionalization of dendrimer-like poly(L-lactide) (PLLA) star polymer for drug delivery studies [209].

Polymer vesicles commonly referred to as polymersomes have recently received significant attention for biological applications [213,214,215,216,217,218,219,220,221]. Polymersomes can be readily accessed from a wide range of block copolymers and they typically exhibit much lower critical aggregation concentrations and enhanced thermodynamic and kinetic stabilities [222,223]. Recently, Gillies and coworkers exploited the multivalent and multifunctional capabilities of polymersomes in a dendritic sialopolymersome system designed to interact with the influenza virus at two different stages in the infection process [103]. First, the sialic acid *N*-acetylneuraminic acid (Neu5Ac) was conjugated to the polymersome surface in order to inhibit the binding of viral hemagglutinin to sialic acids on host cells, thus preventing viral entry. Second, the neuraminidase inhibitor zanamivir was encapsulated into the polymersome core in order to prevent the release of progeny virus from the host cells, thus inhibiting viral replication. With the aim of maximizing multivalent effects at the polymersome surface, polyester dendrons functionalized with Neu5Ac were synthesized and conjugated to polymersomes. The binding of the resulting dendritic sialopolymersomes to Limax flavus agglutinin was studied and compared to the sialodendron and a monovalent Neu5Ac derivative using an enzyme-linked lectin inhibition assay. The results of this study revealed that while the sialodendron exhibited a 17-fold enhancement (per sialoside) relative to the small molecule, the dendritic sialopolymersomes resulted in an almost 2000-fold enhancement in binding affinity. It was also found that encapsulation of zanamivir into the dendritic sialopolymersomes could be performed with the same efficiency as for naked polymersomes to provide a drug loading of about 35 wt%. Drug release rates were similar for both systems with sustained release over a period of 4 days. The results described in this paper indicate that multifunctional polymersome systems can be used for the interaction with and inhibition of influenza viruses [103].

Polyester dendrimers are often synthesized by repeated esterification of bis-HMPA dendron followed by deprotection. This synthetic strategy is straightforward, but when the protection/deprotection reactions are incomplete, defects and thus polydispersity are introduced. Shen and coworkers [19] suggest that aliphatic polyester dendrimers without heterocyclics have better biocompatibility and biodegradability for translational nanocarriers. Using the highly efficient thiol/acrylate Michael addition reactions, a strategy for the synthesis of bis-HMPA-based dendrimers without any protection/deprotection steps was developed. Scheme 6 shows the preparation of a dendrimer bearing 128 terminal hydroxyl groups in five steps. To investigate the potential of this type of dendrimers as drug carriers, G5-128_{OH} was pegylated to obtain a water-soluble biocompatible dendrimer capable of encapsulation and controlled release of a hydrophobic anticancer drug, doxorubicin. The esterification of G5-128$_{OH}$ using PEG2k-COOH and the loading of G5-PEG with DOX is shown in Scheme 7.

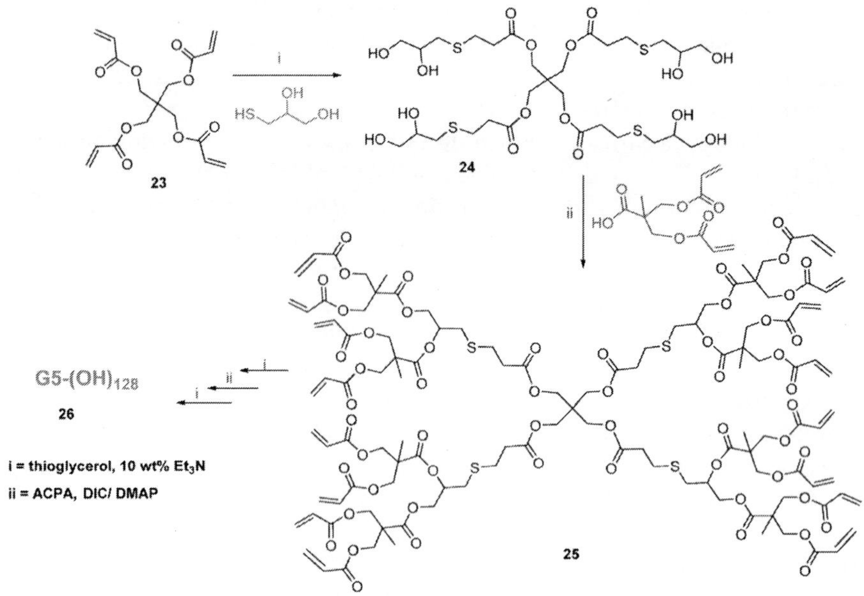

Scheme 6. Efficient synthesis of a fifth generation aliphatic polyester dendrimer [19].

Evaluation of the G5-PEG/ DOX complex revealed that DOX could be released with a slight burst at pH 7.4 and 37 °C followed by a very slow release. About 40% of the DOX was released in 24 h and less than 60% in 100 h. This sustained release is an improvement and is in contrast to the usually severe burst release of most micellar drug carriers [224,225]. DOX release was greatly enhanced at acidic pH. Upon evaluation of the cytotoxicity of free DOX, G5-PEG/ DOX (15.2 wt% DOX), and G5-PEG to ovarian cancer cells, it was found that G5-PEG was not toxic even at high doses. The IC_{50} of the DOX in the G5-PEG/ DOX to SKOV-3 ovarian cancer cells was 0.085 μg/mL, not significant different from that of free DOX (0.056 μg/mL). Further evaluations of this type of dendrimers as drug carriers are currently underway [19].

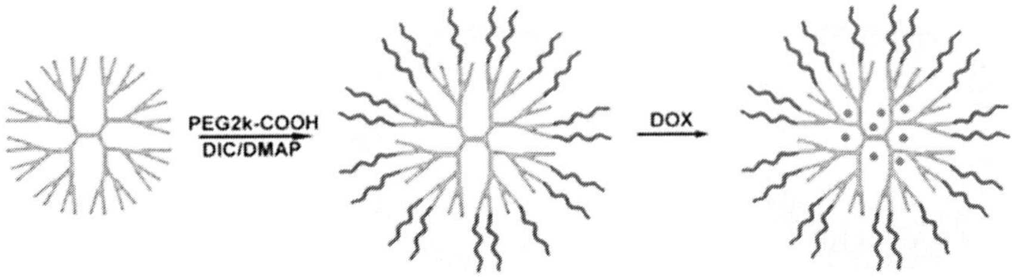

G5-128OH
25

G5-PEG
26

G5-PEG/DOX
27

Scheme 7. Preparation of G5-PEG and its loading with DOX [19].

5. CONCLUSIONS

Various types of delivery vehicles including linear polymers, micellar assemblies, liposomes, polymersomes, and dendrimers have been studied in an effort to identify an ideal drug carrier. The use of dendrimers as drug carriers by encapsulating hydrophobic drugs is an attractive method for delivering highly active pharmaceutical compounds that may not be in clinical use due to their limited water solubility and suboptimal pharmacokinetics. There has been a substantial interest in the area of polyester dendrimers as potential drug delivery carriers because of their relatively easy preparation, biodegradability, and biocompatibility. Encapsulation and conjugation of drugs with polyester dendrimers have shown immense employment for the improvement of pharmacokinetic profiles of hydrophobic and labile drugs. *In vitro* and *in vivo* studies have shown that, in contrast to other dendrimers and polymers, the polyester dendrimer scaffold is hydrolytically degradable and less toxic and does not accumulate in vital organs. Activity in the evaluation of polyester dendrimers as drug carriers has intensified over the last few years and the trend is expected to continue.

ACKNOWLEDGMENTS

We thank Natural Sciences and Engineering Research Council of Canada (NSERC) for support.

CONFLICT OF INTEREST

The authors declare no conflict of interest.

REFERENCES

1. Ringsdorf, H. Structure and properties of pharmacologically active polymers. J. Polym. Sci. Pol. Sym. 1975, 51, 135–153.

2. Bader, H.; Ringsdorf, H.; Schmidt, B. Water soluble polymers in medicine. Angew. Makromol. Chem. 1984, 123, 457–485.

3. Kopeček, J. Soluble biomedical polymers. Polym. Med. 1977, 7, 191–221.

4. Kopeček, J.; Kopeckova, P.; Minko, T.; Lu, Z.R. HPMA copolymer-anticancer drug conjugates: Design, activity, and mechanism of action. Eur. J. Pharmaceut. Biopharmaceut. 2000, 50, 61–81.

5. Duncan, R. Drug-polymer conjugates: Potential for improved chemotherapy. Cancer Res. 1992, 46, 175–210.

6. Maeda, H.; Seymour, L.W.; Miyamoto, Y. Conjugates of anticancer agents and polymers-Advantages of macromolecular therapeutics in vivo. Bioconjugate Chem. 1992, 3, 351–362.

7. Seymour, L.W.; Miyamoto, Y.; Maeda, H.; Brereton, M.; Strohalm, J.; Ulbrich, K.; Duncan, R. Influence of molecular weight on passive tumor accumulation of a soluble macromolecular drug carrier. Eur. J. Cancer 1995, 31A, 766–770.

8. Matsumura, Y.; Maeda, H. A new concept for macromolecular therapeutics in cancer chemotherapy: Mechanism of tumoritropic accumulation of proteins and the antitumor agent smancs. Cancer Res. 1986, 46, 6387–6392.

9. Maeda, H.; Wu, J.; Sawa, T.; Matsumura, Y.; Hori, K. Tumor vascular permeability and the EPR effect in macromolecular therapeutics: A review. J. Control. Release 2000, 65, 271–284.

10. Seymour, L.W. Passive tumor targeting of soluble macromolecules and drug conjugates. Crit. Rev. Ther. Drug 1992, 9, 135–187.

11. Duncan, R.; Sat, Y.N. Tumour targeting by enhanced permeability and retention (EPR) effect. Ann. Oncol. 1998, 9, 39–39.

12. Wang, Z.; Itoh, Y.; Hosaka, Y.; Kobayashi, I.; Nakano, Y.; Maeda, I.; Umeda, F.; Yamakawa, J.; Nishimine, M.; Suenobu, T.; Fukuzumi, S.; Kawase, M.; Yagi, K. Mechanism of enhancement effect of dendrimer on transdermal drug permeation through polyhydroxyalkanoate matrix. J. Biosci. Bioeng. 2003, 96, 537–540.

13. Gillies, E.R.; Fréchet, J.M.J. Designing macromolecules for therapeutic applications: Polyester dendrimer-poly(ethylene oxide) "bow-tie" hybrids with tunable molecular weight and architecture. J. Am. Chem. Soc. 2002, 124, 14137–14146.

14. Kolhe, P.; Misra, E.; Kannan, R.M.; Kannan, S.; Lieh-Lai, M. Drug complexation, in vitro release and cellular entry of dendrimers and hyperbranched polymers. Int. J. Pharmaceut. 2003, 259, 143–160.

15. Baker, J.R. Why I believe nanoparticles are crucial as a carrier for targeted drug delivery. Wiley Interdiscip. Rev. Nanomed. Nanobiotechnol. 2013, 5, 423–429.

16. Gu, L.; Wu, Z.H.; Qi, X.L.; He, H.; Ma, X.L.; Chou, X.H.; Wen, X.G.; Zhang, M.; Jiao, F. Polyamidomine dendrimers: An excellent drug carrier for improving the solubility and bioavailability of puerarin. Pharm. Dev. Technol. 2013, 18, 1051–1057.

17. Zhou, Z.Y.; D'Emanuele, A.; Attwood, D. Solubility enhancement of paclitaxel using a linear-dendritic block copolymer. Int. J. Pharmaceut. 2013, 452, 173–179.

18. Gula, A.; Ren, L.; Zhou, Z.; Lu, D.D.; Wang, S.Q. Design and evaluation of biodegradable enteric microcapsules of amifostine for oral delivery. Int. J. Pharmaceut. 2013, 453, 441–447.

19. Ma, X.P.; Zhou, Z.X.; Jin, E.L.; Sun, Q.H.; Zhang, B.; Tang, J.B.; Shen, Y.Q. Facile synthesis of polyester dendrimers as drug delivery carriers. Macromolecules 2013, 46, 37–42.

20. Thomas, T.P.; Joice, M.; Sumit, M.; Silpe, J.E.; Kotlyar, A.; Bharathi, S.; Kukowska-Latallo, J.; Baker, J.R.; Choi, S.K. Design and in vitro validation of multivalent dendrimer methotrexates as a folate-targeting anticancer therapeutic.Curr. Pharm. Design 2013, 19, 6594–6605.

21. Leng, Z.H.; Zhuang, Q.F.; Li, Y.C.; He, Z.; Chen, Z.; Huang, S.P.; Jia, H.Y.; Zhou, J.W.; Liu, Y.; Du, L.B. Polyamidoamine dendrimer conjugated chitosan nanoparticles for the delivery of methotrexate. Carbohyd. Polym.2013, 98, 1173–1178.

22. Murugan, E.; Rani, D.P.G.; Srinivasan, K.; Muthumary, J. New surface hydroxylated and internally quaternised poly(propylene imine) dendrimers as efficient biocompatible drug carriers of norfloxacin. Expert Opin. Drug. Del.2013, 10, 1319–1334.

23. Sadekar, S.; Thiagarajan, G.; Bartlett, K.; Hubbard, D.; Ray, A.; McGill, L.D.; Ghandehari, H. Poly(amido amine) dendrimers as absorption enhancers for oral delivery of camptothecin. Int. J. Pharmaceut. 2013, 456, 175–185.

24. Wang, L.; Xu, X.P.; Zhang, Y.; Zhang, Y.Q.; Zhu, Y.; Shi, J.Y.; Sun, Y.H.; Huang, Q. Encapsulation of curcumin within poly(amidoamine) dendrimers for delivery to cancer cells. J. Mater. Sci Mater. M. 2013, 24, 2137–2144.

25. Yellepeddi, V.K.; Vangara, K.K.; Palakurthi, S. Poly(amido)amine (PAMAM) dendrimer-cisplatin complexes for chemotherapy of cisplatin-resistant ovarian cancer cells. J. nanopart. Res. 2013, 15.

26. Koc, F.E.; Senel, M. Solubility enhancement of non-steroidal anti-inflammatory drugs (NSAIDs) using polypolypropylene oxide core PAMAM dendrimers. Int. J. Pharmaceut. 2013, 451, 18–22.

27. Yabbarov, N.G.; Posypanova, G.A.; Vorontsov, E.A.; Obydenny, S.I.; Severin, E.S. A new system for targeted delivery of doxorubicin into tumor cells. J. Control. Release 2013, 168, 135–141.

28. Agrawal, U.; Mehra, N.K.; Gupta, U.; Jain, N.K. Hyperbranched dendritic nano-carriers for topical delivery of dithranol. J. Drug Target. 2013, 21, 497–506.

29. Daneshvar, N.; Abdullah, R.; Shamsabadi, F.T.; How, C.W.; Aizat, M.M.H.; Mehrbod, P. PAMAM dendrimer roles in gene delivery methods and stem cell research. Cell Biol. Int. 2013, 37, 415–419.

30. Richardson, R.K.; Dougherty, C.; DiMaggio, S.; Banaszak-Holl, M. Synthesis, isolation, and characterization of dendrimer conjugates as potential chemotherapy drug delivery systems. Abstr. pap. Am. Chem. S. 2013, 245, 856.

31. Cai, X.P.; Hu, J.J.; Xiao, J.R.; Cheng, Y.Y. Dendrimer and cancer: A patent review (2006–2013). Expert Opin. Ther. Pat.2013, 23, 515–529.

32. Garea, S.A.; Ghebaur, E.V. Hybrid drug release systems based on dendrimers and montmorillonite. Mater. Plast. 2013,50, 8–11.

33. Ly, T.U.; Tran, N.Q.; Thi, K.D.H.; Phan, K.N.; Truong, H.N.; Nguyen, C.K. Pegylated dendrimer and its effect in fluorouracil loading and release for enhancing antitumor activity. J. Biomed. Nanotechnol. 2013, 9, 213–220.

34. Wen, S.H.; Li, K.G.; Cai, H.D.; Chen, Q.; Shen, M.W.; Huang, Y.P.; Peng, C.; Hou, W.X.; Zhu, M.F.; Zhang, G.X.; et al. Multifunctional dendrimer-entrapped gold nanoparticles for dual mode CT/MR imaging applications. Biomaterials2013, 34, 1570–1580.

35. Sharma, A.; Jain, N.; Sareen, R. Nanocarriers for diagnosis and targeting of breast cancer. Biomed. Res. Int. 2013, 2013, 960821:1–960821:10.

36. Xu, L.Y.; Yeudall, W.A.; Yang, H. Tailored Polymer Architectures for Pharmaceutical and Biomedical Applications; Scholz, C., Kressler, J., Eds.; American Chemical Society: Washington, DC, USA, 2013; Volume 1135, pp. 197–213.

37. Zhu, J.Y.; Shi, X.Y. Dendrimer-based nanodevices for targeted drug delivery applications. J. Mater. Chem. 2013, 1, 4199–4211.

38. Huang, C.H.; Nwe, K.; Al Zaki, A.; Brechbiel, M.W.; Tsourkas, A. Biodegradable polydisulfide dendrimer nanoclusters as MRI contrast agents. ACS Nano 2012, 6, 9416–9424.

39. Lim, J.; Turkbey, B.; Bernardo, M.; Bryant, L.H.; Garzoni, M.; Pavan, G.M.; Nakajima, T.; Choyke, P.L.; Simanek, E.E.; Kobayashi, H. Gadolinium MRI contrast agents based on triazine dendrimers: Relaxivity and in vivopharmacokinetics. Bioconjugate Chem. 2012, 23, 2291–2299.

40. Carberry, T.P.; Tarallo, R.; Falanga, A.; Finamore, E.; Galdiero, M.; Weck, M.; Galdiero, S. Dendrimer functionalization with a membrane-interacting domain of herpes simplex virus type 1: Towards intracellular delivery. Chem. Eur. J. 2012, 18, 13678–13685.

41. Gardikis, K.; Micha-Screttas, M.; Demetzos, C.; Steele, B.R. Dendrimers and the development of new complex nanomaterials for biomedical applications. Curr. Med. Chem. 2012, 19, 4913–4928.

42. Klajnert, B.; Rozanek, M.; Bryszewska, M. Dendrimers in photodynamic therapy. Curr. Med. Chem. 2012, 19, 4903–4912.

43. Wate, P.S.; Banerjee, S.S.; Jalota-Badhwar, A.; Mascarenhas, R.R.; Zope, K.R.; Khandare, J.; Misra, R.D.K. Cellular imaging using biocompatible dendrimer-functionalized graphene oxide-based

fluorescent probe anchored with magnetic nanoparticles. Nanotechnology 2012, 23.

44. Andreani, T.; Macedo, A.S.; Ferreira, S.F.; Silva, A.M.; Rosmaninho, A.; Souto, E.B. Topical targeting therapies for sexually transmitted diseases. Curr. Nanosci. 2012, 8, 486–490.

45. Guo, R.; Shi, X.Y. Dendrimers in Cancer therapeutics and diagnosis. Curr. Drug Metab. 2012, 13, 1097–1109.

46. Thomas, T.P.; Huang, B.H.; Choi, S.K.; Silpe, J.E.; Kotlyar, A.; Desai, A.M.; Zong, H.; Gam, J.; Joice, M.; Baker, J.R. Polyvalent dendrimer-methotrexate as a folate receptor-targeted cancer therapeutic. Mol. Pharmaceut. 2012, 9, 2669–2676.

47. Holden, C.A.; Tyagi, P.; Thakur, A.; Kadam, R.; Jadhav, G.; Kompella, U.B.; Yang, H. Polyamidoamine dendrimer hydrogel for enhanced delivery of antiglaucoma drugs. Nanomed Nanotechnol. 2012, 8, 776–783.

48. Lim, J.; Simanek, E.E. Triazine dendrimers as drug delivery systems: From synthesis to therapy. Adv. Drug Delivery Rev. 2012, 64, 826–835.

49. Haque, S.; Md, S.; Alam, M.I.; Sahni, J.K.; Ali, J.; Baboota, S. Nanostructure-based drug delivery systems for brain targeting. Drug Dev. Ind. Pharm. 2012, 38, 387–411.

50. Svenson, S.; Tomalia, D.A. Commentary-dendrimers in biomedical applications—Reflections on the field. Adv. Drug Delivery Rev. 2005, 57, 2106–2129.

51. D'Emanuele, A.; Attwood, D. Dendrimer-drug interactions. Adv. Drug Delivery Rev. 2005, 57, 2147–2162.

52. Wolinsky, J.B.; Grinstaff, M.W. Therapeutic and diagnostic applications of dendrimers for cancer treatment. Adv. Drug Delivery Rev. 2008, 60, 1037–1055.

53. Cheng, Y.Y.; Xu, T.W. The effect of dendrimers on the pharmacodynamic and pharmacokinetic behaviors of non-covalently or covalently attached drugs. Eur. J. Med. Chem. 2008, 43, 2291–2297.

54. Nanjwade, B.K.; Bechra, H.M.; Derkar, G.K.; Manvi, F.V.; Nanjwade, V.K. Dendrimers: Emerging polymers for drug-delivery systems. Eur. J. Pharmaceut. Sci. 2009, 38, 185–196.

55. Svenson, S. Dendrimers as versatile platform in drug delivery applications. Eur. J. Pharmaceut. Biopharmaceut. 2009,71, 445–462.

56. Gillies, E.R.; Dy, E.; Fréchet, J.M.J.; Szoka, F.C. Biological evaluation of polyester dendrimer: Poly(ethylene oxide) "Bow-Tie" hybrids with tunable molecular weight and architecture. Mol. Pharmaceut. 2005, 2, 129–138.

57. Lee, C.C.; Gillies, E.R.; Fox, M.E.; Guillaudeu, S.J.; Fréchet, J.M.J.; Dy, E.E.; Szoka, F.C. A single dose of doxorubicin-functionalized bow-tie dendrimer cures mice bearing C-26 colon carcinomas. Proc. Natl. Acad. Sci. USA 2006, 103, 16649–16654.

58. Carlmark, A.; Malmström, E.; Malkoch, M. Dendritic architectures based on bis-MPA: Functional polymeric scaffolds for application-driven research. Chem. Soc. Rev. 2013, 42, 5858–5879.

59. Feliu, N.; Walter, M.V.; Montanez, M.I.; Kunzmann, A.; Hult, A.; Nyström, A.; Malkoch, M.; Fadeel, B. Stability and biocompatibility of a library of polyester dendrimers in comparison to polyamidoamine dendrimers. Biomaterials2012, 33, 1970–1981.

60. Walter, M.V.; Malkoch, M. Simplifying the synthesis of dendrimers: Accelerated approaches. Chem. Soc. Rev. 2012, 41, 4593–4609.

61. Medina, S.H.; El-Sayed, M.E.H. Dendrimers as carriers for delivery of chemotherapeutic agents. Chem. Rev. 2009, 109, 3141–3157.

62. Ihre, H.R.; Padilla de Jesús, O.L.; Szoka, F.C.; Fréchet, J.M.J. Polyester dendritic systems for drug delivery applications: Design, synthesis, and characterization. Bioconjugate Chem. 2002, 13, 443–452.

63. Padilla de Jesús, O.L.; Ihre, H.R.; Gagne, L.; Fréchet, J.M.J.; Szoka, F.C. Polyester dendritic systems for drug delivery applications: In vitro and in vivo evaluation. Bioconjugate Chem. 2002, 13, 453–461.

64. Lazniewska, J.; Milowska, K.; Gabryelak, T. Dendrimers—Revolutionary drugs for infectious diseases. Wiley Interdiscip. Rev. Nanomed. Nanobiotechnol. 2012, 4, 469–491.

65. El Kazzouli, S.; El Brahmi, N.; Mignani, S.; Bousmina, M.; Zablocka, M.; Majoral, J.P. From metallodrugs to metallodendrimers for nanotherapy in oncology: A concise overview. Curr. Med. Chem. 2012, 19, 4995–5010.

66. Malik, N.; Evagorou, E.G.; Duncan, R. Dendrimer-platinate: A novel approach to cancer chemotherapy. Anticancer Drugs 1999, 10, 767–776.

67. Ahn, S.; Lee, I.H.; Lee, E.; Kim, H.; Kim, Y.C.; Jon, S. Oral delivery of an anti-diabetic peptide drug via conjugation and complexation with low molecular weight chitosan. J. Control. Release 2013, 170, 226–232.

68. Sangwai, M.; Vavia, P. Amorphous ternary cyclodextrin nanocomposites of telmisartan for oral drug delivery: Improved solubility and reduced pharmacokinetic variability. Int. J. Pharmaceut. 2013, 453, 423–432.

69. Higuchi, W.I.; Ho, N.F.H.; Merkle, H.P. Design of oral-drug delivery systems—Past, present and future. Drug Dev. Ind. Pharm. 1983, 9, 1227–1239.

70. Mitra, S.B. Oral sustained-release drug delivery system using polymer film composites. Abstr. Pap. Am. Chem. S. 1983,185, 119.

71. Kulhari, H.; Kulhari, D.P.; Prajapati, S.K.; Chauhan, A.S. Pharmacokinetic and pharmacodynamic studies of poly(amidoamine) dendrimer based simvastatin oral formulations for the treatment of hypercholesterolemia. Mol. Pharmaceut. 2013, 10, 2528–2533.

72. Gajbhiye, V.; Kumar, P.V.; Sharma, A.; Agarwal, A.; Asthana, A.; Jain, N.K. Dendrimeric nanoarchitectures mediated transdermal and oral delivery of bioactives. Indian J. Pharm. Sci. 2008, 70, 431–439.

73. Ke, W.L.; Zhao, Y.S.; Huang, R.Q.; Jiang, C.; Pei, Y.Y. Enhanced oral bioavailability of doxorubicin in a dendrimer drug delivery system. J. Pharm. Sci. 2008, 97, 2208–2216.

74. Kolhatkar, R.B.; Swaan, P.; Ghandehari, H. Potential oral delivery of 7-Ethyl-10-hydroxy-camptothecin (SN-38) using poly(amidoamine) dendrimers. Pharm. Res. 2008, 25, 1723–1729.

75. Najlah, M.; Freeman, S.; Attwood, D.; D'Emanuele, A. Design and assessment of drug-dendrimer conjugates for oral drug delivery. J. Pharm. Pharmacol. 2004, 56, S67–S67.

76. Kalhapure, R.S.; Akamanchi, K.G. Oleodendrimers: A novel class of multicephalous heterolipids as chemical penetration enhancers for transdermal drug delivery. Int. J. Pharmaceut. 2013, 454, 158–166.

77. Filipowicz, A.; Wolowiec, S. Solubility and in vitro transdermal diffusion of riboflavin assisted by PAMAM dendrimers. Int. J. Pharmaceut. 2011, 408, 152–156.

78. Borowska, K.; Laskowska, B.; Magon, A.; Mysliwiec, B.; Pyda, M.; Wolowiec, S. PAMAM dendrimers as solubilizers and hosts for 8-methoxypsoralene enabling transdermal diffusion of the guest. Int. J. Pharmaceut. 2010, 398, 185–189.

79. Venuganti, V.V.K.; Perumal, O.P. Poly(amidoamine) dendrimers as skin penetration enhancers: Influence of charge, generation, and concentration. J. Pharm. Sci. 2009, 98, 2345–2356.

80. Cheng, Y.Y.; Man, N.; Xu, T.W.; Fu, R.Q.; Wang, X.Y.; Wang, X.M.; Wen, L.P. Transdermal delivery of nonsteroidal anti-inflammatory drugs mediated by polyamidoamine (PAMAM) dendrimers. J. Pharm. Sci. 2007, 96, 595–602.

81. Chauhan, A.S.; Sridevi, S.; Chalasani, K.B.; Jain, A.K.; Jain, S.K.; Jain, N.K.; Diwan, P.V. Dendrimer-mediated transdermal delivery: Enhanced bioavailability of indomethacin. J. Control. Release 2003, 90, 335–343.

82. Gaudana, R.; Ananthula, H.; Parenky, A.; Mitra, A. Ocular drug delivery. AAPS J. 2010, 12, 348–360.

83. Yang, H.; Kao, W.J. Dendrimers for pharmaceutical and biomedical applications. J. Biomat. Sci Polym. E. 2006, 17, 3–19.

84. Kambhampati, S.P.; Kannan, R.M. Dendrimer nanoparticles for ocular drug delivery. J. Ocul. Pharmacol. Ther. 2013,29, 151–165.

85. Fernandez, L.; Calderon, M.; Martinelli, M.; Strumia, M.; Cerecetto, H.; Gonzalez, M.; Silber, J.J.; Santo, M. Evaluation of a new dendrimeric structure as prospective drugs carrier for intravenous administration of antichagasic active compounds. J. Phys. Org. Chem. 2008, 21, 1079–1085.

86. Kaminskas, L.M.; Kota, J.; McLeod, V.M.; Kelly, B.D.; Karellas, P.; Porter, C.J.H. PEGylation of polylysine dendrimers improves absorption and lymphatic targeting following SC administration in rats. J. Control. Release 2009, 140, 108–116.

87. Merkel, O.M.; Mintzer, M.A.; Librizzi, D.; Samsonova, O.; Dicke, T.; Sproat, B.; Garn, H.; Barth, P.J.; Simanek, E.E.; Kissel, T. Triazine dendrimers as nonviral vectors for in vitro and in vivo RNAi: The effects of peripheral groups and core structure on biological activity. Mol. Pharmaceut. 2010, 7, 969–983.

88. Navath, R.S.; Kurtoglu, Y.E.; Wang, B.; Kannan, S.; Romero, R.; Kannan, R.M. Dendrimer-drug conjugates for tailored intracellular drug release based on glutathione levels. Bioconjugate Chem. 2008, 19, 2446–2455.

89. Ward, B.B.; Huang, B.H.; Desai, A.; Cheng, X.M.; Vartanian, M.; Zong, H.; Shi, X.Y.; Thomas, T.P.; Kotlyar, A.E.; van der Spek, A.; et al. Sustained analgesia achieved through esterase-activated morphine prodrugs complexed with PAMAM dendrimer. Pharm. Res. 2013, 30, 247–256.

90. Duncan, R. Polymer conjugates as anticancer nanomedicines. Nat. Rev. Cancer 2006, 6, 688–701.

91. Harris, J.M.; Chess, R.B. Effect of pegylation on pharmaceuticals. Nat. Rev. Drug Discov. 2003, 2, 214–221.

92. Bae, Y.; Fukushima, S.; Harada, A.; Kataoka, K. Design of environment-sensitive supramolecular assemblies for intracellular drug delivery: Polymeric micelles that are responsive to intracellular pH change. Angew. Chem. Int. Ed.2003, 42, 4640–4643.

93. Kataoka, K.; Harada, A.; Nagasaki, Y. Block copolymer micelles for drug delivery: Design, characterization and biological significance. Adv. Drug Delivery Rev. 2001, 47, 113–131.

94. Kataoka, K.; Harashima, H. Gene delivery systems: Viral vs. non-viral vectors. Adv. Drug Delivery Rev. 2001, 52, 151–151.

95. Vasey, P.A.; Kaye, S.B.; Morrison, R.; Twelves, C.; Wilson, P.; Duncan, R.; Thomson, A.H.; Murray, L.S.; Hilditch, T.E.; Murray, T.; et al. Phase I clinical and pharmacokinetic study of PK1 N-(2-hydroxypropyl)methacrylamide copolymer doxorubicin: First member of a new class of chemotherapeutic agents—Drug-polymer conjugates. Clinic. Cancer Res.1999, 5, 83–94.

96. Gillies, E.R.; Fréchet, J.M.J. Dendrimers and dendritic polymers in drug delivery. Drug Discov. Today 2005, 10, 35–43.

97. Gillies, E.R.; Goodwin, A.P.; Fréchet, J.M.J. Acetals as pH-sensitive linkages for drug delivery. Bioconjugate Chem.2004, 15, 1254–1263.

98. Van der Poll, D.G.; Kieler-Ferguson, H.M.; Floyd, W.C.; Guillaudeu, S.J.; Jerger, K.; Szoka, F.C.; Fréchet, J.M. Design, synthesis, and biological evaluation of a robust, biodegradable dendrimer. Bioconjugate Chem. 2010, 21, 764–773.

99. Nakanishi, T.; Fukushima, S.; Okamoto, K.; Suzuki, M.; Matsumura, Y.; Yokoyama, M.; Okano, T.; Sakurai, Y.; Kataoka, K. Development of the polymer micelle carrier system for doxorubicin. J. Control. Release 2001, 74, 295–302.

100. Haag, R. Supramolecular drug-delivery systems based on polymeric core-shell architectures. Angew. Chem. Int. Ed.2004, 43, 278–282.

101. Morgan, M.T.; Nakanishi, Y.; Kroll, D.J.; Griset, A.P.; Carnahan, M.A.; Wathier, M.; Oberlies, N.H.; Manikumar, G.; Wani, M.C.; Grinstaff, M.W. Dendrimer-encapsulated camptothecins: Increased solubility, cellular uptake, and cellular retention affords enhanced anticancer activity in vitro. Cancer Res. 2006, 66, 11913–11921.

102. Dhanikula, R.S.; Hildgen, P. Synthesis and evaluation of novel dendrimers with a hydrophilic interior as nanocarriers for drug delivery. Bioconjugate Chem. 2006, 17, 29–41.

103. Nazemi, A.; Haeryfar, S.M.M.; Gillies, E.R. Multifunctional dendritic sialopolymersomes as potential antiviral agents: Their lectin binding and drug release properties. Langmuir 2013, 29, 6420–6428.

104. Kim, S.H.; Tan, J.P.K.; Nederberg, F.; Fukushima, K.; Yang, Y.Y.; Waymouth, R.M.; Hedrick, J.L. Mixed micelle formation through stereocomplexation between enantiomeric poly(lactide) block copolymers. Macromolecules 2009,42, 25–29.

105. Skey, J.; Hansell, C.F.; O'Reilly, R.K. Stabilization of amino acid derived diblock copolymer micelles through favorable D:L side chain interactions. Macromolecules 2010, 43, 1309–1318.

106. Moughton, A.O.; O'Reilly, R.K. Noncovalently connected micelles, nanoparticles, and metal-functionalized nanocages using supramolecular self-assembly. J. Am. Chem. Soc. 2008, 130, 8714–8725.

107. Fukushima, K.; Pratt, R.C.; Nederberg, F.; Tan, J.P.K.; Yang, Y.Y.; Waymouth, R.M.; Hedrick, J.L. Organocatalytic approach to amphiphilic comb-block copolymers capable of stereocomplexation and self-assembly. Biomacromolecules2008, 9, 3051–3056.

108. Nederberg, F.; Appel, E.; Tan, J.P.K.; Kim, S.H.; Fukushima, K.; Sly, J.; Miller, R.D.; Waymouth, R.M.; Yang, Y.Y.; Hedrick, J.L. Simple approach to stabilized micelles employing miktoarm terpolymers and stereocomplexes with application in paclitaxel delivery. Biomacromolecules 2009, 10, 1460–1468.

109. Weaver, J.V.M.; Tang, Y.Q.; Liu, S.Y.; Iddon, P.D.; Grigg, R.; Billingham, N.C.; Armes, S.P.; Hunter, R.; Rannard, S.P. Preparation of shell cross-linked micelles by polyelectrolyte complexation. Angew. Chem. Int. Ed. 2004, 43, 1389–1392.

110. Giacomelli, C.; Schmidt, V.; Borsali, R. Specific interactions improve the loading capacity of block copolymer micelles in aqueous media. Langmuir 2007, 23, 6947–6955.

111. Chiang, Y.T.; Cheng, Y.T.; Lu, C.Y.; Yen, Y.W.; Yu, L.Y.; Yu, K.S.; Lyu, S.Y.; Yang, C.Y.; Lo, C.L. Polymer-liposome complexes with a functional hydrogen-bond cross-linker for preventing protein adsorption and improving tumor accumulation. Chem. Mater. 2013, 25, 4364–4372.

112. Hutin, M.; Burakowska-Meise, E.; Appel, W.P.J.; Dankers, P.Y.W.; Meijer, E.W. From molecular structure to macromolecular organization: Keys to design supramolecular biomaterials. Macromolecules 2013, 46, 8528–8537.

113. Zhu, Z.C.; Gao, N.; Wang, H.J.; Sukhishvili, S.A. Temperature-triggered on-demand drug release enabled by hydrogen-bonded multilayers of block copolymer micelles. J. Control. Release 2013, 171, 73–80.

114. Tadi, K.K.; Motghare, R.V. Rational synthesis of pindolol imprinted polymer by non-covalent protocol based on computational approach. J. Mol. Model. 2013, 19, 3385–3396.

115. Sanyakamdhorn, S.; Agudelo, D.; Tajmir-Riahi, H.A. Encapsulation of antitumor drug doxorubicin and its analogue by chitosan nanoparticles. Biomacromolecules 2013, 14, 557–563.

116. Kim, S.H.; Tan, J.P.K.; Nederberg, F.; Fukushima, K.; Colson, J.; Yang, C.A.; Nelson, A.; Yang, Y.Y.; Hedrick, J.L. Hydrogen bonding-enhanced micelle assemblies for drug delivery. Biomaterials 2010, 31, 8063–8071.

117. Zhou, J.; Soontornworajit, B.; Martin, J.; Sullenger, B.A.; Gilboa, E.; Wang, Y. A hybrid DNA aptamer-dendrimer nanomaterial for targeted cell labeling. Macromol. Biosci. 2009, 9, 831–835.

118. Battig, M.R.; Soontornworajit, B.; Wang, Y. Programmable release of multiple protein drugs from aptamer-functionalized hydrogels via nucleic acid hybridization. J. Am. Chem. Soc. 2012, 134, 12410–12413.

119. Zhang, Z.Y.; Chen, N.C.; Li, S.H.; Battig, M.R.; Wang, Y. Programmable hydrogels for controlled cell catch and release using hybridized

aptamers and complementary sequences. J. Am. Chem. Soc. 2012, 134, 15716–15719.

120. Soontornworajit, B.; Zhou, J.; Zhang, Z.Y.; Wang, Y. Aptamer-functionalized in situ injectable hydrogel for controlled protein release. Biomacromolecules 2010, 11, 2724–2730.

121. Zhou, J.; Soontornworajit, B.; Wang, Y. A temperature-responsive antibody-like nanostructure. Biomacromolecules2010, 11, 2087–2093.

122. Morgan, M.T.; Carnahan, M.A.; Immoos, C.E.; Ribeiro, A.A.; Finkelstein, S.; Lee, S.J.; Grinstaff, M.W. Dendritic molecular capsules for hydrophobic compounds. J. Am. Chem. Soc. 2003, 125, 15485–15489.

123. Antoni, P.; Hed, Y.; Nordberg, A.; Nyström, D.; von Holst, H.; Hult, A.; Malkoch, M. Bifunctional dendrimers: From robust synthesis and accelerated one-pot postfunctionalization strategy to potential applications. Angew. Chem. Int. Ed. 2009, 48, 2126–2130.

124. Jain, K.; Kesharwani, P.; Gupta, U.; Jain, N.K. Dendrimer toxicity: Let's meet the challenge. Int. J. Pharmaceut. 2010,394, 122–142.

125. Bernkop-Schnurch, A.; Scholler, S.; Biebel, R.G. Development of controlled drug release systems based on thiolated polymers. J. Control. Release 2000, 66, 39–48.

126. Hawker, C.J.; Fréchet, J.M.J. Unusual macromolecular architectures—The convergent growth approach to dendritic polyesters and novel block copolymers. J. Am. Chem. Soc. 1992, 114, 8405–8413.

127. Haddleton, D.M.; Sahota, H.S.; Taylor, P.C.; Yeates, S.G. Synthesis of polyester dendrimers. J. Chem. Soc. Perkin Trans. 1 1996, 649–656.

128. Antoni, P.; Nyström, D.; Hawker, C.J.; Hult, A.; Malkoch, M. A chemoselective approach for the accelerated synthesis of well-defined dendritic architectures. Chem. Commun. 2007, 2249–2251.

129. Ihre, H.; Hult, A.; Söderlind, E. Synthesis, characterization, and H-1 NMR self-diffusion studies of dendritic aliphatic polyesters based on 2,2-bis(hydroxymethyl)propionic acid and 1,1,1-tris(hydroxyphenyl)ethane. J. Am. Chem. Soc.1996, 118, 6388–6395.

130. Ihre, H.; Padilla de Jesús, O.L.; Fréchet, J.M.J. Fast and convenient divergent synthesis of aliphatic ester dendrimers by anhydride coupling. J. Am. Chem. Soc. 2001, 123, 5908–5917.

131. Parrott, M.C.; Benhabbour, S.R.; Saab, C.; Lemon, J.A.; Parker, S.; Valliant, J.F.; Adronov, A. Synthesis, radiolabeling, and bio-imaging of high-generation polyester dendrimers. J. Am. Chem. Soc. 2009, 131, 2906–2916.

132. Bouillon, C.; Tintaru, A.; Monnier, V.; Charles, L.; Quelever, G.; Peng, L. Synthesis of poly(amino)ester dendrimers via active cyanomethyl ester intermediates. J. Org. Chem. 2010, 75, 8685–8688.

133. Twibanire, J.K.; Al-Mughaid, H.; Grindley, T.B. Synthesis of new cores and their use in the preparation of polyester dendrimers. Tetrahedron 2010, 66, 9602–9609.

134. Keefe, G.E.; Twibanire, J.K.; Grindley, T.B.; Shaver, M.P. Poly(lactic acid) polymer stars built from early generation dendritic polyols. Can. J. Chem. 2013, 91, 392–397.

135. Twibanire, J.K.; Grindley, T.B. Polyester dendrimers. Polymers 2012, 4, 794–879.

136. Knorr, R.; Trzeciak, A.; Bannwarth, W.; Gillessen, D. New coupling reagents in peptide chemistry. Tetrahedron Lett.1989, 30, 1927–1930.

137. Carpino, L.A. 1-Hydroxy-7-azabenzotriazole-An efficient peptide coupling additive. J. Am. Chem. Soc. 1993, 115, 4397–4398.

138. El-Faham, A.; Subirós Funosas, R.; Prohens, R.; Albericio, F. COMU: A safer and more effective replacement for benzotriazole-based uronium coupling reagents. Chem. Eur. J. 2009, 15, 9404–9416.

139. Twibanire, J.K.; Grindley, T.B. Efficient and controllably selective preparation of esters using uronium-based coupling agents. Org. Lett. 2011, 13, 2988–2991.

140. Twibanire, J.K.; Omran, R.P.; Grindley, T.B. Facile synthesis of a library of lyme disease glycolipid antigens. Org. Lett.2012, 14, 3909–3911.

141. Paul, N.K.; Twibanire, J.K.; Grindley, T.B. Direct synthesis of maradolipids and other trehalose 6-monoesters and 6,6′-diesters. J. Org. Chem. 2013, 78, 363–369.

142. Hawker, C.J.; Fréchet, J.M.J. Preparation of polymers with controlled molecular architecture—A new convergent approach to dendritic macromolecules. J. Am. Chem. Soc. 1990, 112, 7638–7647.

143. Hawker, C.J.; Fréchet, J.M.J. A new convergent approach to monodisperse dendritic macromolecules. J. Chem. Soc. Chem. Commun. 1990, 1990, 1010–1013.

144. Hawker, C.J.; Lee, R.; Fréchet, J.M.J. One-step synthesis of hyperbranched dendritic polyesters. J. Am. Chem. Soc.1991, 113, 4583–4588.

145. Hawker, C.J.; Fréchet, J.M.J. Monodispersed dendritic polyesters with removable chain ends—A versatile approach to globular macromolecules with chemically reversible polarities. J. Chem. Soc. Perkin Trans. 1 1992, 2459–2469.

146. Guillaudeu, S.J.; Fox, M.E.; Haidar, Y.M.; Dy, E.E.; Szoka, F.C.; Fréchet, J.M.J. PEGylated dendrimers with core functionality for biological applications. Bioconjugate Chem. 2008, 19, 461–469.

147. Gillies, E.R.; Fréchet, J.M.J. Synthesis and self-assembly of supramolecular dendritic "Bow-Ties": Effect of peripheral functionality on association constants. J. Org. Chem. 2004, 69, 46–53.

148. Krishna, R.; Mayer, L.D. Liposomal doxorubicin circumvents PSC 833-free drug interactions, resulting in effective therapy of multidrug-resistant solid tumors. Cancer Res. 1997, 57, 5246–5253.

149. Kaneko, T.; Willner, D.; Monkovic, I.; Knipe, J.O.; Braslawsky, G.R.; Greenfield, R.S.; Vyas, D.M. New hydrazone derivatives of Adriamycin and their immunoconjugates: A correlation between acid stability and cytotoxicity.Bioconjugate Chem. 1991, 2, 133–141.

150. Lee, C.C.; Cramer, A.T.; Szoka, F.C.; Frechet, J.M.J. An intramolecular cyclization reaction is responsible for the in vivo inefficacy and apparent pH insensitive hydrolysis kinetics of hydrazone carboxylate derivatives of doxorubicin.Bioconjugate Chem. 2006, 17, 1364–1368.

151. Duncan, R. The dawning era of polymer therapeutics. Nat. Rev. Drug Discov. 2003, 2, 347–360.

152. Seymour, L.W.; Ulbrich, K.; Steyger, P.S.; Brereton, M.; Subr, V.; Strohalm, J.; Duncan, R. Tumor tropism and anticancer efficacy of polymer-based doxorubicin prodrugs in the treatment of subcutaneous murine b16f10 melanoma. Brit. J. Cancer 1994, 70, 636–641.

153. Huang, S.K.; Mayhew, E.; Gilani, S.; Lasic, D.D.; Martin, F.J.; Papahadjopoulos, D. Pharmacokinetics and therapeutics of sterically

stabilized liposomes in mice bearing C-26 colon-carcinoma. Cancer Res. 1992, 52, 6774–6781.

154. Mayhew, E.G.; Goldrosen, M.H.; Vaage, J.; Rustum, Y.M. Effects of liposome-entrapped doxorubicin on liver metastases of mouse colon carcinoma-26 and carcinoma-38. J. Natl. Cancer Inst. 1987, 78, 707–713.

155. Namazi, H.; Bahrami, S.; Entezami, A.A. Synthesis and controlled release of biocompatible prodrugs of beta-cyclodextrin linked with PEG containing ibuprofen or indomethacin. Iran. Polym. J. 2005, 14, 921–927.

156. Namazi, H.; Adeli, M. Novel linear-globular thermoreversible hydrogel ABA type copolymers from dendritic citric acid as the A blocks and poly(ethyleneglycol) as the B block. Eur. Polym. J. 2003, 39, 1491–1500.

157. Namazi, H.; Adell, M. Dendrimers of citric acid and poly (ethylene glycol) as the new drug-delivery agents.Biomaterials 2005, 26, 1175–1183.

158. Hawthorne, M.F. The role of chemistry in the development of boron neutron-capture therapy of cancer. Angew. Chem. Int. Ed. Engl. 1993, 32, 950–984.

159. Soloway, A.H.; Tjarks, W.; Barnum, B.A.; Rong, F.G.; Barth, R.F.; Codogni, I.M.; Wilson, J.G. The chemistry of neutron capture therapy. Chem. Rev. 1998, 98, 1515–1562.

160. Kawabata, S.; Hiramatsu, R.; Kuroiwa, T.; Ono, K.; Miyatake, S.-I. Boron neutron capture therapy for recurrent high-grade meningiomas Clinical article. J. Neurosurg. 2013, 119, 837–844.

161. Sun, T.; Zhang, Z.; Li, B.; Chen, G.; Xie, X.; Wei, Y.; Wu, J.; Zhou, Y.; Du, Z. Boron neutron capture therapy induces cell cycle arrest and cell apoptosis of glioma stem/progenitor cells in vitro. Radiat. Oncol. 2013, 8.

162. Hawthorne, M.F.; Lee, M.W. A critical assessment of boron target compounds for boron neutron capture therapy. J. NeuroOncol. 2003, 62, 33–45.

163. Parrott, M.C.; Marchington, E.B.; Valliant, J.F.; Adronov, A. Synthesis and properties of carborane-functionalized aliphatic polyester dendrimers. J. Am. Chem. Soc. 2005, 127, 12081–12089.

164. Newkome, G.R.; Moorefield, C.N.; Keith, J.M.; Baker, G.R.; Escamilla, G.H. Chemistry within a unimolecular micelle precursor: Boron superclusters by site-specific and depth-specific transformations of dendrimers. 37. Chemistry of micelles. Angew. Chem. Int. Ed. Engl. 1994, 33, 666–668.

165. Cragg, G.M.; Newman, D.J.; Snader, K.M. Natural products in drug discovery and development. J. Nat. Prod. 1997,60, 52–60.

166. Cragg, G.M.; Newman, D.J.; Weiss, R.B. Coral reefs, forests, and thermal vents: The worldwide exploration of nature for novel antitumor agents. Semin. Oncol. 1997, 24, 156–163.

167. Oberlies, N.H.; Kroll, D.J. Camptothecin and taxol: Historic achievements in natural products research. J. Nat. Prod.2004, 67, 129–135.

168. Garcia-Carbonero, R.; Supko, J.G. Current perspectives on the clinical experience, pharmacology, and continued development of the camptothecins. Clinic. Cancer Res. 2002, 8, 641–661.

169. Thomas, C.J.; Rahier, N.J.; Hecht, S.M. Camptothecin: Current perspectives. Bioorg. Med. Chem. 2004, 12, 1585–1604.

170. Sriram, D.; Yogeeswari, P.; Thirumurugan, R.; Bal, T.R. Camptothecin and its analogues: A review on their chemotherapeutic potential. Nat. Prod. Res. 2005, 19, 393–412.

171. Hecht, J.R. Gastrointestinal toxicity of irinotecan. Oncology NY 1998, 12, 72–78.

172. Armstrong, D.K. Topotecan dosing guidelines in ovarian cancer: Reduction and management of hematologic toxicity.Oncologist 2004, 9, 33–42.

173. Feng, X.S.; Pinaud, J.; Chaikof, E.L.; Taton, D.; Gnanou, Y. Sequential functionalization of janus-type dendrimer-like poly(ethylene oxide)s with camptothecin and folic acid. J. Polym. Sci. Part A Polym. Sci. 2011, 49, 2839–2849.

174. Fox, M.E.; Guillaudeu, S.; Fréchet, J.M.J.; Jerger, K.; Macaraeg, N.; Szoka, F.C. Synthesis and in vivo antitumor efficacy of pegylated poly(l-lysine) dendrimer-camptothecin conjugates. Mol. Pharmaceut. 2009, 6, 1562–1572.

175. Thiagarajan, G.; Ray, A.; Malugin, A.; Ghandehari, H. PAMAM-camptothecin conjugate inhibits proliferation and induces nuclear

fragmentation in colorectal carcinoma cells. Pharm. Res. 2010, 27, 2307–2316.

176. Bolten, B.M.; DeGregorio, T. Trends in development cycles. Nat. Rev. Drug Discov. 2002, 1, 335–336.

177. Langer, R. Drug delivery and targeting. Nature 1998, 392, 5–10.

178. Dhanikula, R.S.; Hildgen, P. Influence of molecular architecture of polyether-co-polyester dendrimers on the encapsulation and release of methotrexate. Biomaterials 2007, 28, 3140–3152.

179. Lee, C.C.; Yoshida, M.; Fréchet, J.M.J.; Dy, E.E.; Szoka, F.C. In vitro and in vivo evaluation of hydrophilic dendronized linear polymers. Bioconjugate Chem. 2005, 16, 535–541.

180. Lee, C.C.; Grayson, S.M.; Fréchet, J.M.J. Synthesis of narrow-polydispersity degradable dendronized aliphatic polyesters. J. Polym. Sci. Part A Polym. Sci. 2004, 42, 3563–3578.

181. Goldspiel, B.R. Clinical overview of the taxanes. Pharmacotherapy 1997, 17, S110–S125.

182. Wang, T.H.; Wang, H.S.; Soong, Y.K. Paclitaxel-induced cell death—Where the cell cycle and apoptosis come together. Cancer 2000, 88, 2619–2628.

183. Szebeni, J.; Muggia, F.M.; Alving, C.R. Complement activation by cremophor EL as a possible contributor to hypersensitivity to paclitaxel: An in vitro study. J. Natl. Cancer Inst. 1998, 90, 300–306.

184. Hennenfent, K.L.; Govindan, R. Novel formulations of taxanes: A review. Old wine in a new bottle? Ann. Oncol. 2006,17, 735–749.

185. Wu, J.; Liu, Q.; Lee, R.J. A folate receptor-targeted liposomal formulation for paclitaxel. Int. J. Pharmaceut. 2006, 316, 148–153.

186. Ooya, T.; Lee, J.; Park, K. Hydrotropic dendrimers of generations 4 and 5: Synthesis, characterization, and hydrotropic solubilization of paclitaxel. Bioconjugate Chem. 2004, 15, 1221–1229.

187. Le Garrec, D.; Gori, S.; Luo, L.; Lessard, D.; Smith, D.C.; Yessine, M.A.; Ranger, M.; Leroux, J.C. Poly(N-vinylpyrrolidone)-block-poly(D,L-lactide) as a new polymeric solubilizer for hydrophobic anticancer drugs: In vitroand in vivo evaluation. J. Control. Release 2004, 99, 83–101.

188. Lee, S.C.; Huh, K.M.; Lee, J.; Cho, Y.W.; Galinsky, R.E.; Park, K. Hydrotropic polymeric micelles for enhanced paclitaxel solubility: In vitro and in vivo characterization. Biomacromolecules 2007, 8, 202–208.

189. Khandare, J.J.; Jayant, S.; Singh, A.; Chandna, P.; Wang, Y.; Vorsa, N.; Minko, T. Dendrimer versus linear conjugate: Influence of polymeric architecture on the delivery and anticancer effect of paclitaxel. Bioconjugate Chem. 2006, 17, 1464–1472.

190. Majoros, I.J.; Myc, A.; Thomas, T.; Mehta, C.B.; Baker, J.R. PAMAM dendrimer-based multifunctional conjugate for cancer therapy: Synthesis, characterization, and functionality. Biomacromolecules 2006, 7, 572–579.

191. Zhang, Z.P.; Feng, S.S. The drug encapsulation efficiency, in vitro drug release, cellular uptake and cytotoxicity of paclitaxel-loaded poly(lactide)-tocopheryl polyethylene glycol succinate nanoparticles. Biomaterials 2006, 27, 4025–4033.

192. Ceruti, M.; Crosasso, P.; Brusa, P.; Arpicco, S.; Dosio, F.; Cattel, L. Preparation, characterization, cytotoxicity and pharmacokinetics of liposomes containing water-soluble prodrugs of paclitaxel. J. Control. Release 2000, 63, 141–153.

193. Crosasso, P.; Ceruti, M.; Brusa, P.; Arpicco, S.; Dosio, F.; Cattel, L. Preparation, characterization and properties of sterically stabilized paclitaxel-containing liposomes. J. Control. Release 2000, 63, 19–30.

194. Kontoyianni, C.; Sideratou, Z.; Theodossiou, T.; Tziveleka, L.A.; Tsiourvas, D.; Paleos, C.M. A novel micellar PEGylated hyperbranched polyester as a prospective drug delivery system for paclitaxel. Macromol. Biosci. 2008, 8, 871–881.

195. Malmström, E.; Johansson, M.; Hult, A. Hyperbranched aliphatic polyesters. Macromolecules 1995, 28, 1698–1703.

196. Gupta, U.; Agashe, H.B.; Asthana, A.; Jain, N.K. Dendrimers: Novel polymeric nanoarchitectures for solubility enhancement. Biomacromolecules 2006, 7, 649–658.

197. Reul, R.; Renette, T.; Bege, N.; Kissel, T. Nanoparticles for paclitaxel delivery: A comparative study of different types of dendritic polyesters and their degradation behavior. Int. J. Pharmaceut. 2011, 407, 190–196.

198. Chen, S.; Zhang, X.Z.; Cheng, S.X.; Zhuo, R.X.; Gu, Z.W. Functionalized amphiphilic hyperbranched polymers for targeted drug delivery. Biomacromolecules 2008, 9, 2578–2585.

199. Wang, J.; Xu, T. Facile construction of multivalent targeted drug delivery system from Boltorn-® series hyperbranched aliphatic polyester and folic acid. Polym. Adv. Technol. 2011, 22, 763–767.

200. Zeng, X.H.; Zhang, Y.N.; Wu, Z.H.; Lundberg, P.; Malkoch, M.; Nyström, A.M. Hyperbranched copolymer micelles as delivery vehicles of doxorubicin in breast cancer cells. J. Polym. Sci. Part A Polym. Sci. 2012, 50, 280–288.

201. Fox, M.E.; Szoka, F.C.; Fréchet, J.M.J. Soluble polymer carriers for the treatment of cancer: The importance of molecular architecture. Acc. Chem. Res. 2009, 42, 1141–1151.

202. Akiyoshi, K.; Deguchi, S.; Moriguchi, N.; Yamaguchi, S.; Sunamoto, J. Self-aggregates of hydrophobized polysaccharides in water-Formation and characteristics of nanoparticles. Macromolecules 1993, 26, 3062–3068.

203. Kwon, G.S.; Kataoka, K. Block-copolymer micelles as long-circulating drug vehicles. Adv. Drug Delivery Rev. 1995, 16, 295–309.

204. Torchilin, V.P. Structure and design of polymeric surfactant-based drug delivery systems. J. Control. Release 2001, 73, 137–172.

205. Jones, M.C.; Leroux, J.C. Polymeric micelles-A new generation of colloidal drug carriers. Eur. J. Pharmaceut. Biopharmaceut. 1999, 48, 101–111.

206. Lawrence, M.J. Surfactant systems-Their use in drug-delivery. Chem. Soc. Rev. 1994, 23, 417–424.

207. Cao, W.Q.; Zhou, J.; Mann, A.; Wang, Y.; Zhu, L. Folate-functionalized unimolecular micelles based on a degradable amphiphilic dendrimer-like star polymer for cancer cell-targeted drug delivery. Biomacromolecules 2011, 12, 2697–2707.

208. Cao, W.Q.; Zhu, L. Synthesis and unimolecular micelles of amphiphilic dendrimer-like star polymer with various functional surface groups. Macromolecules 2011, 44, 1500–1512.

209. Cao, W.Q.; Zhou, J.; Wang, Y.; Zhu, L. Synthesis and in vitro cancer cell targeting of folate-functionalized biodegradable amphiphilic

dendrimer-like star polymers. Biomacromolecules 2010, 11, 3680–3687.

210. Pan, X.Q.; Wang, H.Q.; Lee, R.J. Antitumor activity of folate receptor-targeted liposomal doxorubicin in a KB oral carcinoma murine xenograft model. Pharm. Res. 2003, 20, 417–422.

211. Lu, Y.J.; Low, P.S. Folate-mediated delivery of macromolecular anticancer therapeutic agents. Adv. Drug Delivery Rev.2002, 54, 675–693.

212. Wang, S.; Low, P.S. Folate-mediated targeting of antineoplastic drags, imaging agents, and nucleic acids to cancer cells. J. Control. Release 1998, 53, 39–48.

213. Brinkhuis, R.P.; Rutjes, F.; van Hest, J.C.M. Polymeric vesicles in biomedical applications. Polym. Chem. 2011, 2, 1449–1462.

214. Pourtau, L.; Oliveira, H.; Thevenot, J.; Wan, Y.L.; Brisson, A.R.; Sandre, O.; Miraux, S.; Thiaudiere, E.; Lecommandoux, S. Antibody-functionalized magnetic polymersomes: In vivo targeting and imaging of bone metastases using high resolution MRI. Adv. Heathc. Mater. 2013, 2, 1420–1424.

215. Huang, Z.H.; Teng, W.; Liu, L.S.; Wang, L.C.; Wang, Q.M.; Dong, Y.G. Efficient cytosolic delivery mediated by polymersomes facilely prepared from a degradable, amphiphilic, and amphoteric copolymer. Nanotechnology 2013,24.

216. Oliveira, H.; Perez-Andres, E.; Thevenot, J.; Sandre, O.; Berra, E.; Lecommandoux, S. Magnetic field triggered drug release from polymersomes for cancer therapeutics. J. Control. Release 2013, 169, 165–170.

217. Debets, M.F.; Leenders, W.P.J.; Verrijp, K.; Zonjee, M.; Meeuwissen, S.A.; Otte-Holler, I.; van Hest, J.C.M. Nanobody-functionalized polymersomes for tumor-vessel targeting. Macromol. Biosci. 2013, 13, 938–945.

218. Spulber, M.; Najer, A.; Winkelbach, K.; Glaied, O.; Waser, M.; Pieles, U.; Meier, W.; Bruns, N. Photoreaction of a hydroxyalkyphenone with the membrane of polymersomes: A versatile method to generate semipermeable nanoreactors. J. Am. Chem. Soc. 2013, 135, 9204–9212.

219. Petersen, M.A.; Hillmyer, M.A.; Kokkoli, E. Bioresorbable polymersomes for targeted delivery of cisplatin.Bioconjugate Chem. 2013, 24, 533–543.

220. Qiao, Z.Y.; Ji, R.; Huang, X.N.; Du, F.S.; Zhang, R.; Liang, D.H.; Li, Z.C. Polymersomes from dual responsive block copolymers: Drug encapsulation by heating and acid-triggered release. Biomacromolecules 2013, 14, 1555–1563.

221. Stano, A.; Scott, E.A.; Dane, K.Y.; Swartz, M.A.; Hubbell, J.A. Tunable T cell immunity towards a protein antigen using polymersomes vs. solid-core nanoparticles. Biomaterials 2013, 34, 4339–4346.

222. Cui, H.G.; Chen, Z.Y.; Zhong, S.; Wooley, K.L.; Pochan, D.J. Block copolymer assembly via kinetic controlled. Science2007, 317, 647–650.

223. Zhang, S.Y.; Zhao, Y. Rapid release of entrapped contents from multi-functionalizable, surface cross-linked micelles upon different stimulation. J. Am. Chem. Soc. 2010, 132, 10642–10644.

224. Tong, R.; Cheng, J.J. Anticancer polymeric nanomedicines. Polym. Rev. 2007, 47, 345–381.

225. Danhier, F.; Lecouturier, N.; Vroman, B.; Jerome, C.; Marchand-Brynaert, J.; Feron, O.; Preat, V. Paclitaxel-loaded PEGylated PLGA-based nanoparticles: In vitro and in vivo evaluation. J. Control. Release 2009, 133, 11–17.

Chapter 3

Enzymatic Polymerization of Cyclic Monomers in Ionic Liquids as a Prospective Synthesis Method for Polyesters Used in Drug Delivery Systems

Urszula Piotrowska [1,*] and Marcin Sobczak [1,2]

[1]Department of Inorganic and Analytical Chemistry, Faculty of Pharmacy, Medical University of Warsaw, Banacha 1, Warsaw 02-097, Poland

[2]Chair of Chemistry, Department of Organic Chemistry, Faculty of Materials Science and Design, Kazimierz Pulaski University of Technology and Humanities in Radom, Chrobrego 27, Radom 26-600, Poland

ABSTRACT

Biodegradable or bioresorbable polymers are commonly used in various pharmaceutical fields (e.g., as drug delivery systems, therapeutic systems or macromolecular drug conjugates). Polyesters are an important class of polymers widely utilized in pharmacy due to their biodegradability and biocompatibility features. In recent years, there has been increased interest in enzyme-catalyzed ring-opening polymerization (e-ROP) of cyclic esters as an alternative method of preparation of biodegradable or bioresorbable polymers. Ionic liquids (ILs) have been presented as green solvents in enzymatic ring-opening polymerization. The activity, stability, selectivity of enzymes in ILs and the ability to catalyze polyester synthesis under these conditions are discussed. Overall, the review demonstrates that e-ROP of lactones or lactides could be an effective method for the synthesis of useful biomedical polymers.

Keywords: biomedical polymers; macromolecular conjugates of drugs; enzymatic ring opening polymerization; ionic liquids; biodegradable polyesters; drug delivery systems

1. INTRODUCTION

A large part of currently used chemotherapeutic agents are low molecular weight compounds (e.g., nucleic acids, peptides, enzymes). They are characterized by fast metabolism and fast excretion from the organism as well as adverse biodistribution and low therapeutic selectivity. To solve this problem, conventional therapies focus on dosage of active pharmaceutical ingredients (APIs) in a high frequency manner. The disadvantages of such a solution are the possibility of adverse reactions resulting in variable concentration of chemotherapeutic agents or their excessive level in a healthy tissues [1].

A promising approach to safely achieving desired therapeutic effect of APIs are polymer-based drug delivery systems (DDS) [2]. Polymeric carriers exhibit suitable pharmacokinetics, biodistribution, and pharmacological efficacy. They increase the bioavailability of the therapeutic agents by modification of the API's solubility. Polymeric carriers also provide protection against endocytosis, phagocytosis, enzymatic degradation and cause reduction in antigenic activity of the drug leading to less pronounced immunological body responses. The tissue types or disease-specific structures are taken into account. It results in appropriate matching of distribution place to the drug release mechanism (active or passive transport) [3].

A few fundamental requirements should be met for any polymer material to be used as a drug carrier: excellent biocompatibility, precision biodistribution and predictable release profile of the therapeutic substances. Rationally designed polymeric carriers have some advantages, e.g., elimination of multiple therapeutic substances which are used during the day or reducing the daily dose. Therefore they provide required toxicological safety while maintaining a high efficiency [4,5]. Development of a new DDS is highly prioritized direction of the modern pharmacy and medicine.

Aliphatic polyesters and copolymers of cyclic esters and carbonates are representatives of a family of polymers commonly used in DDS technology. In this paper, we aim to demonstrate some of the current directions in developing synthesis methods for biodegradable or bioresorbable polyester carriers.

2. POLYMERIC CARRIERS

There are currently two main methods for obtaining polymer-based DDS. The first method consists of the usage of therapeutic agents immobilized *via* incorporation into a variety of polymeric biomaterials. The active substances are suspended or dissolved into the polymer matrix. The API's release rate depends on the hydrophilic-hydrophobic properties, degree of crystallinity, molecular weight, polydispersity and architecture of the polymer carriers, as well as the therapeutic agent's properties (e.g., solubility, concentration gradient) and process conditions (pH, temperature, ionic strength, presence of enzymes, *etc.*). It is also possible to modify drug release kinetics by optimizing the matrices' synthesis parameters. The release of APIs from biodegradable matrices can be governed by several mechanisms: (1) diffusion of therapeutic agents through the polymer matrix; (2) degradation (erosion) of the polymer; (3) by the influence the osmotic pressure. However, many biodegradable DDS are very complex and the release occurs through a combination of several concurrent mechanisms [6,7].

3. MACROMOLECULAR CONJUGATES OF ACTIVE SUBSTANCES

Polymeric prodrugs (or macromolecular conjugates of drugs) are a specific type of therapeutic agents in which APIs are linked to a macromolecular carrier (promoiety) through a physiologically labile bond [8,9]. Release of small therapeutic molecules from those systems can be achieved by polymer hydrolysis. APIs are subsequently metabolized into the active precursors through enzymatic or non-enzymatic process. The process takes place prior to their (the APIs') absorption, after absorption, or at a specific site of the system. Macromolecular prodrugs are very promising API carriers. The high potential of these hybrid materials stems from the synergistic interaction between the elements of their composition [10,11].

In 1975 Helmut Ringsdorf proposed a model for the rational design of polymeric prodrug (Figure 1) [12,13]. This model is based on a polymeric matrix linking therapeutic substances *via* covalent bonds. Several types of labile bonds (e.g., amide, carbonate, ester, urethane) can be used to form biodegradable or bioresorbable polymeric-APIs conjugates.

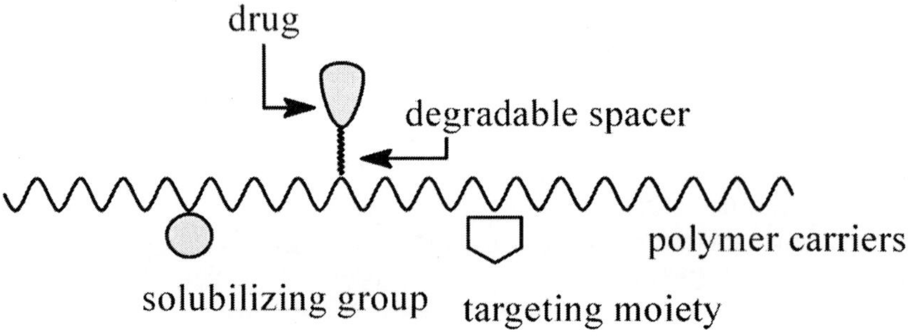

Figure 1. Polymer-drug conjugate model proposed by Ringsdorf.

The therapeutic molecules can be incorporated into the polymer chain, may be linked at the end of macromolecular chains or can form pendant groups on the polymeric chain. Prodrugs usually include several components: (1) polymeric carrier; (2) API; (3) targeting moiety *i.e.*, antibodies, sugars, peptides, proteins or oligonucleotides, which are responsible for the selectively deliver of the APIs to the appropriate tissue; (4) solubilizing group, which is responsible for an increased solubility of low solubility or insoluble therapeutic agents [9,14,15,16].

The use of a properly designed carrier for targeted pharmaceutical delivery leads to an increased accumulation of therapeutic molecules in the target tissue. This is the result of: (1) the appropriate molecular weight of the polymer (a slow degradation of the macromolecules extends the biological half-life of the drug in the tissue); (2) structure and origin of the carrier (synthetic or natural polymers such as proteins, polysaccharides); (3) presence of a specific targeting moiety [11,17].

Polymeric carriers are able to provide active or passive targeting of the APIs specifically to the site of their action. Passive targeting usually depends upon an enhanced permeation and retention (EPR) effect and is widely used as an approach for targeting tumor cells due to the specific differentiated properties of tumor tissues (enhanced vascular permeability, poor lymphatic drainage) [18,19]. High concentrations of pharmaceuticals in tumors have been achieved by entrapping and accumulating API molecules for prolonged periods. Therapeutic agents may also be transported into the cell by concentration differences of APIs on the opposite sides of a cellular membrane [20].

4. ALIPHATIC POLYESTERS AS A CARRIERS OF THERAPEUTIC AGENTS

Biopolymers and their derivatives are commonly used in pharmacy as biomaterials for DDS. Polymers derived from synthetic monomers also show excellent delivery properties. The most promising group are biocompatible and biodegradable polymers (Table 1). They can be readily hydrolyzed into non-toxic and removable products and then excluded by normal metabolic processes [7,15,21].

Table 1. Examples of DDS obtained from polyesters.

Polyesters	Therapeutic Agent	Ref.
poly(lactide-*co*-glycolide) (PLG)	Amphotericin B	[23,24]
	Ciprofloxacin	[25,26]
	Cisplatin	[27]
	Docetaxel	[28]
	Doxorubicin	[29,30]
	Paclitaxel	[31,32]
	Rifampicin	[33]
	r-hGH (recombinant human growth hormone)	[34]
polylactide (PLA)	Camptothecin	[35,36]
	Doxorubicin	[37,38]
	5-fluorouracil	[39]
poly(ε-caprolactone) (PCL)	Amphotericin B	[40]
	Ciprofloxacin	[41]
	Citropin	[42]
	Vancomycin	[43]

Bioresorbable and biodegradable aliphatic polyesters have been extensively investigated as matrices for DDS. They are commonly known as synthetic polymers for biomedical application. The presence of suitable functional groups (hydroxyl and carboxyl) in their molecules allows covalent coupling of therapeutic agents while maintaining their activity. These polyesters include lactides (e.g., dimer of lactic acid, glycolide), lactones (β-propiolactone, δ-valerolactone, ε-caprolactone) and copolymers of various heterocyclic monomers such as *rac*-lactide, L-lactide, glycolide, ε-caprolactone and trimethylene carbonate. They are degraded *in vivo* by hydrolysis reactions into non-toxic products such as glycolic acid, lactic acid or other compounds that become involved in the tricarboxylic acid cycle and are subsequently excreted as carbon dioxide and water. The kinetics of polyester degradation can be tailored by the modifying their morphologies and hydrophilicities during the synthesis [15,21,22].

5. RING OPENING POLYMERIZATION OF CYCLIC ESTERS

There are currently two main methods for the synthesis of aliphatic polyesters, namely polycondensation and ring opening polymerization (ROP) of cyclic monomers. ROP is the most common method for synthesizing aliphatic polyesters with tailored properties and controlled architecture with desired end groups (which is very important in biomedical applications). The ROP process gives polyesters with high molecular weight, high purity and low polydispersity compared to the polycondensation process, so it is the preferred route in controlled release technology. This method also avoids formation of by-product such as water, the presence of which can cause a shift of the thermodynamic equilibrium of the reaction towards hydrolysis. Several possible combinations of type of monomer, temperature, time, initiators and catalysts have been evaluated to achieve the desired polymer architecture and properties. The ROP of cyclic esters can be performed in the presence of cationic or anionic initiators as well as metal coordinate and enzymatic catalysts [44,45,46]. The scheme of preparation of biodegradable or bioresorbable polyesters used in technology of DDS is shown in Scheme 1.

6. BIOCATALYTIC SYNTHESIS OF POLYMERS FOR BIOMEDICAL APPLICATIONS

A large number of enzymes catalyze the synthesis of natural polymers such as polysaccharides, proteins or polyesters in living systems [47]. Enzymes can be highly chemoselective, enantioselective and regioselective. They allow for synthesis of macromolecules with well-defined architectures (end-functional polymers).

Enzyme catalysis has provided a new synthetic strategy for a variety of useful biomaterials, most of which would to be difficult to produce using conventional chemical catalysts [48,49,50,51,52,53,54]. For example, tin(II) 2-ethylhexanoate $Sn(Oct)_2$, probably the most often used catalyst in the polymerization of cyclic esters, has been approved by FDA as a food additive. However, it is difficult to completely remove residual organo-tin catalyst, which leads to toxicity problems for biomedical applications [55].

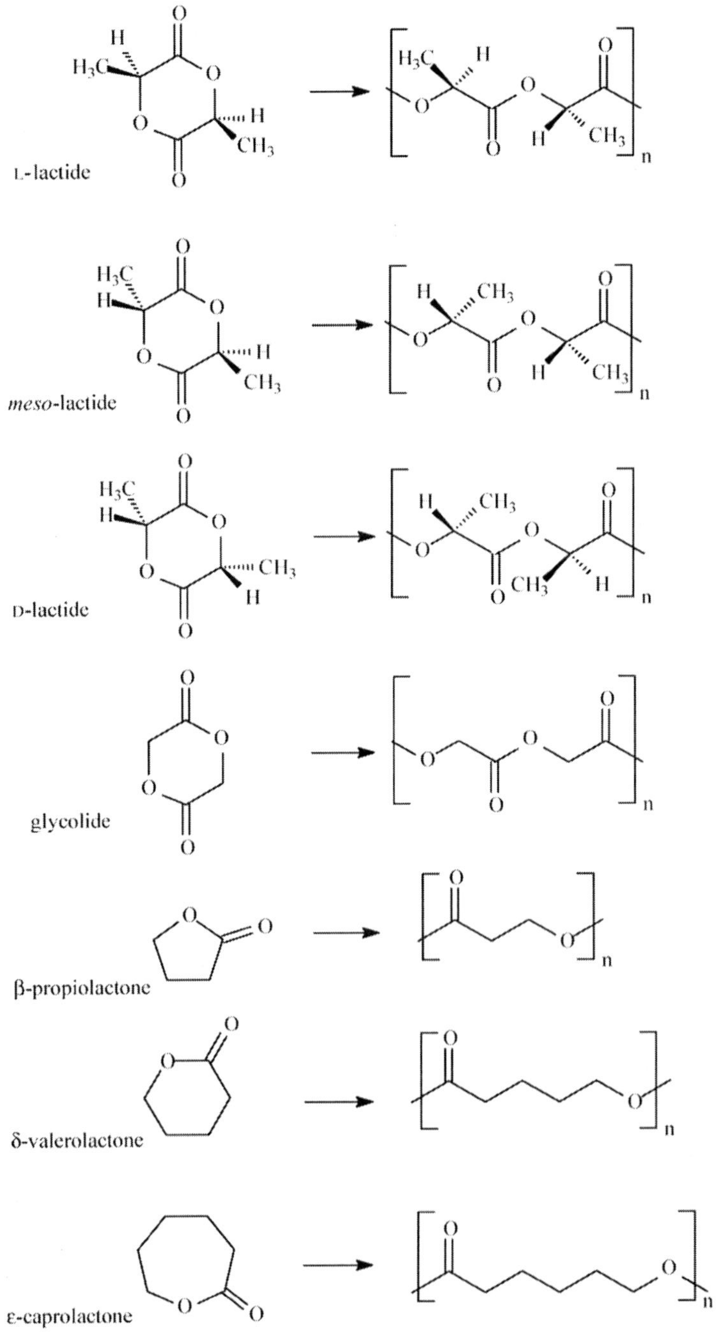

Scheme 1. The synthesis of biodegradable polyesters used in DDS technology.

The particular benefits offered by enzymes are high specificity, and high acceleration rate of reactions under mild conditions of pressure, temperature and pH, which makes enzymatic reactions very energy efficient [56].

Enzymes do not require any co-catalyst and they are recyclable materials derived from renewable sources. Moreover, unlike the conventional anionic initiators, large size lactones (macrolides) can be easily polymerized with a high efficiency*via* enzymatic routes [57,58]. The catalytic activity of enzymes in e-ROP process of cyclic esters has been examined.

It has been found that lipases (triacylglycerol acylhydrolase, EC 3.1.1.3) are the most effective enzymes for the synthesis of polyesters (Table 2). They are ubiquitous enzymes that have been found in most organisms from the microbial, plant and animal kingdoms. In living cells lipases catalyze an ester bond-cleavage in water. In low water environments or non-aqueous systems lipases induce the reverse reaction of hydrolysis, leading to polymer production [59,60,61,62,63].

The most important advantage of lipases are their stability under varying environmental conditions (*i.e.*, high temperature, pH). The majority of the industrial enzymes are usually obtained from microorganisms that produce a wide variety of extracellular lipases. Most lipases of microbial origin exhibit their maximum activity in the pH range 7 to 9 and the temperature range from 30 °C to 40 °C. There are also lipases (e.g., lipase from *Thermomyces lanuginosus*) which show up to 25% of their activity at a temperature of 100 °C. Lipases derived from *Rhizomucor miehei*, *Thermomyces lanuginosus* and produced by the yeast *Candida antarctica* (CA) due to their high activity and stability at temperatures around 80 °C are commonly used as biocatalysts on a laboratory and industrial scale [64].

Manufacturers offer lipolytic enzymes both as lyophilized powders and immobilized forms or poly(ethylene glycol)-modified enzymes. Enzyme immobilization on hydrophobic media such as a macroporous acrylic resin, polystyrene or porous silica can significantly increase their activity and thermal stability compared to the free enzyme. Immobilization techniques allows also one to recover the enzymes from the reaction mixtures, providing a continuous process and minimizing the loss of catalyst [65,66,67,68]. However, it is important to take into account the nature of solid state that may affect the suitability of the reaction media [69].

Table 2. Origin of lipases commonly used in the e-ROP of cyclic esters.

Origin of Lipases	Ref.
Aspergillus niger	[70]
Candida antarctica	[45,71–78]
Candida cylindracea	[45,70,78]
Candida rugosa	[70]
Penicillium roqueforti	[70]
Porcine pancreatic	[45,70,78–82]
Pseudomonas cepacia	[45,70,76,78]
Pseudomonas fluorescens	[45,70,76,78]
Yarrowia lipolytica	[83]

6.1. Influence of the Reaction Media on Activity of Biocatalysts

A number of researchers have developed e-ROP of cyclic monomers in organic solvents due to their many advantages: (1) shifting of the thermodynamic equilibrium toward polyester synthesis; (2) increasing the solubility of non-polar products or substrates; (3) simple removal of solvent and biocatalyst; (4) prevention of microbial contamination as a result of the decreased water activity of the environment [84,85,86,87,88].

However, small amounts of water bound to the enzyme are required to maintain the catalytic activity of the enzyme [84,89]. Access to the active site may be shielded by a mobile, hydrophobic lid, whose position determines the enzyme conformation. The presence of a minimum amount of water assists the reorientation of the catalyst structure at an interface [90]. In non-aqueous systems enzymes can fold into their native structure provided that the essential water layer around them is not stripped off [85]. Hydrophobic, organic solvents leave the hydration shell of the protein intact due to the small redistribution of water molecules. The amount of water required to maintain the native conformation of biocatalyst is mainly dependent on the nature of the catalyst and the type of environment.

Toluene and heptane are organic solvents commonly used during the synthesis of polyesters. They are known as hazardous, toxic and flammable media. Due to the toxicity of the vapors of these typical solvents, recent literature reports suggest the possibility of using thermal and chemically stable 'green solvents'- ionic liquids (ILs) as the reaction media. ILs have thus emerged as promising alternative green solvents due to their favorable properties including: (1) negligible vapor pressure; (2) low flammability; (3) wide liquid range; (4) ability to dissolve polar and non-polar, organic, inorganic, organometallic and polymeric compounds; (5) ability to controlled miscibility with many organic solvents and (6) high reusability [91,92,93,94,95,96,97]. Moreover, the use of ILs does not require special equipment and is very energy efficient, which makes this methodology environmentally friendly.

6.2. Ionic Liquids

ILs are organic salts with melting points below 100 °C. They are also called 'room-temperature ionic liquids', because they remain liquid in the ambient temperature. ILs remain liquid over a wide temperature range from their melting point of approx. −80 °C to their decomposition temperature, which often exceeds 300 °C [91,97,98,99].

Unlike traditional solvents, which can be described as molecular liquids, ILs are composed entirely of ions: large, asymmetrical, organic and heterocyclic cation (*i.e.*, tetraalkylammonium, 1,3-dialkylimidazolium; 1,1-dialkylpyrrolidinium, 1,4-dialkylpyridinium, n-alkylpyridinium) and small, inorganic, organic or complexes anions (*i.e.*, tetrafluoroborate, hexafluorophosphate, bis[(trifluoromethyl)sulfonyl]imide, trifluoromethyl acetate, trifluoromethyl sulfate, chloride) [91,94].

Ionic liquids are called 'tailored solvents' or 'designer solvents' because their physical and chemical properties (e.g., viscosity, density, miscibility with other solvents, melting point) depend on their structure and can be fine-tuned by changing the anion and the cation [100]. The number of possible anion-cation combinations amounts 10^{18} [101]. This allows one to choose appropriate ILs for specific reaction conditions. Given the well-known fact that in some cases enzymes are much more stable in organic solvents than in aqueous solution, it is expected that ILs should have the same effect [89,94,100].

In recent years, ILs have increasingly attracted attention as solvents for biocatalytic polyester synthesis. It has been found that in some cases these "green solvents" improve the solubility of substrates and (or) products and also provide better enzyme stability, activity and selectivity. Moreover, ILs prevent the thermal deactivation of enzymes resulting in the formation of high molecular weight polymers with desired architecture [93]. Enzymatic synthesis of polymers in bulk or in typical organic solvents (like toluene) requires using even 10 times more enzyme in comparison to e-ROP in ILs

[74,77,102]. For these reasons, ILs offer new possibilities for the solvent engineering in e-ROP. Those based on 1-alkyl-3-methylimidazolium cations *i.e.*, 1-butyl-3-methylimidazolium tetrafluoroborate, 1-butyl-3-methylimidazolium bis[(trifluoromethyl)-sulfonyl]imide and 1-butyl-3-methylimidazolium hexafluorophosphate are the most commonly used ILs for enzymatic polyester syntheses (Table 3).

Table 3. Ionic liquids discussed in this review.

ILs	Abbreviation
1-Butyl-3-methylimidazolium tetrafluoroborate	[bmim][BF_4]
1-Butyl-3-methylimidazolium bis((trifluoromethyl)-sulfonyl)imide	[bmim][NTf_2]
1-Butyl-3-methylimidazolium hexafluorophosphate	[bmim][PF_6]
1-Butyl-3-methylimidazolium trifluoromethanesulfonate	[bmim][OTf]
1-Ethyl-3-methylimidazolium tetrafluoroborate	[emim][BF_4]
1-Hexyl-3-methylimidazolium hexafluorophosphate	[hmim][PF_6]
1,4-bis(3-Hexylimidazolium-1-yl)butane bishexafluorophosphate	[$C_4(C_6Im)_2$][PF_6]
1-Dodecyl-3-methylimidazolium bis((trifluoromethyl)-sulfonyl)imide	[C_{12}MIm][NTf_2]
1-Dodecyl-3-methylimidazolium hexafluorophosphate	[C_{12}MIm][PF_6]

6.2.1. Enzyme Stability in Ionic Liquids

Enzyme activity and stability can be improved by adjusting the ILs' properties. High stability and activity of enzymes in ILs are compared with a specific chemical architecture of ionic liquids. ILs are formed by an extensive network of cations and anions linked by hydrogen bonds. For this reason, ILs are named "hydrogen bond polymeric supramolecules" [103]. The inclusion of other molecules in that network allows the existence of both polar and non-polar regions in the IL structure [104]. This arrangement can provide high protection for a biocatalyst. Lozano *et al.* suggest that ILs should be considered as both reaction media and immobilization supports [105]. Moreover, the specific architecture of ILs allows isolation of polymers by extraction using conventional solvents after the completion of a process. Enzymes remain trapped in ILs, which allows one to recover and reuse them for continuous processes, resulting in further process cost reductions [94,100]. However, not all ILs are suitable for biocatalysis. The activity, specificity and stability of the enzyme in ILs depends on the solvent characteristics such as: polarity, hydrophobicity, viscosity, hydrogen-bond capacity, solvent miscibility and impurities [94,100].

6.2.2. Polarity of Ionic Liquids

Enzyme activity strongly depends on the environment's polarity. The solvent polarity is usually determined by an empirical method using the solvatochromic dye Nile Red or Reichardt's dye (Figure 2). The most commonly used method is Reichardt scale (E_T), wherein the polarity is determined based on the shift of the charge-transfer absorption band of a Reichardt's betaine, zwitterions, exhibiting negative solvatochromic properties. The shift is due to the hydrogen bonding between the solvent and the phenoxide oxygen atom present in Reichardt's dye [94,106].

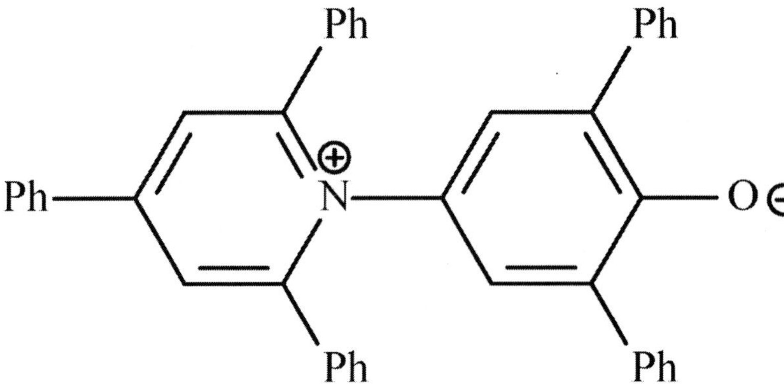

Figure 2. 2,6-Diphenyl-4-(2,4,6-triphenyl-1-pyridinio)phenolate (Reichardt's dye).

On the normalized polarity scale (E_T^N) tetramethylsilane has a polarity of 0.0 and water has a polarity of 1.0. The polarity values of commonly known ILs were found to being close to typical hydrophilic organic solvent *i.e.*, lower alcohols (e.g., methanol, ethanol, 1-butanol) and formamide and varies in a relatively narrow range of 0.6–0.7 [107,108].

The polarity of the imidazolium-based ILs is usually determined by: (1) electrostatic interactions between the anion and cation; (2) the presence of hydrogen bonds between the hydrogen atom of the imidazolium ring and oxygen or halogen atoms in anion; (3) the size of the cation and anion; (4) π–π interactions in aromatic ring. There is a correlation between the decrease of both the alkyl chain length and anion size resulting in increasing polarity [109]. For the 1,3-dialkylimidazolium salts the polarity decreases with increasing anion size ($[BF_4] > [PF_6] > [NTf_2]$), hence a reduction in the effective anion charge density [107].

High polarity values suggest that ILs should exhibit strong hydrogen bonding forces [92]. In general, highly polar media can strip the water from an enzyme due to the fact they can hold water in solution and decrease the activity and selectivity properties of a biocatalyst [62,65,92,110,111,112].

The hydrogen bonding could be the key to understanding the interactions between enzymes and ILs. IL anions can form strong hydrogen bonds that maintain the structural integrity of the enzyme's α-helices and ß-sheets, but also it could cause the catalyst's deactivation. Cations with acidic properties *i.e.*, pyridinium, maintain the enzyme activity [113]. More basic anions may interfere with the enzyme's internal hydrogen bonds [102].

As mentioned earlier, ILs show polarity values comparable to typical organic solvents, but surprisingly they do not inactivate enzymes. Decreased water activity of the enzyme micro-environment as a result of the high polarity of ILs may improve the activity and selectivity of enzymes [114,115]. Lozano *et al.* reported that an increase in the polarity of the imidazolium-based ILs enhanced both synthetic activity and selectivity of free *Candida antarctica* lipase B (CALB) at 2% (v/v) water content in comparison with two typical organic solvents (hexane and 1-butanol) [105]. However, small differences between the polarity values of ILs suggest that there may be no correlation between lipase activity and the normalized polarity scale [116].

6.2.3. Hydrophobicity/Hydrophilicity

Despite their high polarity, most of the ILs commonly used in biocatalytic processes are hydrophobic as a result of the presence of alkyl substituents in the cation molecules. For e.g., [hmim][PF_6] is more hydrophobic (590 ppm of water content obtained after 4 h drying at 70 °C) than [bmim][PF_6] (472 ppm under the same conditions) [117].

They are miscible with polar solvents, *i.e.*, dichloromethane, tetrahydrofuran, but not miscible with *i.e.*, hexane. The miscibility of ILs with water varies widely and unpredictably. Although three ILs based on the 1-butyl-3-methylimidaziolium cation: [bmim][PF_6], [bmim][NTf_2] and [bmim][BF_4] have similar polarity (Table 4), the first two ILs are only slightly soluble in water (0.13 and 1.40% v/v respectively), whereas the latter is completely miscible with water [100]. It is well known that hydrophilic ILs with nucleophilic anions are an ideal medium for polar substrates. However, in biocatalysts, hydrophilic solvents can form covalent interactions (hydrogen bonding) with the active center of the enzymes and cause a decrease in their activity. Therefore, most hydrophilic ILs act as enzyme deactivating agents, with few exceptions, *i.e.*, [bmim][BF_4], [emim][BF_4], [bmim][OTf] [69,113,116].

Table 4. Physicochemical properties of ILs commonly used in biocatalysis.

ILs	Polarity E_T^N (RT)	M_w (g·mol^{-1})	Melting Point (°C)	Viscosity in 20 °C (cP)	Density (g·cm^{-3})	Conductivity (S·m^{-1})	Water Solubility (WS) (%w/v)
[bmim][BF_4]	0.680	226	−82	233	1.17	0.17	100
[bmim][Tf_2N]	0.645	419	−4	52	1.43	0.39	1.40
[bmim][PF_6]	0.676	284	−8	312	1.362	0.14	0.13

Kim *et al.* reported enhanced enantioselectivity of CALB in ILs compared to a typical organic solvent (toluene). Moreover they reported that lipases show higher enantioselectivity in the hydrophobic IL [bmim][PF_6] compared to the hydrophilic IL [emim][BF_4] [118]. Furthermore, hydrophobic ILs have stabilizing effect on hydrolases in non-aqueous environments due to the fact ILs maintain the native conformation of enzymes [69].

Because of the high hydrophobicity of ILs, most lipases do not dissolve in IL environments, but remain in suspension while maintaining high catalytic activity [119]. However, van Rantwijk *et al.* found, that the negative, structural changes of the active site of enzymes, which take place during dissolution in ILs, are reversible [95].

6.2.4. Viscosity

As is shown in Table 4, ILs are highly viscous solvents with viscosity that vary in a relatively narrow range of 35–500 cP, compared with the viscosity of toluene at 25 °C which is 0.6 cP, and that of water, 0.9 cP [94,99,108]. The high viscosity values of ILs are the result of strong intermolecular forces (charge-charge interactions, van der Waals forces) [100]. Increased viscosity is a result of the elongation of the cation's alkyl chain [94]. High viscosity may slow down the conformational changes of biocatalysts, allowing them to maintain their native structures [116,120,121]. Due to the small differences in the polarity of ILs, some reports suggest that solvent viscosity has significant effect on reaction rates and yields [108]. High viscosity values could affect the reaction rate by limiting mass transfer. The addition of organic co-solvents or water can decrease the ILs' viscosity values. Increasing the temperature has the same effect [93,116,122].

6.2.5. Effect of Impurities

An important factor affecting the enzyme activity and polymer yield is the solvent's purity. Contaminants that may be present in ILs are halide anions (*i.e.*, chloride ions), organic compounds and water. Chloride ions may constitute contamination due to incomplete ion exchange during the ILs' synthesis from their chloride precursors. Chloride content below 0.1% w/v does not affect lipase activity, but higher concentrations can cause decreased polymer yields and enzyme deactivation [96]. Madeira Lau *et al.* reported that reduction of the water content in ILs also gives better polymer yields [91].

7. IONIC LIQUIDS AS A MEDIUM FOR THE ENZYMATIC RING-OPENING POLYMERIZATION OF CYCLIC ESTERS

Uyama and Kobayashi were the first to report the e-ROP of ε-caprolactone (CL) in the presence of two ILs based on 1,3-dialkylimidazolium salts: [bmim][PF_6] and [bmim][BF_4] (Table 5). Reactions was carried out in the presence of *Candida antarctica* (CA) lipase at 60 °C in 24–168 h. They obtained polyesters with a number average molecular weight (M_n) in the range from 300 to 4200 g·mol^{-1}. Polymers with the higher M_n were obtained using as solvent [bmim][BF_4] after a reaction time of 168 h. The authors reported also high polydysperisity (*PDI*) values for the polymers ranging from 2.7 to 7.3 [123].

Marcilla *et al.* also investigated the e-ROP of CL in ILs with three different anions: [bmim][X] (X = BF_4, PF_6, NTf_2) at 60 °C for a reaction time of 24 h, using immobilized lipase B from *Candida antarctica* (Novozym 435) as a catalyst. They obtained oligomers with M_n in the range from 10,500 to 12,700 g·mol^{-1} and *PDI* values range from 1.7 to 2.1 after precipitation [124].

Although the abovementioned reactions were carried out under the same conditions, there were significant differences in the polymers' M_n values as a result of the differences in: (1) amounts of monomer and catalyst used; (2) forms of the enzymes (free and immobilized lipases); (3) purity of ILs; (4) the presence of the precipitation process that provided a higher polymer M_n and lower *PDI*.

Table 5. Ring opening enzymatic polymerization and copolymerization of cyclic esters in ionic liquids.

Monomer	ILs	Purity of ILs (%)	Enzyme	Temp. (°C)	Time (h)	M_n (Da)	*PDI*	Y/C (%)	Ref.
	[bmim][BF_4]	-	CA	60	168	4200	2.7	97^{C}	[123]
	[bmim][BF_4]	≥99	CA	60	24	12,700	1.8	35^{Y}	[124]
	[bmim][BF_4]	-	YLL	100	16	1758	1.7	-	[113]
	[bmim][BF_4]	-	YLL	150	6	3092	2.5	-	[113]
	[bmim][PF_6]	-	CA	60	72	540	4.2	62^{C}	[123]
	[bmim][PF_6]	≥99	CA	60	24	12,200	1.7	30^{Y}	[124]
CL	[bmim][NTf_2]	≥99	CA	60	24	10,500	2.1	44^{Y}	[124]
	[bmim][NTf_2]	≥97	CA	90	24	8100	-	85^{Y}	[102]
	[$C_4(C_6Im)_2$][PF_6]	-	CA	90	48	26,200	-	62^{Y}	[125]
	[C_{12}MIm][PF_6]	-	CA	90	48	11,700	-	37^{Y}	[125]
	[C_{12}MIm][NTf_2]	-	CA/ILs	60	48	35,600	-	62^{Y}	[125]
	[C_{12}MIm][NTf_2]	-	CA	60	48	20,300	-	54^{Y}	[125]
	[bmim][BF_4]	≥99	CA	110	24	54,600	1.25	24.3^{Y} 96.2^{C}	[126]
	[bmim][PF_6]	≥99	CA	65	264	581	1.2	29.5^{Y}	[127]
	[bmim][PF_6]	-	CA	90	120	19,600	1.2	-	[128]
LLA	[bmim][PF_6]	≥99	CA	120	24	3900	1.19	0.1^{Y} 90.4^{C}	[126]
	[hmim][PF_6]	≥97	CA	90	168	37,800	1.3	63.2^{Y}	[129]
	[hmim][PF_6]	≥97	CA	65	120	1700	1.3	16.5^{Y}	[129]
	[bmim][NTf_2]	≥99	CA	120	24	50,100	1.42	10.5^{Y}	[126]
DO	[bmim][PF_6]	≥99	CA/ILs	70	18	182,100	-	-	[130]
	[bmim][PF_6]	≥99	CA	70	24	27,700	-	-	[130]
GA	[bmim][PF_6]	≥99	CA	65	96	-	-	-	[127]
LLA:GA	[hmim][PF_6]	≥97	CA	65	120	3500	1.3	40.2^{Y}	[129]
(1:3)	[bmim][PF_6]	≥99	CA	65	96	2400	1.1	36.7^{Y}	[127]
LLA:GA (3:1)	[bmim][PF_6]	≥99	CA	90	144	18,500	1.1	-	[127]

CL: ε-caprolactone; **LLA**: L-lactide; **DO**: (1,4-dioxane)-2-one; **GA**: glycolide; **LLA:GA**: molar ratio of L-lactide to glycolide; **CA**: lipase from *Candida antarctica*; **YLL**: lipase from *Yarrowia lipolytica*; **CA/ILs**: lipase from *Candida antarctica* coated with ionic liquids; **PDI**: polydispersity index; **Y**: yield; **C**: conversion.

7.1. Effect of Monomer and Polymer Solubility in ILs

Low solubility of LA in commonly used organic solvents restrict enzymatic polymerization to bulk reactions. The polar and hydrophilic environment of melted LA results in lipase deactivation (especially at high temperature), limiting the polymer propagation. Yoshizawa-Fujita *et al.* showed that at relatively high temperature (110 °C) in IL media ([bmim][NTf_2] and [bmim][BF_4]) one can obtain high M_n poly-L-lactide (PLLA) (54,600 g·mol^{-1}) compared to toluene and bulk (42,200 g·mol^{-1} and 15,600 g·mol^{-1} respectively) [126].

In the case of CL, despite the high solubility of the monomer in two ILs based on 1,3-dialkylimidazolium cations: [bmim][BF_4] and [bmim][PF_6], the polymer product miscibility is strongly dependent on the nature of the IL anion. It is very important to choose appropriate ILs for polymer synthesis. Poor solubility of the polymer in the ILs could lead to a low molecular weight of products due to the premature precipitation of the polymer from the reaction mixture. On the other hand, better solubility of the polymer in ILs most likely leads to lower polymer yields due to difficulty of polymer extraction from the solvent [102]. Compared to the typical organic solvent, toluene, Marcilla *et al.* showed the lowest M_n of PCL for the reaction conducted at 60 °C in an IL medium due to the differences in polymer's solubility [124]. Marcilla *et al.*suggested that when polymer is insoluble in ILs it is diffusing through the layers of a heterogeneous reaction mixture and this provides a limited monomer conversion degree. The polymerization process carried out under these conditions is, therefore, closer to bulk polymerization than the solution type [124]. Moreover, the heterogeneous system facilitates the polymer extraction from the reaction mixture after the completion of the process [113]. Yoshizawa-Fujita *et al.* and Marcilla*et al.* reported that the lowest polymer yield for e-ROP ocurred in [bmim][PF_6] due to the lowest solubility of the obtained polymers in the IL. The relative solubility values of PLLA in different ILs are in the following order: [bmim][NTf_2] > [bmim][BF_4] > [bmim][PF_6] [124,126].

7.2. Effect of Temperature

Hydrophobic ILs provide better stability of an enzyme compared to hydrophilic solvents, specially at high temperatures. Gorke *et al.* reported the influence of temperature on the e-ROP of CL using as catalyst free CALB in [bmim][NTf_2]. The process was carried out in various temperatures: 25, 60, 90, 100 and 110 °C for 24 h. At 25 and 60 °C, M_n continued to increase till it reached a maximum at 90 °C. Decreased M_n and polymer yield at higher temperatures could be a result of rapid inactivation of the enzyme under those conditions [102].

Yoshizawa-Fujita *et al.* reported the same effect in the lipase-catalyzed synthesis of PLLA in ILs based on 1-butyl-3methylimidazolioum cations: [bmim][NTf_2], [bmim][BF_4], [bmim][PF_6]. However, they reported the highest M_n of PLLA in the 110 to 120 °C temperature range, and further temperature increases caused the deactivation of the enzyme [126].

Barerra-Riverra *et al.* reported decreased monomer (CL) conversion in the presence of enzyme (*Yarrowia lipolytica* lipase, YLL) due to the increased temperature in range of 60 to 90 °C for hydrophilic ILs. This is probably a result of the deactivation and denaturation of the enzyme at relatively high temperatures. Thus, hydrophobic ILs provide better temperature stability of enzymes at high temperatures compared to hydrophilic ILs [113].

As mentioned earlier, ILs are solvents with relatively high viscosity values of up to 500 cP although most of them display Newtonian behavior over a wide temperature range. High viscosity retards mass transfer but increasing temperature can decrease this value. Therefore it is important to describe the solvent viscosity at the polymerization temperature [129]. Chanfreau *et al.* reported relatively low viscosity values for [hmim][PF_6] at 90 °C (<30 cP) compared to viscosity at 1 °C (12,000 cP) which was not expected to be a limiting factor during polymerization in that case [129].

Lipase-mediated polymerization in ILs is a promising method for the synthesis of functional polyesters: PCL, PLA and copolymers of LA and glycolide (GA). However, for LA and GA under relatively high temperature polymer synthesis without catalyst was observed. This probably results from a cationic mechanism induced by traces of hydroxyacid from the monomer. The effect is strongly dependent on the temperature, type of monomer and solvent. For GA polymerization it takes place in [bmim][PF_6] even at 65 °C, whereas for LA polymerization the same effect was observed at 90 °C in [hmim][PF_6] and none was observed at 65 °C [127,131].

7.3. Effect of Enzyme Preparations

The water activity in IL systems are the key factors for evaluation of biocatalytic reactions in organic solvents. Increasing the enzyme concentration may lead to hydrolysis as a result of a higher water content in the reaction environment. It has been shown that reduction of water content as a result of the pre-drying of enzymes could improve the catalytic activation of lipases. Gorke *et al.* carried out the polymerization of CL, β-propiolactone and δ-valerolactone using CALB as catalyst and [bmim][NTf_2] as a reaction medium during 24 h at 60 °C. Pre-treatment of the enzyme allowed them to obtain higherM_n polymers compared to catalyst without pre-drying [102].

As mentioned earlier, ILs can be used both as solvent and as in the pre-treatment of enzyme process. Coating of an enzyme by an IL layer increases the activity, stability and enantioselectivity of the biocatalyst [130,132]. Moreover, coating enzymes by IL layers helps to reduce the IL cost during the synthesis. The coating of the enzyme by an IL layer is based on absorption of ILs on the polymer surface without using chemical bonds. Dong *et al.* carried out the e-ROP of (1,4-dioxane)-2-one (DO) in the presence of immobilized CALB (Novozym 435) coated with [bmim][PF_6], to obtain a polymer having a M_n of 182,000 g·mol^{-1} [130]. Wu *et al.* showed a similar relationship using Novozym 435 coated by [C_{12}Mim][NTf_2] to obtain PCL having a M_n of approx. 35,600 g·mol^{-1}. Use at the same as the above conditions of ILs acting as reaction medium leads to the preparation of polymer with a M_n value of 20,300 g·mol^{-1} [132]. Enzyme pre-incubated in ILs before polymerization can improve the catalytic activity of CALB and this procedure allows one to obtain higher polymerM_n values [130].

7.4. Structure of Polyesters Obtained in ILs

Well-defined macromolecules with appropriate molecular weight, multifunctional terminal groups, narrow polydispersity and steroregularity are receiving increasing attention in biomaterial applications, especially in DDS systems. As mentioned earlier, polymers with suitable structure can achieve more predictability and reproducibility release of APIs.

As shown by Marcilla *et al.* the *PDI* of polyesters synthesized in [bmim][BF_4] and [bmim][PF_6] are lower (*PDI* = 1.7–1.8) compared to those obtained in toluene (*PDI* = 2.3) [124]. Besides the formation of linear polymers, e-ROP catalyzed by lipases in organic solvents (*i.e.*, toluene, heptanes, ILs) favored the formation of macrocycles as a result of inter- and intra-molecular transestrification, end-to-end condensation and backbiting (intermolecular termination) [130,133].

The structure of the obtained polymers depends on the temperature, time, monomer concentration and the nature of the ILs. At low monomer concentrations, mainly linear polymers are obtained in ILs. Prolonged reaction times at 60 °C lead to the formation of low molecular weight products as a result of cyclic species formation [113]. However, the spectra of the polymers obtained in ILs display a lower ratio of rings to linear polymers in comparison to those obtained in heptane and toluene [113,124].

Hyperbranched polyesters (HBPs) are very interesting biomaterials. These polymers are considered to be very attractive for DDS technology. HBPs have been the first obtained in the e-ROP of CL by using CALB with bis(hydroxymethyl)butyric acid (BHB) as AB_2 core in toluene/dioxane mixtures. The degree of branching (DB) of these polymers ranged from 0.03 to 0.33 [134]. López-Luna and co-workers reported the CALB-mediated synthesis of HBPs using BHB in liquid 1,1,1,2-tetrafluoroethane media. In this case the DB was rather low (0.02–0.09) [135]. Recently, imidazolium-based ILs have also been shown to be adequate media which enable sustaining enzyme activities. Moreover, they are a good solvent for LA. The obtained PLA was characterized with rather high molecular weights. In [128] the method of synthesis of hyperbranched PLA in the presence of [bmim][PF_6] has been described. BHB has been used as the AB_2 core co-monomer and immobilized CALB as biocatalyst. The DB of obtained HBPs has been controlled by the reaction conditions (the maximum value was 0.21) [128].

7.5. Kinetics of Polyester Enzymatic Synthesis in ILs

The effect of IL type on the kinetics of e-ROP of cyclic esters has been discussed by many authors. The results indicate that high monomer conversion was possible when the process was carried out for long periods of time at relatively low temperatures. For example Uyama and Kobayashi showed an increased monomer conversion of CL at 60 °C in [bmim][BF_4] from 23% to 97% for 24 to 168 h. A similar effect was reported for e-ROP carried out in [bmim][PF_6] [123].

However, general conclusions about the effect of temperature on the kinetics of e-ROP of polyesters cannot be drawn. High temperatures can cause inactivation of the biocatalyst, although for PLLA synthesis in [bmim][BF_4] high LLA conversion from 67.6% to 100% was reported as a result of increasing the temperature from 90 to 120 °C [126].

Dong *et al.* reported monomer conversion of DO in [bmim][PF_6] in different temperature ranges from 40 to 80 °C using CALB as biocatalyst. The result was an increased conversion value from 30% to 60% at the temperature range from 40 to 70 °C. At higher temperature the conversion value decreased as a result of enzyme denaturation processes. Prolonged polymerization time (from 10 to 30 h) at 70 °C caused an increased conversion value from 54% to 61% in the case of ILs used as a solvent and from 57% to 62% in the case of CALB coated by an IL layer [130].

8. CONCLUSIONS

Biodegradable or bioresorbable polyesters are very important biomaterials expected to make essential contributions to the development of pharmaceutical science in the future. The enzyme-catalyzed ring opening polymerization of lactones or lactides seems to be a promising method of biomedical polyester synthesis. ILs offer new possibilities for solvent engineering in e-ROP of cyclic esters. Many authors believe that e-ROP of cyclic esters in the presence of ILs will be an alternative method for the preparation of functional, stereo- and regioregular biomedical polymers. In DDS technology it is very important to use structurally well-defined matrices. The kinetics of active substance release depend not only on theM_n of the polymer, but polydispersity index, appropriate degree of crystallinity and stereoregularity of the polymer are equally important factors in pharmaceutical fields. The stabilization and chemo- regio- and stereoselectivity of enzymes in ILs are very important aspects of biomedical polymer synthesis. Moreover, some of the polyesters synthesized by e-ROP (in the presence of ILs) have been shown to have higher molecular weight and higher monomer conversion compared to typical organic solvents. However, the total control of the M_n of polymers in e-ROP process is still limited. The use of ILs in the e-ROP of cyclic monomers definitely needs further exploration.

ACKNOWLEDGMENTS

This work was financially supported by the National Science Centre (Poland), decision No. DEC-2013/11/N/NZ7/02342).

AUTHOR CONTRIBUTIONS

The contributions of the respective authors are as follows: U.P. and M.S. proposed the concept of the work, wrote the whole article, discussions and conclusions. All authors have seen and approved the manuscript.

CONFLICTS OF INTEREST

The authors declare no conflict of interest.

REFERENCES

1. Rohini, N.A.; Joseph, A.; Mukerji, A. Polymeric prodrugs: Recent achievements and general strategies. J. Antivir. Antiretrovir. 2013.

2. Allen, T.M.; Cullis, P.R. Drug delivery systems: Entering the mainstream. Science 2004, 303, 1818–1822.

3. Tong, R.; Gabrielson, N.P.; Fan, T.M.; Cheng, J.J. Polymeric nanomedicines based on poly(lactide) and poly(lactide-co-glycolide). Curr. Opin. Solid State Mater. Sci. 2012, 16, 323–332.

4. Sobczak, M.; Oledzka, E.; Kolodziejski, W.L.; Kuzmicz, R. Polymers for pharmaceutical applications. Polimery 2007,52, 411–420.

5. Hoste, K.; de Winne, K.; Schacht, E. Polymeric prodrugs. Int. J. Pharm. 2004, 277, 119–131.

6. Vilar, G.; Tulla-Puche, J.; Albericio, F. Polymers and drug delivery systems. Curr. Drug Deliv. 2012, 9, 367–394.

7. Sobczak, M.; Debek, C.; Oledzka, E.; Kozlowski, R. Polymeric systems of antimicrobial peptides-strategies and potential applications. Molecules 2013, 18, 14122–14137.

8. Marinaro, W.; Stella, V. Macromolecular prodrugs of small molecules. In Prodrugs; Stella, V., Borchardt, R., Hageman, M., Oliyai, R., Maag, H., Tilley, J., Eds.; Springer: New York, NY, USA, 2007; Volume 5, pp. 989–1021.

9. Elvira, C.; Gallardo, A.; San Roman, J.; Cifuentes, A. Covalent polymer-drug conjugates. Molecules 2005, 10, 114–125.

10. Shu, J.Y.; Panganiban, B.; Xu, T. Peptide-polymer conjugates: From fundamental science to application. Annu. Rev. Phys. Chem. 2013, 64, 631–657.

11. Khandare, J.; Minko, T. Polymer-drug conjugates: Progress in polymeric prodrugs. Prog. Polym. Sci. 2006, 31, 359–397.

12. Ringsdorf, H. Structure and properties of pharmacologically active polymers. J. Polym. Sci. Symp. 1975, 51, 135–153.

13. Ringsdorf, H. Synthetic Polymeric Drugs. In Polymeric Delivery Systems; Kostelnik, R.J., Ed.; Gordon and Breach Science Publishers, Inc.: New York, NY, USA, 1978; pp. 197–225.

14. Liu, Z.; Jiao, Y.; Wang, Y.; Zhou, C.; Zhang, Z. Polysaccharides-based nanoparticles as drug delivery systems. Adv. Drug Deliv. Rev. 2008, 60, 1650–1662.

15. Oledzka, E.; Sobczak, M. Polymers in the pharmaceutical applications—natural and bioactive initiators and catalysts in the synthesis of biodegradable and bioresorbable polyesters and polycarbonates. In Innovations in Biotechnology; InTech: Rijeka, Croatia, 2012; pp. 139–160.

16. Solaro, R.; Chiellini, F.; Battisti, A. Targeted delivery of protein drugs by nanocarriers. Materials 2010, 3, 1928–1980.

17. Haag, R.; Kratz, F. Polymer therapeutics: Concepts and applications. Angew. Chem. Int. Ed. 2006, 45, 1198–1215.

18. Maeda, H.; Wu, J.; Sawa, T.; Matsumura, Y.; Hori, K. Tumor vascular permeability and the EPR effect in macromolecular therapeutics: A review. J. Control. Release 2000, 65, 271–284.

19. Maeda, H. The enhanced permeability and retention (EPR) effect in tumor vasculature: The key role of tumor-selective macromolecular drug targeting. Adv. Enzym. Regul. 2001, 41, 189–207.

20. Goodarzi, N.; Varshochian, R.; Kamalinia, G.; Atyabi, F.; Dinarvand, R. A review of polysaccharide cytotoxic drug conjugates for cancer therapy. Carbohyd. Polym. 2013, 92, 1280–1293.

21. Ikada, Y.; Tsuji, H. Biodegradable polyesters for medical and ecological applications. Macromol. Rapid Commun. 2000,21, 117–132.

22. Uhrich, K.E.; Cannizzaro, S.M.; Langer, R.S.; Shakesheff, K.M. Polymeric systems for controlled drug release. Chem. Rev. 1999, 99, 3181–3198.

23. Van de Ven, H.; Paulussen, C.; Feijens, P.B.; Matheeussen, A.; Rombaut, P.; Kayaert, P.; van den Mooter, G.; Weyenberg, W.; Cos, P.; Maes, L.; et al. PLGA nanoparticles and nanosuspensions with amphotericin B: Potent in vitroand in vivo alternatives to fungizone and ambisome. J. Control. Release 2012, 161, 795–803.

24. Nahar, M.; Jain, N.K. Preparation, characterization and evaluation of targeting potential of amphotericin B-loaded engineered PLGA nanoparticles. Pharm. Res. 2009, 26, 2588–2598.

25. Jeong, Y.I.; Na, H.S.; Nah, J.W.; Lee, H.C. Preparation of ciprofloxacin-encapsulated poly(DL-lactide-co-glycolide) microspheres and its antibacterial activity. J. Pharm. Sci. 2009, 98, 3659–3665.

26. Jeong, Y.I.; Na, H.S.; Seo, D.H.; Kim, D.G.; Lee, H.C.; Jang, M.K.; Na, S.K.; Roh, S.H.; Kim, S.I.; Nah, J.W. Ciprofloxacin-encapsulated poly(DL-lactide-co-glycolide) nanoparticles and its antibacterial activity. Int. J. Pharm.2008, 352, 317–323.

27. Verrijk, R.; Smolders, I.J.; Bosnie, N.; Begg, A.C. Reduction of systemic exposure and toxicity of cisplatin by encapsulation in poly-lactide-co-glycolide. Cancer Res. 1992, 52, 6653–6656.

28. Esmaeili, F.; Dinarvand, R.; Ghahremani, M.H.; Ostad, S.N.; Esmaily, H.; Atyabi, F. Cellular cytotoxicity and in vivobiodistribution of docetaxel poly (lactide-co-glycolide) nanoparticles. Anticancer Drugs 2010, 21, 43–52.

29. Tewes, F.; Munnier, E.; Antoon, B.; Ngaboni Okassa, L.; Cohen-Jonathan, S.; Marchais, H.; Douziech-Eyrolles, L.; Soucé, M.; Dubois, P.; Chourpa, I. Comparative study of doxorubicin-loaded poly (lactide-co-glycolide) nanoparticles prepared by single and double emulsion methods. Eur.J. Pharm. Biopharm. 2007, 66, 488–492.

30. Yoo, H.S.; Lee, E.A.; Park, T.G. Doxorubicin-conjugated biodegradable polymeric micelles having acid-cleavable linkages. J. Control. Release 2002, 82, 17–27.

31. Dong, Y.; Feng, S.S. Poly(D,L-lactide-co-glycolide) (PLGA) nanoparticles prepared by high pressure homogenization for paclitaxel chemotherapy. Int. J. Pharm. 2007, 342, 208–214.

32. Kou, G.; Gao, J.; Wang, H.; Chen, H.W.; Li, B.H.; Zhang, D.P.; Wang, S.H.; Hou, S.; Qian, W.Z.; Dai, J.X.; et al. Preparation and characterization of paclitaxel-loaded PLGA nanoparticles coated with cationic SM5-1 single-chain antibody. J. Biochem. Mol. Biol. 2007, 40, 731–739.

33. Esmaeili, F.; Hosseini-Nasr, M.; Rad-Malekshahi, M.; Samadi, N.; Atyabi, F.; Dinarvand, R. Preparation and antibacterial activity evaluation of rifampicin-loaded poly lactide-co-glycolide nanoparticles. Nanomedicine 2007, 3, 161–167.

34. Rafi, M.; Singh, S.M.; Kanchan, V.; Anish, C.K.; Panda, A.K. Controlled release of bioactive recombinant human growth hormone from PLGA microparticles. J. Microencapsul. 2010, 27, 552–560.

35. Tong, R.; Cheng, J.J. Controlled synthesis of camptothecin-polylactide conjugates and nanoconjugates. Bioconjugate Chem. 2010, 21, 111–121.

36. Sobczak, M.; Oledzka, E.; Kwietniewska, M.; Nalecz-Jawecki, G.; Kolodziejski, W. Promising macromolecular conjugates of camptothecin—The synthesis, characterization and in vitro studies. J. Macromol. Sci. A 2014, 51, 254–262.

37. Liu, S.; Zhou, G.Y.; Liu, D.X.; Xie, Z.G.; Huang, Y.B.; Wang, X.; Wu, W.B.; Jing, X.B. Inhibition of orthotopic secondary hepatic carcinoma in mice by doxorubicin-loaded electrospun polylactide nanofibers. J. Mater. Chem. 2013, 1, 101–109.

38. Tong, R.; Tang, L.; Yala, L.; Cheng, J.J. Controlled formulation of doxorubicin-polylactide nanoconjugates for cancer drug delivery. Conf. Proc. IEE Eng. Med. Biol. Soc. 2009, 2400–2402.

39. Nagarwal, R.C.; Singh, P.N.; Kant, S.; Maiti, P.; Pandit, J.K. Chitosan coated PLA nanoparticles for ophthalmic delivery: Characterization, in vitro and in vivo study in rabbit eye. J. Biomed. Nanotechnol. 2010, 6, 648–657.

40. Espuelas, M.; Legrand, P.; Loiseau, P.; Bories, C.; Barratt, G.; Irache, J. In vitro antileishmanial activity of amphotericin B loaded in poly (ε-caprolactone) nanospheres. J. Drug Target. 2002, 10, 593–599.

41. Dang, N.T.T.; Turner, M.S.; Coombes, A.G.A. Development of intra-vaginal matrices from polycaprolactone for sustained release of antimicrobial agents. J. Biomater. Appl. 2013, 28, 74–83.

42. Sobczak, M.; Kamysz, W.; Tyszkiewicz, W.; Dębek, C.; Kozłowski, R.; Olędzka, E.; Piotrowska, U.; Nałęcz-Jawecki, G.; Plichta, A.; Grzywacz, D. Biodegradable macromolecular conjugates of citropin: Synthesis, characterization andin vitro efficiency study. React. Funct. Polym. 2014, 83, 54–61.

43. Le Ray, A.M.; Chiffoleau, S.; Iooss, P.; Grimandi, G.; Gouyette, A.; Daculsi, G.; Merle, C. Vancomycin encapsulation in biodegradable poly(epsilon-caprolactone) microparticles for bone implantation. Influence of the formulation process on size, drug loading, in vitro release and cytocompatibility. Biomaterials 2003, 24, 443–449.

44. Jérôme, C.; Lecomte, P. Recent advances in the synthesis of aliphatic polyesters by ring-opening polymerization. Adv. Drug Deliv. Rev. 2008, 60, 1056–1076.

45. Namekawa, S.; Suda, S.; Uyama, H.; Kobayashi, S. Lipase-catalyzed ring-opening polymerization of lactones to polyesters and its mechanistic aspects. Int. J. Biol. Macromol. 1999, 25, 145–151.

46. Nuyken, O.; Pask, S.D. Ring-opening polymerization-an introductory review. Polymers 2013, 5, 361–403.

47. Varma, I.K.; Albertsson, A.C.; Rajkhowa, R.; Srivastava, R.K. Enzyme catalyzed synthesis of polyesters. Prog. Polym. Sci. 2005, 30, 949–981.

48. Kobayashi, S.; Uyama, H.; Kimura, S. Enzymatic polymerization. Chem. Rev. 2001, 101, 3793–3818.

49. Albertsson, A.C.; Srivastava, R.K. Recent developments in enzyme-catalyzed ring-opening polymerization. Adv. Drug Deliv. Rev. 2008, 60, 1077–1093.

50. Kobayashi, S.; Uyama, H. Enzymatic polymerization to polyesters. Biopolym. Online 2002.

51. Jeon, B.W.; Lee, J.; Kim, H.S.; Cho, D.H.; Lee, H.; Chang, R.; Kim, Y.H. Lipase-catalyzed enantioselective synthesis of (R,R)-lactide from alkyl lactate to produce PDLA (poly D-lactic acid) and stereocomplex PLA (poly lactic acid). J. Biotechnol. 2013, 168, 201–207.

52. Kadokawa, J.; Kobayashi, S. Polymer synthesis by enzymatic catalysis. Curr. Opin. Chem. Biol. 2010, 14, 145–153.

53. Gross, R.A.; Kumar, A.; Kalra, B. Polymer synthesis by in vitro enzyme catalysis. Chem. Rev. 2001, 101, 2097–2124.

54. Kobayashi, S.; Uyama, H.; Ohmae, M. Enzymatic polymerization for precision polymer synthesis. Bull. Chem. Soc. Jpn. 2001, 74, 613–635.

55. Zhang, C.; Liao, L.; Gong, S. Recent developments in microwave-assisted polymerization with a focus on ring-opening polymerization. Green Chem. 2007, 9, 303–314.

56. Adrio, J.L.; Demain, A.L. Microbial enzymes: Tools for biotechnological processes. Biomolecules 2014, 4, 117–139.

57. Duda, A.; Kowalski, A.; Penczek, S.; Uyama, H.; Kobayashi, S. Kinetics of the ring-opening polymerization of 6-, 7-, 9-, 12-, 13-, 16-, and 17-membered lactones. Comparison of chemical and enzymatic polymerizations. Macromolecules2002, 35, 4266–4270.

58. Uyama, H.; Takeya, K.; Kobayashi, S. Enzymatic ring-opening polymerization of lactones to polyesters by lipase catalyst—Unusually high reactivity of macrolides. Bull. Chem. Soc. Jpn. 1995, 68, 56–61.

59. Kobayashi, S. Lipase-catalyzed polyester synthesis—A green polymer chemistry. Proc. Jpn. Acad. Ser. B Phys. Biol. Sci.2010, 86, 338–365.

60. Hasan, F.; Shah, A.A.; Hameed, A. Industrial applications of microbial lipases. Enzym. Microb. Technol. 2006, 39, 235–251.

61. Wehtje, E.; Costes, D.; Adlercreutz, P. Enantioselectivity of lipases: Effects of water activity. J. Mol. Catal. B 1997, 3, 221–230.

62. Mendes, A.A.; Oliveira, P.C.; de Castro, H.F. Properties and biotechnological applications of porcine pancreatic lipase. J. Mol. Catal. B 2012, 78, 119–134.

63. Gupta, R.; Gupta, N.; Rathi, P. Bacterial lipases: An overview of production, purification and biochemical properties.Appl. Microbiol. Biotechnol. 2004, 64, 763–781.

64. Sharma, R.; Chisti, Y.; Banerjee, U.C. Production, purification, characterization, and applications of lipases.Biotechnol. Adv. 2001, 19, 627–662.

65. Idris, A.; Bukhari, A. Immobilized Candida antarctica lipase B: Hydration, stripping off and application in ring opening polyester synthesis. Biotechnol. Adv. 2012, 30, 550–563.

66. Miletic, N.; Nastasovic, A.; Loos, K. Immobilization of biocatalysts for enzymatic polymerizations: Possibilities, advantages, applications. Bioresour. Technol. 2012, 115, 126–135.

67. Uyama, H.; Kuwabara, M.; Tsujimoto, T.; Kobayashi, S. High-performance immobilized lipase catalyst for polyester synthesis. Polym. J. 2002, 34, 970–972.

68. Chen, B.; Miller, M.E.; Gross, R.A. Effects of porous polystyrene resin parameters on Candida antarctica lipase B adsorption, distribution, and polyester synthesis activity. Langmuir 2007, 23, 6467–6474.

69. De Diego, T.; Lozano, P.; Abad, M.A.; Steffensky, K.; Vaultier, M.; Iborra, J.L. On the nature of ionic liquids and their effects on lipases that catalyze ester synthesis. J. Biotechnol. 2009, 140, 234–241.

70. Kobayashi, S. Recent developments in lipase-catalyzed synthesis of polyesters. Macromol. Rapid Commun. 2009, 30, 237–266.

71. Cordova, A.; Iversen, T.; Hult, K. Lipase-catalyzed formation of end-functionalized poly(epsilon-caprolactone) by initiation and termination reactions. Polymer 1999, 40, 6709–6721.

72. Deng, F.; Gross, R.A. Ring-opening bulk polymerization of epsilon-caprolactone and trimethylene carbonate catalyzed by lipase Novozym 435. Int. J. Biol. Macromol. 1999, 25, 153–159.

73. Hans, M.; Keul, H.; Moeller, M. Ring-opening polymerization of DD-lactide catalyzed by Novozyme 435. Macromol. Biosci. 2009, 9, 239–247.

74. Bisht, K.S.; Henderson, L.A.; Gross, R.A.; Kaplan, D.L.; Swift, G. Enzyme-catalyzed ring-opening polymerization of omega-pentadecalactone. Macromolecules 1997, 30, 2705–2711.

75. Meyer, U.; Palmans, A.R.A.; Loontjens, T.; Heise, A. Enzymatic ring-opening polymerization and atom transfer radical polymerization from a bifunctional initiator. Macromolecules 2002, 35, 2873–2875.

76. Sobczak, M. Enzyme-catalyzed ring-opening polymerization of cyclic esters in the presence of poly(ethylene glycol).J. Appl. Polym. Sci. 2012, 125, 3602–3609.

77. Mei, Y.; Kumar, A.; Gross, R. Kinetics and mechanism of Candida antarctica lipase B catalyzed solution polymerization of epsilon-caprolactone. Macromolecules 2003, 36, 5530–5536.

78. Bisht, K.S.; Svirkin, Y.Y.; Henderson, L.A.; Gross, R.A.; Kaplan, D.L.; Swift, G. Lipase-catalyzed ring-opening polymerization of trimethylene carbonate. Macromolecules 1997, 30, 7735–7742.

79. Divakar, S. Porcine pancreas lipase catalyzed ring-opening polymerization of epsilon-caprolactone. J. Macromol. Sci. Pure 2004, A41, 537–546.

80. Yu, X.H.; Zhuo, R.X.; Feng, J. Ring-opening polymerization of trimethylene carbonate catalyzed by PPL immobilized on silica nanoparticles. Chem. J. Chin. Univ. 2005, 26, 978–981.

81. Matsumura, S.; Tsukada, K.; Toshima, K. Novel lipase-catalyzed ring-opening copolymerization of lactide and trimethylene carbonate forming poly(ester carbonate)s. Int. J. Biol. Macromol. 1999, 25, 161–167.

82. Henderson, L.A.; Svirkin, Y.Y.; Gross, R.A.; Kaplan, D.L.; Swift, G. Enzyme-catalyzed polymerizations of epsilon-caprolactone: Effects of initiator on product structure, propagation kinetics, and mechanism. Macromolecules 1996, 29, 7759–7766.

83. Barrera-Rivera, K.A.; Flores-Carreon, A.; Martinez-Richa, A. Enzymatic ring-opening polymerization of epsilon-caprolactone by a new lipase from yarrowia lipolytica. J. Appl. Polym. Sci. 2008, 109, 708–719.

84. Torres, S.; Castro, G.R. Non-aqueous biocatalysis in homogeneous solvent systems. Food Technol. Biotechnol. 2004, 42, 271–277.

85. Sharma, S.; Kanwar, S.S. Organic solvent tolerant lipases and applications. Sci. World J. 2014, 2014.

86. Dong, H.; Wang, H.D.; Cao, S.G.; Shen, J.C. Lipase-catalyzed polymerization of lactones and linear hydroxyesters.Biotechnol. Lett. 1998, 20, 905–908.

87. Zaks, A.; Klibanov, A.M. Enzymatic catalysis in organic media at 100 degrees C. Science 1984, 224, 1249–1251.

88. Zaks, A.; Klibanov, A.M. Substrate-specificity of enzymes in organic solvents vs. water is reversed. J. Am. Chem. Soc.1986, 108, 2767–2768.

89. Zaks, A.; Klibanov, A.M. Enzyme-catalyzed processes in organic-solvents. Proc. Natl. Acad. Sci. USA 1985, 82, 3192–3196.

90. Zaks, A.; Klibanov, A.M. The effect of water on enzyme action in organic media. J. Biol. Chem. 1988, 263, 8017–8021.

91. Madeira Lau, R.; van Rantwijk, F.; Seddon, K.R.; Sheldon, R.A. Lipase-catalyzed reactions in ionic liquids. Org. Lett.2000, 2, 4189–4191.

92. Kaar, J.L.; Jesionowski, A.M.; Berberich, J.A.; Moulton, R.; Russell, A.J. Impact of ionic liquid physical properties on lipase activity and stability. J. Am. Chem. Soc. 2003, 125, 4125–4131.

93. Tavares, A.P.M.; Rodríguez, O.; Macedo, E.A. New Generations of Ionic Liquids Applied to Enzymatic Biocatalysis. In Ionic Liquids-New Aspects for the Future; Kadokawa, J., Ed.; InTech: Rijeka, Croatia, 2013; pp. 537–556.

94. Yang, Z.; Pan, W. Ionic liquids: Green solvents for nonaqueous biocatalysis. Enzym. Microb. Technol. 2005, 37, 19–28.

95. Van Rantwijk, F.; Madeira Lau, R.; Sheldon, R.A. Biocatalytic transformations in ionic liquids. Trends Biotechnol. 2003,21, 131–138.

96. Sureshkumar, M.; Lee, C.-K. Biocatalytic reactions in hydrophobic ionic liquids. J. Mol. Catal. B-Enzym. 2009, 60, 1–12.

97. Kubisa, P. Ionic liquids as solvents for polymerization processes—Progress and challenges. Prog. Polym. Sci. 2009, 34, 1333–1347.

98. Dupont, J.; de Souza, R.F.; Suarez, P.A. Ionic liquid (molten salt) phase organometallic catalysis. Chem. Rev. 2002, 102, 3667–3692.

99. Zhang, S.; Sun, N.; He, X.; Lu, X.; Zhang, X. Physical properties of ionic liquids: Database and evaluation. J. Phys. Chem. Ref. Data 2006, 35, 1475–1517.

100. Park, S.; Kazlauskas, R.J. Biocatalysis in ionic liquids–advantages beyond green technology. Curr. Opin. Biotechnol.2003, 14, 432–437.

101. Keskin, S.; Kayrak-Talay, D.; Akman, U.; Hortaçsu, Ö. A review of ionic liquids towards supercritical fluid applications. J. Supercrit. Fluids 2007, 43, 150–180.

102. Gorke, J.T.; Okrasa, K.; Louwagie, A.; Kazlauskas, R.J.; Srienc, F. Enzymatic synthesis of poly(hydroxyalkanoates) in ionic liquids. J. Biotechnol. 2007, 132, 306–313.

103. Galonde, N.; Nott, K.; Debuigne, A.; Deleu, M.; Jerôme, C.; Paquot, M.; Wathelet, J.P. Use of ionic liquids for biocatalytic synthesis of sugar derivatives. J. Chem. Technol. Biot. 2012, 87, 451–471.

104. Dupont, J. On the solid, liquid and solution structural organization of imidazolium ionic liquids. J. Braz. Chem. Soc.2004, 15, 341–350.

105. Lozano, P.; de Diego, T.; Carrie, D.; Vaultier, M.; Iborra, J. Over-stabilization of Candida antarctica lipase B by ionic liquids in ester synthesis. Biotechnol. Lett. 2001, 23, 1529–1533.

106. Reichardt, C. Solvatochromic dyes as solvent polarity indicators. Chem. Rev. 1994, 94, 2319–2358.

107. Reichardt, C. Polarity of ionic liquids determined empirically by means of solvatochromic pyridinium N-phenolate betaine dyes. Green Chem. 2005, 7, 339–351.

108. Carda–Broch, S.; Berthod, A.; Armstrong, D. Solvent properties of the 1-butyl-3-methylimidazolium hexafluorophosphate ionic liquid. Anal. Bioanal. Chem. 2003, 375, 191–199.

109. Carmichael, A.J.; Seddon, K.R. Polarity study of some 1-alkyl-3-methylimidazolium ambient-temperature ionic liquids with the solvatochromic dye, Nile Red. J. Phys. Org. Chem. 2000, 13, 591–595.

110. Bell, G.; Halling, P.J.; Moore, B.D.; Partridge, J.; Rees, D.G. Biocatalyst behaviour in low-water systems. Trends Biotechnol. 1995, 13, 468–473.

111. Ventura, S.P.; Santos, L.D.; Saraiva, J.A.; Coutinho, J.A. Concentration effect of hydrophilic ionic liquids on the enzymatic activity of Candida antarctica lipase B. World J Microb. Biot. 2012, 28, 2303–2310.

112. Martinelle, M.; Holmquist, M.; Hult, K. On the interfacial activation of Candida antarctica lipase A and B as compared with Humicola lanuginosa lipase. BBA—Lipids Lipid Metab. 1995, 1258, 272–276.

113. Barrera-Rivera, K.A.; Marcos-Fernandez, A.; Vera-Graziano, R.; Martinez-Richa, A. Enzymatic ring-opening polymerization of epsilon-caprolactone by Yarrowia lipolytica lipase in ionic liquids. J. Polym. Sci. A Polym. Chem.2009, 47, 5792–5805.

114. Lozano, P.; de Diego, T.; Iborra, J. Hydrophobicity and water activity relationships of water-miscible aprotic solvents on kyotorphin synthesis catalyzed by α-chymotrypsin. Biotechnol. Lett. 1997, 19, 1005–1009.

115. Levitsky, V.Y.; Lozano, P.; Iborra, J.L. Designing enzymatic kyotorphin synthesis in organic media with low water content. Enzym. Microb. Technol. 2000, 26, 608–613.

116. Zhao, H.; Baker, G.A.; Song, Z.; Olubajo, O.; Zanders, L.; Campbell, S.M. Effect of ionic liquid properties on lipase stabilization under microwave irradiation. J. Mol. Catal. B-Enzym. 2009, 57, 149–157.

117. Huddleston, J.G.; Visser, A.E.; Reichert, W.M.; Willauer, H.D.; Broker, G.A.; Rogers, R.D. Characterization and comparison of hydrophilic and hydrophobic room temperature ionic liquids incorporating the imidazolium cation.Green Chem. 2001, 3, 156–164.

118. Kim, K.-W.; Song, B.; Choi, M.-Y.; Kim, M.-J. Biocatalysis in ionic liquids: Markedly enhanced enantioselectivity of lipase. Org. Lett. 2001, 3, 1507–1509.

119. Baudequin, C.; Baudoux, J.; Levillain, J.; Cahard, D.; Gaumont, A.-C.; Plaquevent, J.-C. Ionic liquids and chirality: Opportunities and challenges. Tetrahedron-Asymmetr 2003, 14, 3081–3093.

120. Van Rantwijk, F.; Sheldon, R.A. Biocatalysis in ionic liquids. Chem. Rev. 2007, 107, 2757–2785.

121. Zhao, H. Methods for stabilizing and activating enzymes in ionic liquids—A review. J. Chem. Technol. Biot. 2010, 85, 891–907.

122. Seddon, K.R.; Stark, A.; Torres, M.-J. Influence of chloride, water, and organic solvents on the physical properties of ionic liquids. Pure Appl. Chem. 2000, 72, 2275–2287.

123. Uyama, H.; Takamoto, T.; Kobayashi, S. Enzymatic synthesis of polyesters in ionic liquids. Polym. J. 2002, 34, 94–96.

124. Marcilla, R.; de Geus, M.; Mecerreyes, D.; Duxbury, C.J.; Koning, C.E.; Heise, A. Enzymatic polyester synthesis in ionic liquids. Eur. Polym. J. 2006, 42, 1215–1221.

125. Wu, C.; Zhang, Z.; He, F.; Zhuo, R. Enzymatic synthesis of poly (ε-caprolactone) in monocationic and dicationic ionic liquids. Biotechnol. Lett. 2013, 35, 879–885.

126. Yoshizawa-Fujita, M.; Saito, C.; Takeoka, Y.; Rikukawa, M. Lipase-catalyzed polymerization of L-lactide in ionic liquids. Polym. Adv. Technol. 2008, 19, 1396–1400.

127. Mena, M.; Chanfreau, S.; Gimeno, M.; Bárzana, E. Enzymatic synthesis of poly-L-lactide-co-glycolide in the ionic liquid 1-butyl-3-methylimidazolium hexafluorophosphate. Bioprocess Biosyst. Eng. 2010, 33, 1095–1101.

128. Mena, M.; López-Luna, A.; Shirai, K.; Tecante, A.; Gimeno, M.; Bárzana, E. Lipase-catalyzed synthesis of hyperbranched poly-L-lactide in an ionic liquid. Bioprocess Biosyst. Eng. 2013, 36, 383–387.

129. Chanfreau, S.; Mena, M.; Porras-Domínguez, J.R.; Ramírez-Gilly, M.; Gimeno, M.; Roquero, P.; Tecante, A.; Bárzana, E. Enzymatic synthesis of poly-L-lactide and poly-L-lactide-co-glycolide in an ionic liquid. Bioprocess Biosyst. Eng.2010, 33, 629–638.

130. Dong, F.-X.; Zhang, L.; Tong, X.-Z.; Chen, H.-B.; Wang, X.-L.; Wang, Y.-Z. Ionic liquid coated lipase: Green synthesis of high molecular weight poly (1, 4-dioxan-2-one). J. Mol. Catal. B-Enzym. 2012, 77, 46–52.

131. Huijser, S.; Staal, B.B.; Huang, J.; Duchateau, R.; Koning, C.E. Topology characterization by MALDI-ToF-MS of enzymatically synthesized poly (lactide-co-glycolide). Biomacromolecules 2006, 7, 2465–2469.

132. Wu, C.; Zhang, Z.; Chen, C.; He, F.; Zhuo, R. Synthesis of poly (ε-caprolactone) by an immobilized lipase coated with ionic liquids in a solvent-free condition. Biotechnol. Lett. 2013, 35, 1623–1630.

133. Córdova, A.; Iversen, T.; Hult, K.; Martinelle, M. Lipase-catalysed formation of macrocycles by ring-opening polymerisation of ε-caprolactone. Polymer 1998, 39, 6519–6524.

134. Skaria, S.; Smet, M.; Frey, H. Enzyme-catalyzed synthesis of hyperbranched aliphatic polyesters. Macromol. Rapid Commun. 2002, 23, 292–296.

135. López-Luna, A.; Gallegos, J.L.; Gimeno, M.; Vivaldo-Lima, E.; Bárzana, E. Lipase-catalyzed syntheses of linear and hyperbranched polyesters using compressed fluids as solvent media. J. Mol. Catal. B-Enzym. 2010, 67, 143–149.

Chapter 4

Controlled Release of Liraglutide using Thermogelling Polymers in Treatment of Diabetes

Yipei Chen[1], Yuzhuo Li[1], Wenjia Shen1, Kun Li[2], Lin Yu[1], Qinghua Chen[2] & Jiandong Ding[1]

[1]*State Key Laboratory of Molecular Engineering of Polymers, Collaborative Innovation Center of Polymers and Polymer Composite Materials, Department of Macromolecular Science, Fudan University, Shanghai, 200433, China.*

[2]*National Pharmaceutical Engineering Research Center, China State Institute of Pharmaceutical Industry, Shanghai, 200437, China.*

ABSTRACT

In treatment of diabetes, it is much desired in clinics and challenging in pharmaceutics and material science to set up a long-acting drug delivery system. This study was aimed at constructing a new delivery system using thermogelling PEG/polyester copolymers. Liraglutide, a fatty acid-modified antidiabetic polypeptide, was selected as the model drug. The thermogelling polymers were presented by poly(ε-caprolactone-*co*-glycolic acid)-poly(ethylene glycol)-poly(ε-caprolactone-*co*-glycolic acid) (PCGA-PEG-PCGA) and poly(lactic acid-*co*-glycolic acid)-poly(ethylene glycol)-poly(lactic acid-*co*-glycolic acid) (PLGA-PEG-PLGA). Both the copolymers were soluble in water, and their concentrated solutions underwent temperature-induced sol-gel transitions. The drug-loaded polymer solutions were injectable at room temperature and gelled *in situ* at body temperature. Particularly, the liraglutide-loaded PCGA-PEG-PCGA thermogel formulation exhibited a sustained drug release manner over one week in both *in vitro* and *in vivo* tests.

This feature was attributed to the combined effects of an appropriate drug/polymer interaction and a high chain mobility of the carrier polymer, which facilitated the sustained diffusion of drug out of the thermogel. Finally, a single subcutaneous injection of this formulation showed a remarkably improved glucose tolerance of mice for one week. Hence, the present study not only developed a promising long-acting antidiabetic formulation, but also put forward a combined strategy for controlled delivery of polypeptide.

INTRODUCTION

Type 2 diabetes mellitus (T2DM) is a global epidemic characterized by hyperglycemia. With the increase of patient number at an alarming rate, T2DM and its complications have got to be one of the most threatening and challenging problems concerning public health around the world, and the consequent health, social and economic burden is great. Recently, incretin-based therapies have been acknowledged as an effective treatment strategy for patients with T2DM1′2′3. Glucagon-like peptide-1 (GLP-1), a hormone of 31 amino acid residues, is released from the L cells in the colon and the ileum, and stimulates insulin secretion in a glucose-dependent manner. Therefore, GLP-1 effectively controls the blood glucose level of T2DM patients without the risk of hypoglycemia1′4. However, the clinical application of GLP-1 is limited by its short half-life (about 2 min) due to the rapid degradation by dipeptidyl peptidase IV (DPP-IV). To resolve this problem, DPP-IV-resistant GLP-1 analogues have been developed1′2.

Liraglutide (Lira) is a fatty acid derivative of GLP-1 and its amino acid sequence is displayed in Fig. 1a. It is formed by attaching a 16-carbon fatty acid molecule at position Lys26 and making an Arg34Lys substitution on GLP-1, and shares approximately 97% sequence homology with GLP-15′6. These structural modifications of Lira increase chain aggregation, promote reversible non-covalent binding to other molecules, such as albumin, and resist DPP-IV degradation. Thus, the half-life of Lira is prolonged to about 13 h after subcutaneous (SC) injection into human body6. Meanwhile, Lira retains the physiological activities of GLP-1, which include stimulating insulin release and suppressing glucagon secretion in a glucose-dependent manner, improving *β*-cell mass and function, decreasing insulin resistance, delaying gastric emptying, and increasing satiety7′8′9.

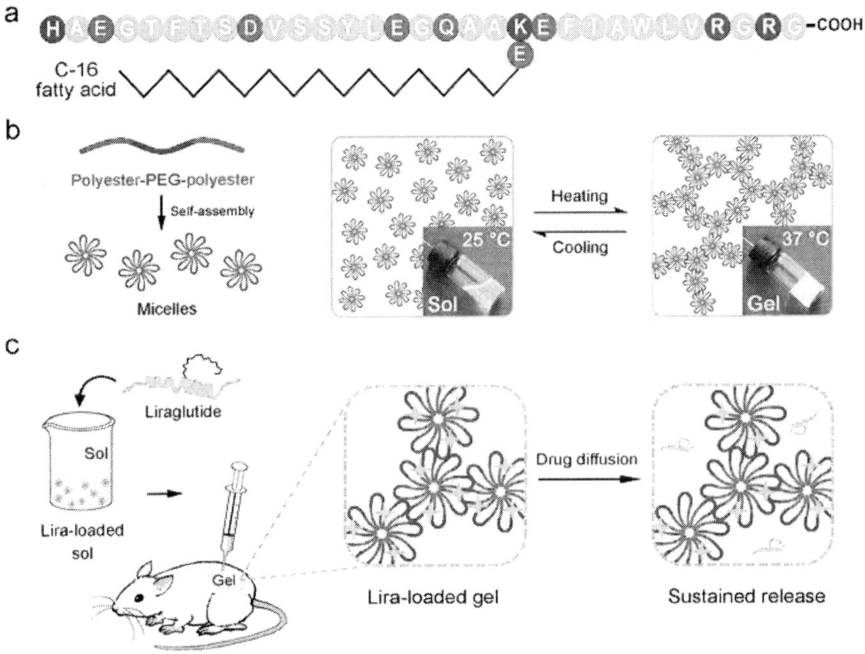

Figure 1: Schematic presentation of a Lira-loaded thermogel formulation as the long-acting drug delivery system. **(a)** Amino acid sequence of Lira with neutral residues in green, acidic ones in red and alkaline ones in blue. **(b)** Amphiphilic polyester-PEG-polyester triblock copolymers self-assemble into micelles in water at room temperature and turn into a physical hydrogel due to the formation of a percolated micelle network at body temperature. **(c)** Main procedures of constructing the Lira-loaded thermogel formulation, its *in vivo* application and the corresponding drug release mechanism.

Victoza, the solution injection of Lira developed by Novo Nordisk Inc., has been approved by both the European Medicine Agency (2009) and the U.S. Food and Drug Administration (FDA) (2010) for the treatment of T2DM. As a blockbuster in the antidiabetic drug market, the global sales of Victoza reached $420 million for the year (2010) and quickly increased to $2700 million in 2015. In general, once-daily SC injection of Victoza is needed for patients with T2DM. The dosage usually begins with 0.6 mg, and then increases to 1.2 mg after one week. It is obvious that the repeated administration and complex treatment regimen is not convenient for patients, and thus a long-acting drug delivery system of Lira is much desired in order to reduce administration frequency and improve patients' compliance. However, no long-acting formulation of Lira has, to the best of our knowledge, been reported.

As minimally invasive depot forming materials, thermogelling polymers have been extensively studied in the past decade10′11′12′13′14′15′16′17. They are dissolved in water at low or room temperature and exhibit a sol-gel transition with increase of temperature. The drugs or cells can be easily incorporated into thermogels by simply mixing them with polymeric aqueous solutions at low temperatures. This procedure avoids the denaturation of sensitive therapeutic agents, such as protein or polypeptide, due to free of any organic solvent and high temperature. Once administrated by a conventional syringe, the polymer aqueous solution spontaneously transforms into a physical hydrogel at the injection site. This *in situ* forming gel containing drugs or cells can act as a sustained drug release depot or a cell-growing matrix12′18′19′20′21′22′23′24. Generally, the delicate balance between hydrophilicity and hydrophobicity of an amphiphilic polymer plays a crucial role in the thermo-induced physical gelation25′26′27. To date, polyester27′28, polypeptide19′29′30, poly(phosphazenes)31′32, and so on have been employed as biodegradable hydrophobic segments, while PEG has been utilized as a hydrophilic block.

Among the polymers undergoing a thermo-reversible sol-gel transition in water, block copolymers composed of hydrophobic polyesters, such as poly(lactic acid-*co*-glycolic acid) (PLGA), poly(ε-caprolactone) (PCL), poly (ε-caprolactone-*co*-glycolic acid) (PCGA), and hydrophilic PEG are particularly interesting and important because of the good safety profile and facile synthesis33′34′35. Their thermogelling properties and degradation behavior can be well-modulated by many molecular parameters including molecular weight (MW), MW distribution, polyester composition, block ratio, sequence of polyester block, as well as end group25′26′28′35′36′37′38. The corresponding mechanism of thermogelation is attributed to the formation of a percolated micelle network as the temperature increases27′39, as illustrated in Fig. 1b. These resulting thermogels have been suggested as promising biomaterials for delivery of a variety of drugs40′41′42, and other biomedical applications18′43′44′45′46′47. Generally, the release profiles of drugs from thermogels can be greatly affected by many factors, such as polymer MW, polymer concentration, drug loading amount and even additive excipient41′48′49′50. Nevertheless, little attention has being paid to the effect of PEG/polyester thermogels with different polyester components on the release behavior of drugs. In fact, various polyester segments differ in their hydrophobicity, chain mobility, degradation rate, permeability to drugs, and so on51′52′53′54.

In this study, a long-acting delivery system of Lira in treatment of T2DM using thermogelling block copolymers as the carriers was examined for the first time. Different from hydrophilic polypeptides such as exenatide and insulin, Lira is of relatively higher global hydrophobicity due to the introduction of 16-carbon fatty acid into the peptide backbone, resulting in the increased capacity of chain aggregation and non-covalent binding to other amphiphilic molecules1′6.

Consequently, we hypothesized that Lira could interact with amphiphilic PEG/polyester polymers. Their appropriate interactions might realize the release of Lira at a relatively slow and consistent rate, as schematically presented in Fig. 1c.

To verify our hypothesis, two thermogelling triblock copolymers poly(ε-caprolactone-*co*-glycolic acid)-poly(ethylene glycol)-poly(ε-caprolactone-*co*-glycolic acid) (PCGA-PEG-PCGA) and poly(lactic acid-*co*-glycolic acid)-poly(ethylene glycol)-poly(lactic acid-*co*-glycolic acid) (PLGA-PEG-PLGA) were synthesized. Their physicochemical properties and thermogelling behavior in water were examined. Micellizations of amphiphilic block copolymers with or without the presence of the drug were monitored, and the secondary structures of the polypeptide in the presence of block copolymers were detected. *In vitro* release behavior of Lira from the two thermogels was investigated, and the effect of polyester component on release profile was discussed. Finally, we evaluated the *in vivo* drug release and efficacy of an optimal Lira-loaded thermogel formulation.

RESULTS

Characterization of triblock copolymers

Two triblock copolymers PCGA-PEG-PCGA and PLGA-PEG-PLGA were synthesized by us, and characterized via proton nuclear magnetic resonance (^{1}H NMR) and gel permeation chromatography (GPC). ^{1}H NMR spectra of both the polymers are presented in the Supplementary Fig. S1. The glass transition temperatures (T_g) of the two specimens were also determined by differential scanning calorimetry (DSC). The $T_g$of PCGA-PEG-PCGA was −57 °C, which was significantly lower than that of PLGA-PEG-PLGA (−4 °C). This feature indicates that the PCGA-PEG-PCGA system has the higher chain mobility at body temperature compared with PLGA-PEG-PLGA. The detailed physical parameters of the two copolymers used in this study are summarized inSupplementary Table S1.

Thermogellability of copolymer aqueous solutions

Both the PCGA-PEG-PCGA and PLGA-PEG-PLGA polymers were soluble in water at ambient temperature and underwent sol-gel transitions with increasing temperature. Figure 2a presents their phase diagrams in phosphate buffer saline (PBS, pH 7.4), which were determined by the vial inverting method25′35. The two specimens exhibited a similar critical gel concentration (about 12 wt%). The sol-gel transition temperatures (T_{gel}) of PCGA-PEG-PCGA and PLGA-PEG-PLGA aqueous solutions with the indicated concentrations were also obtained via the phase diagram. The gel windows of both polymer/water systems covered body temperature, indicating that the two thermogels are suitable for biomedical applications.

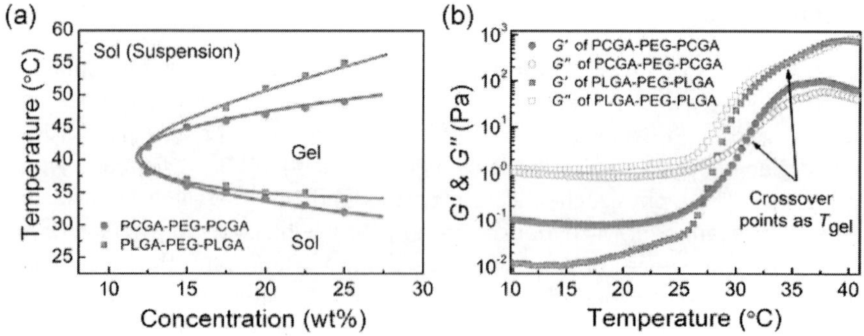

Figure 2: Thermogellability of copolymer aqueous solutions. (a) Phase diagrams of PCGA-PEG-PCGA and PLGA-PEG-PLGA triblock copolymers in PBS (pH 7.4). **(b)** Storage modulus *G'* and loss modulus *G"* of the indicated samples in PBS (pH 7.4, 25 wt%) as a function of temperature. Heating rates: 0.5 °C/min, oscillatory frequency: 10 rad/s.

The sol-gel transitions of triblock copolymers in PBS were further investigated by dynamic rheological measurements. Figure 2b shows the change in modulus of PCGA-PEG-PCGA and PLGA-PEG-PLGA aqueous solutions (25 wt%) as a function of temperature. At low or room temperature, the moduli were low, and the loss modulus *G"* was obviously greater than the storage modulus *G'*. This feature reflected their free-flowing sol states. An abrupt increase in modulus was observed along with the formation of *in situ* physical hydrogels as the temperature increased. The crossover point of *G'* and *G"* is usually regarded as T_{gel}55. The T_{gel} values determined via rheological measurements for the two polymer/water systems (25 wt%) were about 32 °C and 34 °C, which well coincided with those obtained by the vial inverting method. It is noteworthy that the maximum value of *G'* (G'_{max}) of PCGA-PEG-PCGA system was one order of magnitude lower than that of PLGA-PEG-PLGA system, which was attributed to the high flexibility of PCGA chains in PCGA-PEG-PCGA polymers.

Interactions between Lira and PEG/polyester triblock copolymers

The interactions between Lira and copolymers in water were first studied by dynamic laser scattering (DLS). As shown in Fig. 3a, both the PCGA-PEG-PCGA and PLGA-PEG-PLGA triblock copolymers formed micelles in water with sizes of about 40 nm and 30 nm, respectively. The incorporation of Lira did not influence their unimodal distribution, yet a slightly increase in the micelle size was observed.

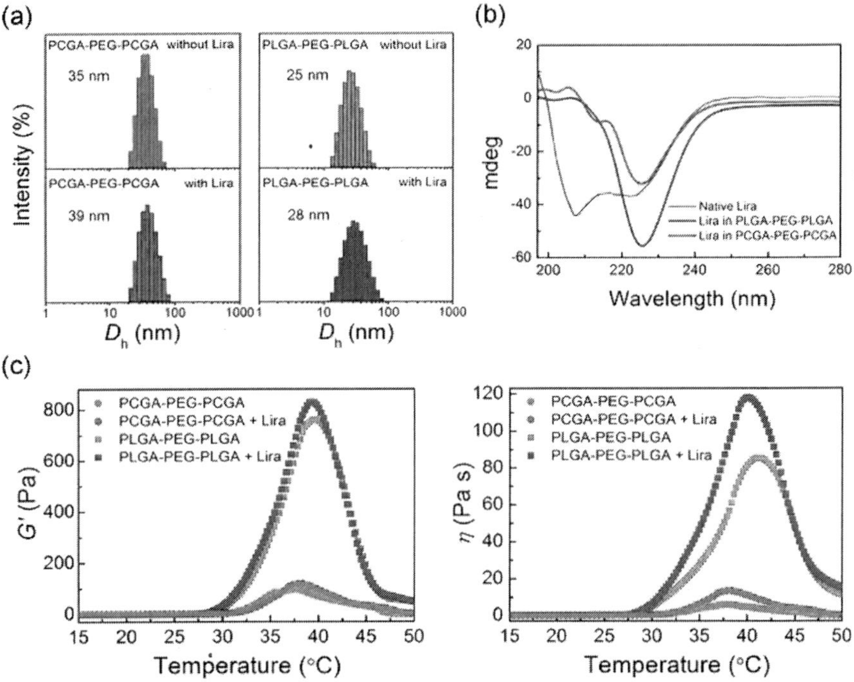

Figure 3: Interactions between Lira and PEG/polyester triblock copolymers. (a) Distribution of hydrodynamic diameters of copolymer micelles in water with or without Lira measured by DLS at 25 °C. The copolymer concentration was 0.1 wt% and Lira loading concentration was 0.008 mg/mL. **(b)** CD spectra of native Lira, Lira in PLGA-PEG-PLGA and Lira in PCGA-PEG-PCGA aqueous solutions. Lira concentration was set as 0.04 mg/mL and the polymer concentration was 0.5 wt%. **(c)** Effects of Lira on storage modulus G' and viscosity η of the indicated copolymer aqueous solutions (pH 7.4, 25 wt%) at different temperatures. Drug loading concentration: 2 mg/mL, heating rates: 0.5 °C/min, oscillatory frequency: 10 rad/s.

The circular dichroism (CD) spectra of Lira were recorded to determine its secondary structure in the different polymer aqueous systems. As shown in Fig. 3b, native Lira showed negative bands with two minima at approximately 208 and 222 nm on the CD spectra, indicating the α-helix conformation of Lira in native state. The secondary structure of Lira underwent a significant change in the presence of triblock copolymers. In the case of PCGA-PEG-PCGA, the shifts of negative bands from 208 nm to 213 nm, 222 nm to 225 nm were observed. For the PLGA-PEG-PLGA system, the negative signal at 208 nm disappeared and a bigger shift of negative band from 222 nm to 225 nm was seen. It is obvious that the interactions between the carrier polymers and drug were responsible for the transition of conformation of Lira.

The rheological properties of PEG/polyester copolymers with or without Lira in PBS (pH 7.4) were further investigated, as shown in Fig. 3c. The incorporation of Lira into the polymer aqueous solutions had no obvious influence on their sol-gel transition temperatures. Nevertheless, the presence of Lira caused an increase in both G' and viscosity η of the polymer/water systems. It is not difficult to infer that the increases of G' and η are also attributed to the interactions between the copolymer chains and polypeptide molecules.

In vitro release of Lira from thermogels

We evaluated the *in vitro* release profiles of Lira from the thermogel systems. The data in Fig. 4 show the cumulative amounts of released Lira during 9 days. Although the release of Lira from the PLGA-PEG-PLGA hydrogel exhibited a low burst with less than 17% of the loaded amount being released in the first day, a significantly incomplete release was observed at the late stage and only 56% loaded drug was released within 9 days. Different from the PLGA-PEG-PLGA system, the PCGA-PEG-PCGA thermogel formulation showed a sustained release profile over 9 days and the cumulative release amount was more than 85%. This finding indicates that the polyester component played an important role in the sustained drug release from the PEG/polyester thermogel systems.

We also utilized a commercial Pluronic F127 gel as the control group. F127 is composed of block copolymer of PEG and poly(propyl glycol) (PPG). The concentrated aqueous solution of F127 underwent a sol-gel transition upon heating as well. The Lira-loaded F127 gel exhibited a rapid release profile and almost all Lira was released within 2 days. It is obvious that the PCGA-PEG-PCGA thermogel is the optimal carrier for long-acting delivery of Lira among the materials examined in this study.

The release data of Lira from the three gel matrix were fitted via zero-order equation $Q = kt$ and Higuchi equation $Q = kt^{1/2}$, where Q is the cumulative release amount, t is release time, k is a constant. The fitted results are shown in Supplementary Table S2. As is well-known, Higuchi equation ($Q < 0.6$) represents a diffusion-controlled mechanism41. The release data of Lira from PCGA-PEG-PCGA and PLGA-PEG-PLGA thermogels well matched with Higuchi equation with the squared correlation coefficient $R^2 > 0.97$, indicating that the diffusion-controlled mechanism governed the release of drug from the PEG/polyester copolymer hydrogels. For Pluronic F127, a nearly zero-order release was observed, which demonstrated that another release mechanism controlled the Lira release from F127 gel. In the section of Discussion, we will further explain the reasons of the different release mechanisms for these gel formulations.

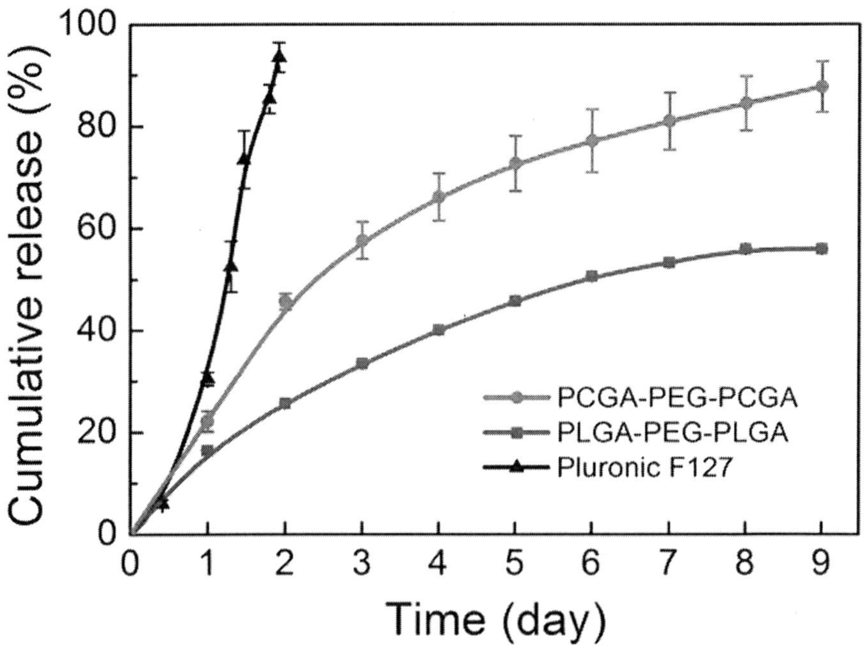

Figure 4: Cumulative release of Lira from the indicated thermogels in PBS (pH 7.4) at 37 °C. The data are represented as the mean ± SD, $n = 3$ for each group. The polymer concentration was 25 wt% and the drug loading amount was 2 mg/mL. The lines are used just for the guides of the eyes.

In vivo imaging of Lira from PCGA-PEG-PCGA thermogel

Non-invasive imaging was further carried out to track the release of Lira from thermogel matrix in ICR mice. Considering that the Lira-loaded PCGA-PEG-PCGA gel formulation exhibited a sustained release profile *in vitro*, we choose it as the optimal formulation for the *in vivo*examination. The drug was fluorescently labeled by Cyanine 5.5 (Cy5.5). A strong NIR fluorescence was observed after SC injection of the thermogel formulation containing Cy5.5-Lira at the backs of ICR mice, as shown in Fig. 5a. The fluorescence was spread to the whole back of mice on day 2, and the core red fluorescence at the injection sites lasted for more than 10 days post-injection. Cy5.5 is a hydrophobic fluorescent probe with MW of 619. The introduction of Cy5.5 significantly increased the total hydrophobicity and MW of Lira, and thus strengthened the hydrophobic interaction and aggregation between polypeptide and carrier polymer, which resulted in a slower release rate from the thermogel depot.

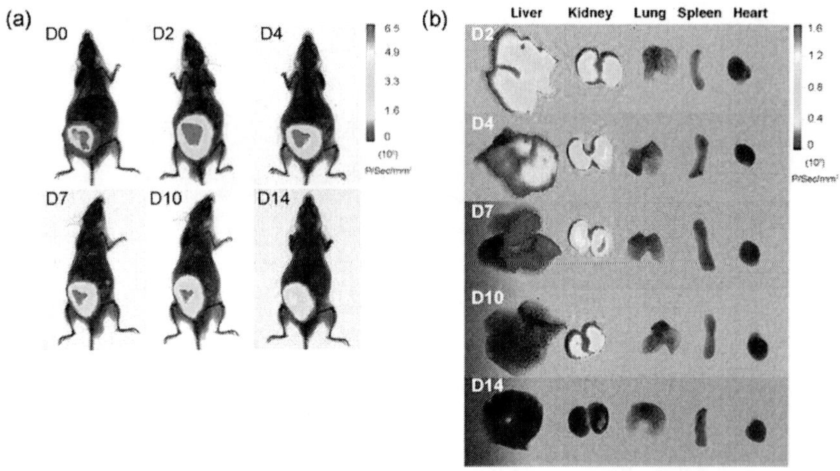

Figure 5: Monitoring of fluorescence-probe-modified peptide Cy5.5-Lira released from PCGA-PEG-PCGA thermogel. (a) The fluorescence of Cy5.5-Lira in ICR mice was monitored by non-invasive live imaging at different time points after SC injection. **(b)** *Ex vivo* organ distributions of degradation segments of Cy5.5-Lira at indicated days after SC injection. The livers, kidneys, lungs, spleens and hearts were isolated from mice at predetermined time points and fluorescence intensities were monitored. "D" denotes "day".

Meanwhile, the major organs of mice were isolated and the fluorescence was observed in livers and kidneys. The fluorescence intensity in both the organs gradually decreased over timescale and almost disappeared on day 14 (Fig. 5b). It is well-known that Lira is metabolized by degradation within the body in multiple organs and tissues after SC administration, and the widely distributed endogenous enzymes, such as DPP-IV, are involved in the degradation of Lira5. Therefore, the fluorescence observed in livers and kidneys is attributed to the degradation segments of released Cy5.5-Lira, and they would be further eliminated from the circulation by glomerular filtration.

In vivo hypoglycemic efficacy

Compared with fasting glucose level, postprandial hyperglycemia is generally considered as a more sensitive indicator of diabetic control. One of widely used models to mimic the postprandial state of hyperglycemia is the oral glucose tolerance test (OGTT), which can rapidly reflect the hypoglycemic effect due to

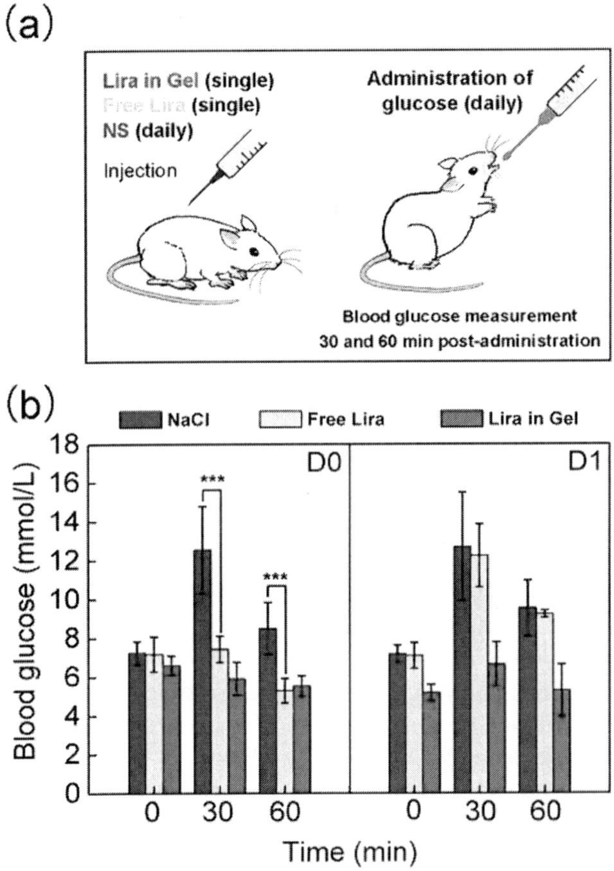

Figure 6: OGTT of ICR mice. (a) Schematic illustration of the procedure of the OGTT. To mimic the postprandial state, the mice were poured by glucose (3 g/10 mL/kg) once daily. Blood samples were collected at $t = 0$, 30 and 60 min for glucose measurements before and after the oral gavage of glucose. The data of blood glucose at $t = 0$ reflects the limosis blood glucose level before the oral gavage of glucose, while the data of blood glucose at $t = 30$ and 60 min after the oral gavage of glucose indicate the postprandial blood glucose levels. **(b)** Blood glucose levels in ICR mice in the groups "NaCl" (injection of 0.9% NS daily) "Free Lira" (a single injection of Lira solution) and "Lira in Gel" (a single injection of the Lira-loaded PCGA-PEG-PCGA gel formulation), $n = 6$ for each group. Here, the normal coordinate indicates the time after oral administration of glucose. "D0" in the legend denotes the day of injection, "D1" indicates the next day after the treatment. The significant differences between the group of "NaCl" and that of "Free Lira" are specifically marked: $^{***}p < 0.001$.

drug action on the glucose utilization41′56. In this study, we carried out OGTTs in ICR mice to evaluate the *in vivo* efficacy of the Lira-loaded PCGA-PEG-PCGA gel formulation on reduction of the blood glucose level at the postprandial state, as schematically presented in Fig. 6a.

The blood glucose levels of mice in the NaCl group rapidly increased after the oral administration of glucose. In contrast, the blood glucose levels of mice received a single SC injection of free Lira or Lira-loaded gel formulation significantly reduced at the time points of 30 and 60 min after the same administration of glucose on D0 (Fig. 6b). Unlike the long-acting Lira-loaded gel formulation, no sign of the hypoglycemic effect was observed for the group of Free Lira after oral gavage of glucose on the next day (D1). This finding coincides with the *in vivo*half-life of Lira1′2, suggesting that the repeated administration is required for the solution injection of Lira and thus the long-acting thermogel formulation is quite meaningful for the treatment of T2DM.

Subsequently, the OGTTs were carried out once per day during the whole experimental period of 10 days. The results in Fig. 7demonstrated that there were significantly statistical differences of glucose level between the group of "NaCl" and that of "Lira in Gel" from D0 to D7 at the time points of 30 and 60 min after the administration of glucose. The *in vivo* tests indicated that the gel formulation of Lira had a significantly hypoglycemic effect up to one week in ICR mice after a single SC administration. This feature is well consistent with the *in vitro*release profile. Meanwhile, the blood glucose levels of mice that didn't receive any treatment throughout the whole experiment period (as the group of "Blank") were also detected as an indicator of the normal glucose level in the mouse blood. Their blood glucose levels were steady and no significant change was observed as a function of administration time, as demonstrated in Supplementary Fig. S2.

Patients with T2DM are highly probably accompanied with obesity. Thus, how about the weight control of animals in the case of the Lira release? The mice were weighed daily, and the results are shown in Fig. 8. We set three control groups, the NaCl group, Gel group (without drugs) and Blank group (without any treatment). The body weight gradually increased over time in all of these control groups, and no statistic difference was observed among them. On the other hand, it has been widely recognized that the reduction of body weight is an index of*in vivo* toxicity of an implanted biomaterial. The change in body weight of mice received the administration of thermogel without any drug was similar to that of the Blank group, demonstrating the good biocompatibility of the thermogel itself.

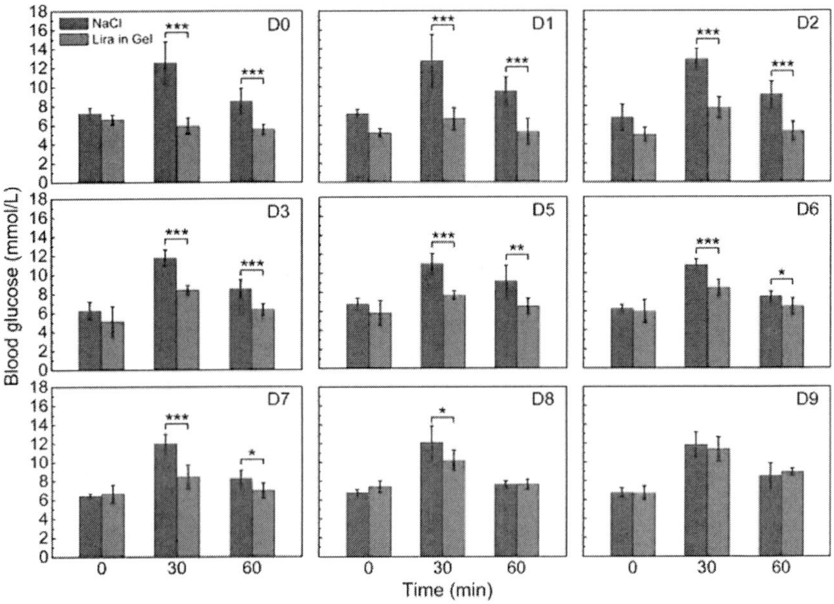

Figure 7: Blood glucose levels of ICR mice in the groups of "NaCl" and "Lira in Gel" during the whole experimental period of 10 days. $n = 6$ for each group. Here, the oral gavage of glucose in mice was once-daily performed, and the time points 0, 30, 60 min in the horizon coordination denotes the time after oral administration of glucose. "D0" in the legend denotes the day of injecting the Lira gel formulation, "D9" in the legend indicates day 9 after the treatment with the Lira gel formulation. In the group of "NaCl", the physiological saline solution was injected daily. The hydrogel formulation of Lira was administrated via a single subcutaneous injection during the whole 10 days of *in vivo* examination. The continuous liberation of Lira from the hydrogel acted significantly the hypoglycemic efficacy within the initial 7 days. Significant differences between the group of "NaCl" and that of "Lira in Gel" are specifically marked: *$p < 0.05$, **$p < 0.01$, ***$p < 0.001$.

In contrast, the body weight gain of mice in the group of Lira in Gel was significantly suppressed after the administration of Lira gel formulation. The mean body weight of mice received the Lira gel formulation was about 10% lower than that of the blank. This feature affirmed that the released Lira has the potency of delaying gastric emptying and reducing appetite, which is in accordance with the pharmacology of Lira as illustrated elsewhere8'9.

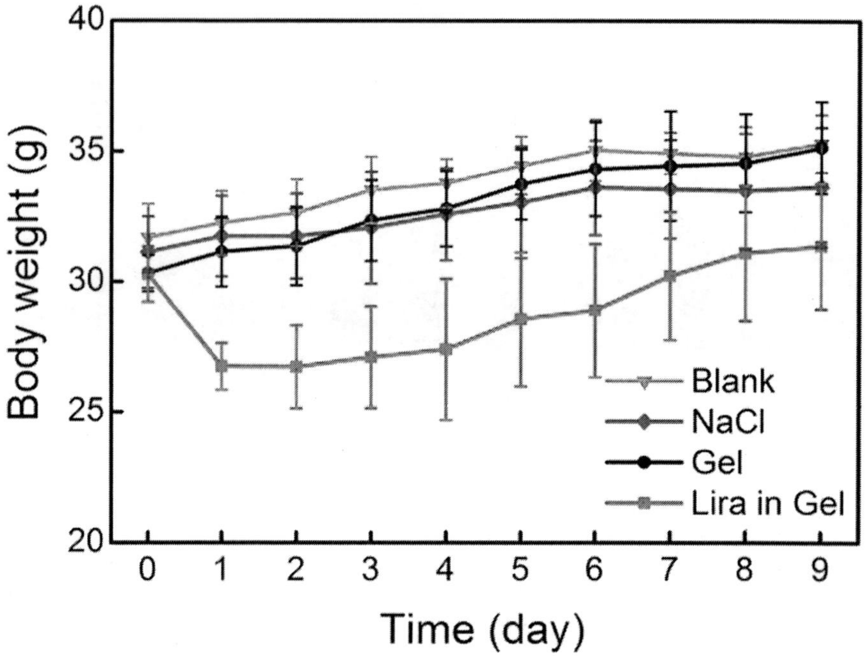

Figure 8: Body weights of ICR mice after the indicated treatments. $n = 6$ for each group. The lines are used just for the guides of the eyes.

DISCUSSION

It is well-recognized that the development of new T2DM treatments should avoid the decline of *β*-cell function, occurrence of hypoglycemia and body weight gain. Lira is a "smart" glucoregulatory agent associated with *β*-cell function improvement, glucose-dependent insulin secretion and body weight reduction, and it exerts the hypoglycemic efficacy only when blood glucose levels are higher than normal[5,6]. Namely, it shows negligible risk of hypoglycemia in spite of the sustained release of Lira. Nevertheless, the solely commercial formulation of Lira is its solution injection and daily injection is still not ideal for the treatment of T2DM. Therefore, the development of long-acting delivery system of Lira is much desired.

Injectable thermogels composed of PEG and biodegradable polyesters have been suggested as potential carriers for sustained delivery of various drugs, such as protein, polypeptide and small-molecule drug[33,42,49,57,58,59]. However, there is little work on release kinetics comparisons between carrier polymers with different polyester components for the same model drug. In the present study, two triblock copolymers PCGA-PEG-PCGA and PLGA-PEG-PLGA with similar MWs were synthesized by us. Both the polymer aqueous solutions underwent reversible sol-gel transitions as the temperature increased and formed semi-solid thermogels at body temperature (Fig. 2). Hence, the two thermogels were selected as the carriers to deliver Lira for the first time, and their release kinetics comparisons were carried out as well.

It is well-known that the PEG/polyester copolymers could form core-corona micelles in water with the hydrophilic PEG blocks locating in the coronas and the hydrophobic polyester blocks in the cores36'39. Herein, the formation of PEG/polyester micelles was also confirmed by DLS measurements, and the size of copolymer micelles slightly increased with addition of Lira (Fig. 3a). Also, the changes in the secondary structure of Lira were observed by CD analysis (Fig. 3b). On a macro level, the introduction of Lira resulted in a significant increase in η of thermogels (Fig. 3c). Taken together, we believe that there were the interactions between Lira and the carrier polymers. Considering that Lira is an amphiphilic polypeptide with a hydrophobic 16-carbon side chain, we further speculate that the C16 side chain probably entered the hydrophobic cores of micelles through the hydrophobic interaction with each other.

Non-degradable F127 hydrogel is easily eroded in water, resulting in its fast disappearance within one or two days34. As a result, Lira was thoroughly released from the F127 gel matrix due to the rapid erosion of carrier polymers (Fig. 4). In contrast, the PEG/polyester thermogels can maintain their *in vivo* integrities from one week to several months, and their degradation mainly depends on the hydrolysis of polyester segments and the final degradation products are lactic acid, glycolic acid, 1,6-hydroxycaproic acid and PEG, which are nontoxic and easily cleared from the body12'33'34'46'57. Consequently, the PEG/polyester thermogels are suitable for long-acting drug delivery. Nevertheless, the hydrophilic polypeptides, such as insulin and exenatide, are often enclosed between micelles after being loaded into the thermogel depots, and thus their release period is only a few days because of the fast diffusion of drugs41'59. In this study, although the release of Lira, an amphiphilic polypeptide, from the thermogels was also governed via diffusion mechanism, a sustained release manner without significant initial burst was observed for the two gel formulations. This feature was attributed to the hydrophobic interactions between C16 fatty side chain of Lira and the hydrophobic cores of copolymer micelles, which effectively delayed the diffusion of drug. And yet, due to the difference of polyester components, the two thermogel systems also exhibited the different diffusion rates of drug.

Now, a question arises: what kind of intrinsic factor leads to the different release profiles? Compared with PLGA segment, the PCGA block was more hydrophobic because of the longer hydrocarbon chain in the PCL backbone54. However, the diffusion of Lira from the PCGA-PEG-PCGA thermogel system was faster even though the hydrophobic interaction between drug and the carrier polymer seemed to be relatively stronger. Hence, the difference of hydrophobic and hydrophilic performance of polyester components was not the intrinsic factor. Over the past decades, PLGA, PCL and their copolymers have been widely utilized as carrier polymers for drug delivery in different forms including microsphere, nanoparticle, micelle and hydrogel[60,61,62,63]. Interestingly, a very similar trend had been reported, namely, the release rate of drug from PCL-based systems was often faster than that of PLGA systems[51,52,60,61,63,64]. The highly flexible nature of PCL chain, which produced the high mobility of chain and the good permeability to drugs, was accounted for the increased release rate. In the present study, a much lower T_g of PCGA-PEG-PCGA when compared to PLGA-PEG-PLGA polymer also reflects the highly flexible nature of PCGA block. Meanwhile, this result suggests that the PCGA-PEG-PCGA system has the higher chain motion at body temperature compared with PLGA-PEG-PLGA, and thus facilitates the diffusion of drug. As a result, the PCGA-PEG-PCGA/Lira system exhibited a sustained release profile *in vitro* over one week. The *in vivo* imaging also demonstrated that this gel formulation exhibited a long-acting drug release manner in an animal model (Fig. 5). In contrast, in the case of PLGA-PEG-PLGA/Lira system, the low mobility of carrier polymer resulted in an incomplete release of Lira at the late stage due to the difficulty of drug diffusion out of the micelles.

After a single SC administration of Lira-loaded PCGA-PEG-PCGA gel formulation in ICR mice, the hypoglycemic effect lasted up to one week (Fig. 7) and such a feature coincided with the *in vitro* release profile.Figure 9 schematically presents the mechanism of the thermogel formulation in controlling blood glucose level. The successful animal testing also affirmed the bioactivity of drug released from the gel depot. This feature indicates that the denaturation of Lira in the gel matrix did not occur even if the secondary conformation of Lira changed due to its interaction with carrier polymers. Moreover, the administration of Lira gel formulation induced modest weight loss (Fig. 8), which is beneficial for some patients of T2DM with obesity. In fact, the Lira solution injection Saxenda (Novo Nordisk Inc.) has been approved by FDA in 2014 as a treatment option for chronic weight management. Hence, besides as a sustained release anti-diabetic system, our Lira-loaded thermogel formulation may also serve as a long-acting weight-manage formulation for patients who are obese or overweight.

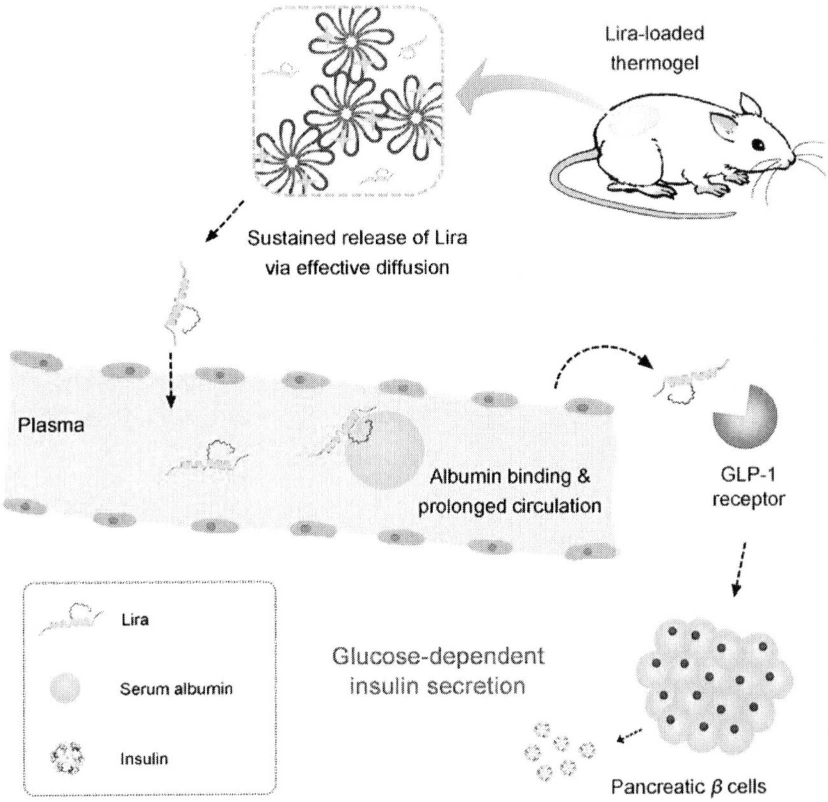

Figure 9: Schematic presentation of controlling blood glucose level by the Lira-loaded PCGA-PEG-PCGA thermogel formulation. The copolymer aqueous system became a physical hydrogel at body temperature after injection due to the formation of a percolated micelle network upon heating. The combination of an appropriate drug/polymer interaction and a high chain mobility of carrier polymers led to a sustained release of Lira from the thermogel matrix. The circulation of Lira was remarkably prolonged via its non-covalent binding to serum albumin. The activation of GLP-1 receptors on pancreatic *β* cells by Lira promoted insulin secretion in a glucose-dependent manner, leading to intelligent blood glucose reduction.

CONCLUSION

This paper reports the first long-acting drug delivery system of Lira, a glucose-dependent insulinotropic hormone. To this end, injectable and biodegradable PCGA-PEG-PCGA and PLGA-PEG-PLGA thermogels were synthesized. Both Lira and the PEG/polyester polymers were amphiphilic, and their mixtures easily formed micelles in water. The significantly different release profiles were observed in the two Lira-loaded thermogel systems with varying polyester components. As one of the two cases, the sustained release of Lira from the PCGA-PEG-PCGA gel formulation with a period of one week was achieved. This result was attributed to both the appropriate drug/carrier polymer interaction and the high chain mobility of carrier polymer. Their combination led to the effective diffusion of drug from the hydrogel matrix for a relative long time.

After a single shot of the Lira-loaded PCGA-PEG-PCGA gel formulation into mice, not only an *in vivo* sustained release was observed, but also a reduced blood glucose level at the postprandial state was achieved up to one week. The *in vivo* therapeutic efficacy was consistent with the *in vitro* release profile. Consequently, the PCGA-PEG-PCGA thermogel holds great promise for once-weekly delivery of Lira, and such a delivery system can improve patient compliance significantly. Meanwhile, the strategy based on the interactions between drugs and carrier polymers and the chain mobility of carrier polymers to control drug release might be helpful for the development of some other kinds of drug delivery systems.

METHODS

Materials

PEG of MW 1500, ε-caprolactone (CL), Pluronic F127, and stannous 2-ethyl-hexanoate (stannous octoate, 95%) were supplied by Sigma-Aldrich (USA). Glycolide (GA) and D,L-lactide (LA) were purchased from Purac (Netherlands). Liraglutide was synthesized by Chinese Peptide Co., Ltd (Hangzhou, China). Cyanine5.5 N-hydroxysuccinimide ester (Cy5.5-NHS) was product of Lumiprobe (USA). All of chemicals were used without further purification.

Experimental animals

ICR mice (male, 30 ± 2 g) were purchased from SLAC Laboratory Animal Co. Ltd (Shanghai, China). The animals were housed in cages at 22~25 °C with 12–12 h light-dark cycle. During acclimation, the mice were fed with a standard laboratory chow diet and tap water. All the animal experiments were carried out in accordance with the approved guidelines of the "Principles of Laboratory Animal Care" (NIH publication #85-23, revised 1985) and were approved by the ethics evaluation board of Fudan University.

Synthesis and physicochemical characterization of polymers

Triblock copolymers of PCGA-PEG-PCGA and PLGA-PEG-PLGA were synthesized via ring-opening polymerization of CL and GA or LA and GA using PEG as the macroinitiator and stannous octoate as the catalyst. The detailed synthetic procedure has been described in our previous publications28'35. ^{1}H NMR was used to determine the composition of triblock copolymers. Spectra were recorded at a 500 MHz Bruker spectrometer (DMX500) using $CDCl_3$ as the solvent. MWs of copolymers and the distribution thereof were measured using a gel permeation chromatography system (GPC, Agilent 1100). The eluent was tetrahydrofuran at a flow rate of 1.0 mL/min at 35 °C. Uniform polystyrene standards were used to obtain a calibration curve. The T_g of copolymers was determined by DSC (Q2000, TA Instruments) in the temperature range from −80 °C to 80 °C with a heating rate of 20 °C/min. The sample was loaded in an aluminum pan and scanned in the instrument to record the thermograms. The midpoint of the transition zone was defined as T_g.

The vial inverting method25'41 with an increment temperature of 1 °C per step was used to determine the sol-gel transition of the polymer aqueous solution. Rheological characteristics of the polymer aqueous solutions with or without drug was also measured using a stress-controlled rheometry (Kinexus Pro, Malvern) equipped with a Peltier plate (1° steel cone, 60 mm diameter with solvent trap)47. The time sweep measurements were carried out at a heating rate of 0.5 °C/min and an oscillatory frequency of 10 rad/s.

Dynamic laser scattering

The hydrodynamic diameters of copolymer micelles in PBS with or without Lira were measured by dynamic light scattering instrument (Zetasizers Nano ZS90, Malvern) with a vertically polarized incident beam at 532 nm and a fixed scattering angle of 90°. All of the samples were filtered through 0.45-μm filters and equilibrated at room temperature for 12 h before measurement.

Circular dichroism spectroscopy

The secondary structures of Lira with or without copolymers were characterized by circular dichroism instrument (Bio-Logic MOS-450, Bio-Logic). Spectra were recorded from 200 to 280 nm using a bandwidth of 1 nm and a scanning rate of 1 nm/s. Aqueous polymer solutions without Lira were also scanned in the same wavelength range as the blank background.

In vitro drug release

Lira was added into polymeric aqueous solutions (PBS, pH 7.4, polymer concentration: 25 wt%) and stirred at 4 °C till it was completely dissolved. Then, 0.5 mL polymer solutions containing 2 mg/mL Lira were transferred into 10-mL test tubes (inner diameter 14 mm), and the samples were converted to physical hydrogels by incubating in water bath at 37 °C for 10 min. Next, 5 mL of PBS (pH 7.4, 37 °C) containing 0.025% NaN_3 was added as release medium. The shaking rate of water bath was fixed at 50 rpm. At designated time intervals, the release medium was totally extracted from the tubes and replaced with the same amount of fresh buffer to maintain the sink condition. The drug amount released into the release medium were measured by high-performance liquid chromatography (HPLC, Waters Separation Module e2695) equipped with a C18 column (5 μm particle, 150 × 4.6 mm, Phenomenex). Mobile phase A was acetonitrile and mobile phase B was water containing 0.1% trifluoroacetic acid. A flow-rate of 1.0 mL/min was set over 20 min with mobile phase A increased from 48% to 56% and mobile phase B decreased from 52% to 44%. Detection was performed with a UV detector (Waters UV/visible detector 2489) at 220 nm.

Monitoring of Lira release from thermogel in ICR mice

In vivo real-time fluorescence imaging was performed in ICR mice for monitoring of Lira release from thermogel. The polypeptide was labeled with a Cy5.5 dye by adding Cy5.5-NHS to Lira solution at pH 8.4 with a molar ratio of 1/1. After incubated at 4 °C for 12 h, the solution was dialyzed to remove the unreacted Cy5.5 and then freeze-dried. PCGA-PEG-PCGA solutions (25 wt%, 0.2 mL) containing Cy5.5-Lira were SC injected into the backs of ICR mice. At predetermined time points, the fluorescence of the whole body and isolated organs including liver, kidney, lung, spleen and heart were monitored by a small animal imaging system (*In-Vivo* Xtreme, Bruker) with an excitation wavelength of 690 nm and emission wavelength of 790 nm.

Mice oral glucose tolerance test

Mice OGTTs[41,56] were performed to evaluate the *in vivo* hypoglycemic efficacy of the Lira-loaded PCGA-PEG-PCGA thermogel formulation at the postprandial state. The experimental mice were randomly divided into 5 groups with 6 mice per group. For the NaCl group, the mice received a SC injection of 0.9% NaCl solution (NS) daily at a dosage of 7.5 mL/kg. For the Gel group, the mice received a single SC injection of thermogel without drugs. The group of Free Lira was administrated by a single SC injection of Lira solution at a dosage of 1.5 mg/7.5 mL/kg. The group of Lira in Gel was administrated by a single SC injection of Lira-loaded gel formulation (15 mg/7.5 mL/kg). For the Blank group, the mice didn't receive any treatment throughout the whole experiment period. The group of Free Lira was only applied for the short-time examination, while the group of Lira in Gel as a long-acting drug delivery system was evaluated in both the short-time (1 day) and long period (10 days), and thus the drug dosage in the group of Lira in Gel was 10-fold of that of the Free Lira group. All of the mice were fasted from 9:00 a.m. for 4 h but allowed to drink water before treatment. For mice of NaCl group, Free Lira group, Lira in Gel group and Blank group, about 30 μL basal blood sample was obtained from the tail vein (defined as $t = 0$) to measure the glucose concentration using a one-touch blood glucose monitoring system (Accu Check Active, Roche Diagnostics).

The mice in the groups of NaCl, Free Lira and Lira in Gel were poured by glucose (3 g/10 mL/kg) after different injections for 15 min. Then, blood samples were collected at $t = 30$ and 60 min for glucose measurements after the oral gavage of glucose.

On the next 9 days post-administration, the mice were fasted from 9:00 a.m. for 4 h. Subsequently, blood samples were taken from the tail vein ($t = 0$) to determine baseline glucose levels before oral administration of glucose (the same as above). And at $t = 30$ and 60 min after oral administration of glucose, blood samples were also collected and detected. Meanwhile, body weights of mice were recorded each day before fasting.

STATISTICAL ANALYSIS

All the results were expressed as mean ± standard deviation (SD). For group comparison, the statistical differences of mean values were analyzed by least significant difference (LSD) *t*-tests. A *p* value of <0.05 was considered as a significant difference.

REFERENCES

1. Drucker, D. J. & Nauck, M. A. The incretin system: glucagon-like peptide-1 receptor agonists and dipeptidyl peptidase-4 inhibitors in type 2 diabetes. Lancet 368, 1696–1705 (2006).

2. Tahrani, A. A., Piya, M. K., Kennedy, A. & Barnett, A. H. Glycaemic control in type 2 diabetes: Targets and new therapies. Pharmacol. Ther. 125, 328–361 (2010).

3. Kim, P. H., Lee, M. & Kim, S. W. Delivery of two-step transcription amplification exendin-4 plasmid system with arginine-grafted bioreducible polymer in type 2 diabetes animal model. J. Control. Release 162, 9–18 (2012).

4. Doyle, M. E. & Egan, J. M. Mechanisms of action of glucagon-like peptide 1 in the pancreas. Pharmacol. Ther. 113, 546–593 (2007).

5. Ryan, G. J., Foster, K. T. & Jobe, L. J. Review of the therapeutic uses of liraglutide. Clin. Ther. 33, 793–811 (2011).

6. Montanya, E. & Sesti, G. A review of efficacy and safety data regarding the use of liraglutide, a once-daily human glucagon-like peptide 1

analogue, in the treatment of type 2 diabetes mellitus. Clin. Ther. 31, 2472–2488 (2009).

7. Mari, A. et al. Effects of the long-acting human glucagon-like peptide-1 analog liraglutide on beta-cell function in normal living conditions. Diabetes Care 30, 2032–2033 (2007).

8. Jelsing, J. et al. Liraglutide: short-lived effect on gastric emptyingulong lasting effects on body weight. Diabetes Obes. Metab. 14, 531–538 (2012).

9. Vilsboll, T. et al. Liraglutide, a long-acting human glucagon-like peptide-1 analog, given as monotherapy significantly improves glycemic control and lowers body weight without risk of hypoglycemia in patients with type 2 diabetes. Diabetes Care 30, 1608–1610 (2007).

10. Jeong, B., Bae, Y. H., Lee, D. S. & Kim, S. W. Biodegradable block copolymers as injectable drug-delivery systems. Nature 388, 860–862 (1997).

11. Park, M. H., Joo, M. K., Choi, B. G. & Jeong, B. Biodegradable thermogels. Acc. Chem. Res. 45, 424–433 (2012).

12. Shi, K. et al. Synthesis, characterization, and application of reversible PDLLA-PEG-PDLLA copolymer thermogels in vitro and in vivo. Sci Rep 6, 19077 (2016).

13. Yang, Y. et al. A novel gene delivery composite system based on biodegradable folate-poly (ester amine) polymer and thermosensitive hydrogel for sustained gene release. Sci Rep 6, 21402 (2016).

14. Yu, L. & Ding, J. D. Injectable hydrogels as unique biomedical materials. Chem. Soc. Rev. 37, 1473–1481 (2008).

15. Chen, S. et al. Mesenchymal stem cell-laden anti-inflammatory hydrogel enhances diabetic wound healing. Sci Rep 5, 18104 (2015).

16. Wang, W. et al. Dual-functional transdermal drug delivery system with controllable drug loading based on thermosensitive poloxamer hydrogel for atopic dermatitis treatment. Sci Rep 6, 24112 (2016).

17. Vermonden, T., Censi, R. & Hennink, W. E. Hydrogels for protein delivery. Chem. Rev. 112, 2853–2888 (2012).

18. Kwon, J. S. et al. Injectable in situ-forming hydrogel for cartilage tissue engineering. J. Mater. Chem. B 1, 3314–3321 (2013).

19. Moon, H. J., Patel, M., Chung, H. & Jeong, B. Nanocomposite versus mesocomposite for osteogenic differentiation of tonsil-derived mesenchymal stem cells. Adv. Healthc. Mater. 5, 353–363 (2016).

20. Jeong, Y. et al. Enzymatically degradable temperature-sensitive polypeptide as a new in-situ gelling biomaterial. J. Control. Release 137, 25–30 (2009).

21. 21.Tirella, A. et al. Nano-in-micro self-reporting hydrogel constructs. J. Biomed. Nanotechnol. 11, 1451–1460 (2015).

22. 22.Fan, M. et al. Dexamethasone-loaded poly(D, L-lactic acid) microspheres/poly(ethylene glycol)-poly(epsilon-caprolactone)-poly(ethylene glycol) micelles composite for skin augmentation. J. Biomed. Nanotechnol. 10, 592–602 (2014).

23. Fu, S. Z. et al. Biodegradable and thermosensitive monomethoxy poly(ethylene glycol)-poly(lactic acid) hydrogel as a barrier for prevention of post-operative abdominal adhesion. J. Biomed. Nanotechnol. 10, 427–435 (2014).

24. Song, F. F., Li, X. Q., Wang, Q., Liao, L. Q. & Zhang, C. Nanocomposite hydrogels and their applications in drug delivery and tissue engineering. J. Biomed. Nanotechnol. 11, 40–52 (2015).

25. Shim, M. S. et al. Poly(D,L-lactic acid-co-glycolic acid)-b-poly(ethylene glycol)-b-poly (D,L-lactic acid-co-glycolic acid) triblock copolymer and thermoreversible phase transition in water. J. Biomed. Mater. Res. 61, 188–196 (2002).

26. Yu, L., Zhang, H. & Ding, J. D. A subtle end-group effect on macroscopic physical gelation of triblock copolymer aqueous solutions. Angew. Chem. Int. Ed. 45, 2232–2235 (2006).

27. Yu, L., Zhang, Z., Zhang, H. & Ding, J. D. Mixing a sol and a precipitate of block copolymers with different block ratios leads to an injectable hydrogel. Biomacromolecules 10, 1547–1553 (2009).

28. Yu, L., Zhang, Z. & Ding, J. D. Influence of LA and GA sequence in the PLGA block on the properties of thermogelling PLGA-PEG-PLGA block copolymers. Biomacromolecules 12, 1290–1297 (2011).

29. He, C. L., Zhuang, X. L., Tang, Z. H., Tian, H. Y. & Chen, X. S. Stimuli-sensitive synthetic polypeptide-based materials for drug and gene delivery. Adv. Healthc. Mater. 1, 48–78 (2012).

30. Park, M. H. et al. 3D culture of tonsil-derived mesenchymal stem cells in poly(ethylene glycol)-poly(L-alanine-co-L-phenyl alanine) thermogel. Adv. Healthc. Mater. 3, 1782–1791 (2014).

31. Park, M. R. et al. Sustained delivery of human growth hormone using a polyelectrolyte complex-loaded thermosensitive polyphosphazene hydrogel. J. Control. Release 147, 359–367 (2010).

32. Seo, B. B., Choi, H., Koh, J. T. & Song, S. C. Sustained BMP-2 delivery and injectable bone regeneration using thermosensitive polymeric nanoparticle hydrogel bearing dual interactions with BMP-2. J. Control. Release 209, 67–76 (2015).

33. Zentner, G. M. et al. Biodegradable block copolymers for delivery of proteins and water-insoluble drugs. J. Control. Release 72, 203–215 (2001).

34. Yu, L., Zhang, Z., Zhang, H. & Ding, J. D. Biodegradability and biocompatibility of thermoreversible hydrogels formed from mixing a sol and a precipitate of block copolymers in water. Biomacromolecules 11, 2169–2178 (2010).

35. Yu, L., Sheng, W. J., Yang, D. C. & Ding, J. D. Design of molecular parameters to achieve block copolymers with a powder form at dry state and a temperature-induced sol-gel transition in water without unexpected gelling prior to heating. Macromol. Res. 21, 207–215 (2013).

36. Chen, L., Ci, T. Y., Li, T., Yu, L. & Ding, J. D. Effects of molecular weight distribution of amphiphilic block copolymers on their solubility, micellization, and temperature-induced sol gel Transition in water. Macromolecules 47, 5895–5903 (2014).

37. .Lei, K. W., Shen, W. J., Cao, L. P., Yu, L. & Ding, J. D. An injectable thermogel with high radiopacity. Chem. Commun. 51, 6080–6083 (2015).

38. Petit, A. et al. Effect of polymer composition on rheological and degradation properties of temperature-responsive gelling systems composed of acyl-capped PCLA-PEG-PCLA. Biomacromolecules 14, 3172–3182 (2013).

39. Yu, L., Chang, G. T., Zhang, H. & Ding, J. D. Temperature-induced spontaneous sol-gel transitions of poly(D,L-lactic acid-co-glycolic acid)-b-poly(ethylene glycol)-b-poly(D,L-lactic acid-co-glycolic acid) triblock copolymers and their end-capped derivatives in water. J. Polym. Sci., Part A: Polym. Chem. 45, 1122–1133 (2007).

40. .Ma, H. C. et al. Localized co-delivery of doxorubicin, cisplatin, and methotrexate by thermosensitive hydrogels for enhanced osteosarcoma treatment. ACS Appl. Mater. Interfaces 7, 27040–27048 (2015).

41. Li, K. et al. A long-acting formulation of a polypeptide drug exenatide in treatment of diabetes using an injectable block copolymer hydrogel. Biomaterials 34, 2834–2842 (2013).

42. Ci, T. Y., Chen, L., Yu, L. & Ding, J. D. Tumor regression achieved by encapsulating a moderately soluble drug into a polymeric thermogel. Sci Rep 4, 5473 (2014).

43. Ni, P. et al. Injectable thermosensitive PEG-PCL-PEG hydrogel/acellular bone matrix composite for bone regeneration in cranial defects. Biomaterials 35, 236–248 (2014).

44. Chen, L. et al. An injectable hydrogel with or without drugs for prevention of epidural scar adhesion after laminectomy in rats. Chin. J. Polym. Sci. 34, 147–163 (2016).

45. Wu, Q. J. et al. Thermosensitive hydrogel containing dexamethasone micelles for preventing postsurgical adhesion in a repeated-injury model. Sci Rep 5, 13553 (2015).

46. .Zhang, Z. et al. Biodegradable and thermoreversible PCLA-PEG-PCLA hydrogel as a barrier for prevention of post-operative adhesion. Biomaterials 32, 4725–4736 (2011).

47. Cao, L. et al. Safe and efficient colonic endoscopic submucosal dissection using an injectable hydrogel. ACS Biomater. Sci. Eng. 2, 393–402 (2016).

48. Tang, Y. & Singh, J. Biodegradable and biocompatible thermosensitive polymer based injectable implant for controlled release of protein. Int. J. Pharm. 365, 34–43 (2009).

49. Yu, L. et al. In vitro and in vivo evaluation of a once-weekly formulation of an antidiabetic peptide drug exenatide in an injectable thermogel. J. Pharm. Sci. 102, 4140–4149 (2013).

50. Petit, A. et al. Release behavior and intra-articular biocompatibility of celecoxib-loaded acetyl-capped PCLA-PEG-PCLA thermogels. Biomaterials 35, 7919–7928 (2014).

51. Pitt, C. G., Jeffcoat, A. R., Zweidinger, R. A. & Schindler, A. Sustained drug delivery systems.1. permeability of poly(epsilon-caprolactone),

poly(DL-lactic acid), and their copolymers. J. Biomed. Mater. Res. 13, 497–507 (1979).

52. Pitt, C. G., Gratzl, M. M., Jeffcoat, A. R., Zweidinger, R. & Schindler, A. Sustained drug delivery systems. 2. factors affecting release rates from poly(epsilon-caprolactone) and related biodegradable polyesters. J. Pharm. Sci. 68, 1534–1538 (1979).

53. Sinha, V. R., Bansal, K., Kaushik, R., Kumria, R. & Trehan, A. Poly-epsilon-caprolactone microspheres and nanospheres: an overview. Int. J. Pharm. 278, 1–23 (2004).

54. Lemoine, D. et al. Stability study of nanoparticles of poly(epsilon-caprolactone), poly(D,L-lactide) and poly(D,L-lactide-co-glycolide). Biomaterials 17, 2191–2197 (1996).

55. Cao, L. P. et al. An injectable hydrogel formed by in situ cross-linking of glycol chitosan and multi-benzaldehyde functionalized PEG analogues for cartilage tissue engineering. J. Mater. Chem. B 3, 1268–1280 (2015).

56. Chuang, E. Y. et al. Noninvasive imaging oral absorption of insulin delivered by nanoparticles and its stimulated glucose utilization in controlling postprandial hyperglycemia during OGTT in diabetic rats. J. Control. Release 172, 513–522 (2013).

57. Jeong, B., Lee, K. M., Gutowska, A. & An, Y. H. H. Thermogelling biodegradable copolymer aqueous solutions for injectable protein delivery and tissue engineering. Biomacromolecules 3, 865–868 (2002).

58. Choi, S., Baudys, M. & Kim, S. W. Control of blood glucose by novel GLP-1 delivery using biodegradable triblock copolymer of PLGA-PEG-PLGA in type 2 diabetic rats. Pharm. Res. 21, 827–831 (2004).

59. Choi, S. & Kim, S. W. Controlled release of insulin from injectable biodegradable triblock copolymer depot in ZDF rats. Pharm. Res. 20, 2008–2010 (2003).

60. Ge, H. X., Hu, Y., Yang, S. C., Jiang, X. Q. & Yang, C. Z. Preparation, characterization, and drug release behaviors of drug-loaded epsilon-caprolactone/L-lactide copolymer nanoparticles. J. Appl. Polym. Sci. 75, 874–882 (2000).

61. Jiao, Y. Y. et al. Preparation and characterization of heparin-loaded polymeric microparticles. Drug Dev. Ind. Pharm. 28, 1033–1041 (2002).

62. Dash, T. K. & Konkimalla, V. B. Poly-epsilon-caprolactone based formulations for drug delivery and tissue engineering: A review. J. Control. Release 158, 15–33 (2012).

63. Cha, Y. & Pitt, C. G. A one-week subdermal delivery system for L-methadone based on biodegradable microcapsules. J. Control. Release 7, 69–78 (1988).

64. McDonald, P. F., Lyons, J. G., Geever, L. M. & Higginbotham, C. L. In vitro degradation and drug release from polymer blends based on poly(DL-lactide), poly(L-lactide-glycolide) and poly(epsilon-caprolactone). J. Mater. Sci. 45, 1284–1292 (2010).

Chapter 5

High Throughput Screening of Valganciclovir in Acidic Microenvironments of Polyester Thin Films

Teilo Schaller [1,†], Tobias Wenner [1,†], Rupesh Agrawal [2], Stephen Teoh [2], Li Ting Phua [1], Joachim S. C. Loo [1] and Terry W. J. Steele [1,*]

[1]*School of Materials Science & Engineering, Nanyang Technological University, 50 Nanyang Drive, Singapore 639798, Singapore*

[2]*National Healthcare Group Eye Institute, Tan Tock Seng Hospital, 11 Jalan Tan Tock Seng, Singapore 308433, Singapore*

ABSTRACT

Ganciclovir and valganciclor are antiviral agents used for the treatment of cytomegalovirus retinitis. The conventional method for administering ganciclovir in cytomegalovirus retinitis patients is repeated intravitreal injections. In order to obviate the possible detrimental effects of repeated intraocular injections, to improve compliance and to eliminate systemic side-effects, we investigated the tuning of the ganciclovir pro-drug valganciclovir and the release from thin films of poly(lactic-co-glycolic acid) (PLGA), polycaprolactone (PCL), or mixtures of both, as a step towards prototyping periocular valganciclovir implants. To investigate the drug release, we established and evaluated a high throughput fluorescence-based quantification screening assay for the detection of valganciclovir. Our protocol allows quantifying as little as 20 ng of valganciclovir in 96-well polypropylene plates and a 50× faster analysis compared to traditional HPLC measurements. This improvement can hence be extrapolated to other polyester matrix thin film formulations using a high-throughput approach. The acidic microenvironment within the polyester matrix was found to protect valganciclovir from degradation with resultant increases in the half-life of the drug in the periocular implant to 100 days. Linear release profiles were obtained using the pure polyester polymers for 10 days and 60 days formulations; however, gross phase separations of PCL and acid-terminated PLGA prevented tuning within these timeframes due to the phase separation of the polymer, valganciclovir, or both.

Keywords: poly(lactic-co-glycolic acid) (PLGA); polymeric biomaterials; ophthalmic drug delivery; high-throughput; fluorescence spectroscopy; drug-excipient interaction

1. INTRODUCTION

The cytomegalovirus (CMV) is a member of the herpesviridae family and infects approximately 50% of the European population [1,2]. As a herpes virus, CMV is characterized by lifelong persistence in the host [3,4]. Chronic infection of the host usually remains subclinical, as the virus count is actively kept under control by the immune system. Nonetheless, in immunocompromised patients, such as HIV patients, latent cytomegalovirus may reactivate and become life threatening. Cytomegalovirus retinitis (CMVR) is the most common opportunistic AIDS-related ocular complication and occurs in 40% of all HIV patients with CD4 counts of less than 50 units [5].

Ganciclovir, an inhibitor of the viral DNA polymerase is the conventional drug to treat CMVR [6]. However, due to the poor oral bioavailability, it requires intravenous injections, intravitreal injections, or ocular implants [7]. High therapeutic serum concentration is needed for the parenteral treatment of CMVR requiring hospitalization with an increased risk for adverse systemic reactions [8]. In addition to the induction regimen (intravitreal injections of ganciclovir twice a week for one month), a further maintenance phase is required (weekly injection) until resolution of the lesion and reconstitution of the immune system, eventually requiring patients to undergo a minimum of 16 intravitreal injections over a period of three months. Repeated intravitreal injections are prone to cause detrimental effects in the eye including, but not limited to, retinal detachment, cataract, endophthalmitis, vitreous hemorrhage, and blindness [1,9]. The advent of valganciclovir, an L-valyl ester prodrug of ganciclovir, shows marked improvement in bioavailability of ganciclovir due to its transport via the peptide transporter 1 (PEPT1), hence allowing peroral intake of the drug [10,11]. However, due to its prohibitive cost and dubious efficacy for vision threatening CMVR, the popularity of this regimen is still very limited amongst physicians. Nonetheless, to obviate the systemic administration and frequent repeated intravitreal injections, scientists have shifted their focus on new methods for localized drug delivery.

The spectrum of ocular drug delivery systems cover a variety of classes, including biodegradable and non-biodegradable intravitreal implants, emulsions, microspheres, and polymer formulations [12]. The main advantage of drug delivery systems is a controlled drug release near the target area which results in stable drug concentrations. This reduces the risk of toxicity caused by peak concentrations and lowers the risk of resistance due to constant drug levels. Furthermore, drug delivery systems result in improved patient compliance due to long-term release formulas that eliminate treatments consisting of undesirable injections or the need for a daily pill regimen.

Polyesters, particularly poly(lactic-co-glycolic acid) (PLGA) and polycaprolactone (PCL), have been incorporated into numerous biodegradable drug delivery systems due to their proven biocompatibility and bioresorption properties [12].

The proposed development of a prototype biodegradable thin film valganciclovir-eluting disc designed for periocular implantation may facilitate long-term CMVR treatment, obviating the need for systemic or intravitreal therapy for CMVR. The major benefits speculated for such a prototype would be sustained release drug levels, higher compliance, cost-effective implantation, and the avoidance of complications from intravitreal injections. The rationale for using valganciclovir instead of ganciclovir for the proposed therapy is increased membrane permeability of valganciclovir due to its lesser hydrophilic character and its transport via PEPT1 expressed in the eye [13].

Our laboratory has previously published on both high-throughput drug release measurements and on tuning the drug release of fluorescein diacetate in polyester thin film using acidic terminal end-groups to control the rate of degradation [14,15,16]. However, the measurement of valganciclovir in drug release studies has only been conducted with time-consuming analytical methods such as HPLC.

High-throughput fluorescent screening of valganciclovir drug release and the ability to tune that drug release is explored in this research project for the first time. Furthermore, there are no reports of factors affecting valganciclovir stability inside polyester mixtures, an important prerequisite which will be investigated in this study. We hypothesize that the drug release of valganciclovir can be tuned by varying the acidity of homogenous polyester thin films using differing ratios of the acid-terminated PLGA and PCL, which can best be assessed with a high-throughput quantitation method.

2. MATERIALS AND METHODS

2.1. Materials

Poly (DL-lactide-co-glycolide) 53/47 (lactide-glycolide ratio) (PLGA) #PDLG 5002A with inherent viscosity 0.2 dL/g was purchased from Purac, Gorinchem, Netherlands; valganciclovir from Afine Chemicals Ltd., Hangzhou, China; and ganciclovir from Sinoright, Dalian, China.

2.2. Preparation and Casting of PLGA/PCL Thin Films

A total of 800 mg of one or both polymers was weighed and dissolved in dichloromethane. In addition to dissolving the polymers alone, ratios of 10:1, 8:1, 6:1, 4:1, 2:1, 1:1, 1:4, and 1:10 poly(lactic-co-glycolic acid) (PLGA) to polycaprolactone (PCL) (w:w) mixtures were prepared. 5%, 10%, and 20% (w/w) valganciclovir were dissolved in methanol and added to each polymer solution. The solutions were cast on polyethylene terephthalate (PET) using the 1137 Automatic Film Applicator from Paul N. Gardner Company, Pompano Beach, FL, USA. Punchouts of the films were made using a stancing tool.

2.3. Spectrofluorometer Measurements of Valganciclovir

Valganciclovir punchouts were incubated in 200 μL of PBS media. Samples were incubated at 37 °C in an oven, with media change and fluorescence measurements occurring at baseline (0 h), 1 h, and 6 h, every day until day seven, every 2 days until day 21, and every 4 days until 60 days. Remaining valganciclovir left inside the films after 60 days was measured by dissolving the films in dimethylformamide (DMF). Spectrofluorometer measurements were done by pipetting 150 μL of release medium (PBS buffer at 7.4 pH) into polypropylene wells and subsequently adding 6 μL of 18.5% hydrochloric acid (HCl). Fluorescence of valganciclovir in Greiner 96-well black polypropylene plates from Sigma-Aldrich, Singapore was measured using an Infinite 200 Pro Plate Fluorescence Reader from Tecan Group Ltd., San Jose, CA, USA.

2.4. Polymer, Valganciclovir, and Thickness Quantification by 1H-NMR

Three dried punchouts of each film were dissolved in 700 μL of deuterated DMF and vortexed before transferring them to NMR tubes. 1H-NMR spectra were recorded on a Bruker Advance Spectrometer at 400 MHz using 0.05% Benzene as an internal standard. 1H-NMR (400 MHZ, d-DMF, δ) 0.7–0.8 [s, valganciclovir 6H, -C(CH3)2], 2.05–2.2 [t, PCL 2H], 2.65–2.75 [s, dDMF], 4.75–4.85 [m, PLGA 2H, -C(=O)-(CH3)-O-], 5.0–5.1 [m, PLGA 1H, -C(=O)-CH(CH3)-O-], 7.1–7.2 [s, Benzene]. The NMR error was calculated using the combined error from d6-DMF peak deviations (weigh in error) and the standard deviation of the lactide/glycolide ratios (integration and machine error). Film thickness was estimated from the calculated punchout density using the known densities of PLGA, PCL, and valganciclovir combined with the NMR composition data. The punchout density (in $\mu g/cm^3$) was divided by the NMR generated mass of PLGA, PCL, and valganciclovir per punchout (in $\mu g/cm^2$), giving the average film thickness. The method has been described previously [15,17].

2.5. Valganciclovir Conversion to Ganciclovir Inside of Thin Film by HPLC Quantification

Punchouts with a 1:1 polymer ratio from 10% and 20% valganciclovir films were incubated in drug release study conditions at 37 °C in 200 μL of PBS. PBS was replaced daily. After every 24 h, three punchouts from each of the two films were removed, rinsed with PBS, dried under a vacuum, and dissolved in 0.5 mL of chloroform. Next, 1 mL of PBS was added, and the mixture was shaken and sonicated for 15 min. After separation of the phases, the valganciclovir and/or ganciclovir containing solution was removed and filtered with a 0.22 syringe filter. For HPLC analysis, 40 μL were injected into the Agilent 1100 chromatographic system using a Poroshell 120 EC-C18 column and a spectrofluorometer (Model 1260). Valganciclovir and ganciclovir were separated isocratically with a flow rate of 0.9 mL/min, using 3.2% acetonitrile in 0.05 M dihydrogen phosphate buffer with added phosphoric acid at 2.5 pH. Measurements were done at λ(EX) = 265 nm and λ(EM) = 375 nm. Half-life determination was assessed by measuring the fluorescence of valganciclovir (F) over time (t) allows calculating the degradation constant (k) according to the equation $A(t) = A(0) \exp(-kt)$. Half-life ($t_{1/2}$) was determined by the equation $t_{1/2} = \ln(2)/k$.

2.6. Statistics Method Analysis

Linear regressions and Pearson's correlations were calculated with Origin 8.5 SRI. Pearson's correlations were determined with a minimum of n = 5 data points.

3. RESULTS

3.1. High-Throughput Screening Leads to 50x Faster Development

To develop a high-throughput screening for valganciclovir detection, buffer conditions were optimized using a quartz cuvette. Optimization screening found a pH-dependent fluorescence increase in acid conditions with a maximum fluorescence below pH 1. pH 1 was used for all subsequent fluorescence measurements (Figure 1A). The excitation maximum was 280 nm at valganciclovir concentrations at or below 10 μg/mL (Figure 1B; data points only shown for 10 μg/mL).

Different 96-well plate materials were tested to minimize autofluorescence. polystyrene showed an autofluorescence signal of 302 ± 8.2 fluorescence units (FLU) at the measurement wavelength, which is 1.7 times higher than the noise fluctuations of the detector. Autofluorescence of the polypropylene and quartz glass plates at 175 ± 3.3 and 183 ± 3.8 was minimal and showed no significant difference when compared to the fluorescence noise of the detector. All subsequent fluorescence measurements were therefore done with disposable 96-well polypropylene plates.

Calibration curves from 100 ng/mL to 100 μg/mL valganciclovir were made. A limit of quantitation (LOQ) of 100 ng/mL was calculated for valganciclovir using the polypropylene plates in the Tecan plate reader.

Previous investigations have shown that the phenylglyoxal can fluorescently label guanine-like structures, such as ganciclovir and valganciclovir [18,19]. However, the LOQ in the Tecan Plate reader showed no improvement over valganciclovir's intrinsic fluorescence (data not shown), and the required additional labor and reagents hindered the high throughput nature of the bioassay. Therefore, phenylglyoxal labeling wasn't utilized in our investigations. Nevertheless, one advantage of the phenylglyoxal labeling is a shift in excitation to a lower energy wavelength (365 *vs.* 280 nm), which allows for detection in a broader spectrum of release mediums such as those that may contain proteins or other nucleic acids, e.g., human blood plasma.

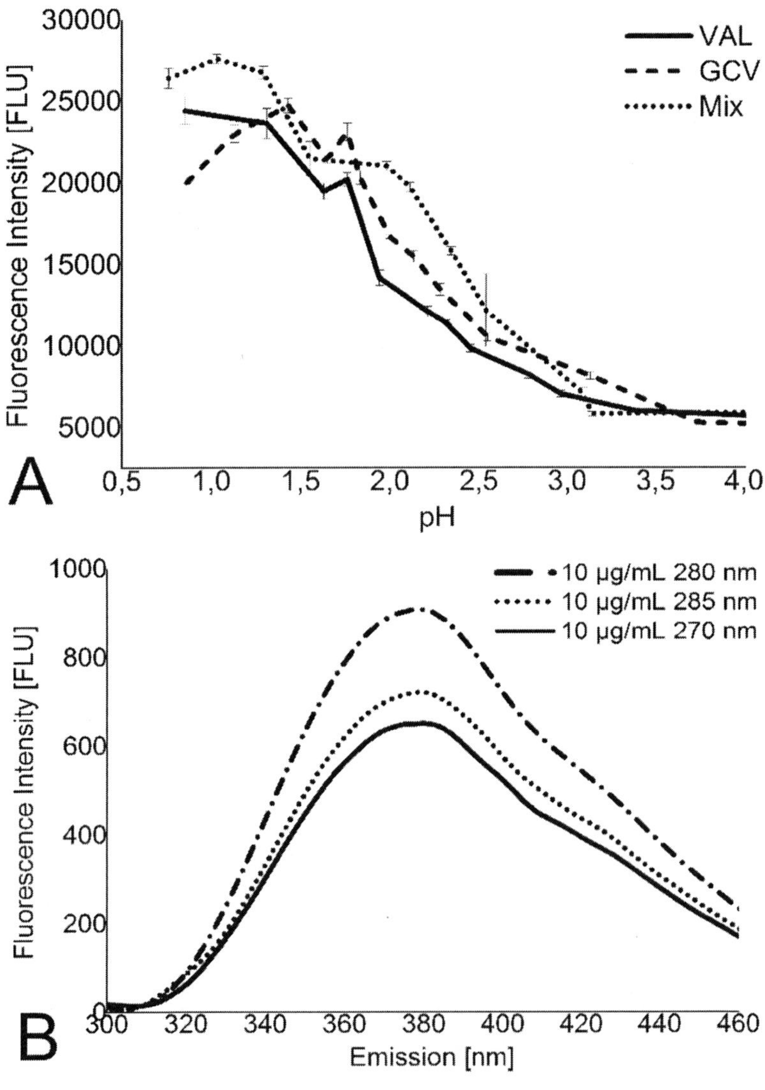

Figure 1. Optimization for parameters for fluorescence measurement. (**A**) Equimolar concentrations of valganciclovir (VAL) and ganciclovir (GCV) as well as a 1:1 mixture (Mix) were tested for pH-dependent fluorescence change. Valganciclovir and ganciclovir seem to overlap at a pH value close to 1.2 and close to 3.6. The overlap close to pH 1 has the higher fluorescence intensity of the two pH values; (**B**) Enlarged emission spectrum of valganciclovir at 10 µg/mL showing the global maximum for different excitation wavelength.

Half-life determination of valganciclovir showed that the degradation followed first order kinetics. The half-life in PBS with pH 7.4 at T = 23.5 °C was calculated at $t_{1/2}$ = 36.7 h ± 0.3. At T = 37 °C, a $t_{1/2}$ = 10.7 ± 0.3 h was measured, which agrees with the 11 h half-life determined by Li *et al.* in similar conditions [20]. At pH 1 and T = 23.5 °C, valganciclovir showed virtually no degradation over a time period of 22 h, signifying that the drug is stable for several hours before quantitation needs to be done—an important aspect for automated high-throughput screening protocols.

The NMR measurements of four thin film formulations, listed in Table 1, revealed that the PLGA:PCL ratios, valganciclovir content, and thickness measurements matched the predicted results. Film thickness measurements using NMR are more time efficient compared to other methods, such as microscopy [15,17].

Table 1. NMR quantification of the valganciclovir polymer films.

Thin Film	Valganciclovir (μg/cm²)	Valganciclovir added (%)	PLGA (μg/cm²)	PCL (μg/cm²)	PLGA:PCL	NMR estimated * thickness (μm)
PLGA	106 ± 4	2.8 ± 0.1	3900 ± 130	0.0 ± 0.0	N/A	29.4 ± 1.0
1:4 PLGA: PCL	805 ± 27	9.9 ± 0.3	1540 ± 50	7260 ± 250	1:4.71	79.1 ± 2.7
1:10 PLGA: PCL	352 ± 12	7.1 ± 0.2	506 ± 17	4800 ± 160	1:9.54	47.8 ± 1.6
PCL	411 ± 14	12.6 ± 0.4	196 ± 7	3500 ± 120	N/A	34.2 ± 1.2

* based on density and mass per cm².

The time required for the high throughput fluorescence assay, including setup of the machine, sample preparation, and running samples, is less than 20 min per 96-well plate. Running 96 samples using the standard HPLC based detection assay requires approximately 16 h. When using the high throughput fluorescence assay we developed, there is an approximate 50-fold increase in throughput as well as significant savings in consumables (no HPLC solvents or columns).

3.2. Valganciclovir Proves to be Stable within Polyester Films

HPLC analysis showed that there was minimal degradation of valganciclovir to ganciclovir in the films containing 1:1 PLGA to PCL inside of the thin film after 7 days of incubation at 37 °C. Peaks for the two valganciclovir diastereomers and the ganciclovir as well as the retention times can be seen in Figure 2. Day 0 punchouts of the 20% valganciclovir films showed a 99.5% ± 0.3% valganciclovir to 0.5% ± 0.3% ganciclovir ratio (mol/mol). After 7 days, the valganciclovir proportion dropped to 96.8% + 0.1%. For the 10%

valganciclovir films, the unincubated punchouts after 7 days showed a 100.1% ± 0.1% valganciclovir proportion and the incubated punchouts showed a 95.9% ± 0.8% valganciclovir proportion. The half-life for valganciclovir in the 20% drug polyester film was calculated to be 95.0 days (81.5 days to 113.6 days) and 118.5 days (109.5 days to 129.1 days) for the 10% valganciclovir film. Comparing these two half-lives to the half-lives of valganciclovir reported by Li *et al.* [20] 1999 at different pH, suggests an environmental pH of approximately 4.4 ± 0.3. Although there are numerous reports on the pH microclimate of PLGA with varying pH values, they all agree on an increasingly acidic pH ranging from 1.5 to 4.7 [21,22,23]. Comparing the half-life of valganciclovir in PBS at pH 7.4, measured to be 10.6 h (10.2 to 11.1 h), to in-film degradation shows a dramatic increase in stability.

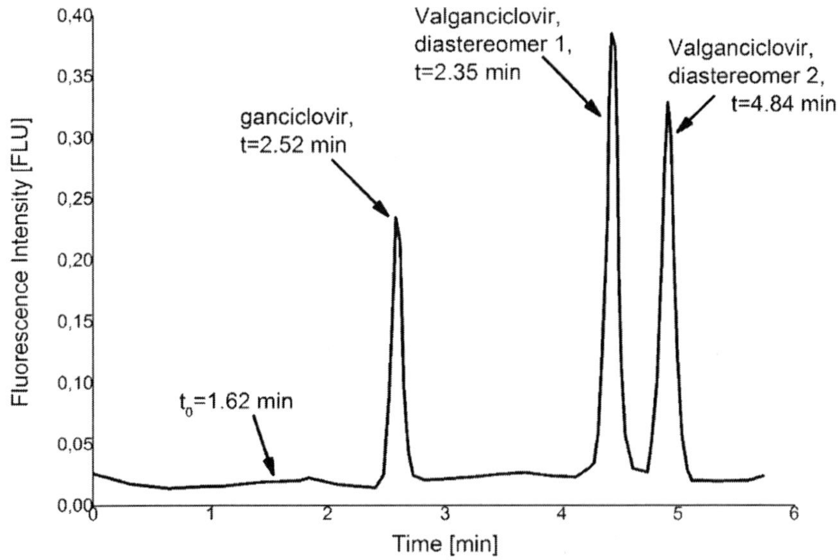

Figure 2. Replotted HPLC chromatogram of valganciclovir normalized with blank. Inj. Volume: 40 µL; ganciclovir is eluted after t(GCV) = 2.52 ± 0.01 min and the two peaks representing the diastereomers of valganciclovir eluted at t(VAL1) = 4.35 ± 0.06 min and t(VAL2) = 4.84 ± 0.06 min. All peaks are separated and allow quantitation.

3.3. Pure Films Allow Short and Long Term Valganciclovir Drug Delivery, but Polymer Phase Separation Prevents Tuning of Drug Release

Casting of the thin films revealed phase separations in all of the mixed polymer films, which increased with higher PLGA to PCL ratios (Figure 3). Tuning of the long-term drug release study for these polymer mixtures was effectively prevented by this phase separation.

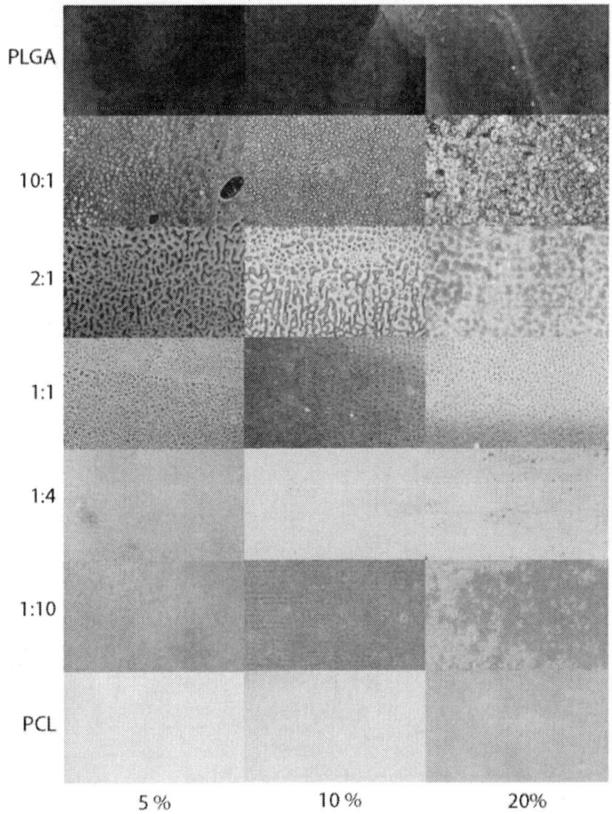

Figure 3. Surface of the thin films. Matrix showing the casted thin films with differing ratios of PLGA to PCL. From top to bottom the PCL content in the films increases, from left to right the valganciclovir content increases from 5% over 10% to 20% drug added. The following polymer ratios are shown: Pure PLGA (row 1), PLGA:PCL = 10:1 (row 2), 2:1 (row 3), 1:1 (row 4), 1:4 (row 5), 1:10 (row 6) and pure PCL (row 7). A phase separation seems to have occurred in the films with more PLGA than PCL and in the films with a 1:1 ratio.

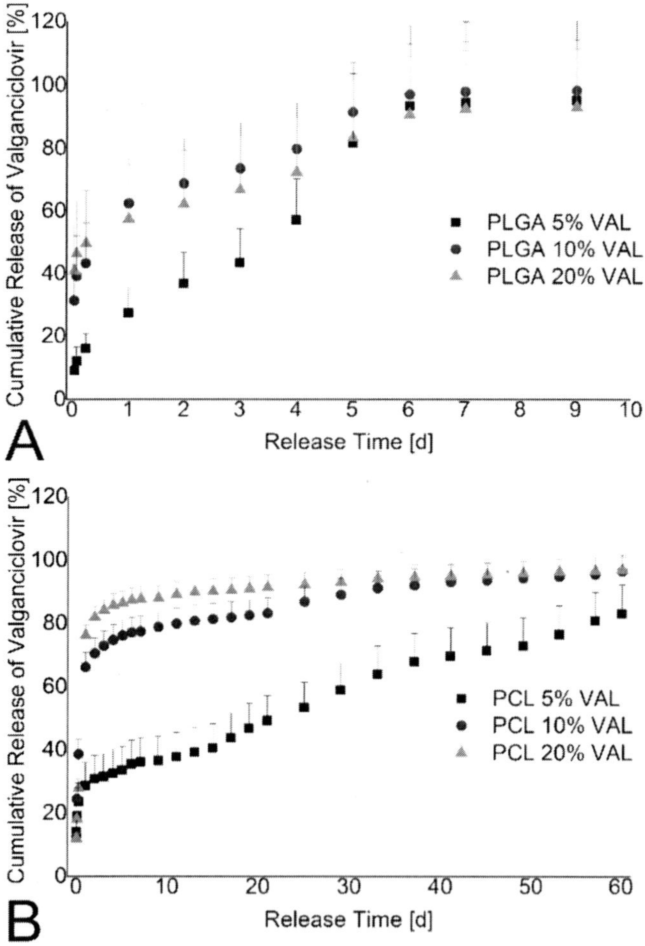

Figure 4. Cumulative release of valganciclovir in percent. The release is plotted in percent of total drug amount of each punchout *versus* the incubation time. The rectangles are the 5% valganciclovir films, the circle the 10% valganciclovir films, and the triangle the 20% valganciclovir films. Both PLGA and PCL films show significant burst releases in the first day. (**A**) Drug release profile of PLGA thin film over a time period of 10 days showing that drug release can be controlled, but with limited dependence on valganciclovir content. After six days, all three thin films have completely released their valganciclovir content; (**B**) Drug release profile of PCL thin film with a controlled release over a time period of 60 days showing a burst release dependent on the amount of valganciclovir added. The 5% pure PCL film shows a lower than usual amount of drug release (<50 μg/cm^2); however, a clear drug release profile can be seen.

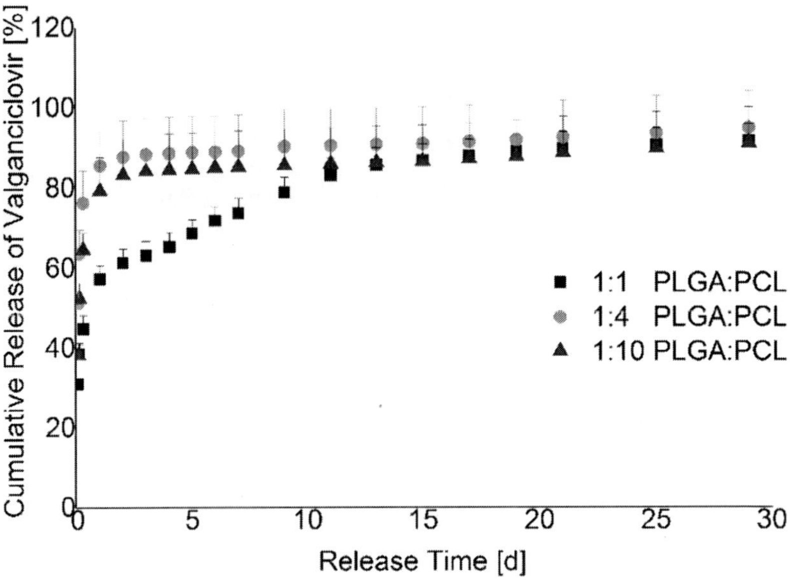

Figure 5. Cumulative release of valganciclovir out of films with more PCL. The graph shows the percentage of released drug out of 5% valganciclovir films *versus* the release time. Data for the film with PLGA and PCL in equal mass concentrations are depicted by the rectangles, the 1:4 PLGA to PCL film by the circles, and the 1:10 PLGA to PCL film by the triangles. All other polymer ratio films showed phase separation and were not evaluated. Nevertheless, the plotted films show a high burst release, even without visible phase separation.

Nevertheless, the pure PLGA and PCL films allow short and long term valganciclovir drug delivery, respectively (Figure 4). Increasing the initial amount of valganciclovir in the PCL film increases the burst release, which was not observed for the PLGA film (Figure 4).

Figure 5 shows the drug release of 5% valganciclovir thin films with 1:1, 1:4, and 1:10 PLGA to PCL ratios. These are the films with the least amount of visible phase separation. Nevertheless, over a time period of 30 d, little to no drug release tuning could be realized. Should phase separation be improved or eliminated in further studies, the thickness differences seen in the thin films, as shown by ^{1}H NMR measurements in Table 1, may still interfere with comparing drug release from thin films with different ratios of PLGA to PCL.

4. DISCUSSION

4.1. High-Throughput Screening Shows Significant Improvement Compared to HPLC

The benefits of high-throughput methods are obvious: more analysis in a shorter time results in more time for research experiments. In most cases, such as in this study, high-throughput also increases cost-effectiveness.

The establishment of a high-throughput valganciclovir detection method in a plate reader based upon the drug's intrinsic fluorescence is described in this paper for the first time. The 50× rate increase of sample throughput, when compared to the standard valganciclovir detection method in the HPLC, is substantial and changes the rate limiting factor from the machine to the scientist.

Using a fluorescence plate reader allows for the measurement of one 96 sample set in less than 20 min, whereas the HPLC requires around 16 h. This efficiency increase makes it possible to increase the measurement interval of the drug release study and thereby allows for more exact drug release curves, or for an increase in the number of sample sets. Hypothetically, a scientist working 8 h/d would be able to prepare and measure more than 2304 drug release samples (or 24 plates/d). In addition to the economic benefits that arise from the substantial speed increase, use of the plate reader also provides environmental benefits in comparison to the HPLC. At a flow rate of 0.9 mL/min, the HPLC consumes 9.8 L of buffer per sample set, requires 96 one-time-use HPLC vials and micro vial insets, and degrades the column for 14.7 h—All of which can be avoided by using the fluorescence plate reader.

The sensitivity of the method was optimized by adjusting the pH, tuning excitation and emission wavelengths, and minimizing the autofluorescence of the 96-well plates. Our study demonstrates that the fluorescence of valganciclovir and ganciclovir is strongly pH-dependent and the fluorescence intensity improves with low pH. These results correlate with the findings of Mascher *et al.* [24] which demonstrated the same for aciclovir, another guanine-like drug. The long stability of valganciclovir in acidic conditions is a benefit for this detection method because degradation will occur neither during analysis nor during storage of the valganciclovir solutions [2]. Polypropylene plates are ideal for the detection of valganciclovir as they show negligible autofluorescence, are sterile, disposable, compatible with most solvents (unlike polystyrene), and cost-efficient.

The 100 ng/mL limit of quantification for valganciclovir that we determined for our high-throughput fluorescence measuring system is one order of magnitude higher than the traditional HPLC [25]. Given the typical valganciclovir concentrations generated by drug eluting matrices, the loss in sensitivity is irrelevant for assessment of *in vitro* release kinetics, but may not be sensitive enough for tissue distribution analyses. Towards *in vitro* release assessment, the loss of sensitivity compared to HPLC is more than compensated by the increase in throughput.

4.2. Acidic Microenvironment of Polyester Films Protects Valganciclovir from Physiological pH Degradation

Drugs can be released out of polymer matrices by different mechanisms. A common method is to modify the drug release by adding specific substances called additives or excipients. These components have to be biocompatible.

We demonstrate that a polymer matrix, consisting of two different biocompatible polymers, has an influence on the drug behavior. By varying the ratio of the two components PLGA and PCL, one varies the acidity of the PLGA:PCL film. The acidity can influence the degradation rate of the polymers as well as the degradation rate of valganciclovir [2]. We show that the half-life of valganciclovir is prolonged from 10.6 hours in PBS buffer to approximately 100 days inside of 1:1 PLGA to PCL thin films.

The microenvironment of PLGA is acidic in nature [23]. With a direct link between the half-life of valganciclovir to pH, we suggest that the intrinsic low pH of the polymer mixture provides an acidic microenvironment that inhibits valganciclovir from degrading during our drug release trials [20]. It is this increase in half-life inside of the polymer that makes it feasible to consider PLGA thin films as well-suited drug reservoirs for valganciclovir.

The drawbacks of other ophthalmic drug delivery systems, such as microemulsions, microspheres, and liposomes, indicate that the development of a valganciclovir release system is challenging [26,27,28]. Our approach shows that using PLGA and PCL thin films provides a biodegradable and stable release platform for valganciclovir drug release. We speculate that by implanting the valganciclovir-infused thin films into sub-tenon's or periocular space, it would be possible to prevent rapid valganciclovir degradation and allow transport into the intravitreal space via the PEPT1 peptide transporter as well as transport by diffusion [11].

4.3. Pure Films Allow Short and Long Term Valganciclovir Drug Delivery, but Polymer Phase Separation Prevents Tuning of Drug Release

The phase separation between acid-terminated PLGA and PCL in the thin films effectively prevented the tuning of the drug release due to high burst release of valganciclovir from the thin films. The burst release is caused by the phase separation of PLGA, PCL, and valganciclovir as it allows for rapid diffusion of PBS into the thin film, subsequently allowing valganciclovir to rapidly dissolve into the surrounding medium. Interestingly, phase separation is most visible in films with high PLGA to PCL ratios. As the polymer ratio shifts toward PCL, the phase separation appeared to decrease (Figure 3). The opacity of the PCL-containing thin films may also be an indication that valganciclovir is incorporated in a crystalline form, leading to a high burst release as seen in Figure 4B. It is apparent that the burst release increases with higher valganciclovir concentrations. However, after accounting for drug lost due to the burst release, the pure PCL films, despite differing initial concentrations of valganciclovir, contain a similar concentration of drug. This leads to the hypothesis that we have reached the solubility limit of valganciclovir in PCL. While burst release is normally hard to control, it should be evaluated as to whether or not a small burst release can be used as a strategy to shorten the initial time needed to reach therapeutic concentrations. *In vitro* drug release studies using scleral tissues are needed in order to test whether the burst release in combination with the subsequent drug release from the thin films allow reaching the minimum inhibitory concentration needed for the treatment of CMVR.

In contrast to the other thin films, the pure PLGA thin films seem to show no phase separation and allows for short term controlled drug release over 10 days (Figure 4A).

We speculate that the three compounds must be completely miscible for tuning and that their properties are too different to be miscible and homogeneous when dried [29,30]. The leakage of hydrophilic drugs from polymer drug delivery systems is known from nanoparticle formulations [31]. One possible alternative is to vary the PGA to PLA ratio of PLGA, as a higher PLA content increases the hydrophobicity and a higher PGA content increases the hydrophilicity [32,33]. The number of free carboxyl groups can increase the incorporation rate of proteins or amino acids, suggesting a higher interaction with valganciclovir [33]. In addition, by changing the polymers we may also be able to improve the miscibility of valganciclovir.

5. CONCLUSIONS

By optimizing medium pH and by decreasing microplate autofluorescence, we developed an analytical method that provides high-throughput screening of ganciclovir-related adducts. The ability to measure the drug release of valganciclovir from polyester thin films using 96-well plate fluorescence measurements represents a dramatic increase in throughput when compared to standard HPLC protocols. We calculate a 50-fold increase in measurement efficiency, which significantly raises the productivity in *in vitro* drug release experiments, while minimizing consumables and solvents.

The high stability of valganciclovir in low pH makes the acidic microenvironment of the polyester films an ideal drug delivery matrix for short to long-term medical implants. Furthermore, the prolonged half-life of 100 days would allow valganciclovir to retain its superior bioavailability properties, in comparison to ganciclovir, towards ocular treatment of cytomegalovirus retinitis.

ACKNOWLEDGMENTS

Funding from the NTU-NHG Innovation Seed Grant: "Development of sustained release ganciclovir implant for treatment of CMV retinitis in HIV-AIDS patients" and the Ministry of Education Tier 1 Grant: "Rapid Development of biocompatible surfaces through acrylate combinatorial libraries (RG 46/11)" and Ministry of Education Tier 2 Grant: Tailored soft-tissue bioadhesives for site-specific therapy (MOE2012-T2-2-046) was greatly appreciated.

AUTHOR CONTRIBUTIONS

Teilo Schaller and Tobias Wenner conceived and designed the experiments. Both performed the experiments and analyzed the data. Li Ting Phua did the setup and preliminary experiments. Teilo Schaller and Tobias Wenner wrote the manuscript. Joachim S.C. Loo and Stephen Teoh contributed to the medical and experimental design. Terry Steele and Rupesh Agrawal conceived and funded the project.

CONFLICTS OF INTEREST

The authors declare no conflict of interest.

REFERENCES

1. Tseng, A.; Foisy, M. The role of ganciclovir for the management of cytomegalovirus retinitis in HIV patients: Pharmacological review and update on new developments. Can. J. Infect. Dis. 1996, 7, 183–194.

2. Stefanidis, D.; Brandl, M. Reactivity of valganciclovir in aqueous solution. Drug Dev. Ind. Pharm. 2005, 31, 879–884.

3. Alcami, A.; Koszinowski, U.H. Viral mechanisms of immune evasion. Immunol. Today 2000, 21, 447–455.

4. Morlet, N.; Young, S.; Naidoo, D.; Graham, G.; Coroneo, M.T. High dose intravitreal ganciclovir injection provides a prolonged therapeutic intraocular concentration. Br. J. Ophthalmol. 1996, 80, 214–216.

5. Jabs, D.A. Ocular manifestations of HIV infection. Trans. Am. Ophthalmol. Soc. 1995, 93, 623–683.

6. Moss, P.; Rickinson, A. Cellular immunotherapy for viral infection after HSC transplantation. Nat. Rev. Immunol.2005, 5, 9–20.

7. Loregian, A.; Gatti, R.; Palu, G.; de Palo, E.F. Separation methods for acyclovir and related antiviral compounds. J. Chromatogr. B 2001, 764, 289–311.

8. Daikos, G.L.; Pulido, J.; Kathpalia, S.B.; Jackson, G.G. Intravenous and intraocular ganciclovir for CMV retinitis in patients with AIDS or chemotherapeutic immunosuppression. Br. J. Ophthalmol. 1988, 72, 521–524.

9. Stewart, J.M.; Srivastava, S.K.; Fung, A.E.; Mahmoud, T.H.; Telander, D.G.; Hariprasad, S.M.; Ober, M.D.; Mruthyunjaya, P. Bacterial contamination of needles used for intravitreal injections: A prospective, multicenter study. Ocul. Immunol. Inflamm. 2011, 19, 32–38.

10. Jung, D.; Dorr, A. Single-dose pharmacokinetics of valganciclovir in HIV- and CMV-seropositive subjects. J. Clin. Pharmacol. 1999, 39, 800–804.

11. Sugawara, M.; Huang, W.; Fei, Y.J.; Leibach, F.H.; Ganapathy, V.; Ganapathy, M.E. Transport of valganciclovir, a ganciclovir prodrug, via peptide transporters PEPT1 and PEPT2. J. Pharm. Sci. 2000, 89, 781–789.

12. Choonara, Y.E.; Pillay, V.; Danckwerts, M.P.; Carmichael, T.R.; du Toit, L.C. A review of implantable intravitreal drug delivery technologies for the treatment of posterior segment eye diseases. J. Pharm. Sci. 2010, 99, 2219–2239.

13. Kadam, R.S.; Vooturi, S.K.; Kompella, U.B. Immunohistochemical and functional characterization of peptide, organic cation, neutral and basic amino acid, and monocarboxylate drug transporters in human ocular tissues. Drug Metabol. Dispos. 2013, 41, 466–474.

14. Huang, C.L.; Kumar, S.; Tan, J.J.Z.; Boey, F.Y.C.; Venkatraman, S.S.; Steele, T.W.J.; Loo, J.S.C. Modulating drug release from poly(lactic-co-glycolic acid) thin films through terminal end-groups and molecular weight. Polymer Degrad. Stab. 2013, 98, 619–626.

15. Steele, T.W.J.; Huang, C.L.; Kumar, S.; Iskandar, A.; Baoxin, A.; Boey, F.Y.C.; Loo, J.S.C.; Venkatraman, S.S. Tuning drug release in polyester thin films: Terminal end-groups determine specific rates of additive-free controlled drug release. NPG Asia Mater. 2013, 5, e46.

16. Steele, T.W.J.; Huang, C.L.; Kumar, S.; Widjaja, E.; Boey, F.Y.C.; Loo, J.S.; Venkatraman, S.S. High-throughput screening of PLGA thin films utilizing hydrophobic fluorescent dyes for hydrophobic drug compounds. J. Pharm. Sci.2011, 100, 4317–4329.

17. Steele, T.W.J.; Huang, C.L.; Kumar, S.; Irvine, S.; Boey, F.Y.C.; Loo, J.S.; Venkatraman, S.S. Novel gradient casting method provides high-throughput assessment of blended polyester poly(lactic-co-glycolic acid) thin films for parameter optimization. Acta Biomater. 2012, 8, 2263–2270.

18. Kai, M.; Ohkura, Y.; Yonekura, S.; Iwasaki, M. Selective determination of guanine and its nucleosides and nucleotides by reaction with phenylglyoxal as a fluorogenic reagent. Anal. Chim. Acta 1988, 207, 243–249.

19. Rao, M.; Prahhaka, T.; Sankar, G.; Jyothi, N. Development and validation of new stability indicating HPLC method for the determination of valganciclovir in tablet dosage forms. Int. J. Pharm. Sci. 2012, 2, 101–104.

20. Li, W.; Anwar, F.; Jesurrun, J.; Erice, A. Cytomegalovirus UL97 and glycoprotein B (gB) sequences in tissues from immunocompromised patients with ganciclovir-resistant virus infection. Scand. J. Infect. Dis. 1999, 31, 549–553.

21. Fu, K.; Pack, D.W.; Klibanov, A.M.; Langer, R. Visual evidence of acidic environment within degrading poly(lactic-co-glycolic acid) (PLGA) microspheres. Pharm. Res. 2000, 17, 100–106.

22. Li, L.; Schwendeman, S.P. Mapping neutral microclimate pH in PLGA microspheres. J. Control. Release 2005, 101, 163–173.

23. Mader, K.; Nitschke, S.; Stosser, R.; Borchert, H.H.; Domb, A. Non-destructive and localized assessment of acidic microenvironments inside biodegradable polyanhydrides by spectral spatial electron paramagnetic resonance imaging. Polymer 1997, 38, 4785–4794.

24. Mascher, H.; Kikuta, C.; Metz, R.; Vergin, H. New, high-sensitivity high-performance liquid-chromatographic method for the determination of acyclovir in human plasma, using fluorometric detection. J. Chromatogr. Biomed. Appl. 1992, 583, 122–127.

25. Dogan-Topal, B.; Uslu, B.; Ozkan, S.A. Development and validation of an RP-HPLC method for determination of valganciclovir in human serum and tablets. Chroma 2007, 66, 97–101.

26. Yasukawa, T.; Tabata, Y.; Kimura, H.; Ogura, Y. Recent advances in intraocular drug delivery systems. Recent Pat. Drug Deliv. Formul. 2011, 5, 1–10.

27. Soppimath, K.S.; Aminabhavi, T.M.; Kulkarni, A.R.; Rudzinski, W.E. Biodegradable polymeric nanoparticles as drug delivery devices. J. Control. Release 2001, 70, 1–20.

28. Honda, M.; Asai, T.; Oku, N.; Araki, Y.; Tanaka, M.; Ebihara, N. Liposomes and nanotechnology in drug development: Focus on ocular targets. Int. J. Nanomed. 2013, 8, 495–503.

29. Diban, N.; Haimi, S.; Bolhuis-Versteeg, L.; Teixeira, S.; Miettinen, S.; Poot, A.; Grijpma, D.; Stamatialis, D. Hollow fibers of poly(lactide-co-glycolide) and poly(epsilon-caprolactone) blends for vascular tissue engineering applications. Acta Biomater. 2013, 9, 6450–6458.

30. Lao, L.L.; Venkatraman, S.S.; Peppas, N.A. Modeling of drug release from biodegradable polymer blends. Eur. J. Pharm. Biopharm. 2008, 70, 796–803.

31. Barichello, J.M.; Morishita, M.; Takayama, K.; Nagai, T. Encapsulation of hydrophilic and lipophilic drugs in PLGA nanoparticles by the nanoprecipitation method. Drug Dev. Ind. Pharm. 1999, 25, 471–476.

32. Panyam, J.; Williams, D.; Dash, A.; Leslie-Pelecky, D.; Labhasetwar, V. Solid-state solubility influences encapsulation and release of hydrophobic drugs from PLGA/PLA nanoparticles. J. Pharm. Sci. 2004, 93, 1804–1814.

33. Hans, M.L.; Lowman, A.M. Biodegradable nanoparticles for drug delivery and targeting. Curr. Op*in. Solid State Mater. Sci.* **2002**, *6*, 319–327.

Chapter 6

Tuning Drug Release in Polyester Thin Films: Terminal End-Groups Determine Specific Rates of Additive-Free Controlled Drug Release

Terry W J Steele[1], Charlotte L Huang[1], Saranya Kumar[1], Aneesa Iskandar[1], Aw Baoxin[1], Freddy Yin Chiang Boey[1], Joachim S C Loo[1] and Subbu S Venkatraman[1]

[1]*Division of Materials Technology, Materials and Science Engineering, Nanyang Technological University, Singapore, Singapore*

ABSTRACT

Modulating the drug release from polyester matrices independently of material properties would be beneficial to those designing biodegradable medical implants, such as drug delivery devices, stents and screws. However, the most common approaches use additives that often drastically alter the desired material properties. Recently, we have developed tools that allow gradient film formulations and high-throughput drug quantitation for the determination of parameter-specific correlations. We propose that modulated drug release can be obtained via additive-free mechanisms in polyesters by simply controlling polymer erosion through acidic terminal functional groups. Our results showed that drug release in poly(lactic-co-glycolic acid) (PLGA) formulations could be tuned to produce large ranges in drug release with relatively small changes in terminal acidic functional groups. For example, PLGA 53/47 thin films could be tuned to have 10–60%drug release at 14 days or 10–90% drug release at 20 days, depending on the PLGA/PLGA blend formulation and concentration of acidic terminal functional groups. A linear R-square correlation of up to 0.9 was observed for the acidic groups and percent drug release. Below a threshold of 1 part per thousand acidic groups, there was no increase in drug release, which has implications for polymer processing and film integrity.

Keywords: drug delivery; fluorescein; gradient; knife casting; PLGA; screening

INTRODUCTION

Biodegradable polyesters, such as poly(lactic-co-glycolic acid) (PLGA), have been incorporated into a number of drug delivery medical devices because of their numerous advantages, that is, they are commercially available in a range of formulations, approved by the Food and Drug Administration for implants, and tend to be predictable in drug release and degradation. In this respect, polyesters are unique among the many raw materials available for drug delivery. Natural polymers, such as polysaccharides and proteins, have inherent advantages, but these materials lack simple methods for controlling mechanical properties and biodegradability.[1] Polyesters have been successful in the release of therapeutics that span the range from hydrophilic macromolecules (for example, small interfering RNA, growth factors and vaccines) to hydrophobic small molecule drugs (see reviews Mundargi *et al.*[2] and Rytting *et al.*[3]).

However, for each therapeutic delivered, the rate of drug delivery from PLGA needs to be modified to specific parameters based on the needs of the medical device. After choosing the geometry (thin film vs nano/microparticle), the formulation scientist must decide which strategy is best suited for tailoring the required drug delivery. The most common method is the addition of additives (for example, polyethylene glycol (PEG)). Although the addition of additives is the simplest option, additives have wide ranging effects on drug/matrix phase separations and can substantially change the material properties.[4, 5, 6]

Ideally, the best matrices would be composed of pure polyester and use alternative methods to modulate drug release without the addition of additives. This narrows the parameters to molecular weight (MW), polydispersity or changes in the polyester matrix environment, such as polyester blends or varying the terminal functional groups. Blending has been commonly used in a number of applications. Two such examples include poly(D,L-lactic acid)/PLGA (PLA/PLGA) for the delivery of betamethasone or poly(ε-caprolactone)/PLGA for cell adhesion studies.[7, 8] Similarly, protein and ganciclovir controlled release matrices using PLGA/PLGA blends that differed in their MW and terminal functional groups and small MW PLGA with a carboxylic acid functional group blended with a large MW PLGA with an ester terminal group have been reported.[9, 10] Others studies have used carboxylic acid functional groups within the PLGA to increase the rate of drug delivery.[11, 12]

These studies suggest that PLGA matrices can be tailored via MW, terminal functional groups or both without the inclusion of additives. Despite these observations, no systematic study has been performed to quantify the influence on controlled drug release comparing both MW and terminal functional groups, especially for thin films used in medical devices. This lack of research is most likely due to the large number of film formulations that would need to be cast under specific conditions to determine the parameter-specific correlations. In addition, a high-throughput method is required to quantify the controlled release in a routine and timely manner.

Recently, our laboratory has developed such tools to allow tuning of PLGA controlled release using both MW and terminal functional groups, which can be characterized in a systematic, high-throughput method. We have previously published a method for gradient casting films with ~1% cm^{-1} change in the PLGA/PEG and polypropylene composition. These gradient films allowed us to determine which additive was more efficient for tuning drug release and simultaneously evaluate how the various additives affected the mechanical properties.[6] A high-throughput method was concurrently used to quantify the controlled release of model hydrophobic drugs with octanol/water partition coefficients (log P) of ~4.[13]

We proposed that the controlled release of PLGA could be tuned to specific controlled delivery rates through gradients by altering the MW and terminal functional groups, especially acid-terminal functional groups, of PLGA. For the terminal functional groups, we chose either a hydrophilic, more soluble carboxylic acid terminal group or the standard, hydrophobic ester terminal functional group. We have previously published the drug release of paclitaxel and fluorescein diacetate (FDAc) as well as the MW decay constant k, mass loss, water absorption, differential scanning calorimetry scans, mechanical properties and the statistical correlations of five 'neat' PLGA films reported in the gradient formulations found in the article (that is, P02A, P02E, P04A, P04E and P103E).[14]This previously published manuscript also suggested that acid terminal end-groups could be used to tailor the drug release kinetics from PLGA blended thin films. These concepts are more thoroughly explored in the article.

MATERIALS AND METHODS

Materials

Poly (DL-lactide-co-glycolide) 53/47 (PLGA), which is summarized in Table 1, was purchased from Purac (Gorinchem, The Netherlands). High-performance liquid chromatography grade dichloromethane and acetonitrile were purchased from Tritech Scientific Pte Ltd, Singapore. Deuterated chloroform ($CDCl_3$+0.03% v/v tetramethysilane D99.8%+silver foil) was purchased from

Cambridge Isotope Laboratories, Andover, MA, USA. FDAc was purchased from TCI Japan, Singapore, Singapore. All of the other polar solvents used were of high-performance liquid chromatography grade and purchased from Sigma-Aldrich, Singapore, Singapore. All of the chemicals and materials were used as received.

Table 1 - Properties of poly (DL-lactide-co-glycolide) 53/47 (PLGA) used in gradient casting.

PLGA 53/47 abbreviation	*Purac purasorb product #*	*Intrinsic viscosity ($dl\,g^{-1}$)[a]*	*Molecular weight, MW (kDa)[b]*	*Terminal functional group*
P103E	PDLG 5010	1.03	110	Methyl ester
P04E	PDLG 5004	0.4	50	Methyl ester
P04A	PDLG 5004A	0.4	40	Carboxylic acid
P02E	PDLG 5002	0.2	20	Methyl ester
P02A	PDLG 5002A	0.2	15	Carboxylic acid

Abbreviations: PLGA, poly(lactic-co-glycolic acid); SEC, size exclusion chromatography.
[a]Manufacturer supplied data.
[b]Calculated by multi-angle laser light scattering coupled to size exclusion chromatography (see section 'Quantitative analysis of PLGA mixtures by SEC-MALLS').

RESULTS

Knife casting gradient PLGA/PLGA blends

The overall description, gradient caster dimensions and limitations of the technique have previously been described for gradient knife casting of PLGA/additive blended films.[6] Only trivial changes in the methodology were used for the PLGA/PLGA blends (that is, addition of a peristaltic pump for more accurate flow control, 5 mm diameter punch-outs for drug release studies and shorter gradient lengths of 110–140 cm). The shorter gradients were possible because of the thicker viscosity of the PLGA polymer solution compared with oligomer additives with similar w/w ratios.

^{1}H NMR quantitation of total PLGA and FDAc

The total mass of PLGA and the amount of FDAc was determined with ^{1}H NMR. Previously, we were able to determine the ratios of PLGA and additive on dissolution in $CDCl_3$ followed by NMR characterization. However, with the PLGA blends, no discernment was possible between varying PLGA MWs in the same sample via NMR analysis. The lactide and glycolide ^{1}H NMR peaks exhibit the same chemical shifts independent of the PLGA MW. For high MW PLGA, the peaks are broader, but the measurements of polydispersity and PLGA ratios by NMR were not possible. However, spiking one of the PLGA mixtures with trace amounts of a non-volatile additive with intense NMR signals, such as pyrene, would allow straightforward PLGA ratio determination. For this initial PLGA/PLGA gradient characterization, we chose to keep all additives to a minimum and no spiked PLGAs were used.

SEC for P0XX/P103E ratio quantitation

Calculation of the P0XX/P103E (P0XX refers to P02A, P02E, P04A or P04E) ratios was found to be considerably more laborious than originally envisioned. SEC was used for the determination of the P0XX/P103E ratios. However, the hydrodynamic sizes of P103E mixed with any P0XX were similar, yielding co-eluting 'camel back' peaks. Gaussian deconvolution analyses were either not repeatable, inaccurate or both. The co-elution was most prominent between the P103E and P04X (or 0.4 intrinsic viscosity) blends. Although the samples had different MWs, the polymer peaks eluted fairly close together, even with three SEC columns serially connected (data not shown). To overcome this obstacle, SEC deconvolution techniques were performed according to previously published protocols.[15, 16] Briefly, mathematical models were constructed from the SEC chromatograms of the five pure PLGA injections to predict the height ratios of the P0XX/P103E PLGA blends. After subtraction of the baseline, the pure PLGA elution peaks were normalized to 100 µg mass. For example, to determine the 1:9 relative height ratio for the P02E/P103E standard curve, 10% of the refractive index signal of the 100 µg P02E baselined/normalized SEC chromatogram was added to 90% of the refractive index signal for the 100 µg P103E baselined/normalized SEC chromatogram. In this method, a standard curve was constructed by plotting the relative peak height ratios as a function of the P0XX/P103E ratios (see Figure 1). Then, the baseline was subtracted from the analyzed data, and the peak height ratio was converted to the P0XX/P103E ratios (normalizing the unknowns was not necessary). After testing three ratios of known composition, (P0XX/P103E ratios of 3:7, 5:5 and 7:3), the maximum s.d. was found to be ⩽±8% for the P04X and ⩽±5% for the P02X blended films.

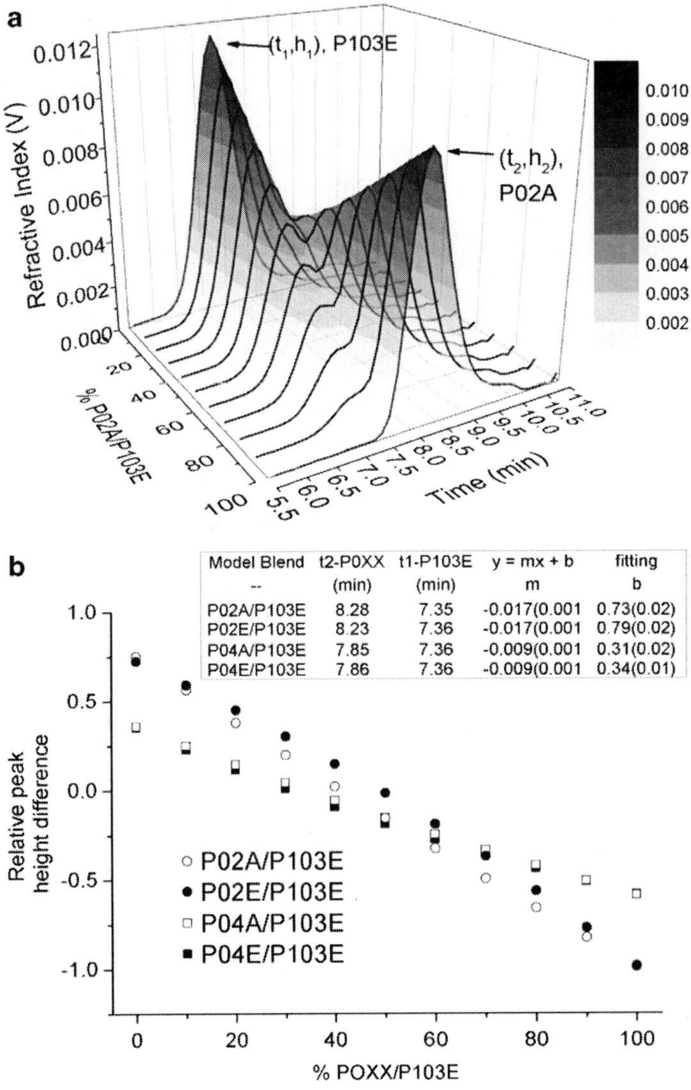

Figure 1. Mathematical deconvolution model for determining the ratios of the P0XX/P103E blends. (a) Construction of P02A/P103E simulated ratios (from 1:9 to 9:1) from pure P02A and P103E SEC chromatograms. (b) Linear regression of the relative peak height difference as a function of the P0XX percentage. Relative peak height difference=$(h_1t_1-h_2t_2)/(h_1t_1+h_2t_2)$. h_1 and h_2 are the baseline subtracted refractive index values at the respective t_1 and t_2 time points.

Optimal gradients of acid terminal end-groups depends on the MW of additive PLGA

With our gradient film casting method, a continuous increase in acid concentration can be synthesized into a single thin film. For the results reported herein, only four gradient thin films were cast, as shown in Scheme 1. This method allows for a more confident 'freezing' of the myriad parameters that can affect the synthesis of thin films or the final dried thin films themselves. The addition of PLGA with a terminal acid group must be balanced between two factors because an increased acid gradient can result in a wider range of polymer degradation with more variations possible for the subsequent drug release. However, the addition of small (<5 kDa) PLGA oligomer acids would likely do little to catalyze drug release because they may quickly diffuse from the PLGA matrix. To achieve an acceptable balance of these factors, commercially available PLGA containing acid or ester functional groups with an intrinsic viscosity of 0.2 and 0.4 dl g^{-1} and MWs of~20 and 50 kDa were chosen, as shown in Table 1. P02A and P04A yield gradients that have a maximum of 8.9 and 3.3 p.p.t. (parts per thousand), respectively, of the terminal acid monomer to the sum of the lactide and glycolide monomers. As these acid gradients must be formed by the P0XX polymers with P103E, the cumulative MW will also differ across the gradients. To separate the combined effects of MW and acid concentration on drug release, control gradient films of P02E or P04E were also cast with the P103E. These films were methyl ester terminated and contained no acid groups.

Gradient comparisons and respective surface compositions of PLGAs and encapsulated drugs

The average of the four gradient % P0XX additives was 0.73±0.06% per cm when cast at a wet thickness of 500 μm. The small s.d. between the slopes suggests that the casting conditions were fairly reproducible, as shown in Figure 2. The gradient compositions in regards to molar mass (MW—weight-averaged, left axis, black) and % P0XX (right axis, gray) as a function of the gradient length are also compared in Figure 2. Note that the molar mass formulations under 50%were typically analyzed via PEG standards vs laser light scattering because of the small refractive index differential between PLGA and tetrahydrafuran. Figures 3a and b compare the differences in the PLGA gradients with 0.2 and 1.03 dl g^{-1}intrinsic viscosity gradients that have acid (P02A) or ester (P02E) terminated functional groups. Interestingly, small

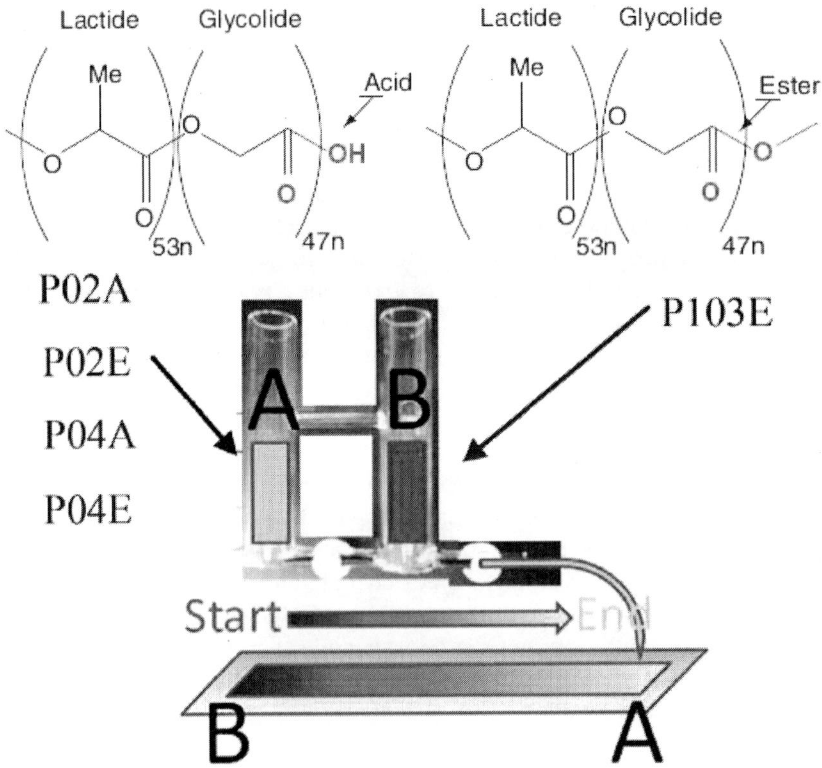

Scheme 1. *Synthesis of POXX/P103E gradient thin films allowing tailored controlled release in the absence of additives.*

differences were observed when the overall composition was compared for the acid and ester terminal groups. For the P02A or P04A total PLGA gradients in Figures 3a and c, the trends were slightly positive, with stable slopes compared with the P02E or P04E gradients inFigures 3b and d. A common empirical observation in the synthesis of thin films was that a lower viscosity resulted in thinner films, as shown in Figures 3b and d. As viscosity was dependent on the MW of the polymer, the knife cast solutions became less viscous or thinner as the smaller MW polymer was mixed into the solutions, even though the polymer concentration remained at 10% w/v. We speculate that the slightly positive and stable slopes observed in Figures 3a and b(total PLGA) may be due to intermolecular hydrogen bonding by the carboxylic acid end-group. The trend was slightly positive for the more carboxylic acid concentrated P02A then the P04A. The thickness (and therefore viscosity) did not decrease on MW dilution for these two polymers that were mixed with

P103E. Such interactions have been observed in other polymer matrices containing acidified carboxylic acid h-donors and oxygen h-acceptors (for example, poly(methacrylic acid)/PEG complexes).[17]

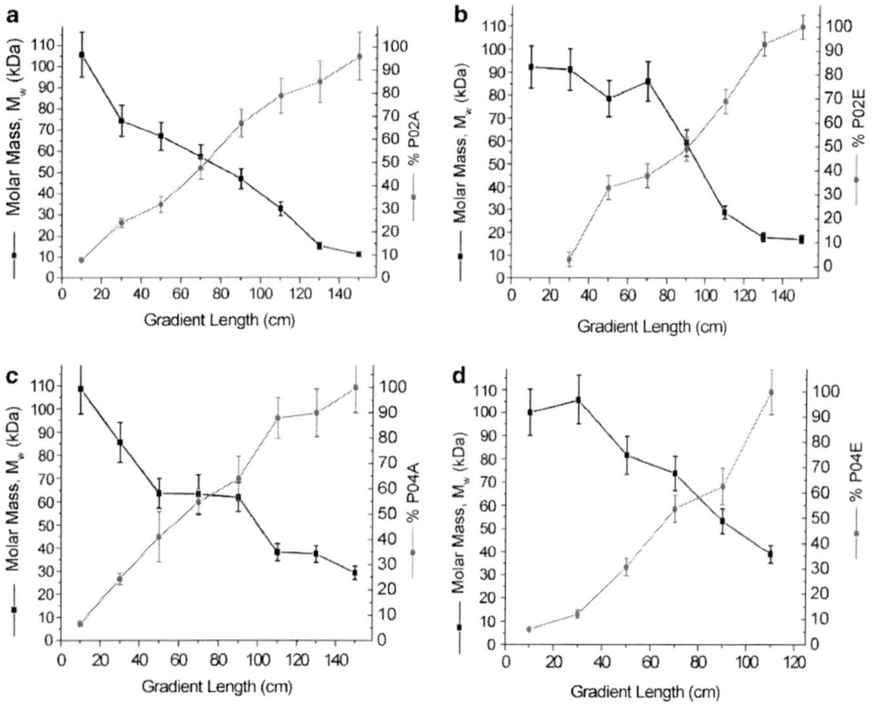

Figure 2. *P02A and P103E gradient blend. Weight averaged molecular weight (MW) for the P02A/P103E blended film and the percentage of P02A at different gradient lengths. For simplicity, total PLGA cm^{-2} can be divided by 122 to yield the thickness in microns. (a) P02A/P103E gradient %P02A slope=(0.68±0.02) % cm^{-1}; (b) P02E/P103E gradient % P02E slope=(0.81±0.05) % cm^{-1}; (c) P04A/P103E gradient % P04A slope=(0.75±0.03) % cm^{-1}; (d) P04E/P103E gradient % P04E slope=(0.66±0.11) % cm^{-1}.*

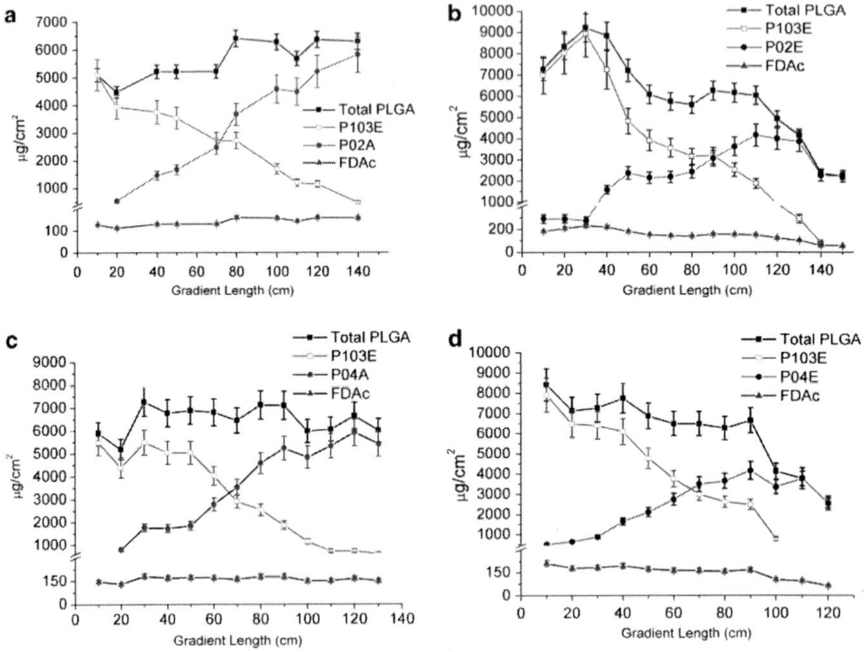

Figure 3. *P0XX/P103E blended film composition and their respective surface concentrations. Fluorescein diacetate (FDAc) was kept at a ~1/40 w/w FDAc/poly(lactic-co-glycolic acid) (PLGA) ratio. Y axis break is from 400 to 1000 μg cm^{-2}. (a) P02A/P103E gradient; (b) P02E/P103E gradient; (c) P04A/P103E gradient; (d) P04E/P103E gradient.*

Controlled drug release of FDAc

A remarkable increase in drug release was observed in the P02A gradients compared with the P02E gradients, as shown in Figures 4a and b, respectively. Most of the P02E gradient formulations required longer than 20 days to release just 10% of the drug (Figure 4b). However, the P02A gradients displayed predictable shifts in drug release as the ratios of P02A/P103E increased over time. For example, depending on the P02A/P103E ratio, one could choose the formulation to have 25% drug release on any day between 10 and 21 days or a 50% drug release between 15 and 30 days. Such flexibility was not possible with the P02E gradients, suggesting that the MW dilution had little to do with the increase in drug release and expanded flexibility. Although not as pronounced, the P04A/P103E ratios displayed similar trends in increased drug release variability compared with P04E/P103E, as shown in Figures 4c and d.

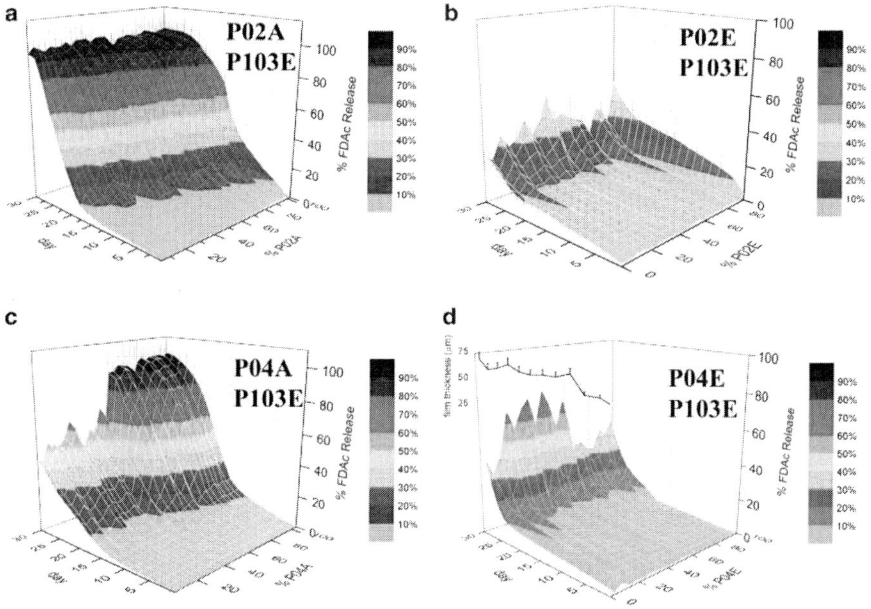

Figure 4. *Cumulative release % of fluorescein diacetate (FDAc; z axis) as a function of time (x axis) and % POXX additive. (a) P02A/P103E gradient; (b) P02E/P103E gradient; (c) P04A/P103E gradient; (d) P04E/P103E gradient; inset) film thickness (μm) vs % P04E.*

One unforeseen result was found in the P04E gradients. In Figure 4, the % FDAc release had a negative correlation to the P04E percentage. The percentage of P04E in the film was not likely to be the dominant factor for the sudden increase in FDAc release. The most plausible explanation was the combined effects of a thicker film and the increase in the amount of P04E. The autocatalysis increased as the thickness of the films increased because of incomplete diffusion from the accumulation of acidic fragments.[16] For example, for the starting conditions of 0% P04E with a relatively thick 70 μm film (see Figure 4d inset), only a 35% FDAc release was observed over 30 days, with the majority of the release occurring in the last few days of measurement. However, when the starting conditions were 20–50% P04E with the ~50-μm thick films, 75% drug release is observed. This release diminished to 35% once the thickness fell below 25 μm. Therefore, the autocatalytic effect was considerably diminished by diffusion of the acidified fragments (see Discussion section below).

Correlation of percent drug release vs acid terminal end-group concentration

Evaluating the amount of drug release over time is often a trial and error task with few tools that control and predict drug release kinetics. To measure the ability of the acid terminal end-groups to control the amount of drug release, the total drug release was plotted as a function of the percent additives of P02A, P04A and P02E, as shown in Figures 5a–c. The data suggest that strong Pearson's r correlations existed for the acid terminal end-group additives. In addition, this correlation grew stronger with time, until a plateau was reached (see Figure 5d). For the P04A gradients, the correlation decreased after 25 days because of drug depletion within the film matrix, as shown in Figure 5d (open squares). When the ester terminal end-groups were similarly analyzed, they displayed a weak (P02E) or negative (P04E) correlation. As described in the previous section, the negative correlation likely arises from the increased thickness of the film.

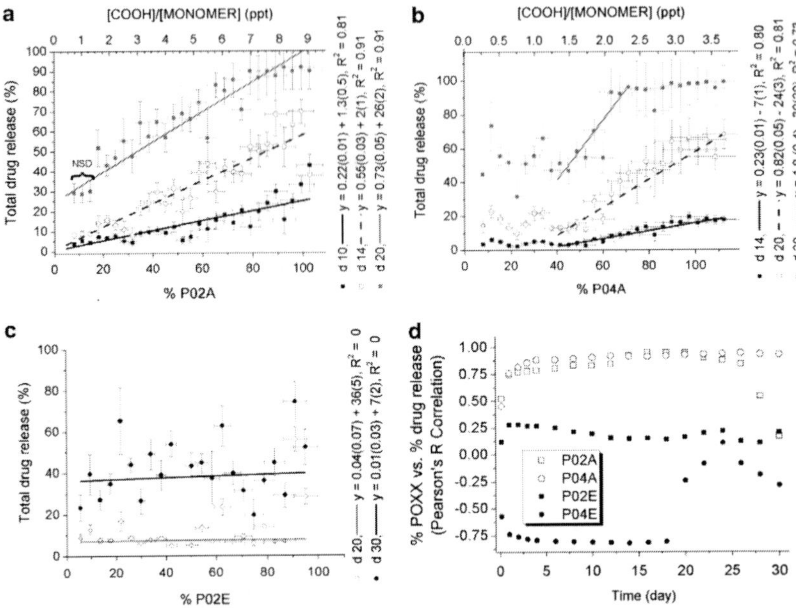

__Figure 5.__Total drug release as a function of acid terminal functional group at certain time points. (a) %P02A as a function of total drug release at 10, 14, and 20 day. p.p.t., parts per thousand monomer lactide/glycolide. (b) %P04A as a function of total drug release at 14, 20 and 30 days. (c)%P04E as a function of total drug release at 20, and 30 days. (d) Pearson's r correlation of the % POXX additive as a function of the %total drug release.

The most useful for the formulation scientist was the observation that the drug release and additive/acid concentration exhibited a nearly linear dependence. For example, at days 10, 14 and 20 for the P02A polyester, linear fits of the total drug release as a function of the percent P02A had R-square values of 0.8, 0.9 and 0.9, respectively. The data suggest that at day 20, a formulation with P02A can be predicted to achieve drug release of from 40 to 90%. However, not every concentration of polyesters was effective in modulating the release. The acid concentration was found to be effective in modulating drug release only above certain concentrations. At a threshold below ~1 p.p.t. of [COOH]/[MONOMER], no trends were observed for the P02A or P04A polyesters.

DISCUSSION

To control rates of drug delivery in biodegradable polymer matrices, one must modify one or more of the four generally accepted release mechanisms: (1) water-saturated pore diffusion, (2) polymer matrix diffusion, (3) osmotic gradients or (4) polymer matrix erosion.[15] The first two mechanisms are based on diffusion and rely on fast-dissolving additives to increase pore networks. These additives are sometimes referred to as 'porogens'. These systems are best suited for hydrophilic therapeutics, but they often exhibit substantial burst release and generally negatively affect the material properties of the drug delivery system.[18] For hydrophobic drug molecules, they tend to partition strongly to the polymer matrix, with diffusion playing a minor role in their release (nanoparticles being an exception). The hydrophobic drugs only release when the polymer fragments or amphiphilic additives diffuse from the matrix.[4,19, 20] Recent investigations of PLGA erosion support this view. PLGA mass loss was largely dependent on the solubility of the degraded fragments, not on diffusion-controlled reactions.[21] PLGA fragments were reported to be soluble after a critical point of 15 000 Da, but are typically soluble at~1000 Da.[21, 22, 23]Therefore, to control the drug delivery of hydrophobic compounds, one must find mechanisms to control the rates of polyester erosion.

Blending of polyesters using carboxylic acid end-groups has previously been reported for microsphere formulations.[9, 10, 11, 12] Acidic groups in polymer matrices are known to catalyze the degradation of polyester polymers. The aggregate results from these microsphere formulations suggested that carboxylic acid end-groups can be used to tailor or modulate the delivery of hydrophobic drugs. Owing to the laborious nature of most drug release protocols, no studies have evaluated the statistical correlations between the amount of acid end-groups and controlled drug release, especially for thin films incorporating hydrophobic drugs for long-term release. With our recent development of high-throughput quantitation and film gradient-casting procedures, drug release profiling of various thin films is now feasible.[6, 13]

We synthesized increasingly acidic gradient films having concentrations of 0–3.3 and 0–8.9 p.p.t. [COOH]/[MONOMER] carboxylic acid terminal end-groups with the usage of commercially available P04A and P02A blended into P103E, respectively. Complete chromatographic separation of the mixed polymers was not possible by size exclusion chromatography. Therefore, a deconvolution analysis was performed, as shown in Figure 1. By having two sets of gradient concentrations, a fine-tuning and extended range acidic analysis could be performed. However, this analysis also set up polymer MW gradients that were proportional to the acid terminal end-groups. Gradients of P04E and P02E were used as controls that had similar MW gradients but no acidic gradients, as demonstrated in Figure 2. To limit drug release by diffusion, a small 1/40 w/w ratio of fluorescent drug/polymer was implemented. The concentrations of FDAc compared with the polymer constituents are shown in Figure 3. Therefore, the controlled drug release was mostly dependent on PLGA erosion.

The results in Figures 4 and 5 display the effects of the acid vs ester terminal groups on the drug release of FDAc, which is a molecule that mimics the release of paclitaxel and allows high-throughput drug release.[13] Using acid end-groups, we were able to tailor a wide range of drug release formulations. For P02A at day 14 and P04A at day 20, a 10–60% range of drug release could easily be predicted and was linearly dependent on the acid end-group concentration. Although these results are for small molecule hydrophobic drugs, previous investigations by Raiche and Puleo[9] suggested that tunable ranges for protein release are feasible through acid gradients. The P04A gradients displayed a short range of tunable drug release because of the small acidic concentration range. However, P04A gradients allowed a better estimate of the threshold of acidic groups required to accelerate controlled drug release. Figures 4c and 5b show that increased drug release was not observed below 40% P04A or below ~1.2 p.p.t. acidic end-groups. Similar results were obtained for <15% P02A, as shown in Figure 5a. In this regard, molecular mass also had a significant effect on drug release. However, we can provide no predictive correlation when drug release was compared with varying MW PLGA with the same acid terminal group. The results must be viewed within the limitations of the two MWs tested, where the range was determined with 20 and 50 kDa. More ranges are required for statistical correlations.

If controlled drug release is directly dependent on the PLGA degradation, this acidic threshold concentration is significant for a number of polyester medical implant processes, such as injection molding, plasma surface modifications and irradiation for sterilization. If not strictly controlled, all of these manufacturing steps cause polyester degradation and acidic end-group formation.[24, 25, 26, 27,28] If the above processes increase the acidic residues to >1 p.p.t. in the PLGA thin films, our results predict an increase in erosion within 30 days.

Alternatively, the linear dependence of the increase in acid end-groups on the total drug release may allow drug delivery implants to dynamically change their delivery rates *in vivo* via specific event triggers. For example, several technologies used by the photolithography industry allow instantaneous formation of carboxylic acid groups through the conversion of ortho-nitrobenzyl esters.[29] Pulses of light create more carboxylic acid end-groups and would allow a gradual increase in drug delivery as needed. Similar formation of acidic end-groups can be envisioned by other 'SMART' triggered events (for example, ultrasound, electrical signal, light, temperature[30]) for switchable hydrophobic/hydrophilic surfaces.[31] This would allow modulation of drug release, and after the drug reservoir is exhausted, subsequent triggers would allow the forced erosion of medical implants, resulting in faster clearance. We will be focusing on this area in our future studies.

We speculate that the dynamic use of acidic terminal functional groups would be applicable to a large number of other implantable polymers and macro-therapeutics. For example, a close polyester relative of PLGA (that is, PLLA) has often been employed for use in stents because of its strong material properties as well as its biodegradability. However, PLLA implants often take years to bioresorb (along with other polyesters like poly-caprolactone, poly-sebacic acid and other poly-alkanoate acids).[32, 33] For longer implant times, the development costs are higher because of animal testing and the long-term risks for inflammation and thrombosis also increase. Degradation times in years exceed the timeframes of how long a stent is actually needed, which is approximately 6 months.[34] By balancing the PLLA MW and the activation of acidic groups within the matrix, one could optimize the material properties for use as a fast resorbable implant.

REFERENCES

1. Li, Y., Rodrigues, J. & Tomas, H. Injectable and biodegradable hydrogels: gelation, biodegradation and biomedical applications. Chem. Soc. Rev. 41, 2193–2221 (2012).

2. Mundargi, R. C., Babu, V. R., Rangaswamy, V., Patel, P. & Aminabhavi, T. M. Nano/micro technologies for delivering macromolecular therapeutics using poly(D,L-lactide-co-glycolide) and its derivatives. J. Control. Release125, 193–209 (2008). ISI | CAS |

3. Rytting, E., Nguyen, J., Wang, X. & Kissel, T. Biodegradable polymeric nanocarriers for pulmonary drug delivery. Expert Opin. Drug Deliv. 5, 629–639 (2008).

4. Steele, T. W., Huang, C. L., Widjaja, E., Boey, F. Y., Loo, J. S. & Venkatraman, S. S. The effect of polyethylene glycol structure on paclitaxel drug release and mechanical properties of PLGA thin films. Acta Biomater. 7, 1973–1983 (2011).

5. Vlachou, M., Hani, N., Efentakis, M., Tarantili, P. A. & Andreopoulos, A. G. Polymers for use in controlled release systems: the effect of surfactants on their swelling properties. J. Biomater. Appl. 15, 65–77 (2000).

6. Steele, T. W. J., Huang, C. L., Kumar, S., Irvine, S., Chiang Boey, F. Y., Loo, J. S. C. & Venkatraman, S. S. Novel gradient casting method provides high-throughput assessment of blended polyester poly(lactic-co-glycolic acid) thin films for parameter optimization. Acta Biomater. 8, 2263–2270 (2012).

7. Ishihara, T., Kubota, T., Choi, T., Takahashi, M., Ayano, E., Kanazawa, H. & Higaki, M. Polymeric nanoparticles encapsulating betamethasone phosphate with different release profiles and stealthiness. Int. J. Pharm.375, 148–154 (2009).

8. Tang, Z. G. & Hunt, J. A. The effect of PLGA doping of polycaprolactone films on the control of osteoblast adhesion and proliferation in vitro.Biomaterials 27, 4409–4418 (2006).

9. Raiche, A. T. & Puleo, D. A. Modulated release of bioactive protein from multilayered blended PLGA coatings. Int. J. Pharm. 311, 40–49 (2006).

10. Duvvuri, S., Gaurav Janoria, K. & Mitra, A. K. Effect of polymer blending on the release of ganciclovir from PLGA microspheres. Pharm. Res-Dordr. 23, 215–223 (2006).

11. Panyam, J., Williams, D., Dash, A., Leslie-Pelecky, D. & Labhasetwar, V. Solid-state solubility influences encapsulation and release of hydrophobic drugs from PLGA/PLA nanoparticles. J. Pharm. Sci. 93, 1804–1814 (2004).

12. Su, Z., Sun, F., Shi, Y., Jiang, C., Meng, Q., Teng, L. & Li, Y. Effects of formulation parameters on encapsulation efficiency and release behavior of risperidone poly(D,L-lactide-co-glycolide) microsphere. Chem. Pharm. Bull. (Tokyo) 57, 1251–1256 (2009).

13. Steele, T. W., Huang, C. L., Kumar, S., Widjaja, E., Chiang Boey, F. Y., Loo, J. S. & Venkatraman, S. S. High-throughput screening of PLGA thin films utilizing hydrophobic fluorescent dyes for hydrophobic drug compounds. J. Pharm. Sci. 100, 4317–4329 (2011).

14. Huang, C. L., Kumar, S., Tan Jun Zhi, J., Boey, F. Y., Venkatraman, S. S., Steele, T. W. & Loo, J. S. Modulating drug release from poly(lactic-co-glycolic acid) films through terminal end-groups and molecular weight.Polym. Degrad. Stabil. 98, 619–626 (2013).

15. Fredenberg, S., Wahlgren, M., Reslow, M. & Axelsson, A. The mechanisms of drug release in poly(lactic-co-glycolic acid)-based drug delivery systems--a review. Int. J. Pharm. 415, 34–52 (2011).

16. Jonnalagadda, S. & Robinson, D. H. Effect of thickness and PEG addition on the hydrolytic degradation of PLLA. J. Biomaterials Sci. Polym. Edn. 15, 1317–1326 (2004).

17. Fortier-McGill, B., Toader, V. & Reven, L. H-1 solid state NMR study of poly(methacrylic acid) hydrogen-bonded complexes. Macromolecules 45, 6015–6026 (2012).

18. Glaessl, B., Siepmann, F., Tucker, I., Rades, T. & Siepmann, J. Deeper insight into the drug release mechanisms in Eudragit RL-based delivery systems. Int. J. Pharm. 389, 139–146 (2010).

19. Kang, J. C. & Schwendeman, S. P. Determination of diffusion coefficient of a small hydrophobic probe in poly(lactide-co-glycolide) microparticles by laser scanning confocal microscopy. Macromolecules 36, 1324–1330 (2003).

20. Mittal, G., Sahana, D. K., Bhardwaj, V. & Kumar, M. N. V. R. Estradiol loaded PLGA nanoparticles for oral administration: effect of polymer molecular weight and copolymer composition on release behavior in vitroand in vivo. J. Control. Release 119, 77–85 (2007).

21. Korber, M. PLGA erosion: solubility- or diffusion-controlled? Pharm. Res-Dordr. 27, 2414–2420 (2010).

22. Park, T. G. Degradation of poly(D,L-lactic acid) microspheres - effect of molecular-weight. J. Control. Release 30, 161–173 (1994).

23. Husmann, M., Schenderlein, S., Luck, M., Lindner, H. & Kleinebudde, P. Polymer erosion in PLGA microparticles produced by phase separation method. Int. J. Pharm. 242, 277–280 (2002).

24. Chia, N. K., Venkatraman, S. S., Boey, F. Y. C., Cadart, S. & Loo, J. S. C. Controlled degradation of multilayered poly(lactide-co-glycolide) films using electron beam irradiation. J. Biomed. Mater. Res. Part A 84A, 980–987 (2008).

25. Ghosh, S., Viana, J. C., Reis, R. L. & Mano, J. F. Effect of processing conditions on morphology and mechanical properties of injection-molded poly(L-lactic acid). Polym. Eng. Sci. 47, 1141–1147 (2007).

26. Koo, G. H. & Jang, J. Surface modification of poly(lactic acid) by UV/Ozone irradiation. Fiber. Polym. 9, 674–678 (2008).

27. Martinez-Sancho, C., Herrero-Vanrell, R. & Negro, S. Study of gamma-irradiation effects on aciclovir poly(D,L-lactic-co-glycolic) acid microspheres for intravitreal administration. J. Control. Release 99, 41–52 (2004).

28. Han, Y. R., Jin, X. Y., Yang, J., Fan, Z. Y., Lu, Z. Q., Zhang, Y. & Li, S. M. Totally bioresorbable composites prepared from poly(L-lactide)-co-(trimethylene carbonate) copolymers and poly(L-lactide)-co-(glycolide) fibers as cardiovascular stent material. Polym. Eng. Sci. 52, 741–750 (2012).

29. Klinger, D. & Landfester, K. Polymeric photoresist nanoparticles: light-induced degradation of hydrophobic polymers in aqueous dispersion.Macromol. Rapid Comm. 32, 1979–1985 (2011).

30. Moon, H. K., Son, M., Park, J. E., Yoon, S. M., Lee, S. H. & Choi, H. C. Significant increase in the water dispersibility of zinc phthalocyanine nanowires and applications in cancer phototherapy. NPG Asia Mater. 4, e12 (2012).

31. Zhang, L. B., Zhang, Z. H. & Wang, P. Smart surfaces with switchable superoleophilicity and superoleophobicity in aqueous media: toward controllable oil/water separation. NPG Asia Mater. 4, E8 (2012).

32. Shazly, T., Kolachalama, V. B., Ferdous, J., Oberhauser, J. P., Hossainy, S. & Edelman, E. R. Assessment of material by-product fate from bioresorbable vascular scaffolds. Ann. Biomed. Eng. 40, 955–965 (2012).

33. Gogotov, I. N., Gerasin, V. A., Kniazev, ,. V., Antipov, E. M. & Barazov, S.[Composite biodegradable materials based on polyhydroxyalkanoate]. Prikl. Biokhim. Mikrobiol. 46, 659–665 (2010). | PubMed |

34. Ormiston, J. A. & Serruys, P. W. Bioabsorbable coronary stents. Circ. Cardiovasc. Interv. 2, 255–260 (2009).

Chapter 7

Polyhydroxyalkanoates: Opening Doors for a Sustainable Future

Zibiao Li[1], Jing Yang[2] and Xian Jun Loh[1,2,3]

[1]*Institute of Materials Research and Engineering (IMRE), A*STAR, Singapore, Singapore*

[2]*Department of Materials Science and Engineering, National University of Singapore, Singapore, Singapore*

[3]*Singapore Eye Research Institute, Singapore, Singapore*

ABSTRACT

Polyhydroxyalkanoates (PHAs) comprise a group of natural biodegradable polyesters that are synthesized by microorganisms. However, several disadvantages limit their competition with traditional synthetic plastics or their application as ideal biomaterials. These disadvantages include their poor mechanical properties, high production cost, limited functionalities, incompatibility with conventional thermal processing techniques and susceptibility to thermal degradation. To circumvent these drawbacks, PHAs need to be modified to ensure improved performance in specific applications. In this review, well-established modification methods of PHAs are summarized and discussed. The improved properties of PHA that blends with natural raw materials or other biodegradable polymers, including starch, cellulose derivatives, lignin, poly(lactic acid), polycaprolactone and different PHA-type blends, are summarized. The functionalization of PHAs by chemical modification is described with respect to two important synthesis approaches: block copolymerization and graft copolymerization. The expanded utilization of the modified PHAs as engineering materials and the biomedical significance in different areas are also addressed.

INTRODUCTION

Polymers from renewable resources have gained significant attention in recent decades due to environmental issues and the realization of limited petroleum resources. Among the natural polymers, polyhydroxyalkanoates (PHAs) comprise a family of biodegradable polyesters that are produced by an extensive variety of microorganisms for intracellular carbon and energy storage purposes (Figure 1a).[1] PHA synthesis is promoted by unbalanced growth during the fermentation and accumulation of PHA granules as part of a survival mechanism of the microbes.[2] The general molecular structure of PHAs is presented in Figure 1b. Depending on the carbon numbers in the monomeric constituents, PHAs can be classified as short-chain-length PHAs (C_3–C_5), which consists of 3–5 carbon monomers, and medium-chain-length PHAs (MCL-PHA, C_6–C_{14}), which consists of 6–14 carbon monomers in the 3-hydroxyalkanoate units (Figure 1b).[3, 4] For example, poly(3-hydroxybutyrate) (PHB), poly(3-hydroxyvalerate) (PHV) and their copolymer poly(3-hydroxybutyrate-*co*-3-hydroxyvalerate) (PHBV) are typical examples of short-chain-length PHAs, whereas poly(3-hydroxyoctanoate) (PHO) and poly(3-hydroxynonanoate) (PHN), which are primarily formed as copolymers with 3-hydroxyhexanoate (HHx), 3-hydroxyheptanoate (HH) and/or 3-hydroxydecanoate (HD), are typical examples of MCL-PHAs. More than 150 different PHA monomers have been identified, which renders them the largest group of natural polyesters.[5]

The applications of PHAs are limited due to several undesirable physical properties. The presence of large crystals in PHB causes poor mechanical properties, which renders PHB unsuitable for various uses, including packaging film and biomedical applications such as heart valves and other vascular applications or controlled drug delivery systems.[6] In addition, the melting temperature (T_m) of PHB is similar to its thermal decomposition temperature. Its poor thermal stability renders PHB incompatible to conventional thermal processing techniques and susceptible to thermal degradation. Although a few studies demonstrated that MCL-PHAs at certain side chain lengths have elastomeric properties at atmospheric temperatures, the corresponding low $T_m$of MCL-PHAs indicates that this behavior is only observed in a narrow temperature window. At temperatures above or close to T_m, the polymers are completely amorphous and sticky.[7] An additional increase in the side chain length of MCL-PHAs will produce even more viscous and tacky polymers, which demonstrates the limitations of modifying PHA properties by side chain adjustment.[8] The development of new MCL-PHA copolymers involves a complicated genetic engineering process. Biosynthetic approaches remain inaccessible to the majority of chemists and material scientists who seek to optimize the properties of PHAs. The high hydrophobicity, lack of advanced functionality and high cost have also restricted further expansion of its utilization. Regarding the biodegradability of PHAs, the slow degradation rate and highly hydrophobic nature of unmodified PHAs are not favored in many advanced biomedical applications. Therefore, the utilization of PHAs as direct substitutes for synthetic plastics remains a significant challenge. PHAs need to be tailored to achieve low cost and better performance, such as tunable mechanical properties, crystallinity, surface features, amphiphilicity and degradation rates to fulfill specific applications.

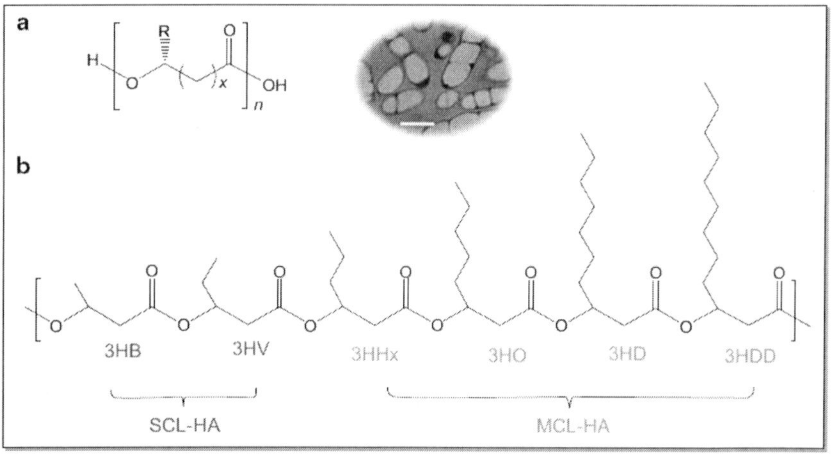

Figure 1. (**a**) General molecular formula of PHAs. Typically, x=1–8, and n ranges from 100 to 1000 s. (**b**) Some commonly synthesized short-chain-length PHA monomers (SCL-HA) and middle-chain-length PHA monomers (MCL-HA). 3HB: 3-hydroxybutyrate, 3HV: 3-hydroxyvalerate, 3HHx: 3-hydroxyhexanoate, 3HO: 3-hydroxyoctanoate, 3HD: 3-hydroxydecanoate, 3HDD: 3-hydroxydodecanoate. Insert TEM image that shows thin sections of recombinant *R. eutropha* PHB–4 cells that contain large amounts of P(3HB-*co*-5mol% 3HHx). The bar represents 0.5 μm. Adapted from ref 78 (2000 Elsevier).

In this review, the modifications of PHAs with improved properties are discussed with respect to two important strategies: physical blends and chemical modifications. Various functionalities that are not typically achieved by biosynthetic processes are introduced to PHAs. Microstructures at different levels and with new material features are elucidated to understand the relationship between the structures and properties of modified PHAs. With enhanced performance, the expanded utilization of the newly developed PHAs from renewable resources into value-added products is also discussed.

PHA modification via blending

Blending is a simple and effective approach for obtaining new polymeric materials with improved properties, in which the drawbacks of the parent components can be suppressed. Typically, the physical and mechanical properties of polymer blends can be tuned by choosing the proper starting materials and varying the compositions of the blend and preparation conditions. In addition, biodegradable blends add interesting properties to PHAs, such as full biodegradability and excellent biocompatibility. These blends have attracted increased interest because they employ conventional technology at low cost and have high potential applications, which range from environmentally degradable resins and biomedical implants to absorbable surgical sutures. A novel blend of PHA with other biodegradable polymers can significantly enhance the performance of PHAs. In this section, blend of PHAs with natural raw materials from sustainable resources or other synthetic biodegradable polymers are discussed. The molecular structures of biodegradable polymers that are commonly employed in PHA blends are presented in Figure 2.

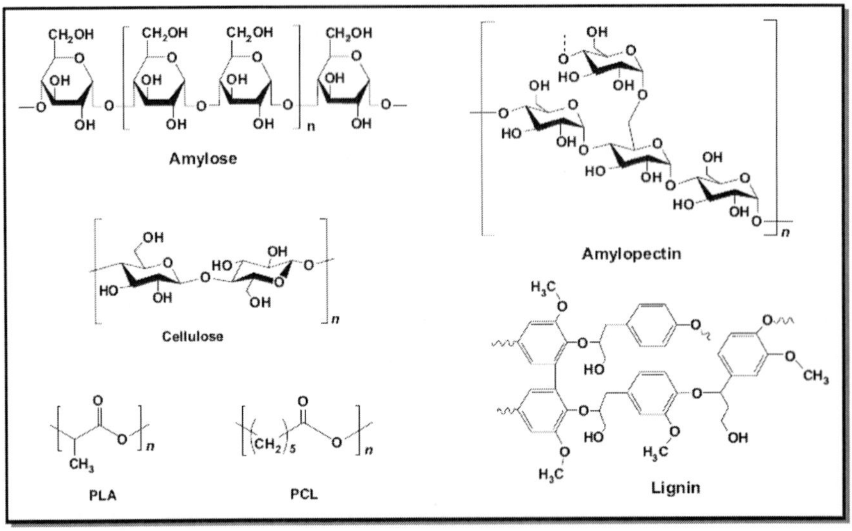

Figure 2. Molecular structures of the most common biodegradable polymers in PHA blends.

PHA blended with starch

Starch is one of the most promising natural polymers due to its inherent biodegradability, overwhelming abundance and annual renewal.[9] Starch consists of two types of molecules: the linear and helical amylose and the branched amylopectin (Figure 2). The blending of PHA, especially PHB with starch, has been extensively investigated. Godbole *et al.*[10] discussed the compatibility of PHB with starch to achieve improved properties and reduce cost. The results revealed that films had a single glass transition temperature (T_g) for all proportions of PHB: starch blends. The nature of all combinations was crystalline. The tensile strength of the blend at a ratio of 30:70% showed a significant increase compared with the virgin PHB. Because starch is abundant at a very low cost, the blending of starch with a maximum percentage of 30 in PHB would substantially reduce the cost of PHB, without compromising its physical properties. These blending materials extended the use of PHB as a coating material on paper or cardboard for food packaging applications.[10] In another study, Zhang *et al.*[11] analyzed the thermal behavior and phase morphology of PHB/starch acetate (SA) blends. The team demonstrated that PHB/SA blends were immiscible and the T_m of PHB in the blends shifted with an increase in SA concentration. The melting enthalpy of the PHB phase in the blend was similar to the value for pure PHB, whereas the T_g of the PHB in the blends remained constant at 9 °C. A differential scanning calorimetry (DSC) cycle test showed that PHB crystallization was affected by the presence of the SA component in the heating and cooling processes. For example, the temperature and enthalpy of the non-isothermal crystallization of the PHB in the blends were substantially lower than the temperature and enthalpy of the non-isothermal crystallization of pure PHB, and the cold crystallization peaks of the PHB in the blends shifted to higher temperatures compared with the cold crystallization peaks of pure PHB.[11]

Although blending of PHA with starch or SA showed some potential for reducing the production cost and improving the mechanical properties, these blends are brittle and do not form intact films due to the incompatibility between the starch/SA and the PHA matrix. To increase the compatibility and produce PHA blends with better mechanical properties, Willett *et al.*[12] employed grafted copolymer of starch and glycidyl methacrylate to improve the mechanical properties of PHBV, which has better mechanical properties than PHB. The tensile and flexural strengths of the blends increased with the use of starch and glycidyl methacrylate compared with the untreated starch; this effect is proportional to the increased graft concentrations. The scanning electron microscope of the cryogenic fracture surface showed improved adhesion between the starch-g-PGMA and the PHBV matrix, which indicates the increased compatibility of the blending components. A promising result of this study was the significant increase in the fracture toughness of these blends due to the incorporation of grafted starch.[12] Recently, poly(vinyl acetate) (PVAc)-modified corn starch (CSV) was exploited to improve the compatibility and flexibility of PHA/starch blends. With a PVAc-grafted ratio of 0.27, the starch-*g*-PVAc possessed a higher T_g at 44 °C compared with 35 °C of neat PVAc, probably due to the hindered molecular mobility that was imposed by starch on the grafted PVAc. After blending PHB with the CSV, only a single T_g was detected for all PHB/CSV blends, which increased from 2 to 37 °C with an increase in the CSV concentration, which indicates that the CSV was compatible with the PHB. The presence of PHB and PVAc components did not hinder the enzymatic degradation of the corn starch by α-amylase.[13]

PHA blended with cellulose derivatives Cellulose derivatives such as ethyl cellulose (EC), cellulose propionate and cellulose acetate butyrate (CAB) are attractive biomaterials that are extensively employed as blood coagulant, a pharmaceutical tablet coating and as carriers for poorly soluble drugs.[14]Cellulose derivatives are susceptible to enzymatic digestion in the human body. Cellulose derivatives have attracted a significant amount of interest as blending components with PHA primarily due to their compatibility with PHA and their ability to enhance the degradation of PHA. Zhang *et al.*[15] investigated the miscibility, crystallization and melting behavior and phase morphology of PHB/EC blends. The results indicated that T_g was composition-dependent; an increase inT_g was observed with a decrease in the PHB concentration in the blends. Unlike the pure PHB component, the blends displayed no crystallization when cooled from a melt state during the DSC non-isothermal crystallization runs, and the growth of the PHB spherulites in the blends was significantly delayed by the EC concentration. Ei-Shafee *et al.*[16] investigated the properties of a blend of PHB and CAB in a film that was formed by solution casting. The single T_g indicated that CAB/PHB blends were miscible. A depression in the equilibrium melting point of PHB and a significant reduction in the spherulites growth rate of PHB in the blends were also observed in the blend films. Additional phase structure analyses showed that the presence of a homogeneous amorphous phase, which consisted of CAB and noncrystalline PHB chains, was situated in the interlamellar regions of the crystalline PHB. In addition, the dispersion of CAB in the PHB-crystallized phase also induced improved mechanical properties with an elongation at break that increased from 2.2 to 7.3%.

PHA blended with lignin Lignin is an amorphous macromolecule that is composed of a phenylpropane repeat unit and possesses aliphatic and aromatic hydroxyl groups, as well as carboxylic acid groups.[17] These active functional groups and their amorphous nature render lignin a suitable candidate for blending with PHA. The amorphous nature of lignin can reduce the formation of large spherulites crystals and secondary nucleation, which has a significant impact on PHB brittleness. Previous studies showed that organosolv lignin and its butyrate derivative achieved higher miscibility with PHB and can significantly retard PHB crystallization.[18] The effect of lignin fine powder on the PHB crystallization process was investigated by Kai *et al.*[19] The results of the kinetic study of the melt for both pure PHB and PHB/lignin blends revealed that the crystallization half-time was reduced by the presence of lignin, which indicates a favorable isothermal crystallization of the PHB/lignin blend compared with pure PHB. With the addition of lignin, the rate of PHB spherulitic growth from the melt increased, the size of the spherulites decreased and the number of the spherulites increased compared with pure PHB.[19] These results indicated that lignin fine powder can be employed as a new type of nucleating agent to modulate PHB crystallization. Recently, Mousavioun *et al.*[20] investigated the thermo–physical properties and rheology of PHB/lignin blends. Soda lignin was employed as a blending component to improve the properties of PHB. The results indicated that soda lignin can improve the total thermal stability of PHB but may reduce the initial decomposition temperature of PHB. The thermogravimetric analysis, DSC and scanning electron microscope results of the PHB/soda lignin blends suggested that the intermolecular interaction between PHB and soda lignin was favored at a maximum soda lignin concentration of 40 wt%. These intermolecular interactions were attributed to the hydrogen bonding formation between the reactive functional groups of lignin and the carbonyl groups of PHB.[20] The degradation behaviors of the PHB/lignin blends were recently investigated by burying the samples in garden soil.[21] The results indicated that PHB films disintegrated with 45 wt% of mass loss within 12 months. However, the mass loss comprised 12 wt% when 10 wt% of lignin was present, which suggests that the presence of lignin can reduce the rate of PHB degradation. This may be caused by the inhibited colonization of the microorganisms that increased the resistance of the blends to microbial attack. Further analysis suggested that lignin can form strong hydrogen bonds with PHB in the buried samples, which likely caused a reduced rate of breakdown of PHB and prevented rapid degradation of the blends.[21] In addition, an accumulation of biofilms was observed on the surface of the buried samples with increased surface roughness during the degradation study, which revealed a biodegradation mechanism.[21]

Blending of different types of PHAs The first member of PHA which was discovered in 1926 is PHB. Previously, more than a hundred different varieties of PHAs have been reported. PHB, PHBV, poly(3-hydroxybutyrate-co-4-hydroxybutyrate) and PHBHHx copolymers with various monomer molar ratios are produced on a large scale by commercial enterprises.[2] As previously mentioned, the properties of PHAs significantly vary due to their monomer structure and composition. For example, PHB is a brittle polymer that forms large crystal spherulitic morphology and has secondary crystallization characteristics, whereas its copolymerization with other MCL-HA monomers, such as 3HHx, 3HO, 3HD and 3HDD, render the resultant SCL-MCL-PHA copolymers more attractive in terms of polyolefin-like thermo/mechanical behaviors, polyester-like physicochemical properties and unique biological characteristics. Another example is P3HB/4HB, which has been shown to exhibit an extensive range of physical properties and morphologies that range from highly crystalline to elastomeric properties, depending on the molar fraction of 4HB. In contrast to other monomers, including 3HB, 3HV, 3HHx and 3HP, 4HB monomer has one more carbon atom in the backbone, which produces unique crystallization behaviors of P3HB/4HB. Consequently, the blending of different types of PHAs offer the potential for alternating the properties of the PHAs, which facilitates expanded applications. For instance, Chen and co-workers systematically investigated PHB/PHBHHx blends and their biomedical applications.[22] The results revealed poor L929 cell growth on PHB films and a significant improvement in the growth on PHB/PHBHHx blending films, which indicated that blending is also an effective method for modifying the bioactive behaviors of the biomaterials. The different cellular behaviors were explained by the crystallization behaviors of the blending films.[22] The following detailed studies have shown that the high degree of crystallization and rapid crystallization rate of PHB generates pores and protrusions on the pure PHB film surface. This coralloid surface may prohibit the attachment and growth of mammalian cells. However, the presence of PHBHHx in PHB substantially reduced both the degree of crystallization and the crystallization rate of PHB. Consequently, the blending films exhibited a fairly regular and smooth surface, which facilitated cell attachment and growth and improved the biocompatibility of PHB.[23]

In addition, blends of different types of PHA members are usually compatible and can be employed as an effective approach for enhancing co-crystallization. For example, Yoshie *et al.* investigated solid-state structures and the crystallization kinetics of PHBV and PHB/PHBV blends.[24] The results indicated that observable phase structures include the co-crystallization of PHB and PHBV, the coexistence of two or more crystalline phases formed by phase segregation upon crystallization and immiscible phase separation, which changes with an increase in the HV content of PHBV. As the HV content increased, phase segregation proceeded to a higher degree prior to co-crystallization; as a result, the copolymer content in the co-crystalline phase decreased and/or the crystalline phases of the component polymers were formed. The final phase structure of the blends was determined by the competition between the co-crystallization and the phase segregation.[24] In another study, Saad analyzed the miscibility, melting and crystallization of PHB and oligo (R,S)-3HB-diol blends using DSC.[25] The thermograms of blends that contained 6 wt% oligo (R,S)-3HB-diol showed behaviors that are characteristic of a single-phase amorphous glass state with a composition-dependent glass transition and depression in the equilibrium T_m of PHB. The negative value of the interaction parameter that was determined from the equilibrium melting depression confirmed the miscibility of the blend components.[25]

PHA blended with synthetic biodegradable polymers

PHA blended with PLA Poly(lactic acid) (PLA) is a chemically synthesized biodegradable polymer from lactic acid, which can also be produced by the fermentation of simple sugars, such as glucose and maltose from corn or potato, sucrose from cane or beet sugar and lactose from cheese. PLA is a linear aliphatic polyester thermoplastic that has been extensively employed as environmentally friendly package materials and biocompatible medical devices. However, low-impact toughness and low end-use temperature are important factors in the large-scale commercial adoption of PLA. Plasticizers, mineral fillers and traditional impact modifiers have been added to overcome the problems associated with PLA.[26] Blending PLA with other biodegradable polymers, such as PHA and PCL, was also shown to be an effective method for altering the properties of the polymer.[27, 28] Several studies have focused on the study of PHA/PLA blends. For example, Gerard and Budtova demonstrated that PHA and PLA are immiscible polymers, and nodular and co-continuous morphologies were observed.[29] From the rheology analysis, the thermal stability of PHBV was extremely low, and the PLA/PHBV blends served a significant role in improving this property. Although PLA and PHBV are brittle polymers, blends that contain a small amount of PHBV in a PLA matrix exhibited a significant ductile plastic deformation.[29]

PHAs that consist of 3HB and a small amount of MCL-HA units have lower crystallinities and T_ms and more ductile properties than short-chain-length PHAs. Noda *et al.*[30] reported that blends of PLA with this type of PHA can form an excellent pair of complementary materials, which can effectively balance the shortcomings of these materials when combined. For example, the results indicated that the toughness and elongation at break of the blends significantly improved when 10% of PHA was added to PLA, which was attributed to an increase in the amorphous phase of the blends and caused unusually slow crystallization kinetics of finely dispersed PHA particles. In addition to short-chain-length PHAs, MCL-PHAs and chemically modified PHAs were also reported to blend with PLA to optimize their physical properties. For instance, Takagi *et al.*[31] blended a series of MCL-PHAs and epoxy-group-modified PHA (e-PHA) with PLA using solution casting methods. In contrast with PHB, the MCL-PHA or e-PHA are amorphous rubbery polymers. Although the PLA/MCL-PHA and the PLA/e-PHA blends were immiscible in the amorphous state, the impact toughness of the PLA increased after blending with these PHAs. The e-PHA with an inserted epoxy group side chain was more effective in improving the morphology and physical properties of the blend than MCL-PHA. The e-PHA exhibited better compatibility with PLA than MCL-PHA. A possible explanation is that the epoxy group is not stable and tends to combine with the hydroxyl group of PLA in the end group, which may increase the interactions between phases.[31]

In addition to the PHA components, which affect their compatibility with PLA, the method of blending will also impact the miscibility of PLA. Zhang *et al.*[32]reported that PHB/PLA blends that were prepared by the solvent casting method were immiscible over the range of the analyzed compositions, whereas the melt-blended sample that was prepared at high temperatures exhibited evidence of greater miscibility. The crystallization of PHB in the blends was affected by the amount of added PLA. The thermal history caused a depression of the melting point and a decrease in the crystallinity of the PHB in the blends.[32] Ohkoshi *et al.*[27] investigated the miscibility and phase structure of the PLA/atactic PHB (a-PHB) of different molecular weights using DSC and optical microscopy. The molecular weight of a-PHB has a substantial impact on the miscibility with PLA. For example, low-molecular-weight a-PHB (M_w=9400) is miscible in the melt at 200 °C with a maximum a-PHB concentration of 50 wt%. Conversely, high-molecular-weight a-PHB (M_w=140 000) revealed two T_g in the melt, which indicates the immiscibility of these two phases.[27] Recently, Furukawa *et al.*[33]compared the properties between blends of PHB/PLA and PHBHHx/PLA. The results revealed that both the PHB/PLLA blends and PHBHHx/PLA blends were immiscible, but the PHBHHx/PLA blends were more compatible. The lattice parameters of each component in the blends were almost constant, which suggested that the crystalline structures in the blends were maintained.[33] The $T_g$for the PHBHHx/PLA components in the blends and the PHB and PLLA components in the PHB/PLLA blends did not significantly change. The observation of the crystallization temperature of PLA in both blend systems suggested that each component was not only the PHB/PLA but also the PHBHHx/PLA blends that formed the mixed semicrystalline structures. The crystallization temperature of PLA in the PHB/PLLA blend and PHBHHx/PLA blend shifted to a lower temperature and higher temperature, respectively, with an increased PHB or PHBHHx component in the blends. These results illustrated that the PHB/Poly(L-Lactic Acid) blends with decreasing crystallization temperature were completely immiscible, whereas the PHBHHx/PLA blends with increasing crystallization temperature were slightly compatible.[33] Recently, blends of poly(3-hydroxybutyrate-co-4-hydroxybutyrate) and stereocomplexed polylactide with improved rheological and mechanical properties were also reported.[34]

PHA blended with PCL

Polycaprolactone (PCL) is a biodegradable semicrystalline aliphatic polyester that has been employed for long-term biomedical applications. PCL possesses superior mechanical strength with high strength and ductility. Consequently, PCL has been extensively explored as a biomaterial in various forms. For example, Lim *et al.*[35] blended PCL with PHBHHx and employed the blends as a substrate for musculoskeletal tissue engineering. PHBHHx possesses a low degree of crystallinity and nontoxic degradation products. In addition, PHBHHx is a soft and flexible polymer with a low tensile strength and Young's modulus.[36] Despite these advantages, PHBHHx exhibits inadequate mechanical strength and toughness for tissue engineering applications. However, the addition of PCL via polymer blends may cause PHBHHx to exhibit enhanced toughness with substantial elasticity. These improvements provided adequate matching of properties with human bone. At an optimal blend ratio of 30:70, the blends exhibited enhanced yield strength, yield strain and Young's modulus, as well as predictable degradation profile. PHBHHx can support human fetal mesenchymal stem cell adhesion and proliferation, which demonstrates significant potential as a bone scaffold material.[35] PHBV and PCL blends have been reported to be miscible. Chiono *et al.*[37] prepared hollow fibers for use as guides for tissue engineering by dry-jet-wet spinning of PHBV and PCL solutions in chloroform. The fibers obtained from these blends exhibited a low degree of surface and bulk porosity depending on the composition. The mechanical properties of PHBV/PCL blends showed increasing ductility of the blend samples with an increasing amount of PCL.[37] Del Gaudio *et al.*[38] developed PCL/PHBV blends using vascular grafts and compared the biological performance with the parent polymers. In their study, rat cerebral endothelial cells were used to assess the biological performance of these grafts. PCL and PCL/PHBV supported adhesion, viability, migration and proliferation of rat cerebral endothelial cells during the 14-day observation period. However, pure PHBV was less suitable for these cells, which may be related to the different mechanical features.[38]

Chemical modification of PHAs

In addition to blending, chemical modification of PHAs enables the easy and precise modulation of the polymer structure with predictable functionalities. Controlled and/or living polymerization techniques that are combined with other new synthetic methodologies enable the synthesis of a large array of new functional PHA-based materials with various architectures and many new accessible materials features for specific applications. In the following sections, the chemically modified PHA-based materials will be discussed with respect to graft and block architectures, with a special focus on the significant impact of the expanded applications that are derived from the enhanced material properties.

PHAs modification via graft copolymerization

PHA grafted on natural polymers

PHA-grafted derivatives were synthesized by conjugation with natural polymers. The amine groups of chitosan react with the carboxyl group-terminated PHB to yield PHB-*g*-chitosan graft copolymers, whereas the esterification between the carboxyl group-terminated PHB and hydroxyl functions in cellulose generates PHB-*g*-cellulose graft copolymers.[39] In a similar approach, PHBV and PHO oligomers have also been reported to graft onto chitosan to yield either PHBV-*g*-chitosan or PHO-*g*-chitosan copolymers.[40]The presence of hydrophilic chitosan caused the PHA-grafted derivatives to exhibit an amphiphilic behavior, in which the solubility of the final product was dependent on the degree of grafting percentage. PHA-*g*-chitosan copolymers with controllable solubility in 2 wt% acetic acid and water can be controlled by changing the grafting percentage. These new grafted materials exhibited high potential in medical applications, such as tissue engineering and drug delivery systems, due to their antimicrobial activity and biocompatibility.[40]

PHA/vinyl- and (meth)acrylate-grafted copolymers

PHA-grafted copolymer can also be produced by radical polymerization of monomers/oligomers that contain vinyl or (meth)acrylate groups. The grafting chains that include Polyethylene glycol (PEG), 2-hydroxyethylmethacrylate (HEMA) and poly(methylmethacrylate) (PMMA) have been previously investigated.[7] For example, PEG that contains acrylate groups were employed to prepare PHA-grafted copolymers by irradiation (Figure 3).[41] The presence of PEG chains in the polymer networks increased the hydrophilicity of the final product. The significant concentrations of water within the PHO-*g*-PEG polymers provided a low interfacial tension with blood and reduced the protein adsorption and platelet adhesion, which has been recognized as an essential requisite for materials that are employed in blood contacting devices. The blood compatibility test confirmed the increasing trend due to an increased fraction of grafted PEG chains, which indicates the potential use of PHO-*g*-PEG polymer networks in blood-compatible biomedical applications.[41] In addition, the mechanical strength was optimized by the PEG concentration. In a typical example, the optimal tensile strength of the PHO-*g*-PEG (50/50, w/w) is 219 kPa, and the elongation at break is 379%, which indicated a significant improvement compared with the pure PHU polymers.[41]

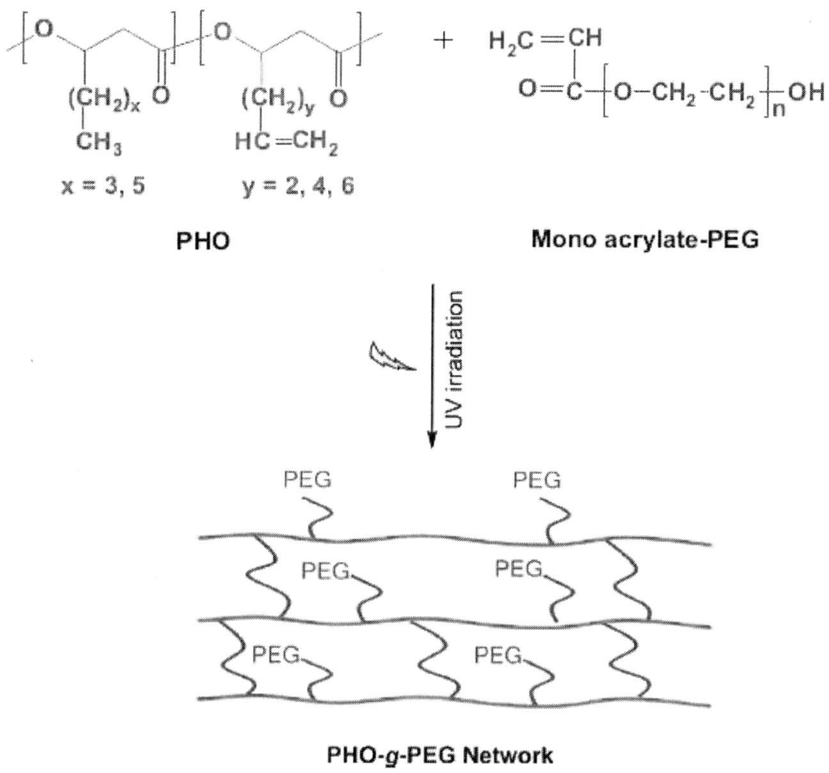

Figure 3. Schematic of the formation of PHO-*g*-PEG copolymers. Adapted from reference 41 (2003 Elsevier).

Active radical sites along the polyhydroxyundecenoate (PHA) main chain can be created by abstracting the proton at the C-3 carbon in PHA to graft vinyl chains by monomer polymerization.[42] For example, when methyl mechacrylate (MMA) was polymerized in the presence of aqueous PHB suspension using benzoyl peroxide (BPO) as an initiator, PMMA branches were able to graft on PHB by the covalent bonding between C-3 carbon of PHB and the vinyl CH of MMA repeating units (Figure 4).[43] However, both PHB-*g*-PMMA and PMMA homopolymer were detected under this grafting mechanism. In another study, PHA-*g*-PMMA grafting copolymers were prepared by irradiation-induced radical polymerization[44] to determine the irradiation-dose-dependent grafting efficiency of MMA onto both PHB and PHBV. However, the higher crystallinity of the PHB compared with PHBV caused a lower degree of grafting for PHB-*g*-PMMA than PHBV-*g*-PMMA. According to a previous study, the degree of grafting was dependent on the differences in regularity in the crystalline regions or the crystallinity and rate of radical decay. In this study, the crystalline regions of PHB remained almost unchanged after grafting, whereas the crystalline regions of PHBV in the PHBV-*g*-PMMA samples were partially destroyed by the introduction of grafting.[44] In addition, the irradiation method was also employed to prepare PHBV-*g*-poly(acrylic acid) (PAA) copolymers.[45] The glucosamine was covalently linked to the functionalized PHBV-*g*-PAA surface by carbodiimide chemistry, which reveals that the modified substrates are suitable for the additional conjugation of bioactive molecules.[45]

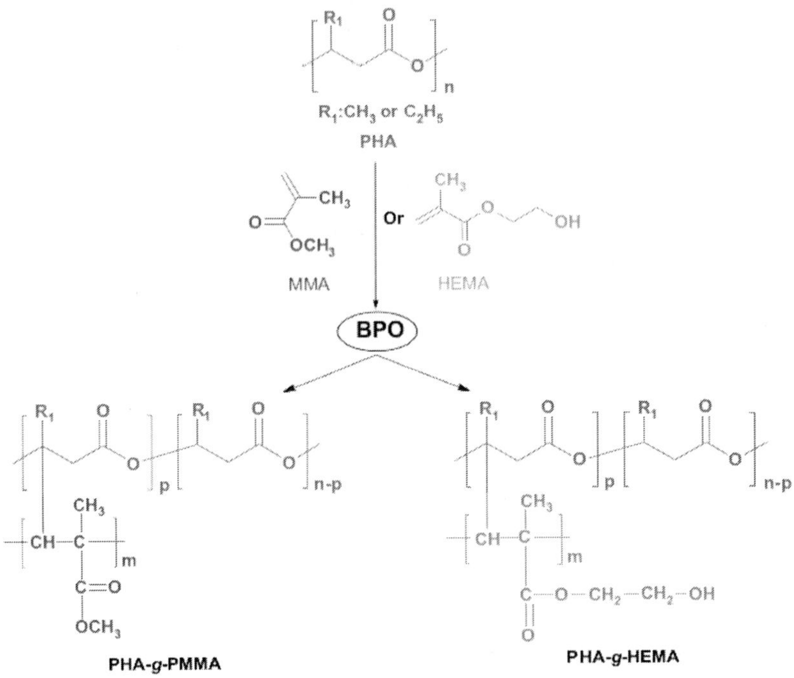

Figure 4. Free radical grafting of MMA and HEMA on PHA using BPO as an initiator.

Recently, 2-hydroxyethylmethacrylate (HEMA)-grafted PHBV films (HEMA-*g*-PHBV) were also prepared using BPO as an initiator (Figure 4).[46] With an increase in HEMA concentration, the graft copolymerization occurred in the bulk of the film and was more prominent at the PHBV surface. Compared with the untreated PHBV, the HEMA-*g*-PHBV showed a significant decrease in crystallinity and improvement of wettability due to the introduction of hydroxyl groups in HEMA. The presence of many hydroxyl groups on the PHBV surface provides a new opportunity to modify the instinct PHAs with bioactive molecules.

Saad *et al.*[47] investigated the grafting behavior of N-vinylpyrrolidone (VP) onto PHBV. The polyvinylpyrrolidone (PVP) grafting content may increase to 45% if the reaction is conducted in a solution using 2,2′-azobisisobutyronitrile as an initiator. Compared with the ungrafted PHBV, the obtained PHBV-*g*-PVP grafting copolymer possessed improved thermal stability. The hydrophilic PVP grafting promoted the degradation of the polymer. In addition, the hydrophilic nature of PVP with a positive charge also enhanced the swelling properties and active antibacterial effect of the grafted PHBV-*g*-PVP copolymer.[47] The graft copolymers that contain PHAs as the branches can also be constructed via the copolymerization of PHA macromonomers with other (meth)acrylic family members. Nguyen *et al.*[48] reported PMMA-*g*-PHB graft copolymers with acrylic-type backbone and side chains that are composed of segments of PHB as branches (Figure 5). The reactivity of PHB macromonomers that were prepared from the esterification of PHB-COOH and HEMA was higher than the macromonomers that were prepared using MMA at a low molar feed ratio but decreased at higher macromonomers proportions. This finding was due to the incompatibility between the macromonomer chains and the propagating comonomer chains, which have a significant influence on the degree of interpenetration and the excluded volume effects around the terminal polymerizable group of the growing chains.[48] PMMA-*g*-PHB-grafted copolymers were evaluated as possible constituents in acrylic bone cements.[49] A formulation with a concentration of PMMA-*g*-PHB copolymer that exceeded 20 wt% produced cement doughs. The ultimate compressive strength test demonstrated that the value exceeded the minimum level and was similar to the value of Antibiotic Simplex or AKZ (Stryker Canada LP, Howmedica Osteonics, Guelph, ON, Canada).[49]

Other functional PHA-grafted copolymers

The unsaturated groups in the pendant chain of PHAs can be employed to conjugate with different oligomers to prepare other types of functional PHA-grafted copolymers. For example, Renard and colleagues reported the synthesis of amphiphilic graft copolymers that consist of hydrophobic PHAs backbone and hydrophilic α-amino-ω-methoxy poly(oxyethylene-*co*-oxypropylene) (Jeffamine) branches via a thiol-ene reaction (Figure 6a).[50] Poly(3-hydroxyoctanoate-co-3-hydroxyundec-10-enoate) (PHOU)-*g*-Jeffamine-grafted copolymers with >13 mol% of Jeffamine were determined to be water soluble and exhibited thermoresponsive behaviors (Figure 6b). In

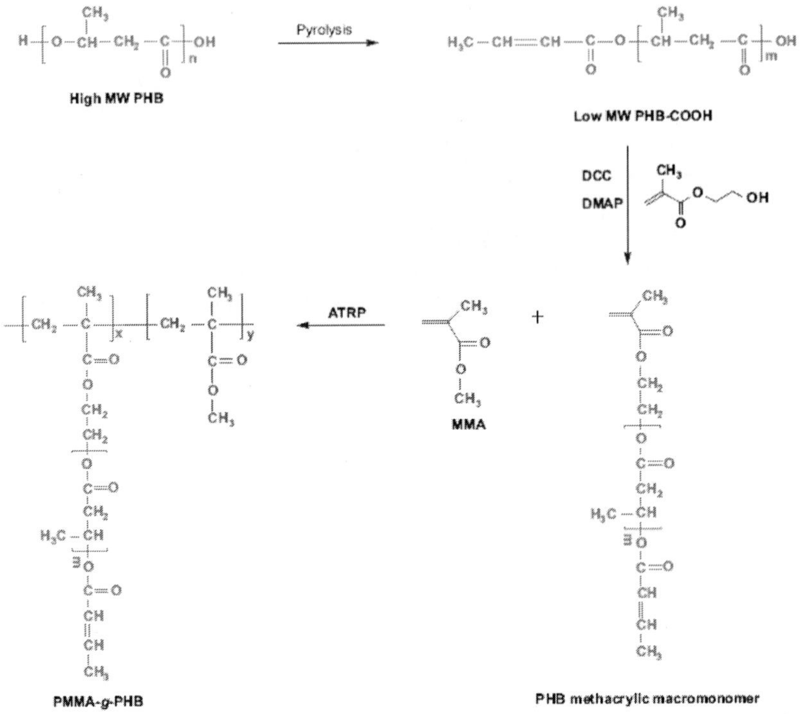

Figure 5. Synthesis route of PMMA-*g*-PHB copolymer by the combination of high-molecular-weight PHB pyrolysis, and the esterification and copolymerization of PHA macromonomers with MMA using ATRP.

addition, the thermoresponsive properties were tunable with different Jeffamine compositions, which encompassed a range of cloud-point temperatures from 17 to 29 °C. In a similar manner, PHOU-*g*-PEG-grafted copolymers were synthesized and formed well-defined nanoscale vesicles in water.[51] In contrast to these strategies, the unsaturated groups in PHAs were also converted to carboxyl groups via oxidation and employed to prepare PHA-graft copolymers by direct esterification with hydroxyl groups of PEG or PLA oligomers (Figure 7).[52]

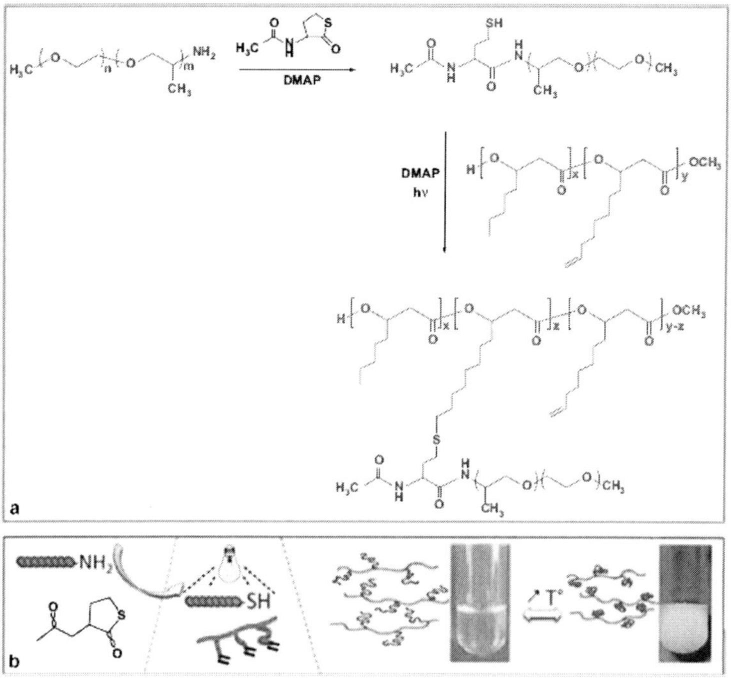

Figure 6. (**a**) Synthesis route of PHOU-*g*-Jeffamine copolymers and (**b**) thermoresponsive illustration of the copolymers in aqueous solution. Adapted from reference 50 (2012 WILEYVCH Verlag GmbH & Co. KGaA, Weinheim).

Zhou *et al.* reported the synthesis of PHA-grafted poly(ethyleneimine) (PEI) copolymers (PHA-*g*-bPEI) by Michael addition between acrylated-PHA and branched PEI (Figure 8a). The hydrophilic nature of PEI rendered P3/4HB-*g*-bPEI copolymer soluble in buffer solution; the surface charge was effectively employed to bind synthetic RNA (siRNA) to prevent its degradation by nucleases. In a typical example, the high intensity of intracellular Cy3-siRNA fluorescence was observed in cells that were transfected with P3/4HB-*g*-bPEI copolymer compared with cells that were incubated with commercial Lipofectamine and PEI, which indicates improved cellular uptake and subcellular distribution (Figures 8b–e).[53] The stability of the P3/4HB-g-bPEI/siRNA complexes was disrupted by the presence of PHA, and the degradation of the ester bonds in P3/4HB simplified the release of siRNA into cytoplasm for efficient gene silencing. In the tested A549-Luc cells and MCF-7-Luc cells, a significant breakdown of luciferase expression from 70 to 90% was observed when the cells were transfected with P3/4HB-g-bPEI copolymers/siRNA complexes, which demonstrated their potential as safe and efficient siRNA carriers for human gene therapy.[53]

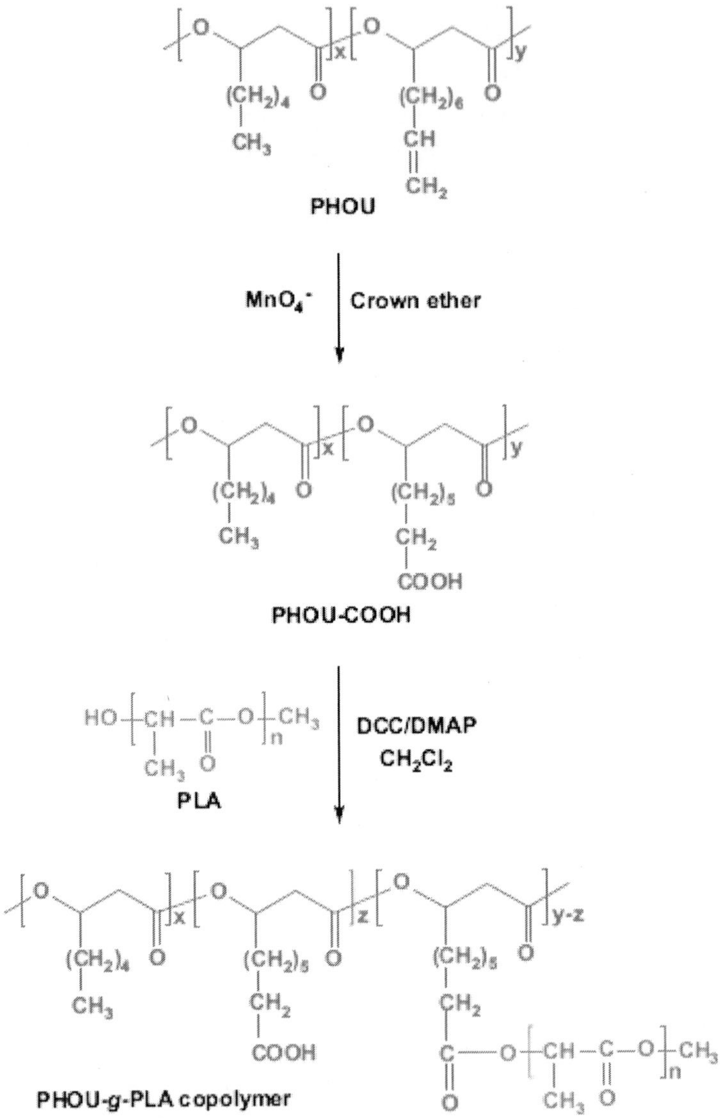

Figure 7. Synthesis route of PHOU-COOH by oxidation and its subsequent preparation of PHOU-*g*-PLA copolymers from esterification with hydroxyl groups of PLA.

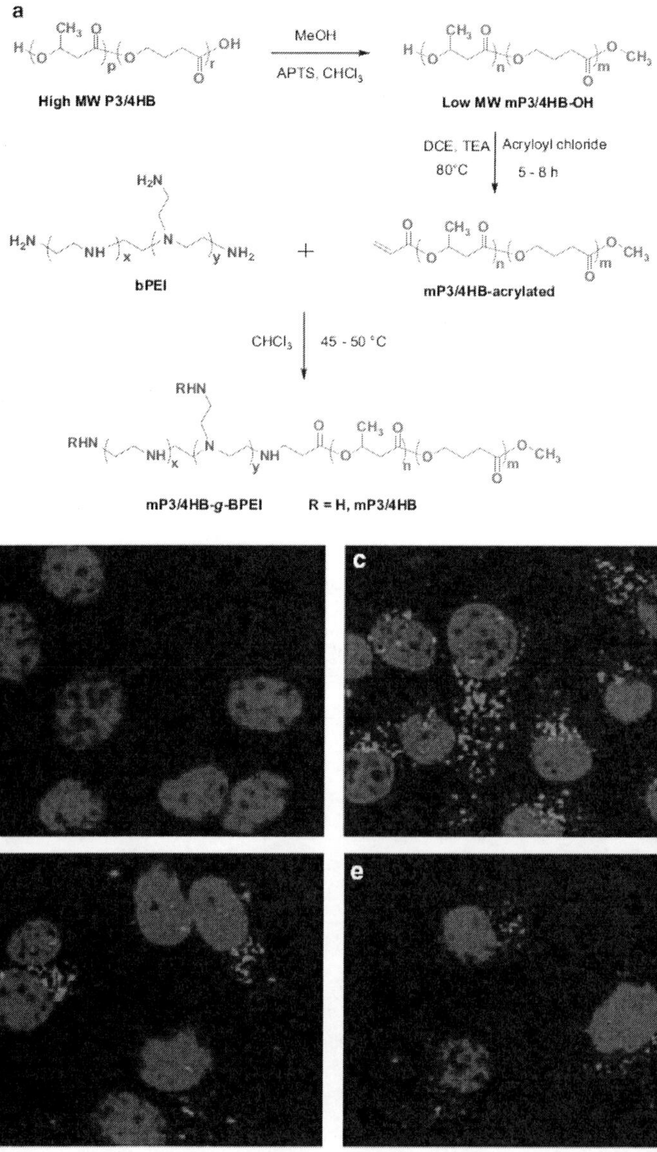

Figure 8. (**a**) Synthesis route of mP3/4HB-acrylate and its preparation of mP3/4HB-*g*-bPEI copolymer by Michael addition. Confocal microscopy images of the A549 cell uptake of (**b**) free siRNA and (**c**) P3/4HB-*g*-bPEI/siRNA complexes. (**d**) Lipofectamine and (**e**) bPEI were employed as the control. Cy3-labeled siRNA appeared red fluorescence and the cell nuclei were stained blue using DAPI. Adapted with permission from reference 53 (2012 Elsevier).

PHAs modification via block copolymerization

Block copolymerization of PHAs with different functional polymers enables the modification of their properties. Many advanced biomedical applications were achieved using the newly developed PHA block copolymers. In this section, PHAs-based block copolymers that contain various types of building blocks will be reviewed.

PHA/polyester block copolymers

Active PHB-O-$AlEt_2$ macroinitiator species were previously prepared from the reaction between mono-hydroxyl-terminated PHB macromonomers and $AlEt_3$. This macroinitiator was employed to conduct the ring opening polymerization of ε-caprolactone (CL) or lactide monomers to obtain PHB-PCL and PHB-PLA diblock copolymers.[54] Similarly, elastmeric soft segments of PHO and PCL were combined to prepare semicrystalline PHO-PCL diblock copolymers, in which the crystallinity of the copolymers were also controlled by the lengths of the two different blocks.[55] Consecutive ROP of lactide followed by CL using PHB as a macroinitiator afforded PHB-PLA-PCL triblock copolymers (Figure 9). The A-B-C type of triblock copolymers are composed of a PHB-PLA hard segment and a PCL soft segment that induced microphase separation in the polymer film. The PHB-PLA hard segment domains serve as physical crosslinkers for the PCL soft segment matrix.[56]

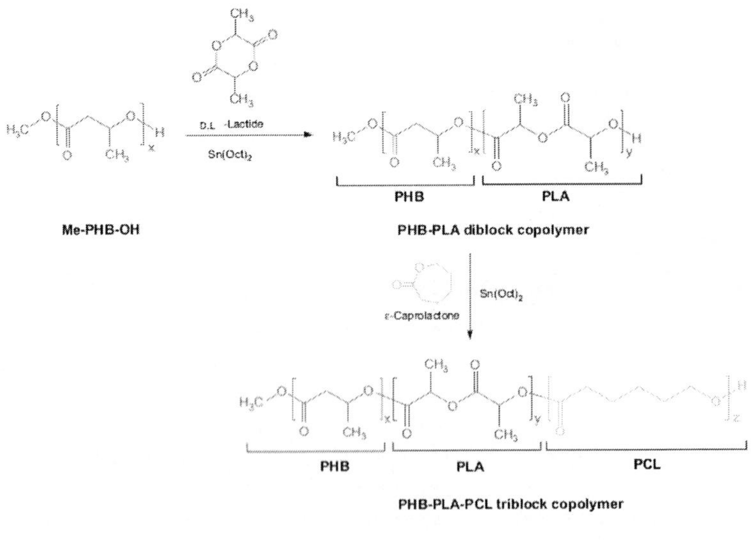

Figure 9. Synthesis of the PHB-PLA-PCL triblock copolymer by consecutive ring opening polymerization.

Another interesting approach to prepare the PHA-polyester block copolymer is to link PHAs and telechelic polyester oligomers with a proper coupling agent, such as diisocyanate and terephthaloyl chloride. Saad *et al.*[57] reported a one-pot solution synthesis of PHB/PCL/1,6-hexamethylene diisocyanate (HDI)-segmented poly(ester urethane)s with different compositions (Figure 10). The results indicated that the thermal and mechanical properties of the PHB/PCL poly(ester urethanes) were successfully manipulated by changing the block lengths of the hard and soft components. In another study, P3/4HB/PCL poly(ester urethane)s that consisted of P3/4HB and PCL were coupled by HDI in a melt state.[58] The P3/4HB/PCL poly(ester urethane)s with a concentration of 4 HB possessed richer platelet adhesion and rapid blood coagulation, as well as lower cytotoxicity toward rat aortic smooth muscle cells, which indicates that P3/4HB/PCL poly(ester urethane)s can be employed as a potential candidate for wound healing applications.[58]

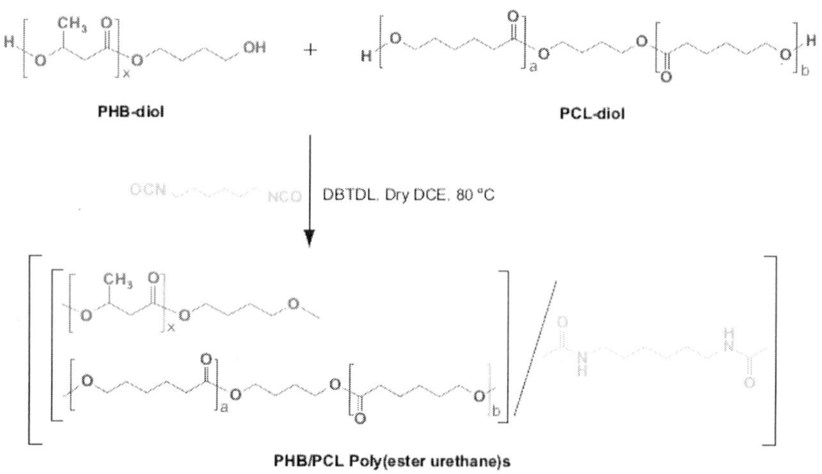

Figure 10. Synthesis of PHB/PCL poly(ester urethane)s block copolymers that use HDI as a coupling agent.

The coupling of different types of PHA segments have diversified a large group of new PHAs-based block copolymers with enhanced properties, such as adjustable mechanical strength, surface features and programmed degradation rate. For example, the physical properties of P3/4HB, which range from soft elastomers to high crystallinity plastics, were produced by altering the 3HB rate in the copolymer to a 4HB rate. Recently, Xu and coworkers reported a coupling synthesis of different types of P3/4HB-diols with a 4HB concentration that varied from 9.3 to 32.3%.[59] The crystallinity, hydrophobicity and surface free energy were tailored by the 4HB content, the P3/4HB segmental length and the urethane linkage concentration in P3/4HB poly(ester urethane)s. From the improved properties of lactate dehydrogenase activity, strong platelet adhesion and cell compatibility, the authors demostrated the use of P3/4HB poly(ester urethane)s as potential hemostatic materials.[59] Similarly, tailored poly(ester urethane)s based on P3/4HB and poly(3-hydroxyhexanoate-*co*-3-hydroxyoctanoate) (PHHxHO) were synthesized (Figure 11).[60] The obtained P3/4HB/PHHxHO poly(ester urethane)s were hydrophobic with a minimum water contact angle of 100°, which is more hydrophobic than the corresponding raw polymers and PLA. Hydrophobicity is an important factor that affects the platelet activation and produces strong platelet adhesion for blood coagulation. The incorporation of PHAs with different side chain lengths can tune the hydrophobicity and platelet adhesion behaviors of P3/4HB/PHHxHO poly(ester urethane)s toward specific requirements as wound healing materials.[60] Andrade *et al.*[61] reported the preparation of novel block copolymers that contain telechelic PHO-diol and telechelic PHB-diol by different coupling methods. The newly chemically synthesized polymer that contained both soft segments and hard segments, that were derived from PHAs showed excellent thermoplastic properties and mechanical properties, which is a potentially useful material for medical applications.

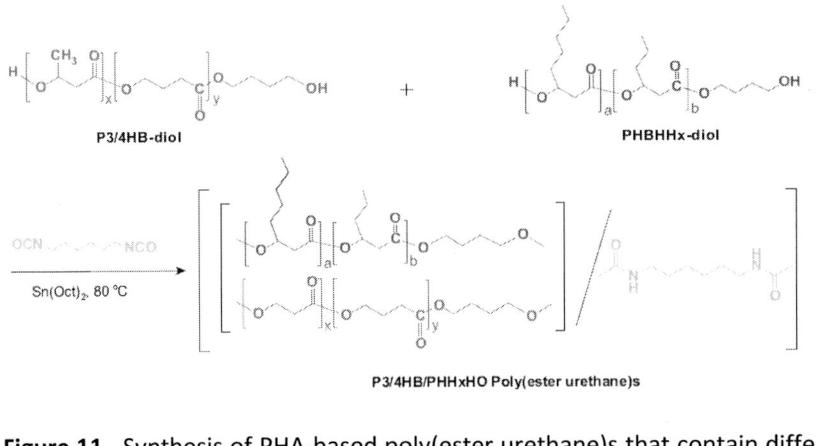

Figure 11. Synthesis of PHA-based poly(ester urethane)s that contain different PHAs as building blocks. Adapted from reference 60 (2009 Elsevier).

PHA-polyether block copolymers

The intrinsic hydrophobicity of natural PHAs and their slow degradation rate have raised many concerns in biomedical applications. The presence of desired hydrophilic components in PHA block copolymers enabled the manipulation of the amphiphilicity and chemicophysical properties. Diblock copolymers that contain high-molecular bacterial PHB with monomethoxy-PEG (mPEG) were synthesized in a melt reaction using *bis*(2-ethylehexanote) tin as a catalyst. This single-step synthesis of mPEGylated PHB proceeded with a concomitant depolymerization of PHB molecular weight to a few thousands.[62] Once formed from oil-in-water emulsion, PHB-PEG diblock copolymer can self-assemble into nanoparticles, which can be potentially employed as drug carriers or binders. Using the same approach, nanometer-sized core-shell micelles were prepared from amorphous amphiphilic block copolymer P(3HV-*co*-4HB)-mPEG and were further explored in cancer therapy. The *in vitro* release profile of cisplatin from P(3HV-*co*-4HB)-mPEG micelles showed a sustained release of the drug, and the drug accumulation became more distinct compared with the free drug in solution.[63] Li *et al.*[64] reported the synthesis of amphiphilic triblock copolymers PEG-PHB-PEG by the coupling reaction between methoxy-PEG-monocarboxylic acid and PHB-diol, which was catalyzed by dicyclohexylcarbodiimide (DCC) and DMAP (Figures 12a and b). Prior to threading with α-CD, PEO–PHB–PEO aqueous solution is a flowable solution; after threading with α-CD, it forms a self-assembled hydrogel (Figures 12c and d). The inner structure α-CD–PEO–PHB–PEO hydrogel formation is also illustrated (Figure 12e). The water-soluble PEG-PHB-PEG copolymer self-assembled into micelles, which are useful for potential drug delivery applications.

a

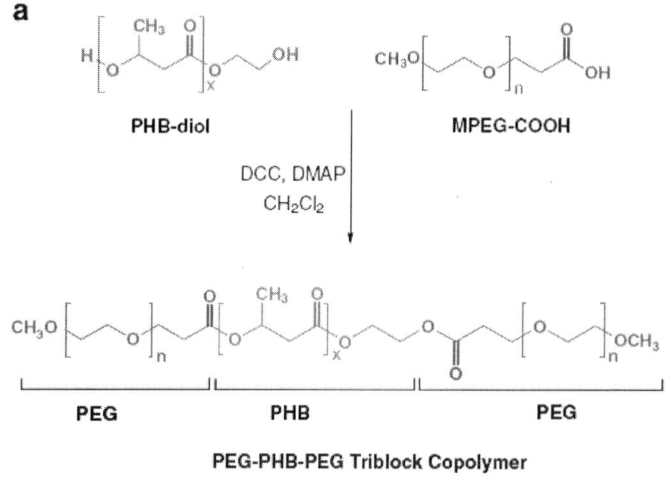

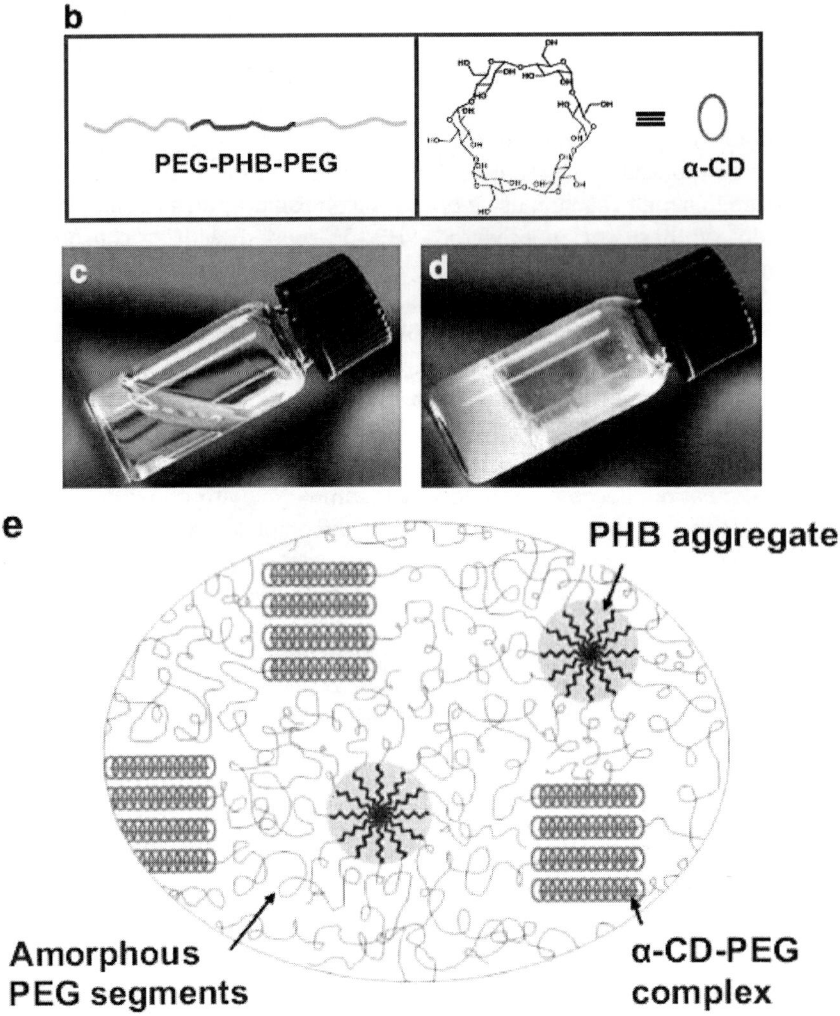

Figure 12. (**a**) Preparation of PEG-PHB-PEG triblock copolymers and (**b**) Schematic of PEG-PHB-PEG triblock copolymer and α-CD; (**c**) Optical photographs of the PEO–PHB–PEO aqueous solution and (**d**) its self-assembled hydrogel with α-CD; (**e**) Illustration of the inner structure of α-CD–PEO–PHB–PEO hydrogel formation. Adapted with permission from reference65 (2006 Elsevier).

The region-selective channel structure of the solution with α-cyclodextrins can trigger the phase transformation from sol to hydrogel formation, which provided a well-controlled long-term release profile of the encapsulated molecules without burst release.[65] PHA-polyether block copolymers were prepared via a diisocyanate chain extension reaction with hydroxyl-capped polyethers such as PEG and Poly(propylene glycol) (PPG). A series of PHB/PEG poly(ether ester urethane)s block copolymers with various PHB and PEG segment lengths were synthesized.[66] The hydrophilicity and water swelling analysis was significantly improved via the incorporation of PEG segments. The degradation studies revealed a random chain scission of the ester backbone bonds of the PHB segments, and the surface roughness of the films increased as the degradation proceeded.[67] The degradation components were water-soluble products, including PEG blocks, 3-hydroxybutyric acid and crotonic acid. The synthesis of alternative block polyurethane copolymers P3/4HB-*alt*-PEG based on the coupling reaction between P3/4HB-diol and PEG-diisocyanate with different segment lengths was reported (Figure 13).[68] The synthetic methodology for P3/4HB-*alt*-PEG poly(ether ester urethane)s provided a method for controlling the exact structure of the biomaterials and tailoring the properties to subtle requirements. The hydrophilic surface and regular surface microstructure endowed the P3/4HB-*alt*-PEG poly(ether ester urethane)s with better hemocompatibility. The cell culture assay revealed that both fibroblasts and rat glial cells were more favorable for the attachment on P3/4HB-*alt*-PEG poly(ether ester urethane)s films, which indicates that the arrangement of PHA/polyether polyurethanes in an alternative block architecture can easily realize the topography control of the materials and achieve the practical structure–property relationship in biomaterial applications.[68]

PPG is a thermoresponsive polymer that undergoes a hydrophilic to hydrophobic transition when the temperature changes across their corresponding lower critical solution temperatures (LCSTs). Our group reported the synthesis of multiblock amphiphilic and thermosensitive poly(ether ester urethane)s, which consist of PHB, PEG and PPG blocks (Figures 14a and b).[69] At PHB concentrations below 11.4 wt%, PHB/PEG/PPG poly(ether ester urethane)s were soluble in water and self-assembled into micelle formation with extremely low concentrations. When the concentration increased from 2 to 5 wt%, the PHB/PEG/PPG poly(ether ester urethane)s solution underwent sol-gel-sol transition as the temperature increased from 4 to 80 °C. The temperature-dependant sol–gel transition of the copolymer solution was attributed to the increased association of the micelles, which was caused by the multiple segments that link the micelles in a network-like gel structure.[69, 70] The hydrolytic degradation of PHB/PEG/PPG poly(ether ester urethane) hydrogels was characterized by an initial incubation period, followed

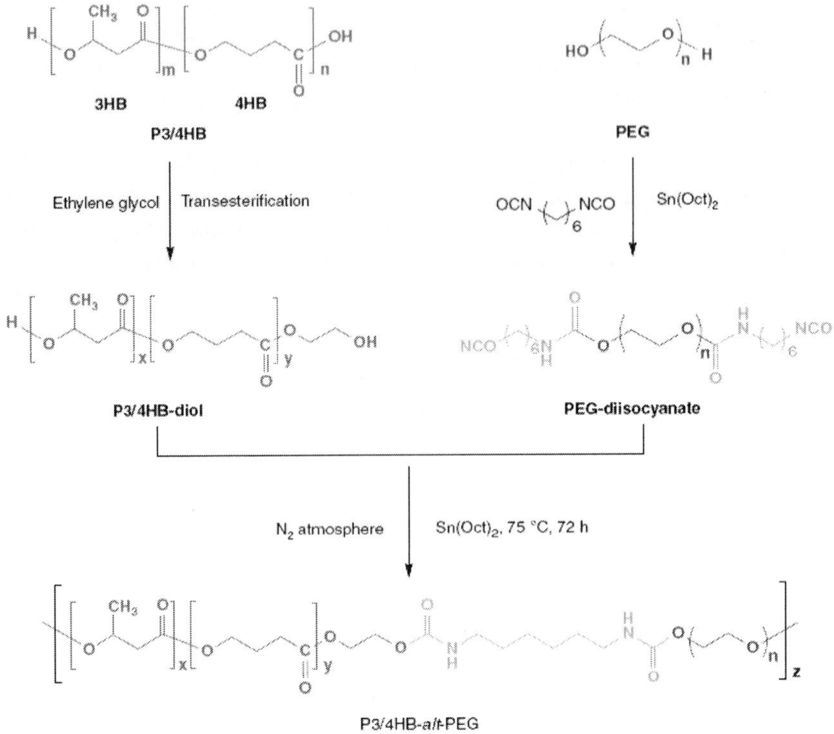

Figure 13. Synthesis of alternative P3/4HB-*alt*-PEG poly(ether ester urethane)s block copolymers. Adapted from reference 68 (2009 Elsevier).

by the erosion of the polymer gel and the random chain scission of the ester bonds in PHB segments.[71] The relationship between the protein release and the hydrogel degradation process was also correlated. Due to control of the gel formulation and polymer composition, the release duration of the protein from 20 to 80 days was successfully demonstrated (Figures 14c, d).[71] In addition, the cell growth on the PHB/PEG/PPG poly(ether ester urethane)s hydrogel surface exhibited a typical spindle-like fibroblast morphology; a healthy morphology was maintained after 72 h of incubation. Conversely, the hydrophilic surface of F127 gels inhibited the growth of cells for longer time periods, which suggests that the incorporation of the PHB segment in PHB/PEG/PPG poly(ether ester urethane)s copolymers significantly increased the hydrophobicity of the gel surface, which enhances the cell adhesion capability and facilitates cell growth.[70]

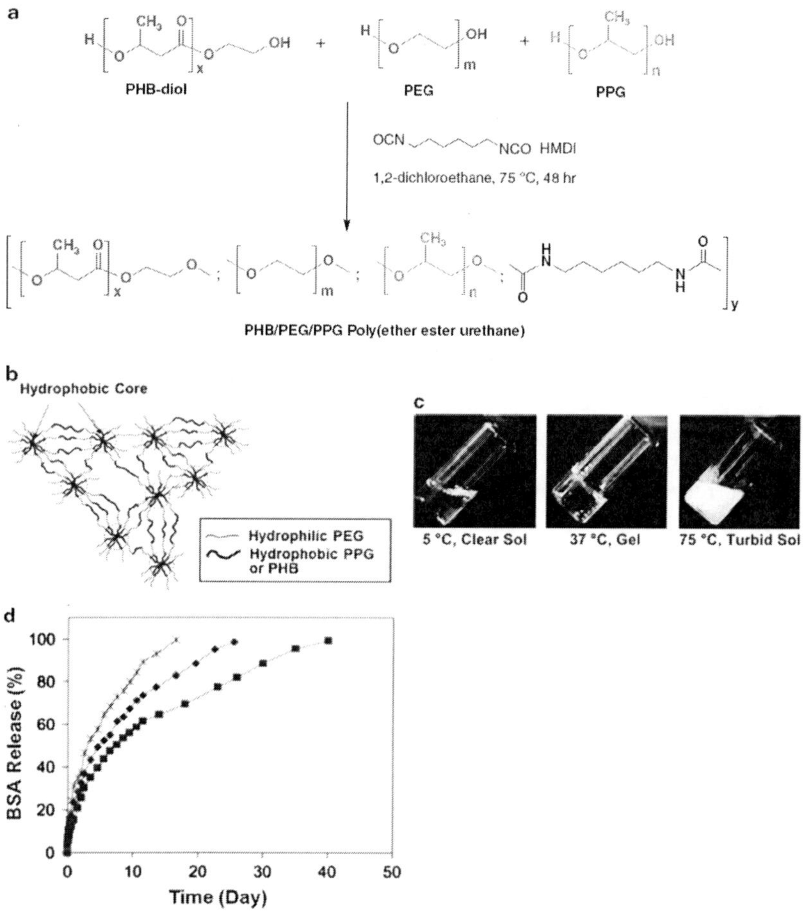

Figure 14. (**a**) Synthesis of PHB/PEG/PPG poly(ether ester urethane) block copolymers, and (**b**) Schematic of associated micelle model depicting network polymer packing gelation; (**c**) Sol-gel-sol transition of the copolymer aqueous solution with increasing temperature. Adapted from reference 69 (2007 American Chemical Society). (**d**) Protein release profiles for PHB/PEG/PPG poly(ether ester urethane) hydrogels of different copolymer compositions. (*: 3 wt%, ♦: 4 wt%, ▪: 5 wt%). Adapted from reference 71 (2007 Elsevier).

PHA-poly(methacrylate) block copolymers and others

The incorporation of poly(meth)acrylates to PHA to form block copolymers is another important strategy for making the newly designed PHA materials accessible to controllable hydrophilicity, pH and temperature responsiveness, as well as therapeutic functions by simple variation of the substitute groups.

Our group previously reported the synthesis of thermoresponsive amphiphilic PNIPAAm-PHB-PNIPAAm triblock copolymers by the combination of esterification and atom transfer radical polymerization (ATRP) (Figure 15a).[72] The obtained PNIPAAm-PHB-PNIPAAm triblock copolymers were water soluble with a LCST range of 28–29 °C in water.[72] At temperatures below the LCST, PNIPAAm-PHB-PNIPAAm self-assembled into core-shell micelle aggregates at 50 mg l^{-1}. At elevated temperatures, the hydrophilic to hydrophobic transition caused the PNIPAAm chains to collapse in the micelle corona, which enabled the formation of smaller particles (Figure 15b). The temperature responsiveness of the micelles was subsequently employed to design a PNIPAAm-PHB-PNIPAAm copolymer-coated surface for nonenzymatic thermal-induced cell detachment in tissue engineering (Figure 15c).[73, 74] In this application, the micelles formed stable coatings on the polyester substrate surface via hydrophobic interactions, which caused the coated surface to exhibit thermoresponsive behaviors, that is, they were hydrophobic at higher temperatures and became hydrophilic when cooled to lower temperatures. Embryonic stem cells and human mesenchymal stem cells were employed in the cell culture to prove the concept of temperature-induced cell detachment. The hydrophobic surface at temperatures above the LCST supports cell adhesion and growth and the detachment of cells at 4 °C without trypsin digestion. Specifically, the embryonic stem cells demonstrated cell morphologies similar to the morphologies cultured using standard cell culture procedure, which indicates that the coatings do not affect the viability of the cells.[74] Human mesenchymal stem cells showed strong intercellular associations, and a sheet of cells was obtained. The preservation of cell–cell and cell–extracellular matrix interactions by this mild technique indicates the high potential of PNIPAAm-PHB-PNIPAAm coating as rapid culture and detachment surfaces, which may be very useful for cell harvesting in tissue regeneration therapies.

Temperature and pH-sensitive amphiphilic triblock copolymers with a central hydrophobic PHB block flanked by two hydrophilic poly(2-(di-methylamino)ethyl methacrylate) (DMAEMA) blocks was prepared.[75] The micelles were employed for drug encapsulation. The effectiveness of pH- and temperature-triggered drug release was investigated. The results revealed a slow rate of drug release at 20 °C, whereas a faster release rate was obtained when the micelle solution was incubated at 37 °C (Figure 16a).[75] The investigation of pH in triggering the drug release demonstrated that a faster rate was obtained at pH 5 compared with the rate at pH 7 (Figure 16b) because the micelles formed at pH 5 were smaller than the micelles formed at pH 7 and possessed a greater surface area for the enhancement of the release rate from the system.[75] These smart micelles were effectively internalized by HeLa cells and exhibited higher *in vitro* drug delivery efficiency than the commercially available Pluronics F127 (Figures 16c and d).[75] With the presence of a positively

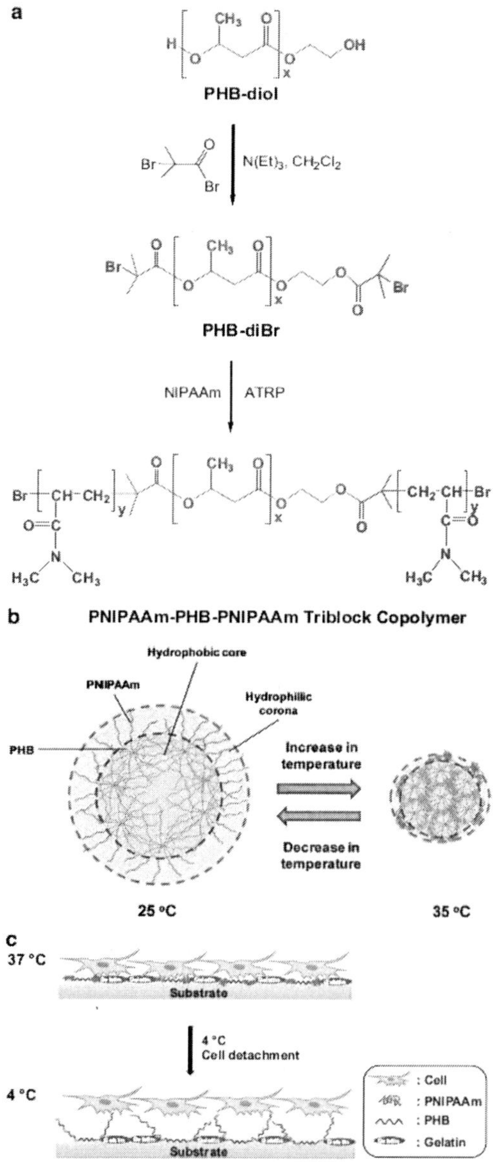

Figure 15. (**a**) Synthesis of PNIPAAm-PHB-PNIPAAm triblock copolymer using PHB-diBr as a macroinitiator in ATRP and (**b**) Thermoresponsive demonstration of PNIPAAm-PHB-PNIPAAm triblock copolymers. Adapted from reference 72 (2009 American Chemical Society). (**c**) Schematic of the temperature-induced cell detachment using a surface that was coated with PNIPAAm-PHB-PNIPAAm triblock copoylmers. Adapted from reference 74 (2009 WILEY-VCH Verlag GmbH & Co. KGaA).

charged tertiary amino group of poly(2-dimethylaminoethyl methacrylate) (PDMAEMA), we also demonstrated that PDMAEMA-PHB-PDMAEMA copolymers can have significant potential as a gene delivery vector to transport plasmid to cells (Figure 16e).[76]

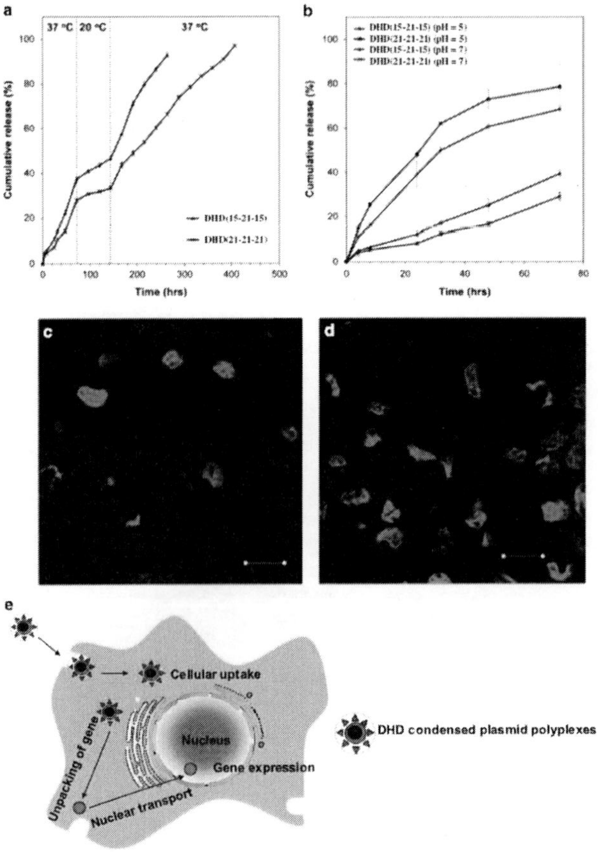

Figure 16. PDMAEMA-PHB-PDMAEMA triblock copolymers are denoted as DHD, and the numbers in brackets indicate the indicative molecular weight of the respective block in hundred g/mol. The effect of temperature (**a**) and pH (**b**) on the drug release profile of PDMAEMA-PHB-PDMAEMA micelles. Confocal images of HeLa cell uptake by incubating with (**c**) Pluronic F127 micelles and (**d**) PDMAEMA-PHB-PDMAEMA, DHD(21-21-21) micelles. The scale bar denotes 20 mm. Adapted from reference 75 (© 2013 Royal Society of Chemistry). (**e**) Schematic of the DHD condensed plasmid polyplexes in gene delivery. Adapted from reference 76 (2013 WILEY-VCH Verlag GmbH & Co. KGaA).

Other types of PHA-modified functional polymers, such as PHA-protein amphiphilic block copolymers were reported via a biosynthetic process. The protein component in this new type of block copolymer can be designed with a specific sequence and end-functionality by genetic engineering. This feature enabled the micelle system to self-assemble from a PHA-protein to a drug carrier with targeting capability (Figure 17). For example, Cys-Asp-Cys-Arg-Gly-Asp-Cys-Phe-Cys (RGD4C) was conjugated to the protein in PHA-protein block copolymer and exhibited strong molecular affinity with integrin overexpressed in cancer cells. The use of PHA as the reservoir of hydrophobic drugs caused RGD4C ligated PHA-protein micelles to exhibit an effective uptake to the targeted MDA-MB-231 breast cancer cells.[77]

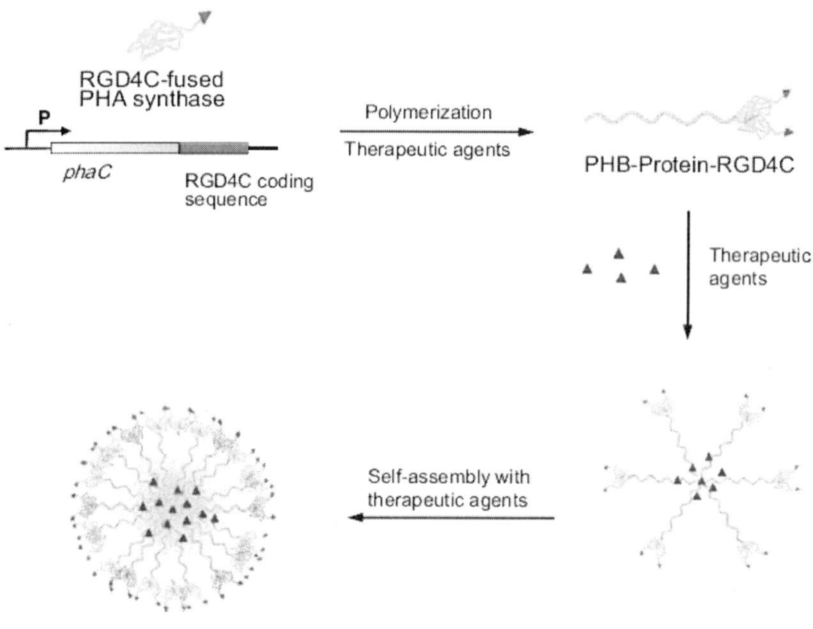

Figure 17. Schematic of PHA-protein block copolymers synthesis with RGD4C as a tumor-targeting ligand in drug delivery. Adapted from reference 77(2013 Royal Society of Chemistry).

CONCLUSIONS AND OUTLOOK

PHAs are a class of diverse polyesters that are naturally produced by various bacteria. These materials are at the forefront of biodegradable and biocompatible polymer research because PHAs and their degradation products are nontoxic after hydrolysis and demonstrate their potential for applications in the medical-related field. Many different approaches have been employed to modify the polyester and its properties. Blending is highlighted due to its ease of processing. Blending enables the facile modification of physical properties, such as T_m, glass transition temperature, crystallinity and mechanical properties. These modifications often produce properties that fall within the extremes yielded by the polymers. This limitation indicates that outstanding properties cannot be formed by blending two different polymers. The blending of polymers is complicated by interfacial interactions between the two polymers. Poor interfacial interactions often cause the deterioration of properties and subsequently poorer mechanical behavior. For this reason, the polymers should be modified by grafting or copolymerization. In these cases, the total polymer property is affected. A hydrophobic polymer can be rendered amphiphilic by these approaches. Analyzing the modification of PHB with PEG enables an understanding of the difference between the two approaches: the blending of PHB with PEG produces a blend system that is inherently hydrophobic, whereas the PEG fraction will leach when exposed to an aqueous solution. The chemical conjugation of the PEG block segment to PHB causes the formation of an amphiphilic copolymer, which is soluble in water. This amphiphilic polymer can be employed in applications, which significantly differs from the potential of applications with simple blends. This polymer can be applied in biomedical applications, such as the solubilization of drugs, the delivery of therapeutics or as carriers of genetic materials. In Table 1, we summarize the properties of the blends and copolymers. In this table, we have also highlighted applications of these materials to showcase the possibilities of these materials.

In addition, some of the PHAs have exhibited features that are similar to the features of conventional synthetic plastics, but with a significantly lower environmental impact on the production process. With an increase in the energy crisis, the renewable and sustainable behaviors of PHAs render them the new generation of eco-friendly plastics based on non-petroleum chemicals. However, many challenges have restrained PHA applications, including complicated genetic engineering processes for producing new PHAs, inadequate mechanical strength and a lack of functionalities. The high production cost and poor processability of PHA have limited their competitive forces to substitute traditional synthetic plastics. Therefore, modification of PHAs to achieve better performance has attracted increasing attention from industry and scientific research organizations and has gained excellent achievements in materials and medical applications.

Table 1 - Material Characteristic Properties of Modified PHAs via Different Methods and Their Applications.

Material type	Polymers	T_m (°C)	T_g (°C)	X_c (%)/T_d (°C)	Mechanical properties	Applications	Reference
Polymer blends	PHB/starch	165.4 to 167.9	67.2 to 87.4	T_d = 200.5 219.7	σ_{max} = 4.99 to 19.7 MPa, E: 578 to 1716 MPa, ε_{max} = 3.5 to 9.8%	Coating materials, cardboard for food package	10
	PHB/SA	171.0 to 175.9	8.6 to 9.9	ND	ND	ND	11
	PHBV/PGA-g-starch	ND	ND	ND	σ_{max} = 16.8 to 24.3 MPa, E: 468 to 539 MPa, ε_{max} = 13 to 18%	ND	12
	PHB/PVAc-g-starch (CSV)	167 to 171	3 to 25	$X_{c,PHB}$ = 32.9 to 66.4 T_d = 268 to 295	ND	ND	13
	PHB/EC	175.3 to 177.0	44.6 to 56.1, annealed samples	$X_{c,PHB}$ = 15.4 to 64.3	ND	ND	15
	PHB/CAB	178.5 to 189.5	6.3 to 12.5	$X_{c,PHB}$ = 40.6 to 53.2	σ_{max} = 13.3 to 29.3 MPa, E: 592.4 to 2288.3 MPa, ε_{max} = 2.2 to 7.3%	ND	16,79
	PHB/lignin	152 to 174	7.0 to 43.0	$X_{c,PHB}$ = 21 to 61	G′ = 3–5 × 10^4 Pa at ω of 1 to 100 rad s^{-1} G″ = 50-1 × 10^5 Pa at ω of 1 to 100 rad s^{-1}	ND	18
	PHB/soda lignin	ND	8.6 to 39.5	T_d = 162 to 212	ND	ND	20
	PHB/PHBHHx	Approximately 152 to 165	Approximately 0.8 to 5.0	ND	E: 500 to 1210 MPa	Scaffolds for tissue engineering with improved biocompatibility	22,23
	PHBV/PLA	PLA:150, PHBV: 170	PLA: 53.2 to 57.6 PHBV: ~3	ND	G′ = 20-1.2 × 10^4 Pa at ω of 0.01 to 100 rad s^{-1}, η = 600 to 1030 Pas at ω of 1 rad s^{-1}	ND	29
	MCL-PHA/PLA	50 to 180	PLA: 55.7 to 57.7, PHA: −32.8– −33.5	$X_{c,PHA}$ = 25 to 58	σ_{max} = 30 to 50 MPa J = 8.1 × 10^{-2}–26.0 × 10^{-2} J	Ductile and tough properties for plastics applications	30,31
	PHB/PLA	174.6 to 175.1	PHB: 9.6 to 11.0 PLA: 48.3 to 54.9	$X_{c,PHB}$ = 55.0 to 56.3	E: 274 to 366 MPa σ_{max} = 6.5 to 8.7 ε_{max} = 3.7 to 27.7%	ND	32
	P3/4HB/PLA stereo-complex (SC)	PLA SC: 218	P3/4HB: -12.5	$X_{c,PLA\ SC}$ = 38.1 to 45.1	σ_{max} = 4.2 to 6.6 MPa, E: 30.8 to 46.7 MPa, ε_{max} = 362.7 to 949.0	Enhanced processabiltiy and enzymatic hydrolysis rates	34
	PHBHHx/PCL	PHBHHx: 95.4 PCL: 61.1	ND	$X_{c,PHBHHx}$ = 10 to 60	E: 190.9 to 324.6 σ_y = 7.7 to 12.2 MPa, T: 0.3 to 3.6 J cm^{-3}	Improved cell adhesion and proliferation for musculoskeletal tissue engineering	35,36
	PHBV/PCL	PCL: 57.0 to 57.5 PHBV: 137 to 152.4	PHBV: 1.3	$X_{c,PHBV}$ = 5 to 40	E: 170 to 1200 MPa σ_y = 9.0 to 12.5 MPa ε_{max} = 8.0 to 25%	Hollow fibers and tubular scaffold in tissue engineering	37,38
Graft copolymer	PHA-g-chitosan PHA: PHB, PHBV, PHO	PHB: 150 to 173 PHBV: 117 to 131 PHO: 80 Chitosan: 105 to 116	ND	T_d = 290 to 308	ND	Drug delivery and tissue engineering	39,40
	PHOU-g-PEG	ND	ND	ND	σ_{max} = 219 to 263 kPa ε_{max} = 379 to 621%	Blood contact device, drug delivery	41,51,52
	PHB-g-PMMA	PHB: 171.8 to 176.8	PHB: 2.5 to 6.0 PMMA: 100 to 102	$X_{c,PHBV}$: 12 to 27	E_b = 3170 to 3300 MPa Gc = 0.7 to 2.3 KJ m^{-2}	Orthopaedic applications.	43,44,49
	PHBV-g-HEMA	138 to 156	2.3 to 63	T_d = 297 to 316	ND	Improved cellular interactions with film	46
	PHBV-g-PVP	140.0 to 158.4	7.7 to 8.6	$X_{c,PHBV}$: 35.5 to 45.9	ND	Increased antibacterial activity	47
Block Copolymer	PHOU-b-PCL	60 to 61.5	−57 – −60	ND	ND	Facilitating biomolecules conjugation	55
	PHB-b-PLA-b-PCL	123.4 to 130.2	−23.5 – −31.2, 11.2 to 32.8	$X_{c,PHB}$: 12.1 to 49.7	ND	Blood contact device	56
	PHB-r-PCL	PCL: 38.0 to 62.7 PHB: 133.0 to 141.0	−18.3 – −62.0	$X_{c,PHB}$: 36.6 to 53.8	σ_{max}: 11.0 to 30.5 MPa ε_{max} = 117 to 990%	nd	57
	P3/4HB-r-PCL	32.3 to 78.4	−21.5 – −40.1	$X_{c,P3/4HB}$: 3.2 to 20.9, T_d = 261.6 to 279.5	ND	Wound-healing materials	58
	P3/4HB-r-P3/4HB[a]	49.8 to 95.4	−10.8 – −48.4	$X_{c,P3/4HB}$: 0.5 to 26.8, T_d = 247.7 to 286.3	ND	Hemostatic materials	59
	P3/4HB-r-P3-/4HB/PHHxHO	44.9 to 75.6	−9.0 – −44.6	$X_{c,P3/4HB}$: 0.4 to 16.9, T_d = 241.9 to 264.8	ND	Hemostatic materials	60
	PHO-r-PHB	61 to 178	−45 –4	ND	E: 200 to 1560 MPa σ_{max} = 7.0 to 38 MPa ε_{max} = 6.3 to 490%		61
						Excellent thermoplastic properties and mechanical properties for medical applications	
	PHB-b-PEG	PEG: 47 to 56 PHB: 122 to 152	ND	ND	ND	Self-assemblies for drug delivery	62
	P (3HV-co-4HB)-b-MPEG	PEG: 53.5	ND	ND	ND	Drug delivery in cancer therapy	63
	PEG-b-PHB-b-PEG	PEG: 23 to 57 PHB: 140 to 153	ND	$X_{c,PHB}$: 53.3 to 73.6 T_d = 382.9 to 391.0	ND	Supramolecular hydrogel for drug delivery	64,80
	PHB-r-PEG	PEG: 31.4 to 61.6 PHB: 82.2 to 148.5	−49 – −33	$X_{c,PHB}$: 9.3 to 44.5 T_d = 260.2 to 279.4	E: 21 to 120 MPa, σ_y: 5.9 to 10.2 MPa, ε_{max}: 11-1912%	Biomaterials with programmed degradation rates	66,67
	P3/4HB-alt-PEG	32.01 to 53.21	−24.16 – −44.26	T_d = 241.7 to 277.9	ND	Hemocompatible materials	68
	PHB-r-PEG-r-PPG	ND	ND	T_d = 227 to 303	η: 0.05 to 0.2 mPa s at 5 °C; 43 to 55 Pa s above 30 °C.	Thermal-responsive hydrogels for protein release and 3D cell culture	69–71
	PNIPAAm-b-PHB-b-PNIPAAM	124.3–142.2	ND	$X_{c,PHB}$: 7.3 to 42.6 T_d = 235.9 to 291.9	ND	Temperature-induced smart surface for cell detachment	72–74
	PDMAEMA-b-PHB-b-PDMAEMA	ND	ND	T_d = 230 to 293	ND	Stimuli-responsive drug delivery and gene delivery	75,76

Abbreviations. CAB, cellulose acetate butyrate; EC, ethyl cellulose; MCL-PHA, medium-chain-length polyhydroxyalkanoates; PGA, polyglycolic acid; PHB, poly(3-hydroxybutyrate); PHBV, poly(3-hydroxybutyrate-co-3-hydroxyvalerate); PLA, Poly(lactic acid); PVAc, polyvinyl acetate); SA, starch acetate.

σ_{max}: Tensile strength, E: Young's modulus, ε_{max}: Elongation at break, G′: Storage modulus, G″: loss modulus, ω: Frequency, J: Total absorbed energy in Charpy impact test, σ_y: yield stress, T: toughness, E_b: Bending modulus in Charpy impact test, G_c: Critical energy release factor, nd: not determined.

[a]P3/4HB with different 4HB contents were employed as prepolymers.

This article summarized the well-established modification approaches of PHAs using two important strategies: physical blending and chemical functionalization. The PHA blends with different types of biodegradable polymers, such as starch, cellulose derivatives, lignin, PLA and PCL, and the chemical modification PHAs to form copolymers in various block/graft architecture were discussed. With significantly altered material properties, modified PHAs have been employed to develop engineering material resins by regulating various physicochemical properties and to enhance the robustness of their use in different biomedical applications, including advanced drug delivery for cancer therapy, gene delivery and tissue engineering in emerging fields. The use of PHAs in the biomedical fields is particularly promising. For biomaterial applications, stringent requirements exist for an implantable system: first, a benign material is required; second, very low toxicity is needed; and third, the material should exhibit long-term stability in a wet, oxygen- and enzyme-rich environment. The living body possesses glutathione and other related enzymes (such as glutathione reductase and glucose-6-phosphate dehydrogenase), which protect various organs from chemical and oxidative stress. The presence of these enzymes can affect the stability of the materials that are implanted in the body. Future PHA material development should emphasize the consideration of these factors. Biodegradable and polymeric soft materials present the future of tissue engineering substrates due to their high water content, density, degradability and rheological properties, which mimic the characteristics of human tissue. Stimuli-responsive PHA-based soft materials have emerged as the material class with the most potential to succeed as an ideal implantable scaffold substitute because it possesses not only the properties of polymeric hydrogels but also added functionalities, such as the change from reversible sol to gel, due to external stimuli that facilitate easy implementation during surgery. In addition, the majority of these hydrogels have shown their efficacy as a drug delivery system. The mechanism and rate of drug release of these systems should be examined if their use for drug release in the body is desired. Additional tests to prove the biocompatibility of PHA with cells should also be performed before *in vivo* studies are conducted. To examine the suitability of the polymeric hydrogels, their material properties and the clinical signs of the study subject must be accurately and comprehensively examined. A collection and thorough analysis of all vital signs and clinical information will enable the well-informed clinician to determine a material's ultimate suitability as a successful long-term biomaterial. With continuous efforts to obtain a large-scale supply of PHA, the development of PHA as new biodegradable material will open doors for a new future.

CONFLICT OF INTEREST

The authors declare no conflict of interest.

REFERENCES

1. Yu, L., Dean, K. & Li, L. Polymer blends and composites from renewable resources. Prog. Polym. Sci. 31, 576–602 (2006).

2. Chen, G. Q. A microbial polyhydroxyalkanoates (PHA) based bio- and materials industry. Chem. Soc. Rev. 38, 2434–2446 (2009).

3. Kai, D., Low, Z. W., Liow, S. S., Abdul Karim, A., Ye, H., Jin, G., Li, K. & Loh, X., J. Development of Lignin Supramolecular Hydrogels with Mechanically Responsive and Self-Healing Properties. ACS Sustain Chem Eng. 3, 2160–2169 (2015).

4. Li, Z. & Loh, X. J. Water soluble polyhydroxyalkanoates: future materials for therapeutic applications. Chem. Soc. Rev. 44, 2865–2879 (2015).

5. Kim, D. Y., Kim, H. W., Chung, M. G. & Rhee, Y. H. Biosynthesis, modification, and biodegradation of bacterial medium-chain-length polyhydroxyalkanoates. J Microbiol 45, 87–97 (2007).

6. Andrade, A. P., Witholt, B., Chang, D. & Li, Z. Synthesis and characterization of novel thermoplastic polyester containing blocks of poly[(R)-3-hydroxyoctanoate] and poly[(R)-3-hydroxybutyrate].Macromolecules 36, 9830–9835 (2003).

7. Hazer, B. & Steinbüchel, A. Increased diversification of polyhydroxyalkanoates by modification reactions for industrial and medical applications. Appl. Microbiol. Biotechnol. 74, 1–12 (2007). CAS

8. Rai, R., Keshavarz, T., Roether, J. A., Boccaccini, A. R. & Roy, I. Medium chain length polyhydroxyalkanoates, promising new biomedical materials for the future. Mater. Sci. Eng. R Rep. 72, 29–47 (2011).

9. Pilkington, S. M., Encke, B., Krohn, N., Hoehne, M., Stitt, M. & Pyl, E. T. Relationship between starch degradation and carbon demand for maintenance and growth in Arabidopsis thaliana in different irradiance and temperature regimes. Plant Cell Environ. 38, 157–171 (2015).

10. Godbole, S., Gote, S., Latkar, M. & Chakrabarti, T. Preparation and characterization of biodegradable poly-3-hydroxybutyrate–starch blend films. Bioresour. Technol. 86, 33–37 (2003).

11. Zhang, L., Deng, X., Zhao, S. & Huang, Z. Biodegradable polymer blends of poly(3-hydroxybutyrate) and starch acetate. Polym. Int. 44, 104–110 (1997).

12. Willett, J. L., Kotnis, M. A., O'Brien, G. S., Fanta, G. F. & Gordon, S. H. Properties of starch-graft-poly(glycidyl methacrylate)–PHBV composites. J. Appl. Polym. Sci. 70, 1121–1127 (1998).

13. Lai, S.-M., Sun, W.-W. & Don, T.-M. Preparation and characterization of biodegradable polymer blends from poly(3-

hydroxybutyrate)/poly(vinyl acetate)-modified corn starch. Polym. Eng. Sci. 55, 1321–1329 (2015).

14. Wang, C., Venditti, R. A. & Zhang, K. Tailor-made functional surfaces based on cellulose-derived materials. Appl. Microbiol. Biotechnol. 99, 5791–5799 (2015).

15. Zhang, L., Deng, X. & Huang, Z. Miscibility, thermal behaviour and morphological structure of poly(3-hydroxybutyrate) and ethyl cellulose binary blends. Polymer 38, 5379–5387 (1997).

16. El-Shafee, E., Saad, G. R. & Fahmy, S. M. Miscibility, crystallization and phase structure of poly(3-hydroxybutyrate)/cellulose acetate butyrate blends. Eur. Polym. J. 37, 2091–2104 (2001).

17. Balahmar, N., Mitchell, A. C. & Mokaya, R. Generalized mechanochemical synthesis of biomass-derived sustainable carbons for high performance CO2storage. Adv. Energy Mater. 5, 1500867 (2015).

18. Mousavioun, P., Halley, P. J. & Doherty, W. O. S. Thermophysical properties and rheology of PHB/lignin blends. Ind. Crops Prod. 50, 270–275 (2013).

19. Weihua, K., He, Y., Asakawa, N. & Inoue, Y. Effect of lignin particles as a nucleating agent on crystallization of poly(3-hydroxybutyrate). J. Appl. Polym. Sci. 94, 2466–2474 (2004).

20. Mousavioun, P., Doherty, W. O. S. & George, G. Thermal stability and miscibility of poly(hydroxybutyrate) and soda lignin blends. Ind. Crops Prod. 32, 656–661 (2010).

21. Mousavioun, P., George, G. A. & Doherty, W. O. S. Environmental degradation of lignin/poly(hydroxybutyrate) blends. Polym. Degrad. Stab.97, 1114–1122 (2012).

22. Yang, X., Zhao, K. & Chen, G.-Q. Effect of surface treatment on the biocompatibility of microbial polyhydroxyalkanoates. Biomaterials 23, 1391–1397 (2002).

23. Kai, Z., Ying, D. & Guo-Qiang, C. Effects of surface morphology on the biocompatibility of polyhydroxyalkanoates. Biochem. Eng. J. 16, 115–123 (2003).

24. Yoshie, N., Saito, M. & Inoue, Y. Effect of chemical compositional distribution on solid-state structures and properties of poly(3-

hydroxybutyrate-co-3-hydroxyvalerate). Polymer 45, 1903–1911 (2004).

25. Saad, G. R. Blends of bacterial poly[(R)-3-hydroxybutyrate] with oligo[(R,S)-3-hydroxybutyrate]-diol. Polym. Int. 51, 338–348 (2002).

26. Tsuji, H. & Fukui, I. Enhanced thermal stability of poly(lactide)s in the melt by enantiomeric polymer blending. Polymer 44, 2891–2896 (2003).

27. Ohkoshi, I., Abe, H. & Doi, Y. Miscibility and solid-state structures for blends of poly[(S)-lactide] with atactic poly[(R,S)-3-hydroxybutyrate].Polymer 41, 5985–5992 (2000).

28. Koyama, N. & Doi, Y. Miscibility of binary blends of poly[(R)-3-hydroxybutyric acid] and poly[(S)-lactic acid]. Polymer 38, 1589–1593 (1997).

29. Gerard, T. & Budtova, T. Morphology and molten-state rheology of polylactide and polyhydroxyalkanoate blends. Eur. Polym. J. 48, 1110–1117 (2012).

30. Noda, I., Satkowski, M. M., Dowrey, A. E. & Marcott, C. Polymer alloys of nodax copolymers and poly(lactic acid). Macromol. Biosci. 4, 269–275 (2004).

31. Takagi, Y., Yasuda, R., Yamaoka, M. & Yamane, T. Morphologies and mechanical properties of polylactide blends with medium chain length poly(3-hydroxyalkanoate) and chemically modified poly(3-hydroxyalkanoate). J. Appl. Polym. Sci. 93, 2363–2369 (2004).

32. Zhang, L., Xiong, C. & Deng, X. Miscibility, crystallization and morphology of poly(β-hydroxybutyrate)/poly(d,l-lactide) blends. Polymer 37, 235–241 (1996).

33. Furukawa, T., Sato, H., Murakami, R., Zhang, J., Noda, I., Ochiai, S. & Ozaki, Y. Comparison of miscibility and structure of poly(3-hydroxybutyrate-co-3-hydroxyhexanoate)/poly(l-lactic acid) blends with those of poly(3-hydroxybutyrate)/poly(l-lactic acid) blends studied by wide angle X-ray diffraction, differential scanning calorimetry, and FTIR microspeçtroscopy. Polymer 48, 1749–1755 (2007).

34. Zhao, H., Bian, Y., Li, Y., Dong, Q., Han, C. & Dong, L. Bioresource-based blends of poly(3-hydroxybutyrate-co-4-hydroxybutyrate) and stereocomplex polylactide with improved rheological and mechanical properties and enzymatic hydrolysis. J. Mater. Chem. A 2, 8881 (2014).

35. Lim, J., Chong, M. S. K., Teo, E. Y., Chen, G.-Q., Chan, J. K. Y. & Teoh, S.-H. Biocompatibility studies and characterization of poly(3-hydroxybutyrate-co-3-hydroxyhexanoate)/polycaprolactone blends. J. Biomed. Mater. Res. Part B Appl. Biomater. 101B, 752–761 (2013).

36. Chen, G.-Q. & Wu, Q. Microbial production and applications of chiral hydroxyalkanoates. Appl. Microbiol. Biotechnol. 67, 592–599 (2005).

37. Chiono, V., Ciardelli, G., Vozzi, G., Sotgiu, M. G., Vinci, B., Domenici, C. & Giusti, P Poly(3-hydroxybutyrate-co-3-hydroxyvalerate)/poly(ε-caprolactone) blends for tissue engineering applications in the form of hollow fibers. J. Biomed. Mater. Res. A 85A, 938–953 (2008).

38. Del Gaudio, C., Fioravanzo, L., Folin, M., Marchi, F., Ercolani, E. & Bianco, A. Electrospun tubular scaffolds: on the effectiveness of blending poly (ε-caprolactone) with poly (3-hydroxybutyrate-co-3-hydroxyvalerate). J. Biomed. Mater. Res. Part B Appl. Biomater. 100, 1883–1898 (2012).

39. Yalpani, M., Marchessault, R. H., Morin, F. G. & Monasterios, C. J. Synthesis of poly(3-hydroxyalkanoate) (PHA) conjugates: PHA-carbohydrate and PHA-synthetic polymer conjugates. Macromolecules 24, 6046–6049 (1991).

40. Arslan, H., Hazer, B. & Yoon, S. C. Grafting of poly(3-hydroxyalkanoate) and linoleic acid onto chitosan. J. Appl. Polym. Sci. 103, 81–89 (2007).

41. Chung, C. W., Kim, H. W., Kim, Y. B. & Rhee, Y. H. Poly(ethylene glycol)-grafted poly(3-hydroxyundecenoate) networks for enhanced blood compatibility. Int. J. Biol. Macromol. 32, 17–22 (2003).

42. Kowalczuk, M., Adamus, G. & Jedlinski, Z. Synthesis of new graft polymers via anionic grafting of.beta.-butyrolactone on poly(methyl methacrylate).Macromolecules 27, 572–575 (1994).

43. Avella, M., Errico, M. E., Immirzi, B., Malinconico, M., Falcigno, L. & Paolillo, L. Preparation of poly(β-hydroxybutyrate)/poly(methyl methacrylate) blends by reactive blending and their characterisation.Macromol. Chem. Phys. 199, 1901–1907 (1998).

44. Mitomo, H., Watanabe, Y., Yoshii, F. & Makuuchi, K. Radiation effect on polyesters. Radiat. Phys. Chem. 46, 233–238 (1995).

45. Grøndahl, L., Chandler-Temple, A. & Trau, M. Polymeric grafting of acrylic acid onto poly(3-hydroxybutyrate-co-3-hydroxyvalerate): surface functionalization for tissue engineering applications. Biomacromolecules 6, 2197–2203 (2005).

46. Lao, H.-K., Renard, E., Linossier, I., Langlois, V. & Vallée-Rehel, K. Modification of poly(3-hydroxybutyrate-co-3-hydroxyvalerate) film by chemical graft copolymerization. Biomacromolecules 8, 416–423 (2007).

47. Saad, G. R., Elsawy, M. A. & Elsabee, M. Z. Preparation, characterization and antimicrobial activity of poly(3-hydroxybutyrate-co-3-hydroxyvalerate)-g-poly(n-vinylpyrrolidone) copolymers. Polym. Plast. Technol. Eng. 51, 1113–1121 (2012).

48. Nguyen, S. & Marchessault, R. H. Atom transfer radical copolymerization of bacterial poly(3-hydroxybutyrate) macromonomers and methyl methacrylate. Macromolecules 38, 290–296 (2005).

49. Nguyen, S. & Marchessault, R. H. Graft copolymers of methyl methacrylate and poly([R]-3-hydroxybutyrate) macromonomers as candidates for inclusion in acrylic bone cement formulations: compression testing. J. Biomed. Mater. Res. B Appl. Biomater. 77B, 5–12 (2006).

50. Le Fer, G., Babinot, J., Versace, D.-L., Langlois, V. & Renard, E. An efficient thiol-ene chemistry for the preparation of amphiphilic pha-based graft copolymers. Macromol. Rapid Commun. 33, 2041–2045 (2012).

51. Babinot, J., Guigner, J.-M., Renard, E. & Langlois, V. Poly(3-hydroxyalkanoate)-derived amphiphilic graft copolymers for the design of polymersomes. Chem. Commun. 48, 5364–5366 (2012).

52. Renard, E., Ternat, C., Langlois, V. & Guerin, P. Synthesis of graft bacterial polyesters for nanoparticles preparation. Macromol. Biosci. 3, 248–252 (2003).

53. Zhou, L., Chen, Z., Chi, W., Yang, X., Wang, W. & Zhang, B. Mono-methoxy-poly(3-hydroxybutyrate-co-4-hydroxybutyrate)-graft-hyper-branched polyethylenimine copolymers for siRNA delivery. Biomaterials33, 2334–2344 (2012).

54. Reeve, M. S., McCarthy, S. P. & Gross, R. A. Preparation and characterization of (R)-poly(.beta.-hydroxybutyrate)-poly(.epsilon.-caprolactone) and (R)-poly(.beta.-hydroxybutyrate)-poly(lactide) degradable diblock copolymers. Macromolecules 26, 888–894 (1993).

55. Timbart, L., Renard, E., Tessier, M. & Langlois, V. Monohydroxylated poly(3-hydroxyoctanoate) oligomers and its functionalized derivatives

used as macroinitiators in the synthesis of degradable diblock copolyesters.Biomacromolecules 8, 1255–1265 (2007).

56. Wu, L. P., Chen, S. T., Li, Z. B., Xu, K. T. & Chen, G. Q. Synthesis, characterization and biocompatibility of novel biodegradable poly ((R)-3-hydroxybutyrate)-block-(D,L-lactide)-block-(epsilon-caprolac tone) triblock copolymers. Polym. Int. 57, 939–949 (2008).

57. Saad, G. R., Lee, Y. J. & Seliger, H. Synthesis and characterization of biodegradable poly(ester-urethanes) based on bacterial poly(R-3-hydroxybutyrate). J. Appl. Polym. Sci. 83, 703–718 (2002).

58. Qiu, H., Li, D., Chen, X., Fan, K., Ou, W., Chen, K. C. & Xu, K Synthesis, characterizations, and biocompatibility of block poly(ester-urethane)s based on biodegradable poly(3-hydroxybutyrate-co-4-hydroxybutyrate) (P3/4HB) and poly(ε-caprolactone). J. Biomed. Mater. Res. A 101A, 75–86 (2013).

59. Ou, W., Qiu, H., Chen, Z. & Xu, K. Biodegradable block poly(ester-urethane)s based on poly(3-hydroxybutyrate-co-4-hydroxybutyrate) copolymers. Biomaterials 32, 3178–3188 (2011).

60. Chen, Z. F., Cheng, S. T. & Xu, K. T. Block poly(ester-urethane)s based on poly(3-hydroxybutyrate-co-4-hydroxybutyrate) and poly(3-hydroxyhexanoate-co-3-hydroxyoctanoate). Biomaterials 30, 2219–2230 (2009).

61. Andrade, A. P., Neuenschwander, P., Hany, R., Egli, T., Witholt, B. & Li, Z. Synthesis and characterization of novel copoly(ester–urethane) containing blocks of poly-[(R)-3-hydroxyoctanoate] and poly-[(R)-3-hydroxybutyrate].Macromolecules 35, 4946–4950 (2002).

62. Ravenelle, F. & Marchessault, R. H. One-Step synthesis of amphiphilic diblock copolymers from bacterial poly([R]-3-hydroxybutyric acid).Biomacromolecules 3, 1057–1064 (2002).

63. Shah, M., Ullah, N., Choi, M. H., Kim, M. O. & Yoon, S. C. Amorphous amphiphilic P(3HV-co-4HB)-b-mPEG block copolymer synthesized from bacterial copolyester via melt transesterification: Nanoparticle preparation, cisplatin-loading for cancer therapy and in vitro evaluation. Eur. J. Pharm. Sci. 80, 518–527 (2012).

64. Li, J., Li, X., Ni, X. P. & Leong, K. W. Synthesis and characterization of new biodegradable amphiphilic poly(ethylene oxide)-b-poly (R)-3-hydroxy butyratel-b-poly(ethylene oxide) triblock copolymers. Macromolecules 36, 2661–2667 (2003).

65. Li, J., Li, X., Ni, X. P., Wang, X., Li, H. Z. & Leong, K. W. Self-assembled supramolecular hydrogels formed by biodegradable PEO-PHB-PEO triblock copolymers and alpha-cyclodextrin for controlled drug delivery.Biomaterials 27, 4132–4140 (2006). CAS |

66. Li, X., Loh, X. J., Wang, K., He, C. & Li, J. Poly(ester urethane)s consisting of poly[(R)-3-hydroxybutyrate] and poly(ethylene glycol) as candidate biomaterials: characterization and mechanical property study.Biomacromolecules 6, 2740–2747 (2005).

67. Loh, X. J., Tan, K. K., Li, X. & Li, J. The in vitro hydrolysis of poly(ester urethane)s consisting of poly[(R)-3-hydroxybutyrate] and poly(ethylene glycol). Biomaterials 27, 1841–1850 (2006).

68. Pan, J. Y., Li, G. Y., Chen, Z. F., Chen, X. Y., Zhu, W. F. & Xu, K. T. Alternative block polyurethanes based on poly(3-hydroxybutyrate-co-4-hydroxybutyrate) and poly(ethylene glycol). Biomaterials 30, 2975–2984 (2009).

69. Loh, X. J., Goh, S. H. & Li, J. New biodegradable thermogelling copolymers having very low gelation concentrations. Biomacromolecules 8, 585–593 (2007).

70. Loh, X. J., Goh, S. H. & Li, J. Biodegradable thermogelling poly[(R)-3-hydroxybutyrate]-based block copolymers: micellization, gelation, and cytotoxicity and cell culture studies. J. Phys. Chem. B 113, 11822–11830 (2009).

71. Loh, X. J., Goh, S. H. & Li, J. Hydrolytic degradation and protein release studies of thermogelling polyurethane copolymers consisting of poly[(R)-3-hydroxybutyrate], poly(ethylene glycol), and poly(propylene glycol).Biomaterials 28, 4113–4123 (2007).

72. Loh, X. J., Zhang, Z. X., Wu, Y. L., Lee, T. S. & Li, J. Synthesis of novel biodegradable thermoresponsive triblock copolymers based on poly[(R)-3-hydroxybutyrate] and poly(n-isopropylacrylamide) and their formation of thermoresponsive micelles. Macromolecules 42, 194–202 (2009).

73. Loh, X. J., Cheong, W. C. D., Li, J. & Ito, Y. Novel poly(N-isopropylacrylamide)-poly (R)-3-hydroxybutyrate -poly(N-isopropyl acrylamide) triblock copolymer surface as a culture substrate for human mesenchymal stem cells. Soft Matter 5, 2937–2946 (2009).

74. Loh, X. J., Gong, J. S., Sakuragi, M., Kitajima, T., Liu, M. Z., Li, J. & Ito, Y Surface coating with a thermoresponsive copolymer for the culture

and non-enzymatic recovery of mouse embryonic stem cells. Macromol. Biosci.9, 1069–1079 (2009). CAS |

75. Loh, X. J., Ong, S. J., Tung, Y. T. & Choo, H. T. Dual responsive micelles based on poly[(R)-3-hydroxybutyrate] and poly(2-(dimethylamino)ethyl methacrylate) for effective doxorubicin delivery. Polym. Chem. 4, 2564–2574 (2013).

76. Loh, X. J., Ong, S. J., Tung, Y. T. & Choo, H. T. Incorporation of poly[(R)-3-hydroxybutyrate] into cationic copolymers based on poly(2-(dimethylamino)ethyl methacrylate) to improve gene delivery. Macromol. Biosci. 13, 1092–1099 (2013).

77. Kim, H. N., Lee, J., Kim, H. Y. & Kim, Y. R. Enzymatic synthesis of a drug delivery system based on polyhydroxyalkanoate-protein block copolymers.Chem. Commun. 46, 7104–7106 (2009).

78. Sudesh, K., Abe, H. & Doi, Y. Synthesis, structure and properties of polyhydroxyalkanoates: biological polyesters. Prog. Polym. Sci. 25, 1503–1555 (2000).

79. Wang, T., Cheng, G., Ma, S., Cai, Z. & Zhang, L. Crystallization behavior, mechanical properties, and environmental biodegradability of poly(β-hydroxybutyrate)/cellulose acetate butyrate blends. J. Appl. Polym. Sci. 89, 2116–2122 (2003).

80. Li, J., Li, X., Ni, X., Wang, X., Li, H. & Leong, K. W. Self-assembled supramolecular hydrogels formed by biodegradable PEO-PHB-PEO triblock copolymers and [alpha]-cyclodextrin for controlled drug delivery.Biomaterials 27, 4132–4140 (2006). CAS |

Chapter 8

Thermo-Responsive Injectable MPEG-Polyester Diblock Copolymers for Sustained Drug Release

Hoon Hyun [1,†], Seung Hun Park [1,†], Doo Yeon Kwon [1], Gilson Khang [2], Hai Bang Lee [1] and Moon Suk Kim [1,*]

[1]*Department of Molecular Science and Technology, Ajou University, Suwon 443-749, Korea*

[2]*Department of BIN Fusion Technology, Chonbuk National University, Jeonju 561-756, Korea*

ABSTRACT

Thermo-responsive diblock copolymers composed of hydrophilic methoxy poly(ethylene glycol) (MPEG) and hydrophobic biodegradable polyesters were prepared for application as injectable drug delivery systems, because they show a thermo-responsive sol-to-gel transition, especially around body temperature, when dispersed in aqueous solutions. The thermogelling hydrogels formed by hydrophobic aggregation could be varied by changing the components of the hydrophobic polyester part. For the polyester block in the present study, 95 mol% of ε-caprolactone (CL) was used for the main polyester chain and 5 mol% of *p*-dioxanone (DO) was copolymerized randomly by the MPEG initiator in the presence of HCl as the catalyst. By adding a small portion of DO into the poly ε-caprolactone (PCL) chains, the temperature range of gelation, the intensity of viscosity and the drug release behavior were changed. The MPEG-*b*-poly(ε-caprolactone-*ran*-*p*-dioxanone) (MPEG-*b*-PCDO) hydrogel showed the enhanced drug release *in vitro* and *in vivo* compared to MPEG-*b*-PCL hydrogel. Therefore, MPEG-polyester hydrogels may serve as minimally invasive and therapeutic, injectable hydrogel systems with adjustable temperature-responsive and biodegradable windows, as well as sustained release of drugs over a certain time period.

Keywords: thermo-responsive hydrogels; biodegradable polyesters; block copolymers; sustained release

1. INTRODUCTION

Thermo-responsive hydrogels have been developed for the delivery of injectable drugs because: (i) the formulation with drugs is relatively easy; and (ii) the drug delivery can be localized and prolonged [1,2,3,4,5]. Thermo-responsive polymers can be composed of amphiphilic block copolymers. If dispersed in aqueous solutions, they initially assemble into micelles and form "bridged" networks of micelles. These bridged micelles undergo arranged packing triggered by temperature changes to form a macroscopic gel. Thus, the sol-to-gel or gel-to-sol phase transitions are affected by the following conditions: concentration of amphiphilic block copolymer, di-, tri- or multi-block structures, the molecular weight (MW) of block components and the interactions of hydrophobic segments (e.g., hydrophobic interactions, crystallinity, stereocomplexation) [6,7,8,9,10,11]. Commercially available poloxamers and pluronics comprising poly(ethylene oxide) (PEO) and poly(propylene oxide) (PPO) are representatives of thermo-responsive hydrogels. However, they have several drawbacks for easy clinical applications, such as poor mechanical properties, high permeability, short persistence time and non-biodegradability [12,13]. As reported by several research groups, the PPO blocks of thermo-responsive hydrogels have been replaced with biodegradable polyester blocks to overcome these limitations. In particular, the aliphatic polyester groups, such as polyglycolide (PGA), polylactic acid (PLA) and poly ε-caprolactone (PCL), have been studied with regard to the preparation of thermosensitive hydrogels and tissue engineering scaffolds, due to their excellent biodegradability and biocompatibility [14,15,16,17,18].

During the last decade, our group has reported a thermo-responsive hydrogel comprising methoxy polyethylene glycol (MPEG) and PCL (MPEG-*b*-PCL) that showed a sol-to-gel phase transition at body temperature when dispersed in aqueous solutions at certain concentrations. In various studies, the MPEG-*b*-PCL diblock copolymer has been used as an *in vivo*carrier for the delivery of protein drugs and as a scaffold for cell growth [19,20,21,22,23,24]. The MPEG-*b*-PCL diblock copolymer was shown to be a good candidate for injectable thermo-responsive hydrogels, and therefore, several approaches to modify the MPEG-*b*-PCL diblock copolymer have been employed for more controllable delivery of drugs [25].

To prepare diverse thermo-responsive hydrogels, we reported that the incorporation of L-lactide (LA), *p*-dioxanone (DO) and trimethylene carbonate (TMC) into the PCL block can be accomplished with PCL in various ratios and that thermosensitive gelation could be maintained at body temperature. Random copolymers using CL, LA, DO and TMC are more favorable than PLA and poly(lactic-*co*-glycolic acid) PLGA copolymers if used for biomedical applications, because their degradation does not result in an acidic environment. However, PLA and PLGA copolymers in biological conditions are degraded rapidly and release acidic byproducts known to be deleterious to bioactive drugs and cells.

By varying the ratio of components and copolymer composition or by modifying the polymer through chemical means, the properties of the carriers (including hydrophobicity and crystallinity) can change and adjust to present suitable degradation behavior and well-designed drug release.

Therefore, in the present study, we prepared MPEG-*b*-poly(ε-caprolactone-*ran*-*p*-dioxanone) (MPEG-*b*-PCDO) diblock copolymer arranged by 95:5 mol% polyester block and examined the sol-to-gel phase transition at body temperature. Furthermore, we demonstrated the sustained release of protein drugs *in vitro* and *in vivo* using MPEG-*b*-PCDO copolymer hydrogels.

2. EXPERIMENTAL SECTION

2.1. Materials

MPEG (number-average molecular weight (M_n = 750 g/mol)) and HCl (1.0 M solution in diethyl ether), both from Sigma-Aldrich (Saint Louis, MO, USA), were used as received. CL was distilled over CaH_2 under reduced pressure. DO (Metabio, Seoul, South Korea) was used as received. CH_2Cl_2 was distilled sequentially from $CaCl_2$ and CaH_2 under nitrogen before use. Pluronic F-127 (BASF, Ludwigshafen, Germany) is a polymer of PEO and PPO with two 100-unit hydrophilic PEO chains surrounding one 65-unit hydrophobic PPO chain and a total weight of 12,600 g/mol; it was used as received. Fluorescein isothiocyanate-labeled bovine serum albumin (BSA-FITC) and bovine-insulin (Zn salt, 28.8 IU/mg) were purchased from Sigma-Aldrich (Saint Louis, MO, USA).

2.2. Characterization

Proton nuclear magnetic resonance (^{1}H NMR) spectra were measured using a Bruker 300-MHz instrument (Billerica, MA, USA) with $CDCl_3$ in the presence of tetramethylsilane (TMS) as the internal standard. Molecular-weight distributions of MPEG-polyester diblock copolymers were measured with an At-3000 GPC system (Shodex RI-71 detector; Futects, Seoul, South Korea) using two columns (Shodex K-802; Futects, Seoul, South Korea) and Shodex Asahipak GF-510; Futects, Seoul, South Korea). $CHCl_3$ was used as the eluent at a flow rate of 0.6 mL/min. The viscosity of polymer solutions was measured using a viscometer (DV-III Ultra; Brookfield Engineering; Middleboro, MA, USA) with a programmable rheometer and circulating baths with a programmable controller (TC-502P). Viscosity measurements in the vessel were undertaken using a tight cap to prevent the evaporation of water in the polymer solution. The viscosity of polymer solutions was investigated using a T-F spindle at 0.2 rpm from 6 to 70 °C in increments of 1 °C.

2.3. Synthesis of MPEG-b-poly(ε-caprolactone) (MPEG-b-PCL) and MPEG-b-poly(ε-caprolactone-ran-p-dioxanone) (MPEG-b-PCDO) Diblock Copolymers

MPEG (M_n = 750 g/mol) (1.5 g, 2 mmol) and toluene (30 mL) were introduced into a flask. The MPEG solution underwent azeotropic distillation to remove water. Toluene was then distilled off completely. CH_2Cl_2 (91 mL) was added to MPEG, followed by the addition of CL (4.8 g, 42 mmol) for MPEG-*b*-PCL, CL (4.8 g, 42 mmol) and DO (0.14 g, 1.7 mmol) for MPEG-*b*-PCDO, respectively. Polymerization was initiated by the addition of a 1.0 M solution of HCl in diethyl ether (4 mL, 4 mmol) at 25 °C. After 24 h, the reaction mixture was poured into *n*-hexane to precipitate a polymer, which was separated from the supernatant by decantation. The obtained polymer was re-dissolved in CH_2Cl_2 and filtered. The polymer solution was concentrated by a rotary evaporator and dried *in vacuo* to give a colorless polymer of quantitative yield. The MW of the PCL and poly(*p*-dioxanone) (PDO) segments in the diblock copolymer was determined by comparison of the intensity of the signal of the terminal methoxy proton of MPEG at δ = 3.38 ppm, the signal of the methylene proton of PCL at δ = 2.31 ppm and the signals of the methylene protons of PDO at δ = 4.15 ppm in ^{1}H NMR spectroscopy.

2.4. In Vitro Gel Formation and Protein Release Study

Vials (10 mL) containing 5-mL solutions of 20 wt% Pluronic F127, MPEG-*b*-PCL and MPEG-*b*-PCDO block copolymers in phosphate-buffered saline (PBS) were immersed in a water bath at 80 °C to dissolve the block copolymer above the melting temperature of PCL. Solutions were then left overnight at 4 °C. For the protein-release experiment, 1 wt% BSA-FITC was added to the diblock copolymer solution at room temperature, and the mixture was mixed gently. A 1-mL aliquot of the diblock copolymer solution containing BSA-FITC was taken from the 5-mL solution, transferred to fresh 5-mL vials and incubated at 37 °C for 1 h to form a gel. Then, 4 mL of PBS at 37 °C was added to each gel, and the vial was shaken at 100 rpm at 37 °C. At specified sample collection times, 1 mL of solution was removed from the vial, and 1 mL of fresh PBS at 37 °C was added to the vial. Fluorescence spectroscopy (F-4500; Hitachi, Tokyo, Japan) was conducted immediately on the removed solution. The amount of cumulatively released BSA was calculated by comparison with a standard calibration curve prepared through measurements of solutions of BSA-FITC in PBS with various known concentrations. The released and remained amounts of BSA-FITC in block copolymer gels were individually calculated and compared with initial loaded BSA-FITC. The initial amount of loaded BSA-FITC showed almost similar amounts with the combined amount of released and remaining BSA-FITC. Three independent protein-release experiments were carried out for each gel composition.

2.5. In Vivo Gel Formation and Protein Release Study

To test the *in vivo* gel formation behavior of the MPEG-*b*-PCDO diblock copolymer, polymer solutions were injected into rats. Polymers were sterilized using ethylene oxide (EO) gas. Twelve Sprague–Dawley (SD) rats (320–350 g, 8 weeks), divided into three groups of four rats each, and were used in the release tests. The protocols of this study were approved by the Institutional Animal Experiment Committee at Ajou University School of Medicine (Gyeonggi-do, South Korea). The protocols of this study were carried out in accordance with the approved guidelines.

Three types of gel formulations were used in the in vivo release experiments: (i) a mixture of 1 mL of 20 wt% MPEG-*b*-PCL solution and 1 mg of BSA-FITC or bovine-insulin; (ii) a mixture of 1 mL of 20 wt% MPEG-*b*-PCDO solution and 1 mg of BSA-FITC or bovine-insulin; and (iii) a mixture of 1 mL of 20 wt% Pluronic F-127 solution and 1 mg of BSA-FITC or bovine-insulin. Each gel formulation was prepared by dissolving the diblock copolymer in PBS and incubating at 4 °C for 1 day. Bovine-insulin was then added, resulting in the mixed solution. Within 5 min of the addition of bovine-insulin, a 1-cm^3 syringe with a 26-G needle was used to inject 0.5 mL of the solution into the subcutaneous dorsum of a rat that had been anesthetized with ethyl ether. Resulting gels were used over 2 months for in vivo release experiments.

For the *in vivo* detection of BSA-FITC and bovine-insulin, an aliquot of blood was drawn from the tail vein of each rat at specified blood-collection times. A 0.3-mL aliquot of blood from the catheterized tail vein was collected in an Eppendorf tube and mixed with 0.2 mL of a 1:499 mixture of heparin and saline, followed by vortex-mixing. To obtain plasma, the blood solution was centrifuged at 10,000 rpm for 5 min at room temperature. Distilled water (100 μL), 66 mM ethylene diamine tetra-acetic acid (300 μL), and 50 mM HEPES (pH 7.4) (400 μL) were then added to the collected plasma. Plasma samples were stored at −20 °C until the assay.

To determine the reliable amount of BSA-FITC for each blood sample, we recorded the spectra of BSA-FITC standard solutions of known concentrations of BSA-FITC in blood. The measurement conditions were an excitation wavelength of 490 nm with a bandwidth at 2.5 nm, an emission wavelength of 525 nm with a bandwidth at 2.5 nm and a response time of 2 s. The amount of cumulatively released BSA was calculated by comparison with the standard calibration curves prepared with known concentrations of BSA-FITC. For each group of four rats treated with a particular gel formulation, the release experiment was separately performed on each rat, and the results were averaged.

For the bovine-insulin detection for each blood sample, the insulin concentration in plasma was determined using a bovine insulin enzyme-linked immunosorbent assay (ELISA) kit (Mercodia AB, Stockholm, Sweden). To run each assay, all reagents and samples were brought to room temperature. An aliquot from each sample (25 μL) was transferred to a well plate strip. After following the manufacturer's instructions, absorbance was measured at 450 nm with an EL808 Ultra Microplate Reader (BioTek Instruments, Winooski, VT, USA). The amount of insulin released *in vivo* was calculated by comparison with standard calibration curves prepared with known concentrations of insulin using the bovine insulin ELISA kit. The area under the plasma insulin concentration *versus* time curve was calculated as the area under the curve (AUC).

3. RESULTS AND DISCUSSION

3.1. Synthesis of MPEG-b-PCL and MPEG-b-PCDO Diblock Copolymers

MPEG-*b*-PCL and MPEG-*b*-PCDO diblock copolymers were synthesized by ring-opening polymerization (ROP) of CL and DO initiated by MPEG in the presence of HCl as the catalyst at room temperature. Typically, stannous octoate has been used for the conventional ROP of cyclic esters, such as CL, LA and GA. The ROP by stannous octoate carried out a reflux of high boiling point solvents, such as toluene. However, for biomedical applications, this organometallic catalyst and toluene are difficult to remove from the products, and the toxic contaminants remaining in the polymers may potentially affect the human body [26,27].

To solve these problems, our group has developed a metal-free ROP method using HCl as a monomer activator [20,23,28]. Preparation of MPEG-*b*-PCL and MPEG-*b*-PCDO diblock copolymers was accomplished by using an HCl catalyst at room temperature (Figure 1). The MPEG-polyesters diblock copolymers were obtained in high yields (>95%) and showed narrow polydispersities (1.14–1.19) as measured by the GPC system. Based on our previous studies, we arranged the MW of MPEG-*b*-PCL diblock copolymers established at 750–2400 g/mol to form thermo-responsive hydrogels at body temperature [19,24]. The unique MW of the MPEG-*b*-PCL and MPEG-*b*-PCDO diblock copolymers was optimized for the balance of amphiphilicity in an aqueous solution resulting in a thermosensitive sol-to-gel phase transition. The 5 mol% portion of PDO added into the PCL main chains was determined to maintain the sol-to-gel transition at body temperature, because it is the gelation range at body temperature if these portions were increased. An MW ratio of 95:5 (PCL:PDO) in the polyester block was calculated by ^{1}H NMR and confirmed to be reasonable (Figure 2).

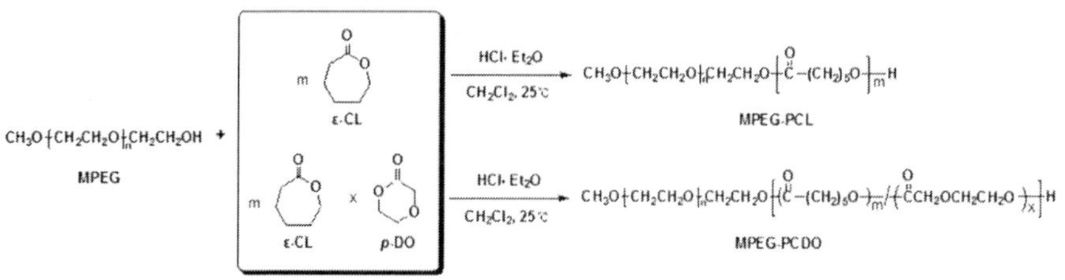

Figure 1. Synthetic scheme of methoxy poly(ethylene glycol) (MPEG) poly ε-caprolactone (PCL) (MPEG-*b*-PCL) and MPEG-*b*-poly(ε-caprolactone-*ran*-*p*-dioxanone) (MPEG-*b*-PCDO).

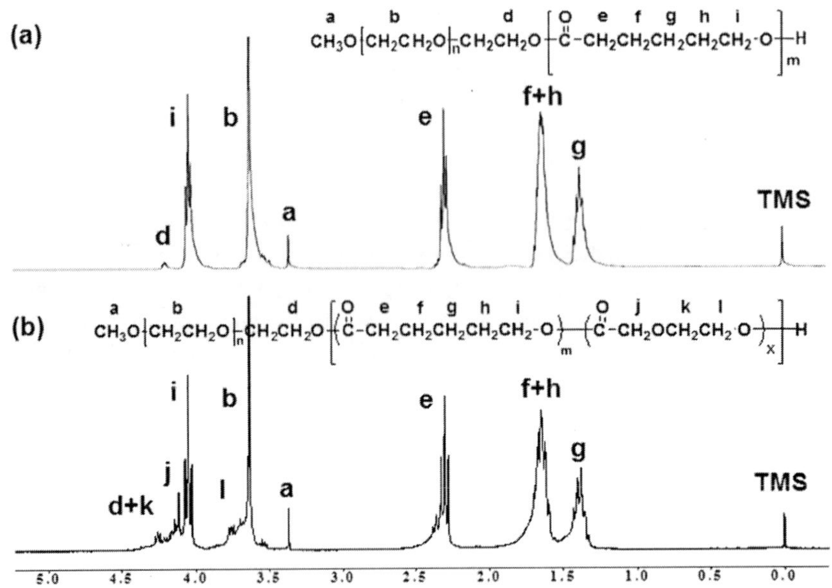

Figure 2. ^{1}H NMR spectra of (**a**) MPEG-*b*-PCL and (**b**) MPEG-*b*-PCDO in $CDCl_3$.

3.2. Temperature- and Time-Dependent Changes in the Viscosity of MPEG-b-PCL and MPEG-b-PCDO Diblock Copolymers

In order to ascertain the diblock copolymers' potential as injectable hydrogels, they were dispersed in aqueous solutions at 20 wt% concentrations to form translucent solutions at room temperature. In addition, the viscosities of the polymer solutions were measured with the gradual increase of temperature from 6 to 70 °C. The 20 wt% concentration of diblock copolymers in aqueous solution was optimized for the sol-to-gel phase transition at body temperature, because the lower concentrations of diblock copolymers in aqueous solution showed gelation outside body temperature, while the higher concentrations had viscosities at room temperature.

The MPEG-*b*-PCDO solution started to form gels at approximately 30 °C, while the MPEG-*b*-PCL solution began gelation at 27 °C. These results suggested that the 5 mol% portion of PDO mixed in 95 mol% PCL chains contributed to the different temperature and range of gelation, as well as the different intensity of viscosity at 37 °C. How the gelation of diblock copolymers responded to temperature changes is shown in Figure 3.

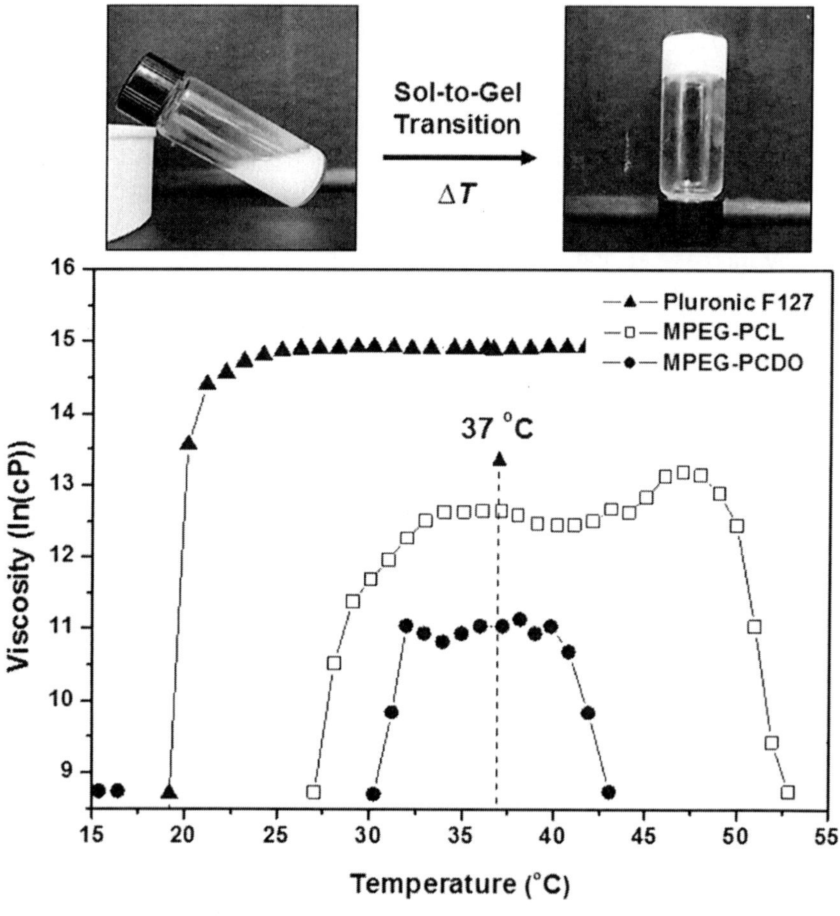

Figure 3. Temperature-dependent viscosity curves of Pluronic F127, MPEG-*b*-PCL and MPEG-*b*-PCDO diblock copolymers dissolved in 20 wt% aqueous solutions. The hydrogel shown in the photos was prepared from an MPEG-*b*-PCDO copolymer, and the gelation photo was taken immediately upon removal from a 37 °C water bath.

Furthermore, the hydrogels of MPEG-polyester diblock copolymers, including Pluronic F127, underwent time-dependent viscosity at 37 °C for 48 h (Figure 4). The viscosities of MPEG-*b*-PCL and MPEG-*b*-PCDO were increased and sustained over 40 h, while the viscosity of Pluronic F127 decreased gradually after 15 h. The slight increase of viscosity with time is generated by the hydrophobic interactions between PCL and PCDO chains in aqueous solutions, as reported in previous works [19,20]. The crystallization process of amphiphilic polymers lad to stronger packing interactions between the hydrophobic blocks, resulting in the increase of viscosity over time.

Although Pluronic F127 hydrogel shows a rapid sol-to-gel phase transition at body temperature, its use for the drug delivery system is limited due to the time-dependent gelation behavior. The hydrophobic interactions between PCL and PCDO chains in aqueous solutions were shown to gradually increase at body temperature. On the other hand, PPO units of Pluronic F127 hydrogel lead to weaker packing interactions between them, resulting in a gel-to-sol phase transition at a certain time.

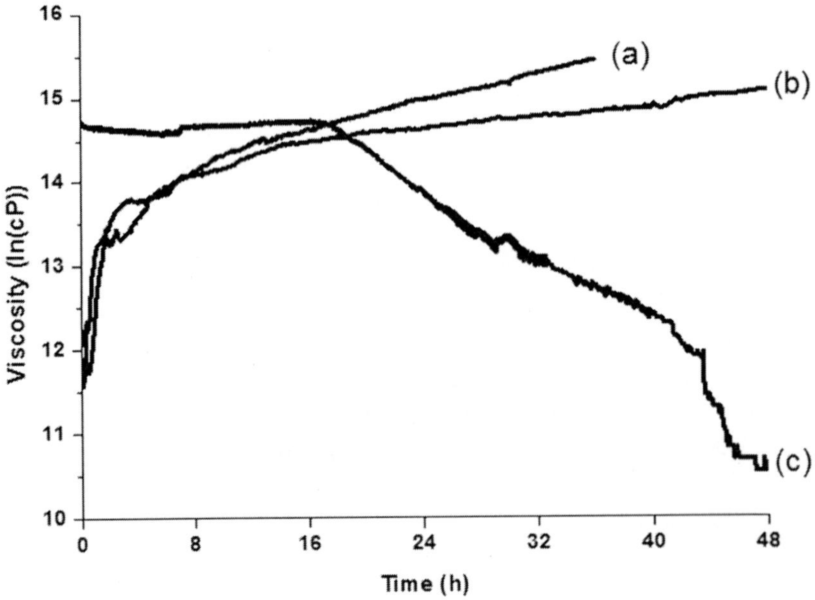

Figure 4. Time-dependent viscosity changes of Pluronic F127, MPEG-*b*-PCL and MPEG-*b*-PCDO diblock copolymers solutions incubated at 37 °C for 48 h. (**a**) MPEG-*b*-PCL; (**b**) MPEG-*b*-PCDO; and (**c**) Pluronic F127.

3.3. In Vitro and in Vivo Release of Proteins from MPEG-b-PCL and MPEG-b-PCDO Hydrogels

The 20-wt% solutions of MPEG-*b*-PCL and MPEG-*b*-PCDO copolymers and Pluronic F127 showed gelation at various intensities of viscosity at body temperature. Pluronic F127 has a 3–6-fold greater intensity of viscosity than that of the MPEG-polyester gels, but its viscosity is retained only for

15 h, thus leading to the conclusion that it is not suitable for long-term drug delivery. When the 20-wt% solutions of MPEG-*b*-PCL and MPEG-*b*-PCDO copolymers, as well as Pluronic F127 were injected subcutaneously into SD rats at room temperature, the copolymers became gels within a few seconds. Furthermore, the MPEG-*b*-PCL and MPEG-*b*-PCDO hydrogels retained their form for over a month at the injection site, whereas the Pluronic F127 gel dissipated 1–2 days post-injection.

For the *in vitro* drug release test, 20-wt% solutions of MPEG-*b*-PCL, MPEG-*b*-PCDO and Pluronic F127 were mixed with BSA-FITC at room temperature and incubated at 37 °C to form gels, followed by the addition of PBS (pH 7.4). BSA-FITC was quantitatively entrapped in MPEG-*b*-PCL, MPEG-*b*-PCDO and Pluronic F127. MPEG-*b*-PCL and MPEG-*b*-PCDO hydrogels were maintained in their initial shapes, and the BSA-FITC release was sustained over a period of time. However, the Pluronic F127 gel dissolved completely in PBS within 24 h, resulting in an uncontrolled release of BSA-FITC. Figure 5shows the cumulative amounts of BSA-FITC release from MPEG-polyester hydrogels and Pluronic F127 gel in various release patterns. The MPEG-*b*-PCL and MPEG-*b*-PCDO hydrogels, respectively, released BSA-FITC at approximately 25% and 45%, for 15 days, whereas the Pluronic F127 hydrogel released over 90% of BSA-FITC within a day. As expected, the MPEG-*b*-PCDO showed a two-fold higher overall release compared to that of the MPEG-*b*-PCL hydrogel. This result indicates that the 5 mol% of PDO block in PCL chains contributed to releasing more BSA-FITC from MPEG-*b*-PCDO hydrogel depending on the viscosity intensities at 37 °C. The remaining BSA-FITC in hydrogels' post-release was confirmed by an excitation of the fluorescein using a blue light (465–490 nm), as shown in the photos of Figure 5.

To verify the *in vivo* drug release behaviors of MPEG-*b*-PCL, MPEG-*b*-PCDO and Pluronic F127 hydrogels, BSA-FITC loaded hydrogels were injected subcutaneously into SD rats. Then, the blood collected from the tail vein at each time point was calculated for the released amounts of BSA-FITC. As shown in Figure 6, the *in vivo* release of BSA-FITC from the MPEG-*b*-PCDO hydrogel was observed only for one week, using a similar pattern as the previous MPEG-*b*-PCL hydrogel study [19]. This was due to the limitation of the fluorescein detected by a fluorometer depending on the fluorescein concentrations, even though the collected blood plasma contained the emitted BSA-FITC. The injection site in an SD rat was resected to confirm the remaining BSA-FITC in the hydrogel by using a blue light (465–490 nm) exciting the fluorescein (see photos in Figure 6). The fluorescence image proves the continuous release of BSA-FITC from the hydrogel by showing the fluorescences on the inside of the skin around the hydrogel.

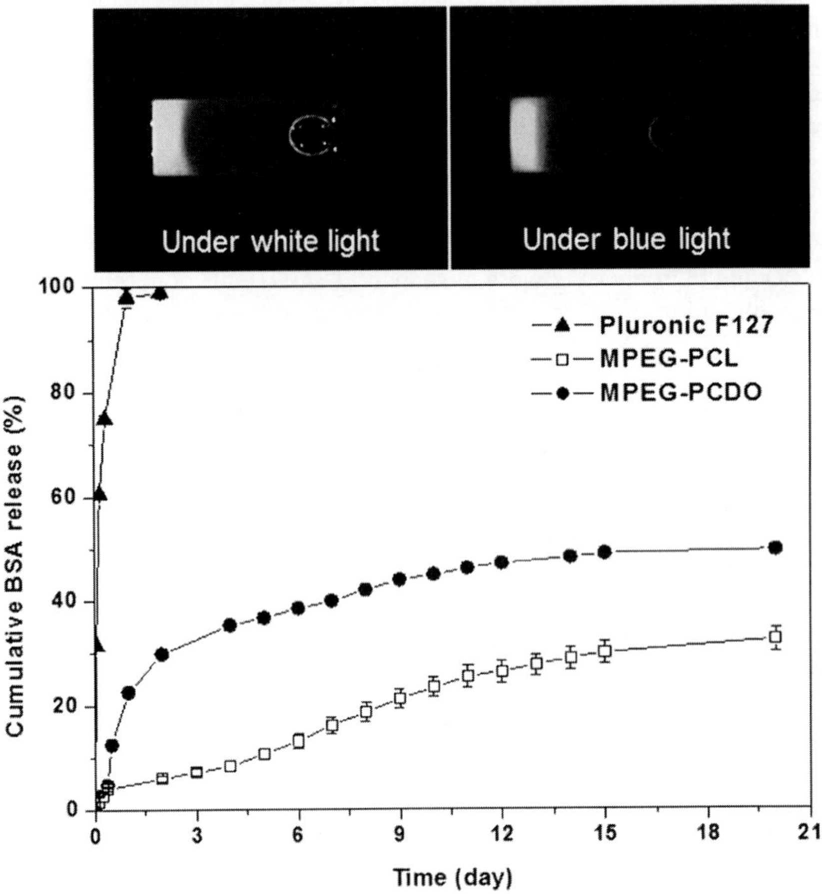

Figure 5. *In vitro* release of BSA-FITC from gels prepared with 20-wt% solutions of MPEG-*b*-PCL and MPEG-*b*-PCDO diblock copolymers. The representative image of MPEG-*b*-PCDO hydrogel shown in the photo indicates the remaining BSA-FITC in the hydrogel three weeks post-release at 37 °C. The fluorescein in PBS solution (pH 7.4) excited by a blue light (465–490 nm).

For a more accurate and reliable *in vivo* test of the model protein drug, bovine insulin was used for the long-term drug release *in vivo*, because even the smallest amount of this drug in the blood plasma can be detected by an ELISA method. As before, the 20-wt% polymer solutions mixed with bovine insulin were injected into SD rats, and blood was collected from the tail vein at each time point to calculate the released amounts of bovine insulin. Insulin concentrations in blood released from MPEG-*b*-PCL and

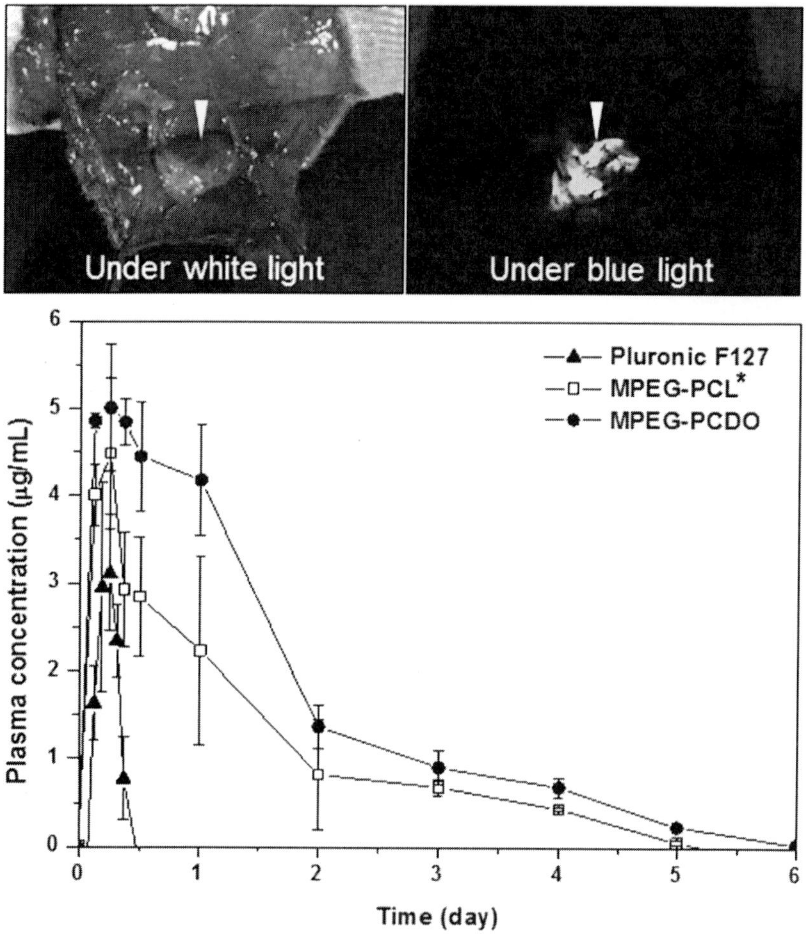

Figure 6. *In vivo* release of BSA-FITC from injected hydrogels in SD rats (n = 4) for one weeks. The photo taken under white light shows an MPEG-*b*-PCDO hydrogel maintained at the injection site in a SD rat after one week. The fluorescence image under blue light (465–490 nm) indicates the remaining BSA-FITC in the hydrogel (arrowhead). * The *in vivo* result of BSA-FITC release from MPEG-*b*-PCL hydrogel is cited from a previous report [19].

MPEG-*b*-PCDO hydrogels increased initially for one day and were sustained for 10 weeks, whereas the Pluronic F127 gel released a small amount of insulin for only two days (Figure 7). The AUC_{0-t} values of MPEG-*b*-PCL and MPEG-*b*-PCDO hydrogels based on the release curves were 33.6 ± 10.9 and 82.3 ± 7.8, respectively, while the AUC_{0-t}value of Pluronic F127 gel was only 3.91 ± 0.53. The MPEG-*b*-PCDO hydrogel showed a two-fold increase in the release of bovine insulin compared to that of the MPEG-*b*-PCL hydrogel for 10 weeks. This result corresponded with the *in vitro*release patterns of MPEG-*b*-PCL, MPEG-*b*-PCDO and Pluronic F127 hydrogels.

The Pluronic F127 hydrogel has high viscosity intensity at body temperature to prevent the initial burst of drug release, but the viscosity of Pluronic F127 hydrogel could not be maintained for over one day, as reported in previous work [19]. The 5 mol% PDO chains distributed randomly in PCL chains enable not only enhanced release of drugs, but also rapid and durable gelation at body temperature. We achieved an enhanced and sustained release of protein drugs *in vivo* for 10 weeks using MPEG-*b*-PCDO hydrogel with an optimized 20-wt% concentration in aqueous solution.

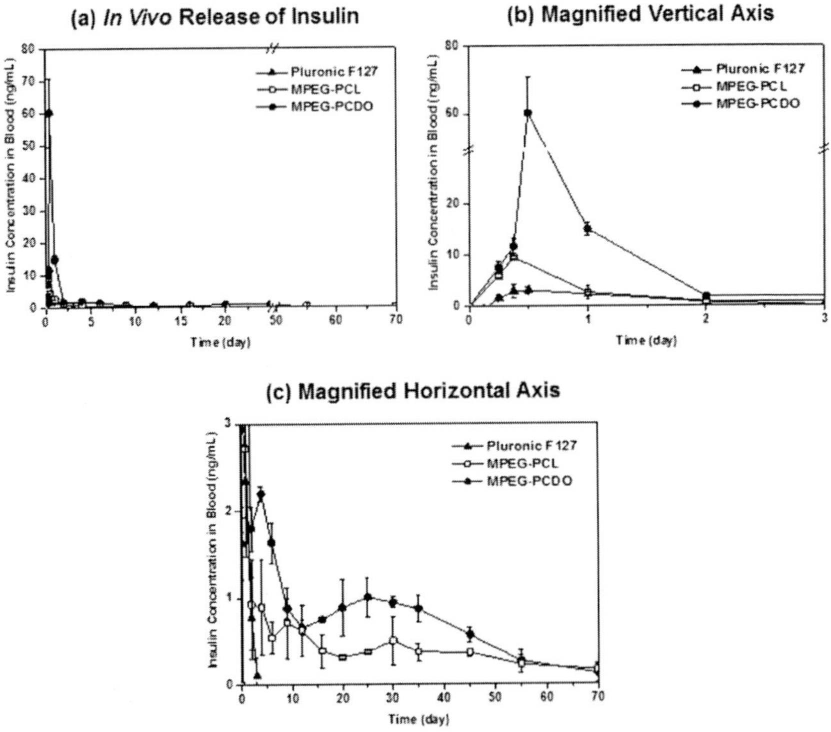

Figure 7. *In vivo* release of bovine insulin from injected hydrogels in SD rats (n = 4) for 10 weeks. (**a**) Release behaviors of Pluronic F127, MPEG-*b*-PCL and MPEG-*b*-PCDO hydrogels at full scale; (**b**,**c**) magnified curves depending on the release time and amount of bovine insulin.

4. CONCLUSIONS

To obtain more controllable hydrogels in terms of the sustained delivery of drugs, we prepared a series of MPEG-*b*-PCDO diblock copolymers by ring-opening random copolymerization of 95:5 mol% CL:DO with MPEG as the initiator in the presence of the HCl catalyst. The copolymers showed sol-to-gel transitions at body temperature when dispersed in aqueous solutions with an optimal 20 wt% concentration. Interestingly, the temperature range of gelation and viscosity intensity were changed by the addition of the PDO segment into PCL chains. At body temperature, the PDO units—components of MPEG-*b*-PCDO diblock copolymer distributed randomly in PCL chains—help to gelate and show a viscosity similar to that of MPEG-*b*-PCL hydrogels. The gelation property was consistently reflected in the release patterns of protein drugs in *in vitro* and *in vivo* experiments.

The *in vitro* release of BSA-FITC from MPEG-*b*-PCDO hydrogels showed a 45% release of BSA for 15 days, whereas the Pluronic F127 gel exhibited an almost complete release of BSA within a day. Furthermore, the sustained *in vivo* release of bovine insulin from MPEG-*b*-PCDO hydrogel was observed for 70 days. Therefore, MPEG-*b*-PCDO thermo-responsive hydrogels can be utilized for drug-delivery applications in terms of the specific gelation temperature, gel strength, degradation rate and controlled release of protein drugs.

ACKNOWLEDGMENTS

This study was supported by a grant from Ministry of Trade, Industry and Energy (MOTIE) (Grant No. 10047811), a Basic Science Research Program (2013R1A2A2A04014200) and Basic Science Research Program through the National Research Foundation of Korea (NRF) funded by the Ministry of Education (NRF-2009-0093826).

AUTHOR CONTRIBUTIONS

Designed the experiments: Moon Suk Kim; Performed the experiments: Hoon Hyun, Seung Hun Park and Doo Yeon Kwon; Analyzed the data: Gilson Khang, Hai Bang Lee and Moon Suk Kim; Wrote the paper: Hoon Hyun and Moon Suk Kim.

CONFLICTS OF INTEREST

The authors declare no conflict of interest.

REFERENCES

1. Kim, M.S.; Park, K. Injectable hydrogel. In Encyclopedia of Nanotechnology; Bhushan, B., Ed.; Springer: Dordrecht, The Netherland, 2012; Volume 2, pp. 1091–1096.

2. Aucoin, H.; Wilson, A.N.; Wilson, A.M.; Ishihara, K.; Guiseppi-Elie, A. Release of potassium ion and calcium ion from phosphorylcholine group bearing hydrogels. Polymers 2013, 5, 1241–1257.

3. Kim, J.I.; Kim, D.Y.; Kwon, D.Y.; Kang, H.J.; Kim, J.H.; Min, B.H.; Kim, M.S. An injectable biodegradable temperature-responsive gel with an adjustable persistence window. Biomaterials 2012, 33, 2823–2834.

4. Seo, H.W.; Kim, D.Y.; Kwon, D.Y.; Kwon, J.S.; Jin, L.M.; Lee, B.; Kim, J.H.; Min, B.H.; Kim, M.S. Injectable intratumoral hydrogel as 5-fluorouracil drug depot. Biomaterials 2013, 34, 2748–2757.

5. Peng, Y.; Li, J.; Li, J.; Fei, Y.; Dong, J.; Pan, W. Optimization of thermosensitive chitosan hydrogels for the sustained delivery of venlafaxine hydrochloride. Int. J. Pharm. 2013, 441, 482–490.

6. He, C.; Kim, S.W.; Lee, D.S. In situ gelling stimuli-sensitive block copolymer hydrogels for drug delivery. J. Control. Release 2008, 127, 189–207.

7. Agrawal, S.K.; Sanabria-DeLong, N.; Tew, G.N.; Bhatia, S.R. Structural characterization of PLA-PEO-PLA solutions and hydrogels: Crystalline vs. amorphous PLA domains. Macromolecules 2008, 41, 1774–1784.

8. Lee, J.; Bae, Y.H.; Sohn, Y.S.; Jeong, B. Thermogelling aqueous solutions of alternating multiblock copolymers of poly(L-lactic acid) and poly(ethylene glycol). Biomacromolecules 2006, 7, 1729–1734.

9. Kim, M.S.; Kim, J.H.; Min, B.H.; Chun, H.J.; Han, D.K.; Lee, H.B. Polymeric scaffolds for regenerative medicine.Polym. Rev. 2011, 51, 23–52.

10. Tsai, Y.; Jheng, L.; Hsu, S.L. Thermogelling polymers composed of poly (cyclohexylenedimethylene adipate) and poly(ethylene glycol). Eur. Polym. J. 2012, 48, 541–548.

11. Wang, F.; Shen, Y.; Xu, X.; Lv, L.; Li, Y.; Liu, J.; Li, M.; Guo, A.; Guo, S.; Jin, F. Selective tissue distribution and long circulation endowed by paclitaxel loaded PEGylated poly(ε-caprolactone-co-L-lactide) micelles leading to improved anti-tumor effects and low systematic toxicity. Int. J. Pharm. 2013, 456, 101–112.

12. Kabanov, A.V.; Batrakova, E.V.; Alakhov, V.Y. Pluronic block copolymers as novel polymer therapeutics for drug and gene delivery. J. Control. Release 2002, 82, 189–212.

13. Lee, S.H.; Lee, J.E.; Baek, W.Y.; Lim, J.O. Regional delivery of vancomycin using pluronic F-127 to inhibit methicillin resistant Staphylococcus aureus (MRSA) growth in chronic otitis media in vitro and in vivo. J. Control. Release 2004,96, 1–7.

14. Jeong, B.; Bae, Y.H.; Kim, S.W. In situ gelation of PEG-PLGA-PEG triblock copolymer aqueous solutions and degradation thereof. J. Biomed. Mater. Res. 2000, 50, 171–177.

15. Kim, M.S.; Hyun, H.; Khang, G.; Lee, H.B. Preparation of thermosensitive diblock copolymers consisting of MPEG and polyesters. Macromolecules 2006, 39, 3099–3102.

16. Jiang, Z.; Hao, J.; You, Y.; Gu, Q.; Cao, W.; Deng, Z. Biodegradable thermogelling hydrogel of P(CL-GL)-PEG-P(CL-GL) triblock copolymer: Degradation and drug release behavior. J. Pharm. Sci. 2009, 98, 2603–2610.

17. Wei, X.W.; Gong, C.Y.; Shi, S.; Fu, S.Z.; Men, K.; Zeng, S. Self-assembled honokiol-loaded micelles based on poly(caprolactone)-poly(ethylene glycol)-poly(caprolactone) copolymer. Int. J. Pharm. 2009, 369, 170–175.

18. Kang, K.N.; Kim, D.Y.; Yoon, S.M.; Lee, J.Y.; Lee, B.N.; Kwon, J.S.; Seo, H.W.; Lee, I.W.; Shin, H.C.; Kim, Y.M.; et al. Tissue engineered regeneration of completely transected spinal cord using human mesenchymal stem cells.Biomaterials 2012, 33, 4828–4835.

19. Hyun, H.; Kim, Y.H.; Song, I.B.; Lee, J.W.; Kim, M.S.; Khang, G.; Park, K.; Lee, H.B. In vitro and in vivo release of albumin using a biodegradable MPEG-PCL diblock copolymer as an in situ gel-forming carrier. Biomacromolecules2007, 8, 1093–1100.

20. Kim, M.S.; Hyun, H.; Seo, K.S.; Cho, Y.H.; Lee, J.W.; Lee, C.R.; Khang, G.; Lee, H.B. Preparation and characterization of MPEG-PCL diblock copolymers with thermo-responsive sol-gel-sol phase transition. J. Polym. Sci. Part A 2006, 44, 5413–5423.

21. Cho, M.H.; Hyun, H.; Shin, Y.N.; Lee, J.W.; Lee, M.S.; Ahn, H.H.; Kim, M.S.; Lee, B.; Khang, G.; Lee, H.B. Release profile of BSA or BDNF from temperature sensitive hydrogels. Key Eng. Mat. 2007, 342–343, 473–476.

22. Kwon, J.S.; Yoon, S.M.; Shim, S.W.; Park, J.H.; Min, K.J.; Oh, H.J.; Kim, J.H.; Kim, Y.J.; Yoon, J.J.; Choi, B.H.; et al. Injectable extracellular matrix hydrogel developed using porcine articular cartilage. Int. J. Pharm. 2013, 454, 183–191.

23. Hyun, H.; Kim, M.S.; Khang, G.; Lee, H.B. Ring-opening polymerization of trimethylene carbonate by poly(ethylene glycol) in the presence of HCl·Et2O as a monomer activator. J. Polym. Sci. Part A 2006, 44, 4235–4241.

24. Kim, M.S.; Kim, S.K.; Kim, S.H.; Hyun, H.; Khang, G.; Lee, H.B. In vivo osteogenic differentiation of rat bone marrow stromal cells in thermosensitive MPEG-PCL diblock copolymer gels. Tissue Eng. 2006, 12, 2863–2873.

25. Shim, S.W.; Kwon, D.Y.; Park, J.H.; Kim, J.H.; Chun, H.J.; Koh, Y.J.; Kim, M.S. Preparation of zwitterionic sulfobetaine end-functionalized poly(ethylene glycol)-b-poly(caprolactone) diblock copolymers and examination of their thermogelling properties. J. Polym. Sci. A 2014, 52, 2185–2191.

26. Davies, A.G. Organotin Chemistry, 2nd ed.; Wiley-VCH: Weinheim, Germany, 2004.

27. Pitt, C.G.; Schindler, A. Long-Acting Contraceptive Delivery Systems; Zatuchni, G.L., Goldsmith, A., Shelton, J.D., Sciarra, J.J., Eds.; Harper and Row Publishers: Philadelphia, PA, USA, 1984; pp. 48–63.

28. Kim, M.S.; Seo, K.S.; Khang, G.; Lee, H.B. Ring-opening polymerization of ε-caprolactone by poly(ethylene glycol) by an activated monomer mechanism. Macromol. Rapid Commun. 2005, 26, 643–648.

Chapter 9

Encapsulation of Docetaxel in Oily Core Polyester Nanocapsules Intended for Breast Cancer Therapy

Ibrahima Youm[1], Xiaoyan Yang[1], James B Murowchick[2] and Bi-Botti C Youan[1*]

[1]*Laboratory of Future Nanomedicines and Theoretical Chronopharmaceutics, Division of Pharmaceutical Sciences, University of Missouri-Kansas City, 2464 Charlotte Street, Kansas City, MO, 64108, USA*

[2]*Department of Geosciences, University of Missouri-Kansas City, 420 Flarsheim Hall, 5110 Rockhill Rd., Kansas City, MO, 64110, USA*

ABSTRACT

This study is designed to test the hypothesis that docetaxel [Doc] containing oily core nanocapsules [NCs] could be successfully prepared with a high percentage encapsulation efficiency [EE%] and high drug loading. The oily core NCs were generated according to the emulsion solvent diffusion method using neutral Labrafac CC and poly(*d, l*-lactide) [PLA] as oily core and shell, respectively. The engineered NCs were characterized for particle mean diameter, zeta potential, EE%, drug release kinetics, morphology, crystallinity, and cytotoxicity on the SUM 225 breast cancer cell line by dynamic light scattering, high performance liquid chromatography, electron microscopies, powder X-ray diffraction, and lactate dehydrogenase bioassay. Typically, the formation of Doc-loaded, oily core, polyester-based NCs was evidenced by spherical nanometric particles (115 to 582 nm) with a low polydispersity index (< 0.05), high EE% (65% to 93%), high drug loading (up to 68.3%), and a smooth surface. Powder X-ray diffraction analysis revealed that Doc was not present in a crystalline state because it was dissolved within the

NCs' oily core and the PLA shell. The drug/polymer interaction has been indeed thermodynamically explained using the Flory-Huggins interaction parameters. Doc release kinetic data over 144 h fitted very well with the Higuchi model (R^2 > 0.93), indicating that drug release occurred mainly by controlled diffusion. At the highest drug concentration (5 μM), the Doc-loaded oily core NCs (as a reservoir nanosystem) enhanced the native drug cytotoxicity. These data suggest that the oily core NCs are promising templates for controlled delivery of poorly water soluble chemotherapeutic agents, such as Doc.

Keywords: docetaxel polylactide emulsion diffusion nanocapsules drug loading

BACKGROUND

In cancer therapy, most of the proposed formulations present certain drawbacks related to the formulation properties including low drug loading, toxicity, and unsuitable release pattern. An ideal formulation should provide biocompatible nanosized particles and high drug loading with sustained-release characteristics. This allows releasing the drug in the target site in its therapeutic concentration and preventing drug inefficiency and side effects. The current research was aimed to prepare highly loaded docetaxel [Doc] oily core nanocapsules [NCs].

Doc, a semisynthetic analog of paclitaxel, is an extract from the needles of the European yew tree *Taxus baccata*[1]. It is prepared by chemical modification of 10-deacetylbacattin III, an inactive precursor compound, and then isolated [2]. Doc is a highly potent, cytotoxic, and antimitotic agent used in the treatment of various types of cancers, including metastatic breast, ovarian, prostate, advanced non-small-cell lung, head/neck, and advanced gastric cancers by inhibiting the microtubule depolymerization of free tubulin [3, 4]. Due to its poor water solubility (10 to 20 μg/l), polysorbate 80 has been markedly used to improve the aqueous solubility of Doc [5, 6, 7]. This currently available, marketed formulation has been associated with the absence of selectivity for target tissues, serious dose limiting toxicities, and hypersensitivity reactions, as well as sensory and motor neuropathies that are sometimes severe and irreversible. Previously, various alternative formulations, including NCs, pegylated liposomes, targeted immunoliposomes, Doc-fibrinogen-coated olive oil droplets, and cyclodextrins [8, 9, 10, 11, 12,13, 14, 15] have been intensively developed for the delivery of Doc. However, the nanosized polymeric nanoparticles represent promising drug-delivery systems which have some advantages such as biodegradability, good biocompatibility, non-toxicity, higher stability, and controlled drug delivery. Polymeric nanoparticles (nanospheres and NCs) not only maintain a prolonged circulation time in the body (especially when pegylated) by avoiding the reticuloendothelial system, but also can extravagate and accumulate into the tumor tissue. This is likely due to the reliance of these nanoparticles on passive accumulation through enhanced permeability and retention, which is highly dependent on adequate blood flow to the tumor [16].

According to the literature, the NCs correspond to nanostructures with polymeric wall enveloping an oily core, whereas the nanospheres consist of a polymeric matrix [17]. There is increasing scientific evidence supporting the notion that certain lipids are able to inhibit both presystemic drug metabolism and P-glycoprotein-mediated drug efflux [18]. Several polymers have been proposed as nanocarriers for drug delivery systems. For example, poly(*d, l*-lactic acid) and poly(ε-caprolactone) [PCL] have been extensively used as nanocarriers because of their excellent biocompatibility and biodegradability. These polyesters have been approved by the US Food and Drug Administration and are the most widely used commercial polymers for drug delivery [19, 20]. Presently, the only available Doc formulations for clinical use consists of intravenous [IV] solutions containing Tween 80® (Sanofi-aventis, Bridgewater, NJ, USA). These solutions namely Taxotere® and Docetaxel®, 10 to 20 mg/ml, are administered IV at a dose ranging from 60 to 100 mg/m^2 over 1 h every 3 weeks [21]). However, such high doses and a long term medication schedule may produce more severe side effects [22]. One of the reasons could be ascribed to the composition of the formulation and the poor control of the drug release rate. Therefore, the development of compatible polymer-based nanocarriers with high drug loading might be a helpful subject in cancer research.

The current research was aimed to prepare highly loaded Doc oily core NCs. However, the relationship between drug and formulation excipients has also been investigated to better control the encapsulation process.

MATERIALS AND METHODS

Materials

Poly(*d, l*-lactide) [PLA], Resomer® R206, Mw 125 kDa, with an inherent viscosity of 1.0 dl/g; PLA, Resomer® R207, Mw 209 kDa, with an inherent viscosity of 1.5 dl/g; and PLA, Resomer® R208, Mw 250 kDa, with an inherent viscosity of 1.8 dl/g were purchased from Boehringer Inc. (Ridgefield, CT, USA). PCL (Mw = 72 kDa) was kindly provided by Union Carbide (Danbury, CT, USA). Polyvinyl alcohol [PVA] (9 to 10 kDa and 30 to 70 kDa) and ethyl acetate were obtained from Sigma-Aldrich (St. Louis, MO, USA). Docetaxel or Doc was purchased from LC Laboratories (Woburn, MA, USA). Labrafac CC (caprylic/capric triglyceride, *d* = 0.945 g/cm^3) was kindly supplied by Gattefosse Corporation (St-Priest, France) as a gift. For the high-performance liquid chromatography

[HPLC] analysis, acetonitrile and methanol were supplied from Fisher (Thermo Fisher Scientific, Fair Lawn, NJ, USA). All the other reagents were of analytical grade and used without further purification.

Preparation of the nanocapsules

Experimental design and general procedure for Doc-loaded nanocapsules

Fifteen formulations of Doc-loaded NCs were prepared by emulsion-diffusion method as previously described [19]. Briefly, the polyester (40 to 360 mg) was solubilized in water-saturated ethyl acetate (10 ml); then, the neutral oil (0.1 to 0.9 ml) containing Doc (2 to 18 mg) was further added to the organic mixture. The resulting solution was emulsified in 40 ml of PVA 2.5% to 5% (*w/v*) aqueous phase solution by homogenization (homogenizer, IKA ULTRA-TURRAX T-25, IKA Labortechnik, Staufen, Germany) at 8,000 rpm for 10 min. A large volume (200 ml) of deionized water was added dropwise into the previous solution to promote the diffusion of ethyl acetate into the aqueous phase. To remove the organic solvent, the nanosuspension was stirred under vacuum at 40°C Rotavapor® RII (BUCHI Labortechnik AG, Flawil, Switzerland) for 30 min. NCs were recovered by ultracentrifugation at 12,000 rpm at 5°C for 30 min, washed twice with deionized water to remove the excess of PVA, and freeze-dried for 12 h (Labconco Corp. Kansas City, MO, USA). Blank NCs were prepared without Doc using the above method. The composition of the 15 formulations is listed in the first four columns of Table S1 in Additional file 1.

Screening for polyester selection based on the blank particle mean diameter

For the first screening test, a set of four biodegradable polymers, including PLA R206, PLA R207, PLA R208, and PCL, was used to obtain a suitable formulation based on the mean diameter of the obtained blank NCs. An amount of 200 mg of polyesters was solubilized in an organic phase containing 10 ml of water-saturated ethyl acetate and 0.5 ml of neutral oil. Each experiment was performed in triplicate.

Screening for stabilizer selection based on the blank particle mean diameter

Since PVA could be used as an emulsion stabilizer in the NCs' formulation process, it was important to first investigate the effect of PVA molecular weight (9 to 10 kDa and 30 to 70 kDa) on the blank NCs' mean diameter. Secondly, the influence of the PVA concentration (2.5% to 5%) on the particle mean diameter and polydispersity index [PDI] was studied.

Physicochemical characterization of docetaxel-loaded nanocapsules

Particles' mean diameter and zeta potential analysis

The particle mean diameter and PDI of the Doc-loaded NCs were measured by dynamic light scattering [DLS] (Zetasizer Nano ZS series from Malvern Instruments Ltd., Worcestershire, UK) as recently reported [23]. The sample to be measured was appropriately diluted with water and briefly sonicated for 2 min. The measurement of each sample was completed at a scattering angle of 175°. Each measurement was done in triplicate, and the average effective diameter and polydispersity were recorded.

Drug loading and percent encapsulation efficiency of docetaxel-loaded nanocapsules

The freeze-dried NCs (2 mg) were dissolved in 0.1 ml of dichloromethane and diluted in methanol at the ratio of 1:14 *v/v*. After suitable dilutions, the amount of the encapsulated Doc was determined by HPLC (Waters Corporation, Milford, MA, USA) equipped with an UV detector at 230 nm. Isocratic flow of the mobile phase, composed of methanol/water/acetonitrile (30:30:40 *v/v/v*), was employed at a flow rate of 1.0 ml·min^{-1} with a 10-µl injection volume. Doc separation was completed using an XBridge™ column C-18, at 4.6 × 150 mm and 3.5 µm (Waters Corporation, Milford, Massachusetts). The experimental Doc loading was quantified using the peak area of each NC formulation. Drug loading [DL] and percent encapsulation efficiency [EE%] were calculated according to Equations 1 and 2, respectively:

$$\mathrm{DL} = \frac{\text{Drug amount}}{\text{Polymer amount} + \text{drug amount}} \times 100\% \tag{1}$$

$$\mathrm{EE} = \frac{\text{Experimental drug loading}}{\text{Theoretical drug loading}} \times 100\% \tag{2}$$

Scanning electron microscopy analysis

Scanning electron microscopy [SEM] was used to assess the NCs' morphology. A droplet of NCs' suspension was put into a grid. The excess of the fluid was removed by wicking it off with an adsorbent paper, and then, it was visualized under a Hitachi S4700 cold-cathode field emission SEM [FESEM] (Hitachi High-Technologies Corporation, Minato-ku, Tokyo, Japan). The particles were sprinkled onto a stub covered with an adhesive conductive carbon tab, then sputter-coated with a fine layer of platinum metal. Then, the particles were imaged in the FESEM at 2 to 5 kV.

Transmission electron microscopy analysis

The selected samples were examined with a JEOL 1400 transmission electron microscope [TEM] (JEOL Ltd., Tokyo, Japan) and photographed digitally on a Gatan axis-mount 2 k × 2 k digital camera (Gatan, Inc., Pleasanton, CA, USA). The freeze-dried samples were put into a small mold, referred to as a BEEM capsule, and then imbedded in liquid epoxy resin (Epon-Araldite, Sigma-Aldrich Corporation, St. Louis, MO, USA). The resin was polymerized at 60°C for 2 days, and then, ultrathin 80-nm sections were cut on a Leica UCT ultramicrotome (Leica Microsystems Ltd., Milton Keynes, UK) with a Diatome diamond knife (Diatome, Hatfield, PA, USA). The sections were collected on 200-mesh copper grids and put into the TEM for imaging on a Gatan digital camera.

Powder X-ray diffraction pattern analysis

Powder X-ray diffraction [PXRD] analysis of the freeze-dried NCs was performed using a MiniFlex automated X-ray diffractometer (Rigaku, The Woodlands, TX, USA) at room temperature. Ni-filtered Cu Kα radiation was used at 30 kV and 15 mA. The diffraction angle covered from $2\vartheta = 5°$ to $2\vartheta = 60°$, with a step size of 0.05°/step and a count time of 3 s/step (effectively 1°/min). The diffraction patterns were processed using Jade 8+ software (Materials Data, Inc., Livermore, CA, USA).

Refractive index measurement

The oil, water-saturated ethyl acetate, and ethyl acetate-saturated water refractive index values were measured experimentally at 25°C (Auto Abbe 10500 Refractometer; Reichert Analytical Instruments, Depew, NY, USA) using Milli-Q water (Millipore Co., Billerica, MA, USA) as a reference. A droplet of liquid was deposited on the prism surface. The obtained values are the average of five measurements.

In vitro drug release kinetics

This experiment was performed using the equilibrium dialysis method for 144 h. Specifically, a known amount of Doc-loaded oily core NCs (1 mg) was suspended in a dialysis bag (Spectra/Float-A-Lyzer, MWCO 3.5-5 kDa, Spectrum Laboratories Inc. Rancho Dominguez, CA, USA) containing 5 ml of phosphate buffer saline [PBS] (Sigma-Aldrich, St. Louis, MO, USA). The bag containing the NCs' suspension was placed in 40 ml of PBS. The system was placed in a shaking water bath (BS-06, Lab. Companion, Des Plaines, IL, USA) at 37°C with an agitation speed of 50 rpm. At predetermined time intervals, 500 μl of PBS solution was withdrawn from the immersion medium and replaced by the same volume of fresh medium. The cumulative percentage of drug released for each time point was calculated as a percentage of the total drug loading of the NCs tested. The quantitative analysis of the data obtained from the study was confirmed using Higuchi's kinetic model [24] to elucidate the mechanism of the drug release.

Solubility parameter determination

To predict the compatibility between the Doc (solubilizate) and polymer (solvent), the Flory-Huggins solubility parameter was evaluated [χ_{sp}]. Our goal was to determine the interaction parameter χ_{sp}[25] using the thermodynamic approach based on the extended Hildebrand solubility. According to Hildebrand, the solubility parameter [δ], defined as the square root of the cohesive energy density [CED], is equal to the energy of vaporization ΔE_v per unit of molar volume (Equation 3) [26]. The solubility parameter is used to calculate χ_{sp} using Equation 3:

$$\delta = (\mathrm{CED})^{1/2} = \left(\Delta E_{\mathrm{v}}/V_{\mathrm{m}}\right)^{1/2} \quad (3)$$

Hansen modified the Hildebrand approach and divided δ into three components that take into account the force of the dispersion [δ_d], the polarity [δ_p], and the hydrogen bonds [δ_h]. Therefore, δ is calculated using Equation 4:

$$\delta_t^2 = \delta_d^2 + \delta_p^2 + \delta_h^2 \quad (4)$$

Equation 5 below was used to estimate the total Hildebrand solubility parameter based on the refractive index [n_D], where δ_t was the Hildebrand solubility parameter in $(\mathrm{cal/cm^3})^{1/2}$, and 304.5 was an empirically determined constant [27]. The refractometer was calibrated using pure water according to the instrument manual. Then, the total solubility parameter was calculated by using Equation 5:

$$\delta_{\mathrm{t}} = \sqrt{304.5 \left(\frac{n_{\mathrm{D}}^2 - 1}{n_{\mathrm{D}}^2 + 2}\right)} \quad (5)$$

An interaction parameter with a value smaller than 0.5 (i.e., $\chi_{sp} < 0.5$) indicates that the solvent polymers are compatible. The interaction parameter can be calculated from the solubility parameters [28]. Considering the corresponding δ_t for each component, the value of the interaction parameter

(χ_{sp}) can be estimated from the Hildebrand solubility parameters δ_s and δ_p (for solubilisant and polymer, respectively). On the basis of regular solution theory, the relationship between the Flory-Huggins interaction parameter and the solubility parameter is defined by using Equation 6:

$$\chi_{sp} = (\delta_s - \delta_p)^2 . V_m/R.T \tag{6}$$

where V_m is the molar volume of the drug, R is the ideal gas constant (8.314 $J \cdot K^{-1} \cdot mol^{-1}$), and T is the temperature in Kelvin (293.15 K) [29].

In vitro evaluation of Doc-loaded nanocapsules' cytotoxicity

The NCs' cytotoxicity was evaluated using the SUM 225 cell line (Asterand, Inc., Detroit, MI, USA). The cytotoxicity after treatment of these cells with native Doc and Doc-loaded NCs at different equivalent drug concentrations (1 nM, 2.5 μM, and 5 μM) was evaluated by the lactate dehydrogenase [LDH] assay. The cells were plated at a density of 5×10^3 cells per well for 24 h in 96-well plates in a standard growth medium prior to exposure to the above materials. Blank NCs, and medium containing 0.5% dimethyl sulfoxide [DMSO] are used as negative controls, while Triton-X 1% (Sigma-Aldrich Corporation, St. Louis, MO) was used as a positive control and incubated for 24 h at 37°C in 5% CO_2. After the treatment, the LDH reagents were used according to the manufacturer's instruction (Promega Life Sciences, Madison, WI, USA). The experimental results were expressed as mean values of six measurements (n = 6), and the cytotoxicity was calculated by the following formula:

$$\text{Cytotoxicity (\%)} = \frac{\text{Experimental} - \text{Background}}{\text{Positive} - \text{Background}} \times 100 \tag{7}$$

where, experimental, background, and positive represent the fluorescence intensity of NC-treated wells, background wells (wells without cells), and positive control wells (cells treated with 1% of Triton X-100), respectively. The fluorescence intensity was detected by using a microplate reader (DTX 800 multimode microplate reader, Beckman Coulter, Brea, CA, USA) at an excitation wavelength of 560 nm and emission wavelength of 590 nm.

RESULTS AND DISCUSSION

Polymer selection based on the mean diameter of blank nanocapsules

This experiment was performed to find out the suitable polymer using small-sized NCs. Four polymers were initially screened including PLA R206, PLA R207, PLA R208, and PCL. Figure 1 shows the effect of different biodegradable polymers on the average diameter of blank NCs. The NCs' mean diameters were 127.5 ± 19.2 nm for NC-PLA206, 123.8 ± 0.9 nm for NC-PLA207, 110.8 ± 8.6 nm for NC-PLA208, and 124.6 ± 3.1 nm for NC-PCL. These findings indicated a statistically significant decrease of PLA NCs' diameters with increasing polymer molecular weights ($P < 0.003$, *T* test). Based on their smaller mean diameter, the NCs prepared with PLA R208 were selected for the subsequent studies. The results did not show any difference regarding the zeta potential values ($\zeta = -36.5 \pm 9$ mV) among the batches of NCs (data not shown). This high potential value also contributed to the stabilization of the nanosuspension.

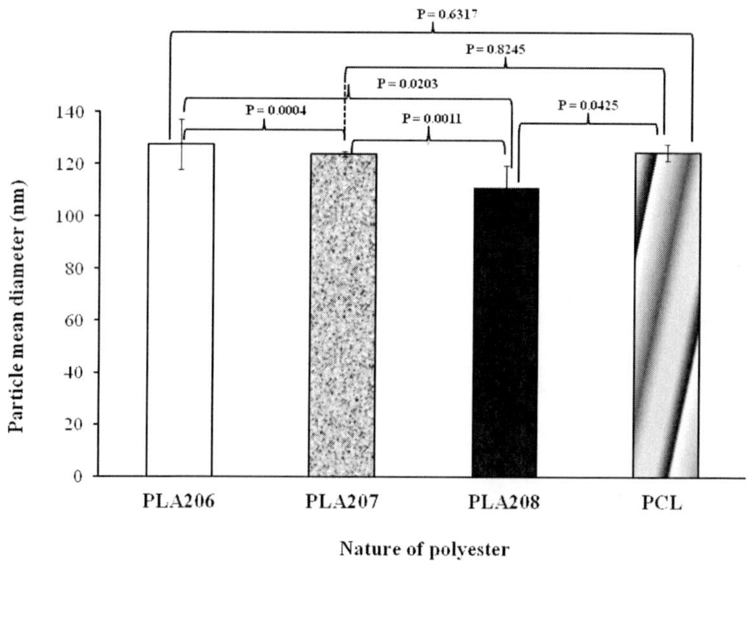

Figure 1. Influence of the nature of biodegradable polyester on blank oily core nanocapsules mean diameter. *n* = 3; S.D.: standard deviation between the three assays: PLA206 (105 kDa), PLA207 (209 kDa), PLA208 (250 kDa), and PCL (72 kDa).

Stabilizer concentration and molecular weight effects on the blank particle mean diameter

This preliminary experiment was performed to select the accurate PVA molecular weight and concentration with the goal of minimizing the particle size. Figure 2A, B, C, D shows that the NCs' mean diameter decreased with increasing both the PVA's molecular weight (9 to 10 kDa, to 30 to 70 kDa) and concentration (2.5% to 5%, *w/w*). Oppositely, previous studies have pointed out the increase of the PLGA NP mean diameter when the concentration of PVA was increased from 2% to 6% [30]. This effect was attributed to the increase of the external phase viscosity, which decreases the molecular diffusion rate and Ostwald ripening phenomenon. This revealed that the PVA concentration is not the only parameter governing the particle mean diameter. According to the overall results, PLA 208 and PVA (30 to 70 kDa, 5%) were finally selected for the following NC preparation.

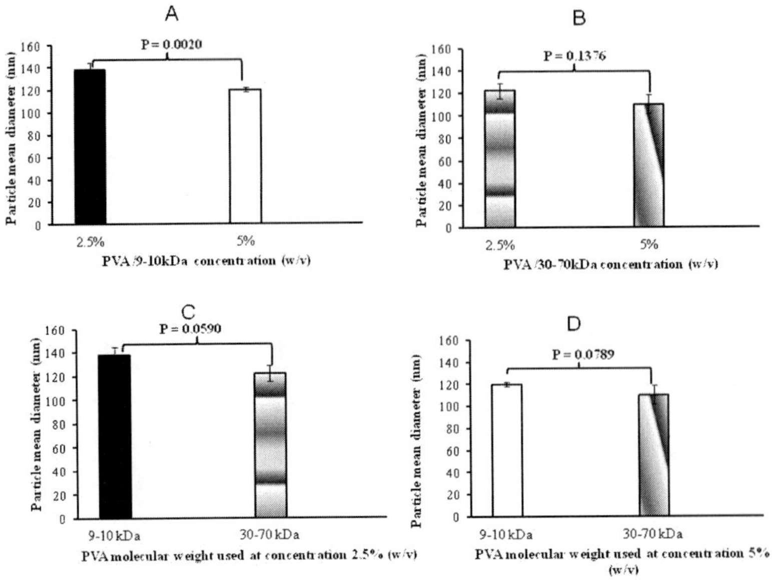

Figure 2. Influence of PVA concentrations (A, B) and molecular weights (C, D) on the blank NC mean diameter. This is detected by DLS (*n* = 3; S.D.: standard deviation between the three assays).

Preparation and characterization of docetaxel-loaded nanocapsules

For optimization purposes, 15 batches of PLA R208 Doc-loaded oily core NCs were prepared using the above method. As shown in Table S1 in Additional file 1, the lowest value of the NCs' diameter was obtained with F_6(115.6 nm), while the largest particle diameter was obtained with F_9 (582.8 nm). The PDI ranged from 0.004 to 0.318 (F_{14} and F_9, respectively). It was found that the particle mean diameter is strongly dependent to the polymer amount. Indeed, at a low PLA amount (40 mg), the particle mean diameter increases with increasing drug amount (see F_9 versus F_{10}, $P < 0.0001$). This might be explained by the fact that the lipophilic feature tends to decrease the leakage of the drug into the external aqueous medium, leading to improved drug content in the nanoparticles (which is consistent with the previous report) [19]. However, at a high PLA amount (360 mg), the particle mean diameter decreases with increasing drug amount (see F_4 versus F_5, $P < 0.0001$). The latter was not consistent with the commonly published report and might be a result of drug solubilization in the polymer matrix, leading to decrease the particle mean diameter. Thus, the solubilization capacity of PLA has a great importance in the preparation of the Doc-loaded NCs.

From Table S1 in Additional file 1, the data suggest that the NCs' mean diameter decreases with increasing oil content from 189 nm to 133 nm (see F_3 versus F_{13}, $P < 0.0001$). The results also show that at a low oil content, the drug level did not have any effect on the NCs' mean diameter, which is consistent with the previous study [31].

From Table S1 in Additional file 1, it appears that for most of the formulations, the PDI value was less than 0.05, indicating a monodispersity according to the National Institute of Standard [32]. However, the polydispersity seems to be increased with decreasing PLA amount (see F_{13} versus F_1, from 0.005 to 0.296, $P = 0.0078$). This suggests that the PLA amount may contribute to ensure the NCs' monodispersity.

Table S1 in Additional file 1 lists also the EE% of the Doc-loaded NCs. Interestingly enough, the results showed that the EE% was mainly governed by the PLA content. A high PLA content led to a high EE% (see pairwise comparison: F_1 to F_{13}, F_3 to F_9, F_4 to F_{11}, F_5 to F_{10}, respectively). At a low PLA content, the EE% was decreasing regardless of the oil content (comparing F_9 to F_{10}, $P = 0.0006$). At a high oil content, a medium content of PLA is at least required to obtain a high EE% (see F_7 and F_{13}, $P = 0.9038$). The lowest EE% (F_9, 65.3%) was obtained when the PLA and oil contents were both at the lowest level (40 mg and 0.1 ml, respectively). This is because the encapsulation process of hydrophobic drugs into these particles results from the interaction between the drug, polymers, and oil. Thus, the drug loading and EE% were found to depend on its solubility in the polymeric material, which is strongly related to the polymer composition, its molecular weight, the drug and polymer interaction, and the presence of end-functional ester or carboxyl groups [31]. These findings were consistent with a previous report [19]. Once the NCs' physicochemical properties have been analyzed, their size and morphology can be most directly monitored by various forms of electron microscopy.

Physicochemical characterization of docetaxel-loaded nanocapsules

Morphological analysis

The particle mean diameter and morphology were analyzed by SEM and TEM. Figure 3 shows a typical SEM picture of spherical NCs with smooth surfaces and undetectable free drug crystals. The NCs' size as estimated by SEM correlated well with the size measured by the DLS showing particles in a nanometric size range. The TEM analysis shows clearly a white and shiny oily core where Doc was well dissolved [33] (Figure 4). Therefore, it is necessary to investigate the drug structure inside the NCs.

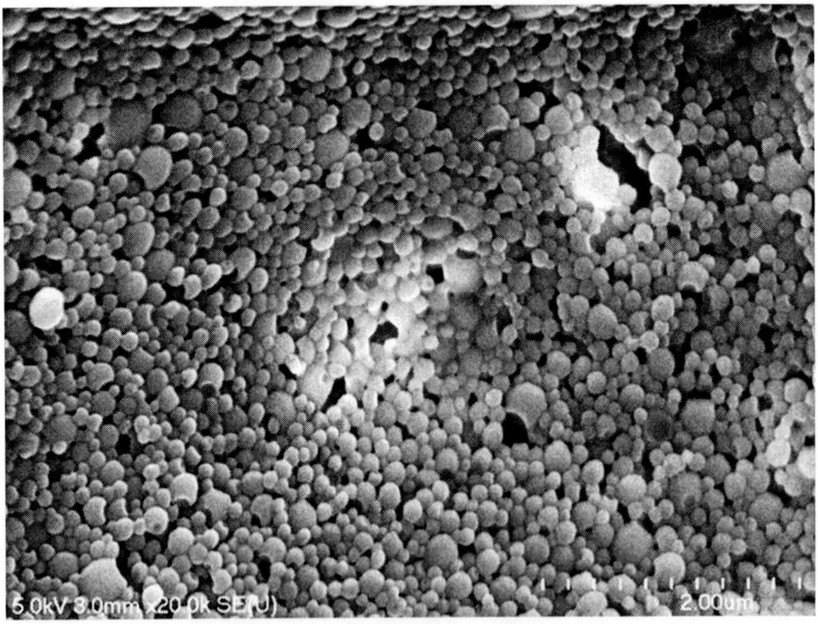

Figure 3. Scanning electron micrographs of Doc-loaded oily core nanocapsules after freeze drying (F6). Scale bar represents 0.2 µm.

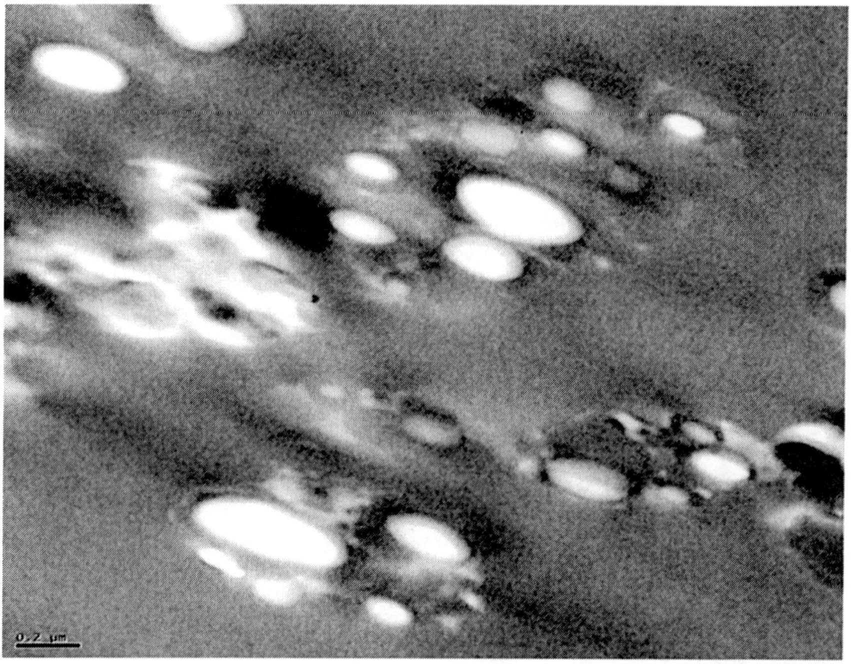

Figure 4. Transmission electron micrographs of PLA 208 oily core nanocapsules after freeze drying (F6). Scale bar represents 0.2 μm.

Powder X-ray diffraction analysis

This experiment aimed to characterize the crystallinity of Doc in the formulated NCs. Figure 5 shows the PXRD results of the formulations containing different amounts of Doc (F_6, F_{12}, and F_{13}) and the individual native chemical compounds used in the tested formulations. The native Doc exhibited sharp and characteristic diffraction peaks at 8.72°, 10.28°, and 11.7°, which is consistent with a previous report [34]. The Doc crystals are orthorhombic. The unit cell parameters (at room temperature) are a = 39.9345 Å, b = 12.7749 Å, c = 8.6644 Å, with V = 4420.2 Å. The number of motifs (Z) per cell is 4, and the density of the crystal is 1.295 [35]. The native PLA is characterized by a broad diffraction peak, which was centered at 25°. The PXRD pattern of the native PVA shows a broad lump between 17° and 20° both in the native component and in the tested formulations, which suggests that the PVA molecule is present in the NCs. The previous study indicated that the OH groups of PVA was adsorbed on the surface of the NCs and can keep the NCs in a pseudo-hydrated state [36]. The diffraction patterns of the native PLA exhibit a broad diffraction peak from 2ϑ = 16.7° to 2ϑ = 35°. These results indicate that Doc is not present as a crystalline state, but is probably dissolved within the NCs' core and shell while some residual PVA might be present on the surface of the NCs.

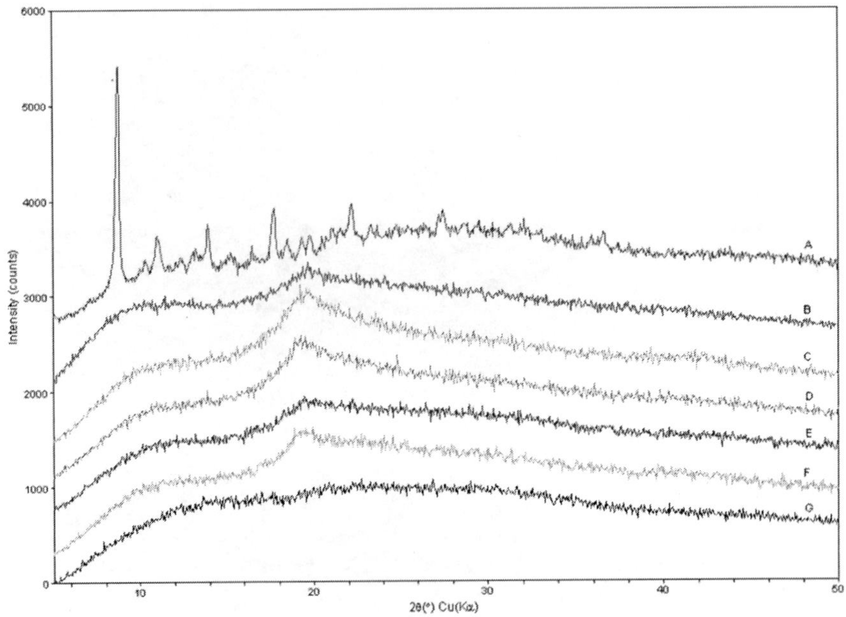

Figure 5. PXRD pattern. A, native Doc; B, F_{13} (PLA, 360 mg; Doc, 10 mg; oil, 0.9 ml); C, F_{12} (200 mg, 10 mg, 0.5 ml); D, F_6 (200 mg, 18 mg, 0.9 ml); E, blank nanocapsules; F, native PVA; and G, native PLA 208.

In vitro drug release study

The purpose of this study was to investigate the drug release mechanisms from Doc-loaded NCs. The cumulative percentages of Doc released from NCs as a function of time are reported in Figure 6. The results indicate that the drug release rate depends on the NCs' properties. The Doc oily core NCs were characterized by a sustained release profile (less than 40% of Doc is released within 60 h). This might be attributed to the hydrophobic interaction between the hydrophobic moiety of PLA, oil, and Doc. Compared to a previous result using nanosphere-based PLA [37], one can assume that the drug release is mainly due to the oil contained inside the NCs' core. The release data of Doc from the NCs (Figure 6) were fitted to the Higuchi model [38] to determine the drug release mechanism. The drug release constant (k) and regression coefficient (R^2) of the Higuchi model are shown in Table S2 in Additional file 1. Accordingly, the Doc release was best supported by Higuchi's model, i.e., based on Fickian diffusion, as it presented the highest values of linearity ($R^2 > 0.93$) for all formulations. From F_6, the release rate of Doc in 24 h corresponds to 0.9 nmol. This concentration is consistent with a previous report where the EC_{50} of

Doc was ranged from 1 to 6.2 nmol. [39]. In these conditions, the low drug level in simulated plasma pH suggests that a triggering mechanism would be required to enhance drug release *in situ* within the targeted cancer cells in order to spare vital organs and significantly reduce the unwanted systemic side effect. To better understand the compatibility between Doc and PLA, as well as the neutral oil, the Flory-Huggins interaction parameter calculations were carried out as shown below.

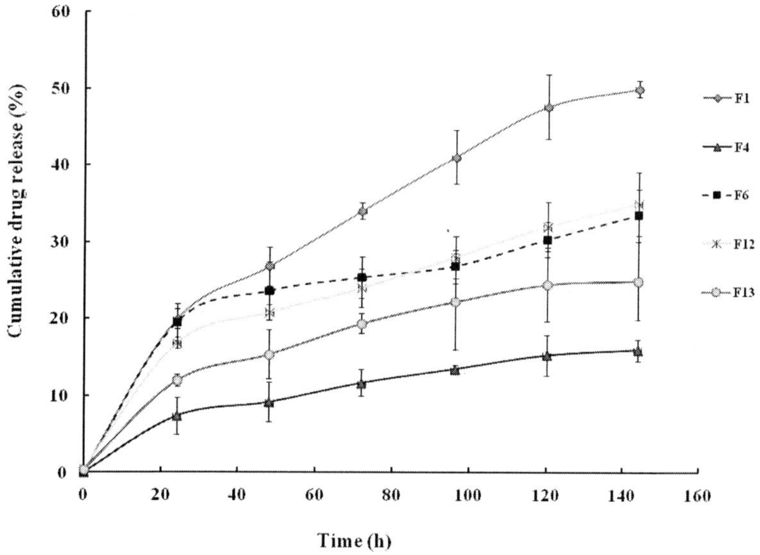

Figure 6. Cumulative drug release from Doc-loaded nanocapsules in PBS (pH 7.4), at 37 ± 0.5°C. Each point represents the mean value of three different experiments ± standard deviation.

Solubility parameter determination

To prove the suitability of PLA and oil for the optimal solubilization of Doc in the nanostructure, the Flory-Huggins interaction parameters were computed. The solubility parameters of Doc (δ_s) and PLA (δ_p) were calculated and listed in Table S3 in Additional file 1. According to the Flory-Huggins theory, the critical χ_{sp} value above which a polymer and a low molecular weight compound (i.e., drug) become miscible is < 0.5. Therefore, a lower value of χ_{sp}should result in a higher solubility. The obtained interaction parameters (χ_{sp}) between Doc and PLA and between Doc and oil were calculated. Table S3 in Additional file 1 shows a low value of the interaction parameter (χ_{sp}) between Doc and

PLA 0.65 $(cal/cm^3)^{1/2}$. In contrast, the interaction solubility value between Doc/oil was relatively high 1.64 $(cal/cm^3)^{1/2}$, indicating that Doc is more compatible with PLA than with the oil. This finding seems to show that a high PLA content may contribute to high drug EE% (up to 93%). To confirm the suitability of the oil/ethyl acetate mixture (phase A) with water (phase B) for the NCs' formation, the interfacial tension (γ_{AB}) between these two immiscible phases (A and B) was predicted by Kim and Burgess [40] using Equation 7:

$$\gamma_{AB} = \gamma_A - \gamma_B \exp\left(-\alpha V^{0.7}\right) + \gamma_B \tag{7.1}$$

where γ_A and γ_B (72 mN/m at 25°C) are the surface tension of each phase (A or B), α is an exponential coefficient, and V is the volume fraction of the oil mixture. The α-value can be calculated by using the following equation:

$$\alpha = 0.178\ (\Delta\gamma) - 0.0132 \tag{8}$$

where $\Delta\gamma$ is the surface tension difference between ethyl acetate and oil, respectively.

The surface tensions of pure oil and ethyl acetate are 30.00 mN/m [41] and 6.80 mN/m [42], respectively. The $\Delta\gamma$ resulting from mixing these two substances is 23.20 mN/m, which is estimated to be γ_A. From Equation 8, α was found to be 4.10 mN/m. However, the obtained value of γ_{AB} from Equation 7 was 7.94 mN/m.

It is important to bear in mind that the interfacial tension of the oil/water system could be altered when another organic liquid is added to the oil phase, resulting in a compositional change at the interface and hence changes in the cohesive and adhesive forces [40]. On the basis of the above result, it is useful to rationalize whether or not the oil droplet entrapment/engulfing inside the polymer shell can occur. To be effective, this should normally occur before the solvent diffusion step, where the polymer forming the shell is in a liquid state. To achieve this goal, the oil droplet inclusion within the polymer shell has been predicted using the interfacial tension between the three phases, A, B, and C, and the spreading coefficients as defined [43, 44]:

$$S_A = \gamma_{BC} - (\gamma_{AB} + \gamma_{AC}) \tag{9}$$

$$S_B = \gamma_{CA} - (\gamma_{BC} + \gamma_{BA}) \tag{10}$$

$$S_C = \gamma_{AB} - (\gamma_{CB} + \gamma_{CA}) \tag{11}$$

where γ is the interfacial tension (A, B, and C refer to the three phases). Based on these conventions, complete engulfing of phase A by phase C will occur if only if $S_A < 0$, $S_B < 0$ and $S_c > 0$. In this study, oil-ethyl acetate mixture is the phase A, water is phase B, and the polymeric phase (PLA) is phase C. The calculation of the spreading coefficients of a specific phase A/phase C system allows predicting the possible formation of oily core NCs.

The corresponding interfacial tension values were obtained as follows: γ_{BC} was obtained from the literature (γ_{BC} = +6.83 mN/m [45], γ_{AC} = +0.06 mN/m was obtained from Table S4 in Additional file 1[46, 47], and γ_{AB} calculated from Equation 7 was 7.94 mN/m, which is comparable to the literature value of 8.42 mN/m [45]. The positive sign of the water-PLA interfacial tension (γ_{BC} = +6.83 mN/m) implies that it tries to reduce its energy by reducing its surface area, and therefore, a spherical shape might be maintained. Based on these data, the obtained spreading coefficients were S_A = -1.17 mN/m (< 0), S_B = -14.71 mN/m (< 0), and S_C = +1.05 mN/m (> 0). Thermodynamically, the driving forces allowed the formation of a PLA layer between the water and oily phase, thus engulfing the oily phase. These data fundamentally explain why the oily core was surrounded by a polymer layer as visually evidenced by the TEM analysis.

In vitro evaluation of Doc-loaded NC cytotoxicity

Figure 7 shows the cytotoxicity from the LDH assay of native Doc and Doc-loaded NCs at three tested different concentrations. The cell culture medium used as a negative control was not cytotoxic. At lower concentrations, the native drug appeared more bioactive perhaps due to rapid diffusion and higher level of interaction with the cells. However, at the highest concentration (5 µM), the drug-loaded NCs' cytotoxicity was significantly higher than that of the native Doc. This data clearly suggests that the oily core NC formulation (as a reservoir system for the drug) could enhance the biological responses of the native Doc with higher drug payload. This might be due to the sustained release properties of the NCs and the enhanced drug internalization by SUM 225 cells in the nanocapsule form. This observation was consistent with a previous report [48] related to a nanoparticulate form of another anticancer drug (doxorubicin) tested on a different breast cancer cell line (MCF7).

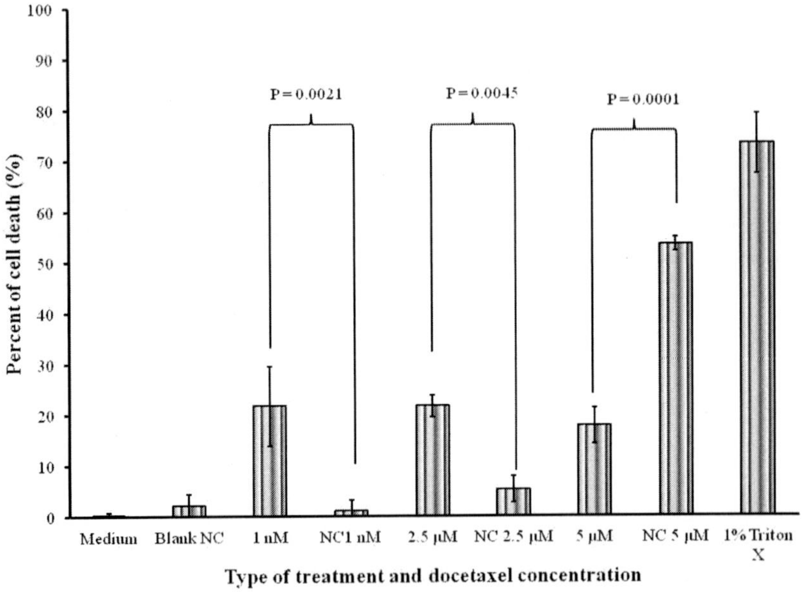

Figure 7. Percent SUM 225 cell death by LDH assay after different treatments for 24 h. See text for details. Pairwise comparison: native drug versus drug loaded NCs at the same concentration. Data are expressed as mean percent ± SD from six measurements (n = 6).

CONCLUSIONS

In this work, we developed PLA-based Doc-loaded oily NCs by solvent diffusion method. The results confirmed the formation of Doc-loaded oily core polyester-shell NCs in the nanosize range (115 to 582 nm) and high EE% (65% to 93%). Most of the NCs were monodisperse in size (PDI = 0.005) with smooth surface. The PXRD data suggested that Doc was dissolved in the NCs. The Doc release data over 144 h fitted well with the Higuchi model ($R^2 > 0.93$), indicating that the drug mainly diffused out of the NCs in this timeframe. Consistent with the analysis of the spreading coefficients and visual evidence from EM, the NCs' oily core was indeed formed. The results from the cytotoxicity study suggested that at a high concentration (5 μM), the enhanced toxicity of the encapsulated drug on the examined cancerous cell line might be due to both the particle's uptake by the SUM 225 cells and the sustained drug release profile from the NCs. In a future work, we plan to investigate the cancer cell targeting capability of pegylated Doc-loaded NCs conjugated to specific ligands for drug delivery applications.

AUTHORS' INFORMATION

IY has a Ph.D. degree in Pharmaceutical Sciences and is a post doctoral research associate in the Division of Pharmaceutical Sciences, School of Pharmacy, University of Missouri-Kansas City. XY is a graduate student in the Division of Pharmaceutical Sciences, School of Pharmacy, University of Missouri-Kansas City. JM has BS, MS, and Ph.D. degrees in Geochemistry and Mineralogy. He is an associate professor in the Department of Geosciences, University of Missouri-Kansas City. BBCY has PharmD and Ph.D. degrees in Pharmaceutical Sciences. He is also an associate professor in the Division of Pharmaceutical Sciences, School of Pharmacy, University of Missouri-Kansas City.

ACKNOWLEDGEMENTS

The authors are thankful to Gattefosse Corporation for providing a gift sample of Labrafac CC, to Dr. Elizabet Kostoryz (Division of Pharmacology, University of Missouri-Kansas City) for assistance with the DLS measurement, and to Randy Tindall (Electron Microscopy Center, University of Missouri-Columbia) for the electron microscopy studies. We are also grateful to Fariba Behbod, PharmD, PhD, Assistant Professor, Pathology and Laboratory Medicine, University of Kansas Medical Center for kindly providing the SUM 225 cell line.

REFERENCES

1. Herbst RS, Khuri FR: Mode of action of docetaxel - a basis for combination with novel anticancer agents. *Cancer Treat Rev*2003, 29: 407–415.

2. Aapro M, Bruno R: Early clinical studies with docetaxel. Docetaxel investigators group. *Eur J Cancer* 1995, 31A: S7–10.

3. Capri G, Tarenzi E, Fulfaro F, Gianni L: The role of taxanes in the treatment of breast cancer. *Semin Oncol* 1996, 23: 68–75.

4. Rowinsky EK: The development and clinical utility of the taxane class of antimicrotubule chemotherapy agents. *Annu Rev Med* 1997, 48: 353–374.

5. Pazdur R, Newman RA, Newman BM, Fuentes A, Benvenuto J, Bready B, Moore D Jr, Jaiyesimi I, Vreeland F, Bayssas MM, Raber MN: Phase I trial of Taxotere: five-day schedule. *J Natl Cancer Inst* 1992, 84: 1781–1788.

6. Tomiak E, Piccart MJ, Kerger J, Lips S, Awada A, de Valeriola D, Ravoet C, Lossignol D, Sculier JP, Auzannet V, Le Bail N, Bayssas M, Klastersky J: Phase I study of docetaxel administered as a 1-hour intravenous infusion on a weekly basis. *J Clin Oncol* 1994, 12: 1458–1467.

7. Bissery MC, Nohynek G, Sanderink GJ, Lavelle F: Docetaxel (Taxotere): a review of preclinical and clinical experience. Part I: preclinical experience. *Anticancer Drugs* 1995, 6: 339–355. 363–338 363-338

8. Liang G, Jia-Bi Z, Fei X, Bin N: Preparation, characterization and pharmacokinetics of N-palmitoyl chitosan anchored docetaxel liposomes. *J Pharm Pharmacol* 2007, 59: 661–667.

9. Immordino ML, Brusa P, Arpicco S, Stella B, Dosio F, Cattel L: Preparation, characterization, cytotoxicity and pharmacokinetics of liposomes containing docetaxel. *J Control Release* 2003, 91: 417–429.

10. Wang QW, Lu HL, Song CC, Liu H, Xu CG: Radiosensitivity of human colon cancer cell enhanced by immunoliposomal docetaxel. *World J Gastroenterol* 2005, 11: 4003–4007.

11. Jakate AS, Einhaus CM, DeAnglis AP, Retzinger GS, Desai PB: Preparation, characterization, and preliminary application of fibrinogen-coated olive oil droplets for the targeted delivery of docetaxel to solid malignancies. *Cancer Res* 2003, 63: 7314–7320.

12. Einhaus CM, Retzinger AC, Perrotta AO, Dentler MD, Jakate AS, Desai PB, Retzinger GS: Fibrinogen-coated droplets of olive oil for delivery of docetaxel to a fibrin(ogen)-rich ascites form of a murine mammary tumor. *Clin Cancer Res* 2004, 10: 7001–7010.

13. Farokhzad OC, Cheng J, Teply BA, Sherifi I, Jon S, Kantoff PW, Richie JP, Langer R: Targeted nanoparticle-aptamer bioconjugates for cancer chemotherapy in vivo. *Proc Natl Acad Sci USA* 2006, 103: 6315–6320.

14. Grosse PY, Bressolle F, Pinguet F: In vitro modulation of doxorubicin and docetaxel antitumoral activity by methyl-beta-cyclodextrin. *Eur J Cancer* 1998, 34: 168–174.

15. Heurtault B, Saulnier P, Pech B, Venier-Julienne M-C, Proust J-E, Phan-Tan-Luu R, Benoît J-P: The influence of lipid nanocapsule composition on their size distribution. *Eur J Pharm Sci* 2003, 18: 55–61.

16. Kennedy L, Bear A, Young J, Lewinski N, Kim J, Foster A, Drezek R: T cells enhance gold nanoparticle delivery to tumors in vivo. *Nanoscale Res Lett* 2011, 6: 283.

17. Couvreur P, Dubernet C, Puisieux F: Controlled drug delivery with nanoparticles: current possibilities and future trends. *Eur J Pharm Biopharm* 1995, 41: 2–13.

18. Wasan KM: The biological functions of lipid excipients and the implications for pharmaceutical products development. *J Pharm Sci* 2009, 98: 379–382.

19. Quintanar-Guerrero D, Ganem-Quintanar A, Allémann E, Fessi H, Doelker E: Influence of the stabilizer coating layer on the purification and freeze-drying of poly(D, L-lactic acid) nanoparticles prepared by an emulsion-diffusion technique. *J Microencapsul* 1998, 15: 107–119.

20. Hans ML, Lowman AM: Biodegradable nanoparticles for drug delivery and targeting. *Cur Opin in Sol State Mater Sci* 2002, 6: 319–327.

21. Wilkes GM, Barton-Burke M: *Oncology Nursing Drug Handbook*. Sudbury, MA: Jones and Bartlett; 2006.

22. Cervin C, Tinzl M, Johnsson M, Abrahamsson P-A, Tiberg F, Dizeyi N: Properties and effects of a novel liquid crystal nanoparticle formulation of docetaxel in a prostate cancer mouse model. *Eur J Pharm Sci* 2010, 41: 369–375.

23. Alukda D, Sturgis T, Youan B-BC: Formulation of tenofovir-loaded functionalized solid lipid nanoparticles intended for HIV prevention. *J Pharm Sci* 2011, 100: 3345–3356.

24. Higuchi T: Rate of release of medicaments from ointment bases containing drugs in suspension. *J Pharm Sci* 1961, 50: 874–875.

25. Hansen CM: Polymer science applied to biological problems: prediction of cytotoxic drug interactions with DNA. *Eur Polym J*2008, 44: 2741–2748.

26. Hildebrand JH, Scott RL: *The Solubility of Nonelectrolytes*. 3rd edition. New York: Reinhold; 1950.

27. Lawson DD, Ingham JD: Estimation of solubility parameters from refractive index data. *Nature* 1969, 223: 614–615.

28. Hansen CM: The three dimensional solubility parameter - key to paint component affinities I. - solvents, plasticizers, polymers, and resins. *J Paint Techn* 1967, 39: 104–117.

29. Latere Dwan'Isa J, Rouxhet L, Préat V, Brewster M, Ariën A: Prediction of drug solubility in amphiphilic di-block copolymer micelles: the role of polymer-drug compatibility. *Pharmazie* 2007, 62: 499–504.

30. Murakami H, Kawashima Y, Niwa T, Hino T, Takeuchi H, Kobayashi M: Influence of the degrees of hydrolyzation and polymerization of poly(vinylalcohol) on the preparation and properties of poly(dl-lactide-co-glycolide) nanoparticle. *Inter J Pharm* 1997, 149: 43–49.

31. Govender T, Riley T, Ehtezazi T, Garnett MC, Stolnik S, Illum L, Davis SS: Defining the drug incorporation properties of PLA-PEG nanoparticles. *Inter J Pharm* 2000, 199: 95–110.

32. Hackley V, Ferraris C: The use of nomenclature in dispersion science and technology. *NIST Recommended Practice Guide: SP* 2001.

33. Mosqueira VCF, Legrand P, Pinto-Alphandary H, Puisieux F, Barratt G: Poly(D, L-lactide) nanocapsules prepared by a solvent displacement process: influence of the composition on physicochemical and structural properties. *J Pharm Sci*2000, 89: 614–626.

34. Chen J, Qiu L, Hu M, Jin Y, Han J: Preparation, characterization and in vitro evaluation of solid dispersions containing docetaxel. *Drug Dev Ind Pharm* 2008, 34(6):588–594.

35. Zaske L, Perrin MA, Leveiller F: Docetaxel: solid state characterization by x-ray powder diffraction and thermogravimetry. *J Phys IVFrance* 2001, 11: Pr10–221-Pr10–226.

36. Abdelwahed W, Degobert G, Fessi H: Investigation of nanocapsules stabilization by amorphous excipients during freeze-drying and storage. *Eur J Pharm Biopharm* 2006, 63: 87–94.

37. Sanna V, Roggio A, Posadino A, Cossu A, Marceddu S, Mariani A, Alzari V, Uzzau S, Pintus G, Sechi M: Novel docetaxel-loaded nanoparticles based on poly(lactide-co-caprolactone) and poly(lactide-co-glycolide-co-caprolactone) for prostate cancer treatment: formulation, characterization, and cytotoxicity studies. *Nanoscale Res Lett* 2011, 6: 260.

38. Higuchi T: Mechanism of sustained action medication. Theoretical analysis of rate of release of solid drugs dispersed in solid matrices. *J Pharm Sci* 1963, 52: 1145–1149.

39. Halder J, Landen CN, Lutgendorf SK, Li Y, Jennings NB, Fan D, Nelkin GM, Schmandt R, Schaller MD, Sood AK: Focal adhesion kinase

silencing augments docetaxel-mediated apoptosis in ovarian cancer cells. *Clin Cancer Res* 2005, 11: 8829–8836.

40. Kim H, Burgess DJ: Prediction of interfacial tension between oil mixtures and water. *J Colloid Interface Sci* 2001, 241: 509–513.

41. Adamson A, Gast A: *Physical Chemistry of Surfaces*. Hoboken: Wiley; 1997.

42. Kobayashi I, Mukataka S, Nakajima M: Effects of type and physical properties of oil phase on oil-in-water emulsion droplet formation in straight-through microchannel emulsification, experimental and CFD studies. *Langmuir* 2005, 21: 5722–5730.

43. Pekarek KJ, Jacob JS, Mathiowitz E: Double-walled polymer microspheres for controled drug release. *Nature* 1994, 367: 258–260.

44. Torza S, Mason SG: Three-phase interactions in shear and electrical fields. *J Colloid Interface Sci* 1970, 33: 67–83.

45. Howard JR, Hadgraft J: The clearance of oily vehicles following intramuscular and subcutaneous injections in rabbits. *Int J Pharm* 1983, 16: 31–39.

46. Biresaw G, Carriere CJ: Interfacial tension of poly(lactic acid)/polystyrene blends. *J Polym Sci B Polym Phys* 2002, 40: 2248–2258.

47. Kirchner B: *Ionic Liquids*. *Volume 290*. Berlin: Springer; 2010.

48. Li PY, Lai PS, Hung WC, Syu WJ: Poly(l-lactide)-vitamin E TPGS nanoparticles enhanced the cytotoxicity of Doxorubicin in drug-resistant MCF-7 breast cancer cells. *Biomacromolecules* 2010, 11: 2576–2582.

Chapter 10

Biodegradable Nanoparticles of Methoxy Poly(Ethylene Glycol)-*b*-Poly(D, L-Lactide)/Methoxy Poly(Ethylene Glycol)-*b*-Poly(ϵ-Caprolactone) Blends For Drug Delivery

Yodthong Baimark* and Yaowalak Srisuwan

Department of Chemistry and Center of Excellence for Innovation in Chemistry, Faculty of Science, Mahasarakham University, Mahasarakham 44150, Thailand

ABSTRACT

The effects of blend weight ratio and polyester block length of methoxy poly(ethylene glycol)-*b*-poly(D, L-lactide) (MPEG-*b*-PDLL)/methoxy poly(ethylene glycol)-*b*-poly(ϵ-caprolactone) (MPEG-*b*-PCL) blends on nanoparticle characteristics and drug release behaviors were evaluated. The blend nanoparticles were prepared by nanoprecipitation method for controlled release of a poorly water-soluble model drug, indomethacin. The drug-loaded nanoparticles were nearly spherical in shape. The particle size and drug loading efficiency slightly decreased with increasing MPEG-*b*-PCL blend weight ratio. Two distinct thermal decomposition steps from thermogravimetric analysis suggested different blend weight ratios. Thermal transition changes from differential scanning calorimetry revealed miscible blending between MPEG-*b*-PDLL and MPEG-*b*-PCL in an amorphous phase. An *in vitro* drug release study demonstrated that the drug release behaviors depended upon the PDLL block length and the blend weight ratios but not on PCL block length.

Keywords: Biodegradable polymers Polymer blends Diblock copolymers Nanoparticles Nanoprecipitation method Controlled release

BACKGROUND

In the past few decades, biodegradable and biocompatible nanoparticles of methoxy poly(ethylene glycol)-*b*-poly(DL-lactide) (MPEG- *b*-PDLL) and methoxy poly(ethylene glycol)- *b*-poly(ϵ-caprolactone) (MPEG- *b*-PCL) amphiphilic diblock copolymers have shown potential as controlled-release drug delivery carriers because of the small size of their nanoparticles, which improves circulation time in the body and decreases the administration frequency when compared to microparticles which are rapidly cleared by the reticuloendothelial tissue [1, 2]. Moreover, for MPEG-*b*-PDLL and MPEG- *b*-PCL nanoparticles suspended in water, PDLL and PCL hydrophobic cores are surrounded by hydrophilic MPEG blocks on the nanoparticle surface to solubilize hydrophobic drugs; this increases blood circulation time and decreases uptake by the liver of the nanoparticles [3, 4, 5, 6]. The need for surfactants when preparing nanoparticles of amphiphilic diblock copolymer by the nanoprecipitation method can be removed. The protective effect of the hydrophilic MPEG block is adequate for preventing nanoparticle aggregation. The poly(vinyl alcohol), Span series, Tween series, poly(ethylene oxide) (PEO), and poloxamer (PEO-poly(propylene oxide) block copolymer) have been used as surfactants to stabilize emulsion droplets [7]. These surfactants remain at the particle surface and are difficult to remove which affect the biodegradability and drug release profile of the drug-loaded particles. Also, these remaining surfactants can influence the human body, for example, causing an allergy-like reaction.

In previous studies, much attention was paid to the drug-loaded nanoparticles of these amphiphilic diblock copolymers with different types of chemical compositions and lengths of polymer blocks used [8, 9, 10, 11]. Drug release profiles of the nanoparticles depended upon these factors. The physical blending of polymers is an alternative method that has been widely used to adjust the properties of biodegradable polyesters [12, 13, 14, 15]. Thus unique properties of polymer blends, quite different from the origin polymers, were obtained. The drug release rate from poly(L-lactide)/PCL blend nanoparticles prepared from the nanoprecipitation method using poloxamer 188 as the surfactant has been adjusted by varying the blend weight ratios [16].

The characteristics and drug release behaviors of the MPEG-*b*-PCL nanoparticles containing drug prepared by the nanoprecipitation method can be controlled by adjusting the processing parameters, such as the organic/water phase volume ratio, polymer concentration, drug/polymer weight ratio, and stirring speed [17]. However, the effect of MPEG-*b*-

PDLL/MPEG- *b*-PCL blending on characteristics and drug release of the nanoparticles has not been reported.

In this study, surfactant-free MPEG-*b*-PDLL/MPEG- *b*-PCL blend nanoparticles containing a model drug were prepared by the nanoprecipitation method. Indomethacin was selected as the model drug because of its poor water solubility. The effects of different polyester block lengths and blend weight ratios on the nanoparticle characteristics, drug loading efficiency, and drug release profiles were studied and discussed.

METHODS

Materials

MPEG-*b*-PDLL and MPEG- *b*-PCL diblock copolymers were synthesized by ring-opening polymerization in bulk under a nitrogen atmosphere as described in the previous works [18, 19]. MPEG with a molecular weight of 5,000 g/mol (Fluka Chemical Corporation, St. Louis, Milwaukee, WI, USA) and stannous octoate (95%, Sigma-Aldrich Corporation, St. Louis, MO, USA) were used as the initiating system. Stannous octoate concentration was kept constant at 0.02 mol%. MPEG-*b*-PDLL and MPEG- *b*-PCL with theoretical PDLL/PCL block lengths of 30,000 (30 K) and 60,000 (60 K) g/mol were called MPEG- *b*-PDLL30K, MPEG- *b*-PDLL60K, MPEG- *b*-PCL30K, and MPEG- *b*-PCL60K, respectively. The resulting number-average molecular weights (M_n) and molecular weight distribution (*MWD*) of diblock copolymers are summarized in Table 1. Indomethacin model drug (99%, Sigma-Aldrich Corporation, St. Louis, MO, USA) was used without further purification. All reagents used were analytical grade.

Table 1. Molecular weight characteristics of diblock copolymers

Diblock copolymer	$M_{n,\ theoretical}$ (g/mol)[a]	$M_{n,\ GPC}$ (g/mol)[b]	*MWD*[b]
MPEG-*b*-PDLL30K	35,000	23,000	1.7
MPEG-*b*-PDLL60K	35,000	49,000	1.8
MPEG-*b*-PCL30K	65,000	25,000	2.2
MPEG-*b*-PCL60K	65,000	47,000	1.6

[a]Calculated based on monomer/MPEG ratio and MPEG molecular weight; [b]obtained from gel permeation chromatography (GPC).

Preparation of drug-loaded blend nanoparticles

Drug-loaded blend nanoparticles were prepared via a nanoprecipitation method. Briefly, 4 mg of indomethacin and 60 mg of copolymer blend were co-dissolved in 6 mL of acetone. The organic solution was added dropwise into 60 mL of distilled water under magnetic stirring. The nanoparticles were immediately formed after solvent extraction. The organic solvent was then evaporated at room temperature for 6 h in a fume hood. The drug-loaded blend nanoparticles with MPEG-*b*-PDLL/MPEG- *b*-PCL blend weight ratios of 100/0, 75/25, 50/50, 25/75, and 0/100 (*w/w*) were investigated. The resultant nanoparticle suspensions were centrifuged at 15,000 rpm 4°C for 2 h. The supernatant was carefully discarded and the precipitated nanoparticles were then resuspended in a phosphate buffer solution media (0.1 M, pH 7.4). The dried drug-loaded nanoparticles were obtained by freeze-drying the precipitated nanoparticles for 48 h.

Characterization of drug-loaded blend nanoparticles

Morphology of the drug-loaded nanoparticles was determined by transmission electron microscopy (TEM) using a JEOL JEM 1230 TEM (JEOL Ltd., Tokyo, Japan). For TEM analysis, a drop of the nanoparticle suspension was placed on a formvar film coated on a copper grid. The specimen on the copper grid was not stained. The average particle sizes of the drug-loaded nanoparticles were measured from the nanoparticle suspension by light scattering analysis using a Coulter LS230 particle size analyzer (Beckman Coulter Inc., Brea, CA, USA) at 25°C. The thermal decomposition behavior of the dried nanoparticles was characterized by thermogravimetry (TG) analysis using a TA-Instrument SDT Q600 TG analyzer (TA Instruments, New Castle, DE, USA). For TG, 5–10 mg of nanoparticles was heated from 50°C to 600°C at the rate of 20°C/min under a nitrogen atmosphere. Thermal transition properties of the dried nanoparticles were determined by mean of non-isothermal differential scanning calorimetry (DSC) using a Perkin-Elmer Pyris Diamond DSC (Perkin-Elmer Inc., Waltham, MA, USA). For DSC, 5–10 mg of nanoparticles was heated at the rate of 10°C/min under helium flow. The degree of crystallinity of the blend nanoparticles due to PCL crystallization was calculated according to the following equation [20],

$$\text{Crystallinity of blend nanoparticles } (\%) = [\Delta H_m / 135.44] \times 100 \tag{1}$$

where ΔH_m is the melting enthalpy of the nanoparticles, and 135.44 J/g is the melting enthalpy for 100% crystalline PCL [21].

The theoretical drug loading content ($DLC_{theoretical}$), actual drug loading content (DLC_{actual}), and drug loading efficiency (DLE) were calculated from Equations 2, 3, and 4, respectively. The DLC_{actual} is an average value from three measurements. For the DLC_{actual} measurement, the dried drug-loaded nanoparticles were dissolved in dichloromethane. The weight of the actual entrapped drug was then determined by ultraviolet (UV)–vis spectrophotometry using a Perkin-Elmer Lambda 25 UV–vis spectrophotometer (Perkin-Elmer Inc., Waltham, MA, USA) at 319 nm and compared to a standard curve of indomethacin.

$$DLC_{theoretical}(\%) = \frac{\text{Weight of feed drug}}{\text{Weight of feed drug and copolymer}} \times 100 \qquad (2)$$

$$DLC_{actual}(\%) = \frac{\text{Weight of actual drug entrapped in nanoparticles}}{\text{Weight of drug} - \text{loaded nanoparticles}} \times 100 \qquad (3)$$

$$DLE(\%) = \frac{DLC_{actual}}{DLC_{theoretical}} \times 100 \qquad (4)$$

In vitro drug release

In vitro release of indomethacin from the blend nanoparticles was performed by dialysis bag diffusion technique. The drug-loaded nanoparticle suspension (10 mL) was placed in a dialysis bag, tied, and immersed into 100 mL of phosphate buffered saline (0.1 M, pH 7.4). The entire system was kept at 37°C under shaking at 100 rpm.

At predetermined time intervals, 5 mL aliquots of the release medium were withdrawn from the release medium, and the same volume of fresh buffer solution was added to continue the release test. The concentration of indomethacin released was monitored using an UV–vis spectrophotometer at 319 nm. According to a predetermined indomethacin concentration-UV absorbance standard curve, indomethacin concentration of the release medium was obtained. Percentage of indomethacin release was calculated based on the ratio of drug release at each release time and initial drug content in the nanoparticles. The average percentage release was calculated from the three experiments.

RESULTS AND DISCUSSION

Morphology and size

Morphology of the blend nanoparticles was investigated by TEM, an example of which is shown in Figure 1 for the MPEG-*b*-PDLL30K/MPEG- *b*-PCL30K blend nanoparticles. It can be seen that they were nearly spherical in shape for all blend weight ratios. The blend nanoparticles of MPEG- *b*-PDLL30K/MPEG- *b*-PCL60K, MPEG- *b*-PDLL60K/MPEG- *b*-PCL30K, and MPEG- *b*-PDLL60K/MPEG- *b*-PCL60K showed similar results. The morphology results suggested that the hydrophilic MPEG blocks act as the nanoparticle shell to stabilize the nanoparticle formation [18, 19]. In these nanoparticles, the hydrophobic core of the PDLL/PCL blocks is surrounded by the water-soluble polar groups of the MPEG blocks that extend into the aqueous medium to prevent nanoparticle aggregation. The polyester block length and blend weight ratio did not affect the morphology of drug-loaded blend nanoparticles. The TEM images also indicate that submicron-sized particles of copolymer blends can be prepared by the nanoprecipitation method.

The particle size results, from light scattering analysis, are illustrated in Figure 2. They were less than 140 nm with a narrow size distribution. The average particle size slightly decreased as the MPEG-*b*-PCL blend weight ratio increased, which may be due to crystallization of the MPEG- *b*-PCL component during particle solidification that induced nanoparticle shrinkage.

THERMAL DECOMPOSITION

Thermal decomposition of the blend nanoparticles was determined by TG. The TG thermograms in Figure 3 (top) showed that the thermal resistance of the drug-loaded nanoparticles of MPEG-*b*- PCL are better than MPEG- *b*-PDLL. The blend nanoparticles, comprised of two decomposition steps, had maintained distinct thermal stability due to MPEG- *b*-PDLL decomposition, followed by degradation of the MPEG- *b*-PCL component. It was found that the TG profiles of the blend nanoparticles strongly depended upon the blend weight ratio. The amount of weight loss in the first step increased significantly when the MPEG- *b*-PDLL blend weight ratio was increased, as would be expected, since the blend nanoparticles with various blend weight ratios were successfully prepared.

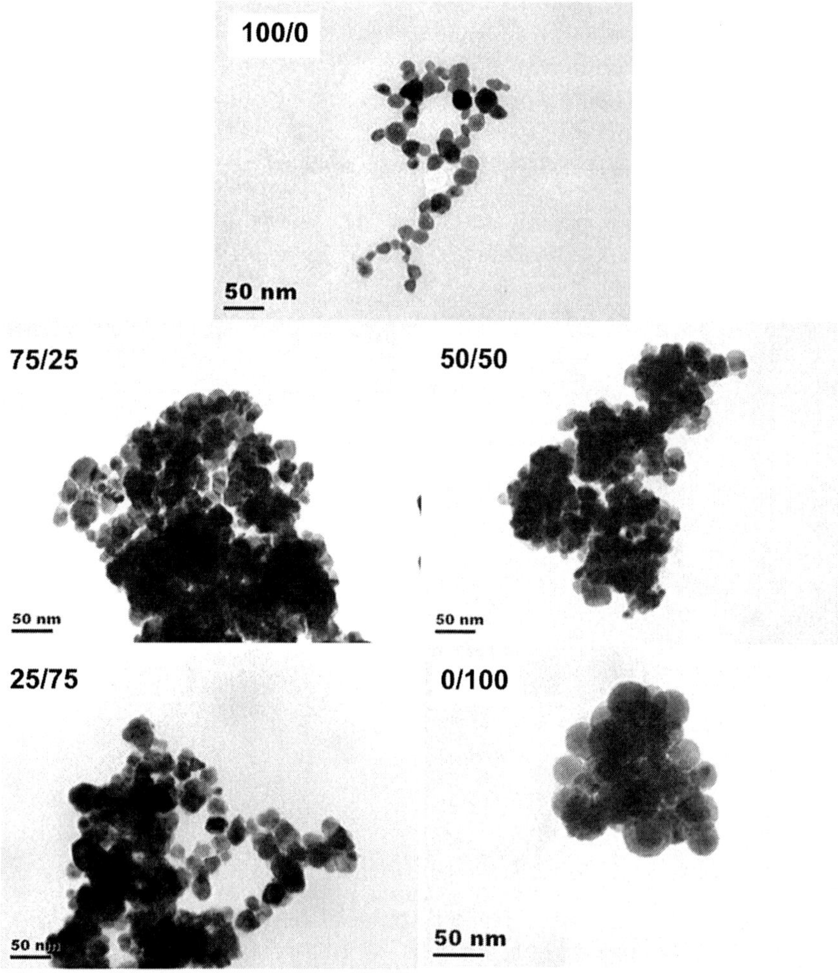

Figure 1. TEM micrographs of drug-loaded nanoparticles with different MPEG- *b* -PDLL30K/MPEG- *b* -PCL30K blend weight ratios. All bars = 50 nm.

Thermal decomposition can be clearly observed from differential TG (DTG) thermograms. Figure 3 (bottom) show DTG thermograms of the MPEG-*b*-PDLL30K/MPEG- *b*-PCL30K blend nanoparticles as examples. The two-step decomposition process of the blend nanoparticles is clearly illustrated. The peak temperature of the DTG thermogram is the temperature of maximum decomposition rate ($T_{d,\ max}$). The lower and higher $T_{d,\ max}$ values of the DTG thermograms are attributed to MPEG-*b*-PDLL and MPEG- *b*-PCL decompositions, respectively. The $T_{d,\ max}$ of MPEG-*b*-PDLL and MPEG- *b*-PCL decomposition peaks are in the range of 343°C to 354°C and 400°C to 418°C, respectively, which also indicates higher thermal stability of the MPEG- *b*-PCL matrix. It should be noted that the peak areas of the DTG thermograms strongly depend on the blend weight ratio. It can be clearly seen that the peak area of the lower temperature peak due to MPEG- *b*-PDLL decomposition decreased steadily as the MPEG- *b*-PDLL blend weight ratio decreased.

The TG and DTG thermograms of the blend nanoparticles of MPEG-*b*-PDLL30K/MPEG- *b*-PCL60K, MPEG- *b*-PDLL60K/MPEG- *b*-PCL30K, and MPEG- *b*-PDLL60K/MPEG- *b*-PCL60K changed with the blend weight ratio similar to the MPEG- *b*-PDLL30K/MPEG- *b*-PCL30K blend nanoparticles. The thermogravimetry results supported the fact that MPEG- *b*-PDLL/MPEG- *b*-PCL blend nanoparticles with different blend weight ratios were obtained.

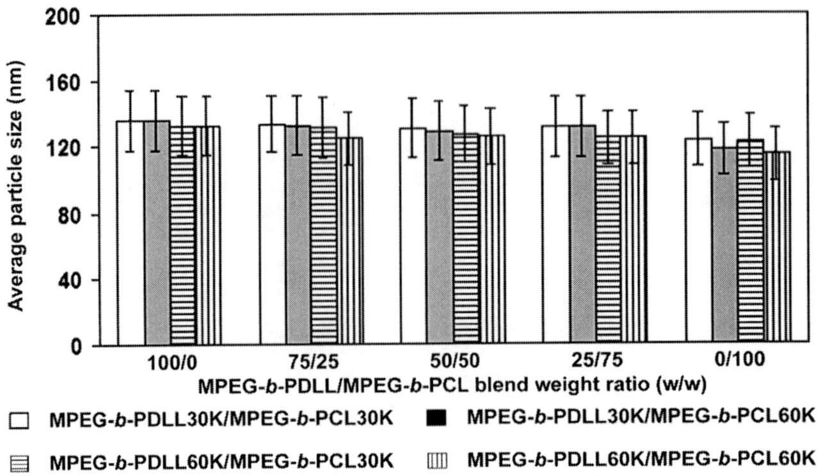

Figure 2. Average particle sizes of drug-loaded blend nanoparticles.

Thermal transition

The thermal transition of the blend nanoparticles was studied by DSC. The DSC thermograms of the MPEG-*b*-PDLL/MPEG- *b*-PCL blend nanoparticles are shown as an example in Figure 4. The melting peak of indomethacin is around 165°C and was not observed for all nanoparticles. This may be explained by the indomethacin molecules being incorporated into the MPEG-*b*-PDLL or MPEG- *b*-PCL in the nanoparticle matrix. The indomethacin crystallizability was then suppressed. Thus the drug was homogeneously dispersed in an amorphous form inside the nanoparticle matrix.

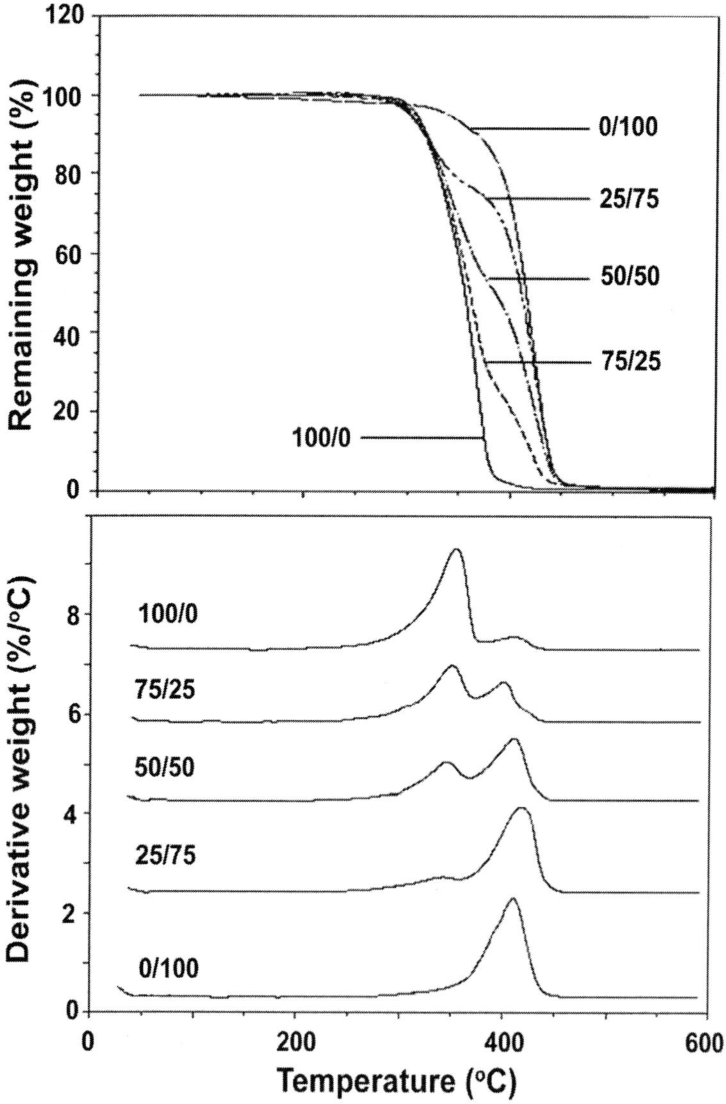

Figure 3. TG (top) and DTG (bottom) thermograms of drug-loaded nanoparticles with different MPEG- ***b*** -PDLL30K/MPEG- ***b*** -PCL30K blend weight ratios.

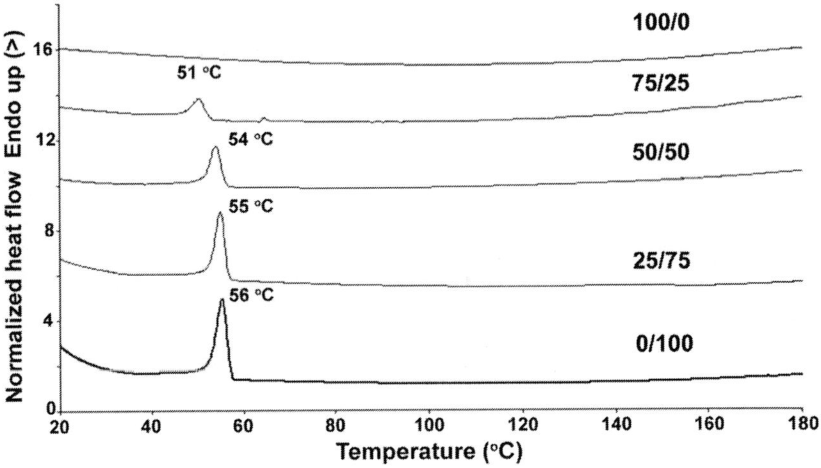

Figure 4. DSC thermograms of drug-loaded nanoparticles with different MPEG-***b*** -PDLL30K/MPEG- ***b*** -PCL30K blend weight ratios.

The drug-loaded MPEG-*b*-PDLL nanoparticles were amorphous (Figure 4a). Meanwhile, the MPEG-*b*-PCL and blend nanoparticles exhibited a single melting peak due to MPEG- *b*-PCL crystalline (Figures 4b,c,d,e). The DSC results, including melting temperature (T_m), melting enthalpy (ΔH_m) and crystallinity of the nanoparticles are given in Figure 5. The T_m, ΔH_m and crystallinity significantly decreased with the MPEG-*b*-PCL blend weight ratio. This may be explained by the MPEG- *b*-PCL crystallization being inhibited by blending with MPEG- *b*-PDLL. The results suggest that the MPEG- *b*-PDLL and MPEG- *b*-PCL can be miscible blended in the amorphous nanoparticle matrix to reduce the T_m, ΔH_m and crystallinity of the MPEG-*b*-PCL.

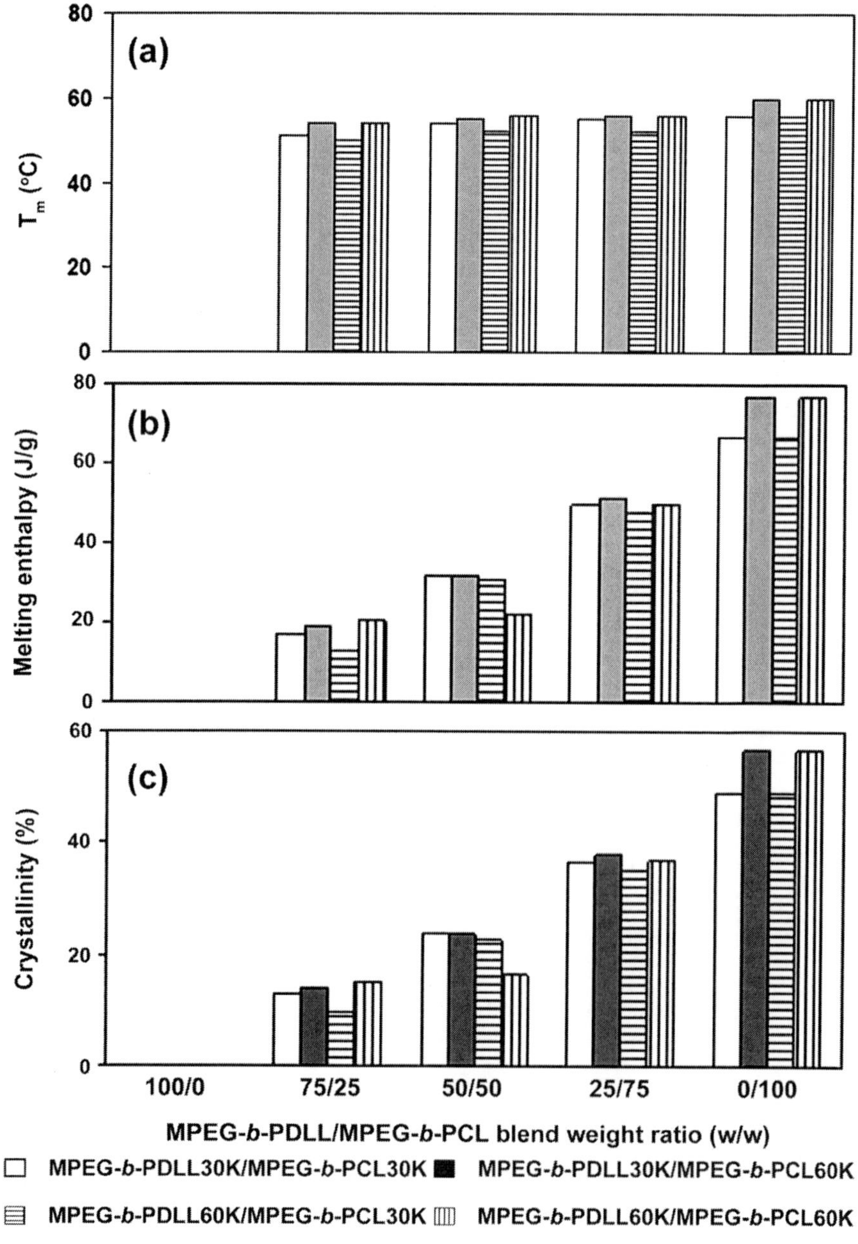

Figure 5. DSC results. (a) T_m, **(b)** melting enthalpy, and **(c)** crystallinity of drug-loaded blend nanoparticles.

Drug loading efficiency

From the feed drug and copolymer blend, the theoretical drug loading contents ($DLC_{theoretical}$) of all blend nanoparticle formulations were calculated from Equation 1, giving the result of 6.25%. The DLE of the blend nanoparticles were calculated from Equation 3 based on the $DLC_{theoretical}$/actual drug loading content (DLC_{actual}) ratios that are shown in Figure 6. The DLE was directly related to the DLC_{actual}. The DLC_{actual} and DLE of MPEG-*b*-PDLL nanoparticles were higher than that of MPEG- *b*-PCL. The higher chain flexibility of MPEG- *b*-PCL is due to its lower glass transition temperature which induced faster outward drug diffusion during nanoparticle solidification. Therefore, the residue drug entrapped in the MPEG- *b*-PCL nanoparticles was less than the MPEG- *b*-PDLL nanoparticles. The DLC_{actual} and DLE of the blend nanoparticles were between MPEG-*b*-PDLL and MPEG- *b*-PCL nanoparticles.

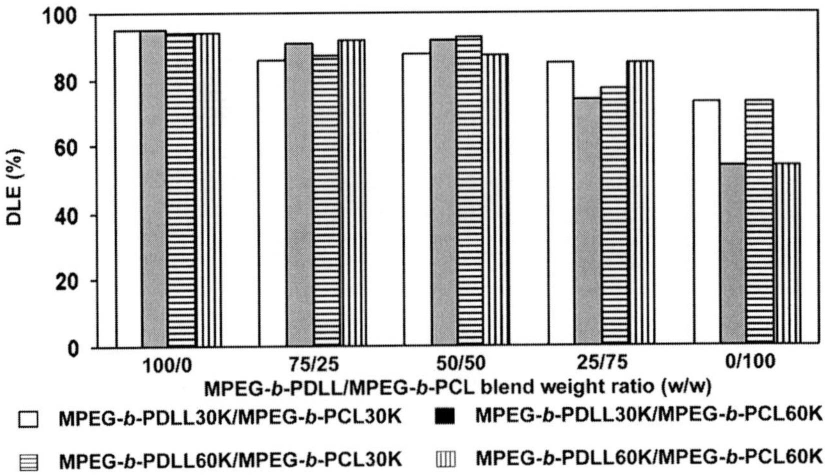

Figure 6. DLE of drug-loaded blend nanoparticles.

In vitro drug release

The *in vitro* drug releases from the blend nanoparticles performed in phosphate buffered saline pH 7.4 at 37°C for 7 days are illustrated in Figure 7. The drug release profiles exhibited biphasic features containing a rapid initial burst release followed by a sustaining release. The rapid initial burst release of the drug from the blend nanoparticles was probably due to the releasing of drug that was entrapped or adsorbed near to the nanoparticle surface. The initial burst release from the blend nanoparticles was found within the first 24 h of release time. After that the slow release may be due to a drug diffusion mechanism.

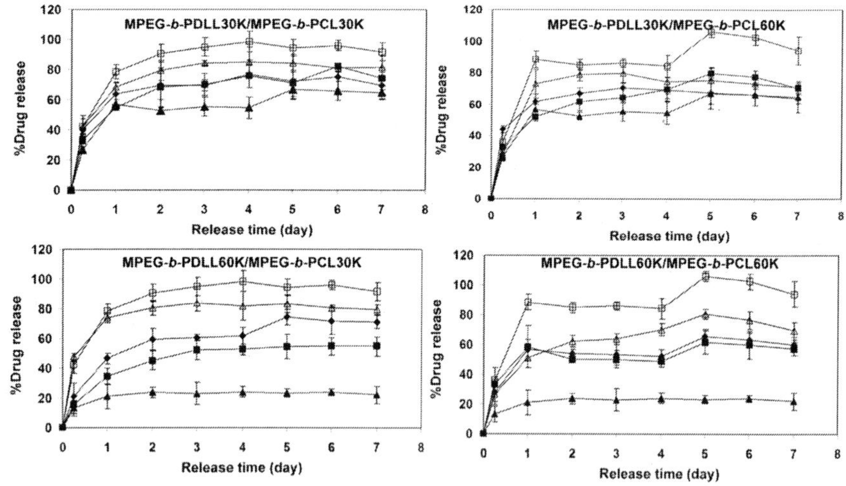

Figure 7. Drug release profiles from drug-loaded blend nanoparticles.

It can be seen that the drug release contents from the nanoparticles are in the order MPEG-*b*-PCL30K ≈ MPEG- *b*-PCL60K > MPEG- *b*-PDLL30K > MPEG- *b*-PDLL60K. The results may be explained due to the crystallinity of the MPEG- *b*-PCL component which could lead to formation of a channel structure in the nanoparticle matrix and results in the drug being easily released from the nanoparticles [10, 16]. Zhang et al. [10] reported that the drug release content from the MPEG-*b*-P(CL- *co*-DLL) nanoparticles increased with the CL content. For the blend nanoparticles, with increasing MPEG- *b*-PCL blend weight ratio, the drug release increased. The higher crystallinity of the blend nanoparticles is due to the larger MPEG- *b*-PCL blend weight ratio, inducing faster drug release from the nanoparticles. The drug release results indicate that the polyester block type and blend weight ratio were important factors for controlling the drug release content from the blend nanoparticles.

CONCLUSIONS

In the present study, drug-loaded MPEG-*b*-PDLL/MPEG- *b*-PCL blend nanoparticles with various polyester block lengths and blend weight ratios were prepared by nanoprecipitation method. They were nearly spherical in shape. The average particle size slightly decreased as the MPEG- *b*-PCL blend weight ratio increased. The thermal decomposition behaviors confirm the difference in MPEG- *b*-PDLL/MPEG- *b*-PCL blend weight ratios of the blend nanoparticles. Melting temperature and melting enthalpy depression of MPEG-

b-PCL indicate the miscibility between MPEG-*b*-PDLL and MPEG-*b*-PCL components in the drug-loaded blend nanoparticle matrix.

The nanoparticles of MPEG-*b*-PDLL and MPEG-*b*-PCL showed the slowest and fastest drug releases, respectively. The drug release behaviors of the blend nanoparticles were between the MPEG-*b*-PCL and MPEG-*b*-PDLL nanoparticles. The drug release from the blend nanoparticles can be tailored by adjusting the PCL block length and blend weight ratio. These blend nanoparticles without any surfactants added are considered to be promising biodegradable drug carriers for sustained release of poorly water-soluble drugs.

ACKNOWLEDGMENTS

The authors would like to acknowledge financial support from the Research, Development and Engineering (RD&E) fund through The National Nanotechnology Center (NANOTEC), The National Science and Technology Development Agency (NSTDA), Thailand (Project No. NN-B-22-EN4-30-52-11) to Mahasarakham University. The authors also thank the Center of Excellence for Innovation in Chemistry (PERCH-CIC), and the Commission on Higher Education, Ministry of Education, Thailand.

REFERENCES

1. Stolnik S, Illum L, Davis SS: Long circulating microparticulate drug carriers. *Adv Drug Deliv Rev* 1995, 16: 195.

2. Stolnik S, Heald CR, Neal J, Garnett MC, Davis SS, Illum L, Purkiss SC, Barlow RJ, Gellert PR: Polylactide-poly(ethylene Glycol) miscellar-like particles as potential drug carriers: production, colloidal properties and biological performance. *J Drug Target* 2001, 9: 361.

3. Tanodekaew S, Pannu R, Heatley F, Attwood D, Booth C: Association and surface properties of diblock copolymers of ethylene oxide and dl-lactide in aqueous solution. *Macromol Chem Phys* 1997, 198: 927.

4. Lemoine D, Francois C, Kedzierewicz F, Preat V, Holman M, Maincent P: Stability study of nanoparticles of poly(ε-caprolactone), poly(d, l-lactide) and poly(d, l-lactide-co-glycolide). *Biomaterials* 1996, 17: 2191.

5. Kim SY, Lee YM, Baik DJ, Kang JS: Toxic characteristics of methoxy poly(ethylene glycol)/poly(ϵ-caprolactone) nanospheres; in vitro and in vivo studies in the normal mice. *Biomaterials* 2003, 24: 55.

6. Otsuka H, Nagasaki Y, Kataoka K: Self-assembly of poly(ethylene glycol)-based block copolymers for biomedical applications. *Curr Opin Colloid Interface Sci* 2001, 6: 3.

7. Jeon H-J, Jeong Y-I, Jang M-K, Park Y-H, Nah J-W: Effect of solvent on the preparation of surfactant-free poly(dl-lactide-co-glycolide) nanoparticles and norfloxacin release characteristics. *Int J Pharm* 2000, 207: 99. S0378-5173(00)00537-8

8. Kim SY, Shin IG, Lee YM, Cho CS, Sung YK: Methoxy poly(ethylene glycol) and epsilon-caprolactone amphiphilic block copolymeric micelle containing indomethacin. II. Micelle formation and drug release behaviours. *J Control Release* 1998, 51: 13.

9. Shuai X, Ai H, Nasongkla N, Kim S, Gao J: Micellar carriers based on block copolymers of poly(ϵ-caprolactone) and poly(ethylene glycol) for doxorubicin delivery. *J Control Release* 2004, 98: 415.

10. Zhang Y, Wang C, Yang W, Shi B, Fu S: Tri-component of diblock polymers of poly(ethylene glycol)-poly(ϵ-caprolactone-co-lactide): synthesis, characterization and loading campothecin. *Colloid Polym Sci* 2005, 283: 1246.

11. Zhang Y, Li X, Zhou Y, Wang X, Fan Y, Huang Y, Liu Y: Preparation and evaluation of poly(ethylene glycol)–poly(lactide) micelles as nanocarriers for oral delivery of cyclosporine A. *Nanoscale Res Lett* 2010, 5: 917.

12. Lopez-Rodriguez N, Lopez-Arraiza A, Meaurio E, Sarasua JR: Crystallization, morphology, and mechanical behavior of polylactide/poly(ϵ-caprolactone) blends. *Polym Eng Sci* 2006, 46: 1299.

13. Dong Y, Feng SS: Nanoparticles of poly(d, l-lactide)/methoxy poly(ethylene glycol)-poly(d, l-lactide) blends for controlled release of paclitaxel. *J Biomed Mater Res* 2006, 78A: 12.

14. Yao M, Deng H, Mai F, Wang K, Zhang Q, Chen F, Fu Q: Modification of poly(lactic acid)/poly(propylene carbonate) blends through melt compounding with maleic anhydride. *Express Polym Lett* 2011, 5: 937.

15. Modi S, Koelling K, Vodovotz Y: Miscibility of poly(3-hydroxybutyrate-co-3-hydroxyvalerate) with high molecular weight poly(lactic acid)

blends determined by thermal analysis. *J Appl Polym Sci* 2012, 124: 3074.

16. Ge H, Hu Y, Yang S, Jiang X, Yang C: Preparation, characterization, and drug release behaviors of drug-loaded ϵ-caprolactone/L-lactide copolymer nanoparticles. *J Appl Polym Sci* 2000, 75: 874.

17. Wei XW, Gong CY, Gou ML, Fu SZ, Guo QF, Shi S, Luo F, Guo G, Qiu LY, Qian ZY: Biodegradable poly(ϵ-caprolactone)-poly(ethylene glycol) copolymers as drug delivery system. *Int J Pharm* 2009, 381: 1.

18. Baimark Y, Srisa-ard M, Threeprom J, Srisuwan Y: Preparation of nanoparticle colloids of methoxy poly(ethylene glycol)-b-poly(d, l-lactide): effects of surfactant and organic solvent. *Colloid Polym Sci* 2007, 285: 1521.

19. Baimark Y: Surfactant-free nanospheres of methoxy poly (ethylene glycol)-b-poly (ϵ-caprolactone) for controlled release of ibuprofen. *J Appl Sci* 2009, 9: 2287.

20. Bai W, Zhang L-F, Li Q, Chen D-L, Xiong C-D: In vitrohydrolytic degradation of poly(para-dioxanone)/poly(d,l-lactide) blends. *Mater Chem Phys* 2010, 122: 79.

21. Nojima S, Akutsu Y, Washino A, Tanimoto S: Morphology of melt-quenched poly(ϵ-caprolactone)-block-polyethylene copolymers. *Polymer* 2004, 45: 7317.

Chapter 11

Nanoparticles of Poly(Lactide-Co-Glycolide)-d-a-Tocopheryl Polyethylene Glycol 1000 Succinate Random Copolymer for Cancer Treatment

Yuandong Ma[1,2] , Yi Zheng[2] , Kexin Liu[3] , Ge Tian[3] , Yan Tian[3] , Lei Xu[3] , Fei Yan[2] , Laiqiang Huang[2] , Lin Mei[1,3]

[1]*School of Life Sciences, Tsinghua University, 100084 Beijing, People's Republic of China*

[2]*The Shenzhen Key Lab of Gene and Antibody Therapy, Center for Biotech and Bio-Medicine and Division of Life Sciences, Graduate School at Shenzhen, Tsinghua University, L401, Tsinghua Campus, Xili University Town, 518055 Shenzhen, Guangdong Province, People's Republic of China*

[3]*College of Pharmacy, Dalian Medical University, 116027 Dalian, Liaoning, People's Republic of China*

ABSTRACT

Cancer is the leading cause of death worldwide. Nanomaterials and nanotechnologies could provide potential solutions. In this research, a novel biodegradable poly(lactide-co-glycolide)-d-a-tocopheryl polyethylene glycol 1000 succinate (PLGA-TPGS) random copolymer was synthesized from lactide, glycolide and d-a-tocopheryl polyethylene glycol 1000 succinate (TPGS) by ring-opening polymerization using stannous octoate as catalyst. The obtained random copolymers were characterized by ^{1}H NMR, FTIR, GPC and TGA. The docetaxel-loaded nanoparticles made of PLGA-TPGS copolymer were prepared by a modified solvent extraction/evaporation method. The nanoparticles were then characterized by various state-of-the-art techniques. The results revealed that the size of PLGA-TPGS nanoparticles was around 250 nm. The docetaxel-loaded PLGA-TPGS nanoparticles could achieve much faster drug release in comparison with PLGA nanoparticles. In vitro cellular uptakes of such nanoparticles were investigated by CLSM, demonstrating the fluorescence PLGA-TPGS nanoparticles could be internalized by human cervix carcinoma cells (HeLa). The results also indicated that PLGA-TPGS-based nanoparticles were biocompatible, and the docetaxel-loaded PLGA-TPGS nanoparticles had significant cytotoxicity against Hela cells. The cytotoxicity against HeLa cells for PLGA-TPGS nanoparticles was in time- and concentration-dependent manner. In conclusion, PLGA-TPGS random copolymer could be acted as a novel and promising biocompatible polymeric matrix material applicable to nanoparticle-based drug delivery system for cancer chemotherapy.

Keywords: PLGA-TPGS Random copolymer Docetaxel Nanoparticle HeLa Cancer chemotherapy

INTRODUCTION

Cancer is the leading cause of death worldwide [1]. Nanotechnology has the potential to have a revolutionary impact on cancer diagnosis and therapy. Drug delivery via nanoparticles presents novel therapeutic opportunities for drugs that were previously unsuited to traditional oral or injectable drug formulations, allowing drugs to be delivered efficaciously while minimizing side effects and leading to better patient compliance. Specifically, nanoparticle-based drug delivery systems have enormous potential in addressing the failures of traditional drugs that could not be effectively formulated due to factors such as poor water solubility or a lack of target specificity [1,2, 3]. Synthetic biodegradable polymers have been widely utilized as the polymeric matrix materials of drug delivery systems. A few synthetic polymers, especially linear polyesters such as poly(ε-caprolactone) (PCL), polylactides (PLA) and poly(lactide-co-glycolide) (PLGA), which have been approved by FDA, are of great interest for medical applications [4]. Among them, PLGA is one of the most widely used biodegradable polymers to make nanoparticles for controlled drug delivery systems [4, 5]. However, these polymers were originally synthesized to be used as surgical sutures, which therefore have disadvantages to be used for drug delivery systems such as too high hydrophobicity and too slow degradation [6]. In addition, long-term incompatibility with blood cells and uptake by the reticuloendothelial system (RES) of PLGA nanoparticles as drug carrier are also a problem [5]. One of the limiting factors in this field is their thrombogenic property. Thus, the surface modification of the nanoparticles with a blood compatible material is important in order to improve the potential of intravenously administered nanoparticles in the drug delivery systems. It has been demonstrated that methoxy poly(ethylene glycol) (mPEG)-modified nanoparticles provides protection against interaction with the blood components, which induce removal of the foreign particles from the blood [7]. D-α-tocopheryl polyethylene glycol 1000 succinate (TPGS) is a water-soluble PEG derivative of natural-source vitamin E, which has amphiphilic structure comprising of hydrophilic polar head group (tocopherol succinate) and lipophilic alkyl tail (polyethylene glycol, PEG). Its bulky structure and large surface area make it become an excellent solubilizer, emulsifier, bioavailability enhancer of hydrophobic drugs [6, 8, 9]. Furthermore, TPGS could improve drug permeability through cell membranes by inhibiting P-glycoprotein (permeability glycoprotein, abbreviated as P-gp), thus enhancing absorption of drugs and reducing P-gp–mediated multi-drug resistance in tumor cells [10, 11, 12, 13]. It was also found that TPGS could effectively inhibit the growth of human lung carcinoma cells from in vitro cell culture and implanted in vivo [14]. The superior anticancer efficacy of TPGS is associated with its increasing ability to induce apoptosis and not due to its increased cell uptake into cells [14, 15,16]. Synergistic effects could be obtained by the use of combinations of vitamin E derivatives in the presence of other anticancer agents [15]. Random copolymerization is known to provide new materials with properties intermediate between those of the parent homopolymers [4]. This is a valuable method to fine-tune properties to the desired parameters. Therefore, in the present study, we synthesized a novel biodegradable poly(lactide-co-glycolide)-d-a-tocopheryl polyethylene glycol 1000 succinate (PLGA-TPGS) random copolymer in order to achieve high drug encapsulation efficiency, desired drug release profiles, good biocompatibility and improvement in drug permeability across cancer cell membranes, resulting in high cellular uptake and good cytotoxicity against human cervix carcinoma cells (HeLa) using docetaxel as a model anticancer drug due to its excellent therapeutic effects against a wide spectrum of cancers and its commercial success as the best seller among all the anticancer agents.

MATERIALS AND METHODS

Materials

D,L-lactide (3,6-dimethyl-1,4-dioxane-2,5-dione, $C_6H_8O_4$) with a purity greater than 99% was purchased from Aldrich, Milwaukee, USA. They were recrystallized at least three times from ethyl acetate before reaction to remove the residual impurities in the monomer. D-α-tocopheryl polyethylene glycol

1000 succinate (TPGS, $C_{33}O_5H_{54}(CH_2CH_2O)_{23}$) was from Sigma (St. Louis, MO, USA). Stannous octoate (Sn(OOCC7H15)2), glycolide (1,4-Dioxane-2,5-dione, $C_4H_4O_4$) (purity >99%) and PLGA (50:50, MW 50,000) were also purchased from Sigma (St. Louis, MO, USA). Docetaxel powder of purity 99.8% was purchased from Shanghai Jinhe Bio-Technology Co. Ltd (Shanghai, China). Acetonitrile and methanol were purchased from EM Science (ChromAR, HPLC grade, Mallinckrodt Baker, USA). All other chemicals used were of the highest quality commercially available. Ultrahigh pure water produced by Boon Environmental Tech. Industry Co., Ltd. (Tianjin, China) was utilized throughout all experiments. Human cervix carcinoma HeLa cells were provided by American Type Culture Collection (ATCC, Rockville, MD).

Synthesis of PLGA-TPGS Random Copolymer

PLGA-TPGS random copolymers were synthesized by ring-opening bulk polymerization of lactide and glycolide monomer with TPGS in the presence of stannous octoate as catalyst. Briefly, weighted amounts of glycolide, lactide, TPGS and 0.5 wt% stannous octoate (in distilled toluene) were added in a reaction flask. The mixture was heated to 145°C and allowed to react for 16 h. Synthesis was carried out under an oxygen- and moisture-free environment. The resulting product was dissolved in DCM and then precipitated in excess cold methanol to remove unreacted monomers and TPGS. The final product was collected by filtration and dried under high vacuum at 45°C for 48 h.

Characterization of PLGA-TPGS Random Copolymer

FTIR spectrophotometer (Thermo Nicolet, Madison, WI, USA) was used to investigate the molecular structure of PLGA-TPGS copolymer. In brief, the samples for FTIR analysis were prepared by grinding 99% KBr with 1% random copolymer and then pressing the mixture into a transparent tablet. The TPGS content and number-averaged molecular weight of the copolymer were determined by ^1H NMR in $CDCl_3$ at 300 Hz (Bruker ACF300). The weight-averaged molecular weight and molecular weight distribution were determined by gel permeation chromatography (Waters GPC analysis system with RI-G1362A refractive index detector, Waters, Milford, USA) column was used. The mobile phase was THF delivered at a flow rate of 1 ml/min. The injection volume was 50 μl sample solution (0.1% w/v polymer in mobile phase). The calibration curve was established by using polystyrene standard sample (molecular weights: 5.51×10^4, 1.39×10^4, 2.97×10^3 and 162, respectively). Thermogravimetric analysis (TGA, TGA 2050 thermogravimetric analyzer, USA) was carried out to investigate the thermal properties of the copolymers. During the TGA analysis, about 5–15 mg of the random copolymer sample was heated from 30 to 600°C at a rate of 10°C/min.

Preparation of Docetaxel-Loaded PLGA-TPGS Nanoparticles

The docetaxel-loaded PLGA-TPGS nanoparticles were prepared by a modified solvent extraction/evaporation method [17]. In brief, a given amount of docetaxel and 100 mg PLGA-TPGS copolymer were dissolved in 8 ml dichloromethane (DCM). The formed solution was poured into 120 ml 0.03% TPGS pure water solution under gentle stirring. The mixture was sonicated for 120 s at 25 W to form O/W single emulsion. The emulsion was then evaporated overnight to remove DCM. The particle suspension was centrifuged at 20,000 rpm for 15 min and then washed three times to remove the unloaded drug and surfactant. The resulted particles were resuspended in 10 ml water and freeze-dried for 2 days. In addition, the fluorescent coumarin-6–loaded nanoparticles were prepared in the same way, except 0.1% (w/v) coumarin-6 was encapsulated instead of docetaxel.

Characterization of Drug-Loaded PLGA-TPGS Nanoparticles

Size and Size Distribution

The particle size and size distribution of the nanoparticles were measured by Dynamic Light Scattering (Zetasizer Nano ZS90, Malvern Instruments LTD., Malvern, UK). One milligram of particles was suspended in 3 ml of pure deionized water before measurement. The measurement was performed in triplicate.

Surface Morphology

The nanoparticles were imaged by a field emission scanning electron microscopy (FESEM) system at an accelerating voltage of 5 kV. The particle surface was coated with platinum layer before being observed.

Surface Charge

The samples were prepared by diluting the nanoparticles suspension with pure deionized water. Zeta potential of the nanoparticles was measured by Laser Doppler Anemometry (LDA; Zetasizer Nano ZS90, Malvern Instruments LTD., Malvern, UK). The data were obtained with the average of three measurements.

Drug Loading and Encapsulation Efficiency (EE)

The docetaxel entrapped in the drug-loaded PLGA-TPGS nanoparticles was measured by HPLC (LC 1200, Agilent Technologies, Santa Clara, CA). A reverse-phase Inertsils C-18 column (150 × 4.6 mm, pore size 5 mm, GL science Inc, Tokyo, Japan) was used. Briefly, 5 mg nanoparticles were dissolved in 1 ml DCM. After DCM was evaporated in nitrogen atmosphere, the samples were extracted by 5 ml mobile phase (50/50 (v/v) acetonitrile/water solution). Twenty microliters of the clear solution was used for HPLC analysis. The flow rate of mobile phase was 1 ml/min. Retention time was controlled at 15 min. The column effluent was detected at 227 nm with a UV/VIS detector. The drug encapsulation efficiency was defined as the ratio between the amount of docetaxel entrapped in nanoparticles and that added in the process.

Differential Scanning Calorimetry (DSC)

The physical status of docetaxel inside the drug-loaded PLGA-TPGS nanoparticles was investigated by differential scanning calorimetry (DSC 822e, Mettler Toledo, Greifensee, Switzerland). The samples were purged with dry nitrogen at a flow rate of 20 ml/min. The temperature was ramped at a rate of 10°C/min.

In Vitro Drug Release

In brief, 15 mg drug-loaded PLGA-TPGS nanoparticles were dispersed in 5 ml release medium (phosphate buffer solution of pH 7.4 containing 0.1% w/v Tween 80) to form a suspension. The suspension was transferred into a Regenerated Cellulose Dialysis Membrane (Spectra/Por 6, MWCO = 1000, Spectrum, Houston, TX, USA). Then, the closed bag was put into a centrifuge tube and immersed in 15 ml release medium. The tube was put in an orbital water bath shaking at 120 rpm at 37.0°C. Ten milliliters of solutions was periodically removed for HPLC analysis and replaced with fresh medium. The collected samples were extracted with 2 ml DCM and reconstituted in 5 ml mobile phase. The DCM was evaporated by nitrogen stream. The analysis procedure was the same as for the measurement of encapsulation efficiency.

Cellular Uptake of Coumarin-6–Loaded PLGA-TPGS Nanoparticles

Human cervical adenocarcinoma cancer cell lines HeLa cells were cultured in Dubelco's modified essential medium (DMEM) supplemented with 10% fetal bovine serum and antibiotics. The culture was maintained in incubator containing 5% CO_2 at 37°C. The cells were incubated with 250 μg/ml coumarin-6–loaded nanoparticles at 37°C for 4 h, rinsed with cold PBS for three times and then fixed by methanol for 10 min. Cells were stained with DAPI for 15 min and washed three with PBS. Finally, cells were observed by confocal laser scanning microscope (CLSM, Olympus Fluoview FV-1000, Olympus Optical. Co., Ltd.,

Tokyo, Japan). The images of the cells were determined with differential interference contrast (DIC) channel, and the images of coumarin-6–loaded nanoparticles and the nuclei of the cells stained by DAPI were recorded with following channels: blue channel (DAPI) with excitation at 340 nm and green channel (coumarin-6) with excitation at 488 nm [18, 19].

In Vitro Cytotoxicity of PLGA-TPGS Nanoparticles

HeLa cells were seeded in 96-well plates at the density of 5,000 viable cells per well and incubated 24 h to allow cell attachment. The cells were incubated with docetaxel-loaded PLGA-TPGS nanoparticle suspension at 0.025, 0.25, 2.5, 10 and 25 μg/ml docetaxel concentrations and drug-free PLGA-TPGS nanoparticle suspension with equivalent nanoparticle concentrations of 0.25, 2.5, 25, 100 and 250 μg/ml for 24, 48 and 72 h, respectively. At the determined time, the formulations were replaced with DMEM containing MTT (5 mg/ml), and cells were then incubated for additional 4 h. MTT was aspirated off, and DMSO was added to dissolve the formazan crystals. Absorbance was measured at 570 nm using a microplate reader (Bio-Rad Model 680, UK). Untreated cells were taken as control with 100% viability, and cells without the addition of MTT were used as blank to calibrate the spectrophotometer to zero absorbance.

Statistical Methodology

The data are expressed as mean ± SD. The significance of differences was assessed by Student's t test and was considered significant when $p = 0.05$.

RESULTS AND DISCUSSIONS

Synthesis and Characterization of PLGA-TPGS Random Copolymer

The PLGA-TPGS random copolymer was synthesized in this research using the stannous octoate as catalyst. The reaction of synthesis is schematically described in Fig. 1. The hydroxyl end of TPGS served as initiator to selectively cleave acyl oxygen chain of lactide or glycolide.

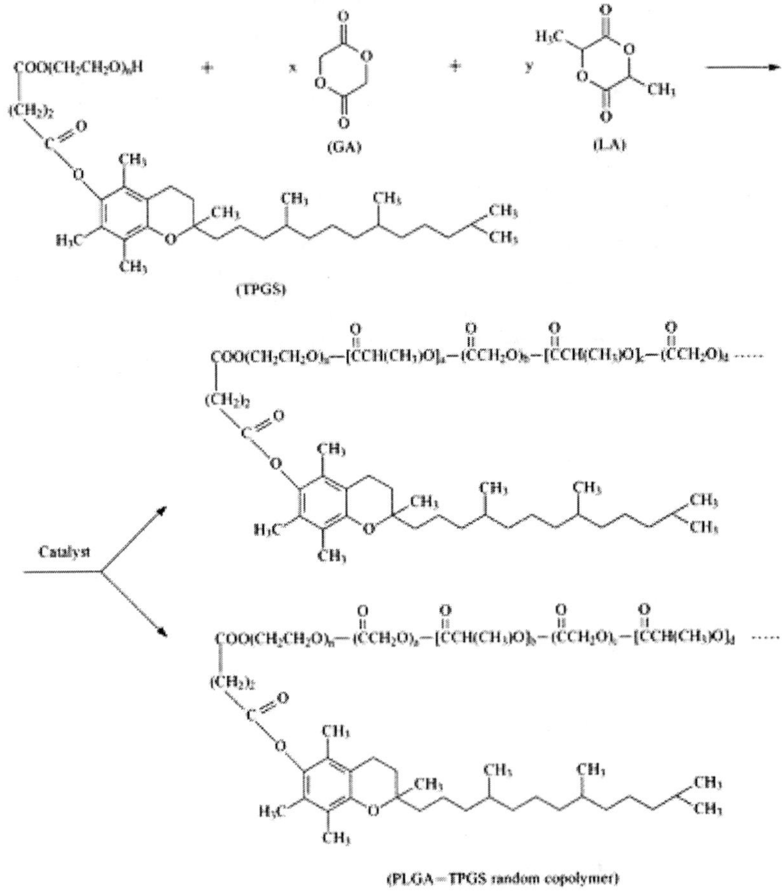

Figure 1. Schematic description of the synthesis of PLGA-TPGS random copolymer

The FTIR spectra of the PLGA-TPGS random copolymer and TPGS were showed in Fig. 2. The carbonyl band of TPGS appears at 1,730 cm^{-1}. For the synthesized random copolymer, the carbonyl band was shifted to 1,754 cm^{-1}. Overlapping of the CH stretching band of PLA at 2,945 cm^{-1} and that of TPGS at 2,880 cm^{-1} was observed. In the PLGA-TPGS copolymer, the CH stretching band of TPGS was decreased. The absorption band at 3,400–3,650 cm^{-1} is attributed to the terminal hydroxyl group and that at 1,045–1,500 cm^{-1} is due to the C–O stretching [20].

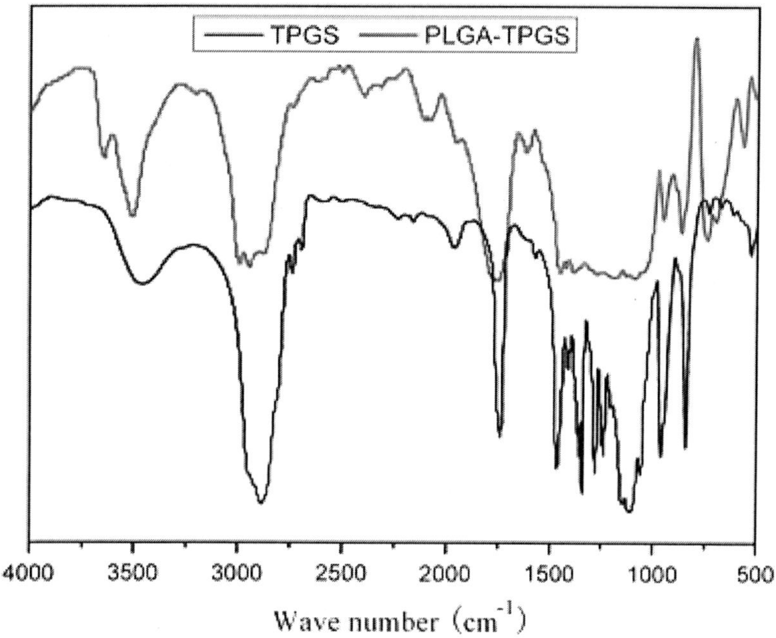

Figure 2. FTIR spectra of PLGA-TPGS random copolymer and TPGS

Figure 3 shows typical ^1H NMR spectra of the PLGA-TPGS random copolymer and TPGS monomer. The signals at 5.2 (peak a) and 1.69 ppm (peak d) were assigned to the –CH protons and methyl protons $–CH_3$ of PLA segment, respectively. The peak at 3.65 ppm (peak c) was assigned to the $–CH_2$ protons of PEO part of TPGS [6]. The peak at 4.82 was assigned to the $–CH_2$ of PGA [21]. The molecular weight of the PLGA-TPGS random copolymer was calculated using the ratio between the peak areas at 5.2 (peak a), 4.8 (peak b) and 3.65 (peak c). The number-averaged molecular weight of the PLGA-TPGS random copolymer was determined to be 21,747. The ratio of glycolide, lactide and TPGS molecular mass, which were integrated into the PLGA-TPGS random copolymers, is 50.61, 38.95 and 10.44%, respectively.

GPC analysis further confirmed that the PLGA-TPGS random copolymer was synthesized by the ring-opening polymerization. Figure 4 shows that the peak for TPGS appeared at 28.23 min. Instead, the peak of the random copolymer shifted to 18.58 min. There was just one narrow peak for the random copolymer, and the TPGS peak could not be detected. The polydispersity of the copolymer molecular weight was narrow, which was around 1.30. The number-averaged molecular weight calculated from the GPC chromatograph was 21,944. It appeared that the molecular weight measured from GPC and NMR could confirm each other.

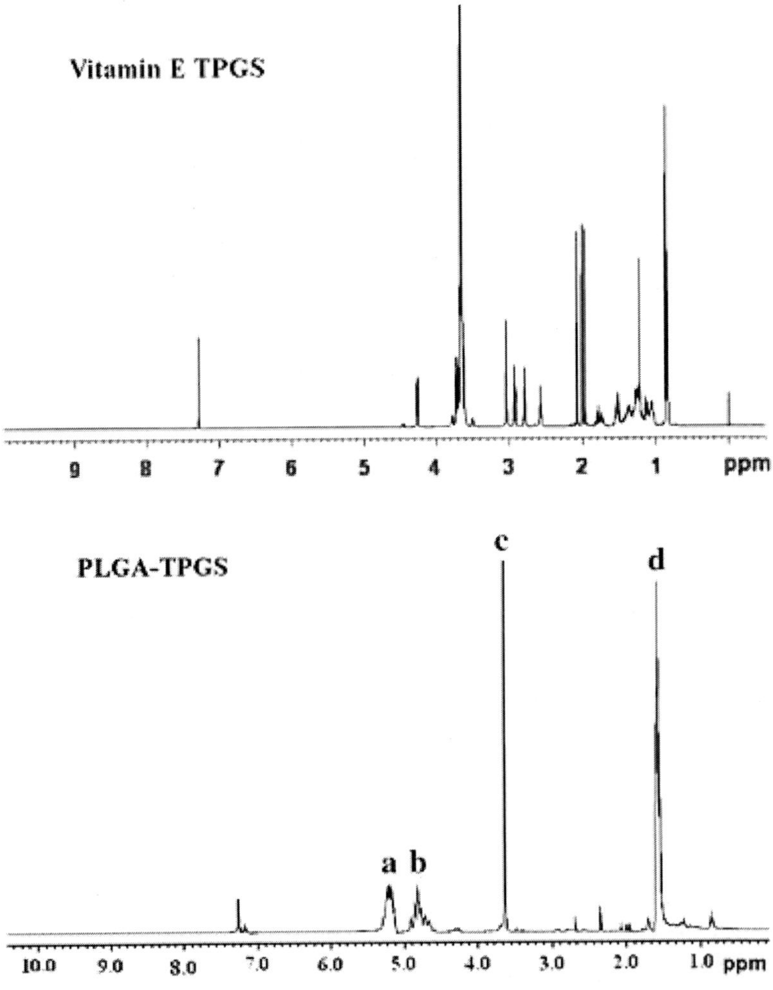

Figure 3. Typical ^{1}H-NMR spectra of PLGA-TPGS random copolymer and TPGS

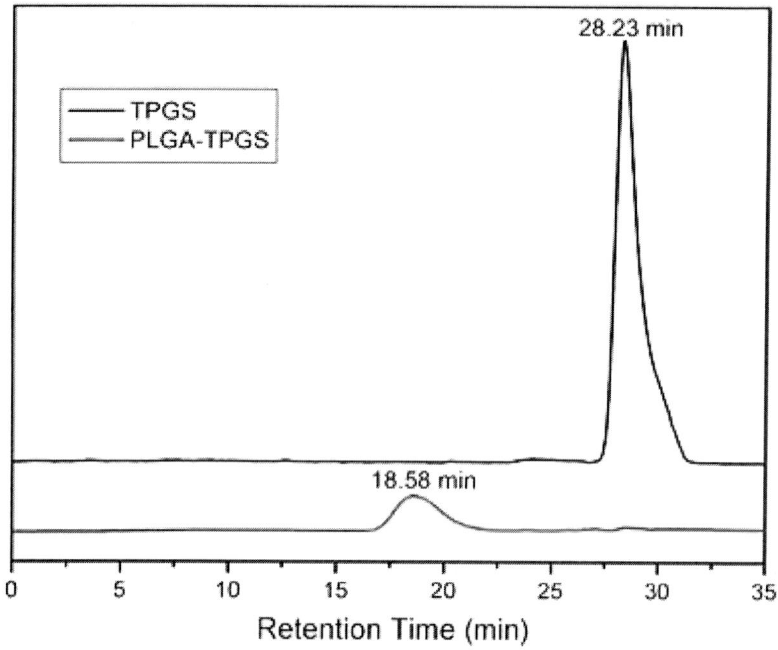

Figure 4. Typical GPC chromatograms of PLGA-TPGS random copolymer and TPGS

Thermogravimetric analysis (TGA) was performed on the synthesized PLGA-TPGS random copolymer in order to investigate its thermal property. Figure 5 shows the typical thermal degradation profiles for TPGS monomer and PLGA-TPGS random copolymer. It was observed that the thermal degradation profile of PLGA-TPGS random copolymer showed two regions of weight loss, which were different from a single mass loss for the TPGS monomer. Each turning point marked the combustion of a new component in the random copolymers. The 200–315°C and 315–450°C combustion zones were attributed to PLGA and TPGS part of copolymer, respectively. The TPGS composition of the PLGA-TPGS copolymer calculated from TGA was 10.71%, which could match very well with NMR result and also confirmed the synthesis of PLGA-TPGS random copolymer. Thus, TGA was a convenient means for evaluating the mass ratios of the PLGA-TPGS random copolymer. Liggins et al. [22] also found that PLA-MPEG copolymers demonstrated a biphasic thermal degradation profile, and TGA was applicable as composition calculation for PEGylated copolymers.

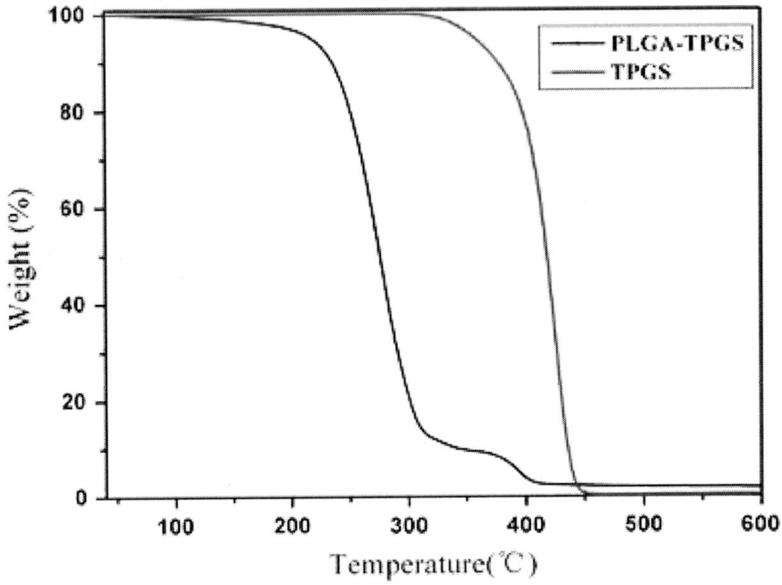

Figure 5. Thermogravimetric profiles of PLGA-TPGS random copolymer and TPGS

CHARACTERIZATION OF DRUG-LOADED NANOPARTICLES

Size, Size Distribution and Drug Encapsulation Efficiency

The size and size distribution of the docetaxel-loaded PLGA-TPGS nanoparticles prepared in this research are shown in Table 1. The particle size was found from 207.15 nm to 244.71 with size distribution of less than 0.4 polydispersity for samples without extra TPGS. Addition of TPGS in the process as emulsifier slightly increased the particle size, which agreed with the previous report [6]. The mean particle size was found around 265.43 nm with size distribution of 0.36 polydispersity for samples with the addition of 0.03% TPGS and around 290.25 nm with size distribution of 0.48 polydispersity for samples with the addition of 0.06% TPGS. The coating effect of TPGS on the particle surface and the aggregation of the formed nanoparticles because of extra TPGS may account for the increases in nanoparticle size.

Table 1. Characterization of drug-loaded nanoparticles

Polymer	Drug loading (%)	Surfactant	Size (nm)	PDI	ZP (mV)	EE (%)
PLGA-TPGS	2.5	No	207.15 ± 8. 46	0.321 ± 0.03		58.87 ± 3.25
PLGA-TPGS	5	No	223.92 ± 6.27	0.372 ± 0.04		52.58 ± 2.94
PLGA-TPGS	10	No	244.71 ± 6.65	0.415 ± 0.02	−24.09 ± 1.45	48.35 ± 5.73
PLGA-TPGS	10	0.03% TPGS	265.43 ± 6.52	0.364 ± 0.03	−18.03 ± 1.89	99.31 ± 0.56
PLGA-TPGS	10	0.06% TPGS	290.25 ± 7.64	0.485 ± 0.01	−15.22 ± 2.12	85.85 ± 3.14
PLGA	10	0.03% TPGS	233.83 ± 9.62	0.293 ± 0.03	−32.10 ± 0.65	75.63 ± 3.42

* *PDI* Polydispersity Index, *EE* Drug encapsulation efficiency, $n = 3$

Table 1 also shows the drug loading and surfactant effects on size and size distribution and the drug EE. The PLGA-TPGS nanoparticles prepared without the addition of emulsifier can result in a relative lower EE, which was found to be 48.35% for 10% drug loading and 58.87% for 2.5% drug loading. For the high drug loading of 10%, however, the EE of the docetaxel-loaded PLGA-TPGS nanoparticles can be improved by the addition of TPGS in the process as emulsifier. The drug EE increased significantly to near 100% for 10% drug loading when 0.03% TPGS was added as emulsifier and to 85.85% when 0.06% TPGS was added. Thus, too little emulsifier would not be enough to cover the interface and too much emulsifier would cause nanoparticle aggregation [23]. It can be seen from Table 1 that 0.03% TPGS used as an emulsifier did improve the EE of the PLGA-TPGS nanoparticles from 48.35 to 99.31% for a high drug loading of 10%.

Surface Charge

Zeta potential determines the particle stability in dispersion. High absolute value of the zeta potential suggests high surface charge of the nanoparticles, which leads to strong repellent interactions among the nanoparticles in dispersion and thus high stability [19]. As shown in Table 1, the absolute value of zeta potential for docetaxel-loaded PLGA-TPGS nanoparticles was found to be about 18.03 mV, which was slightly lower than that of nanoparticles fabricated from PLGA, indicating a slightly lower stability for docetaxel-loaded PLGA-TPGS nanoparticles. The negative surface charge of PLGA-TPGS nanoparticles may be attributed to the presence of ionized carboxyl groups of PLA and PGA segments on the nanoparticles surface.

Surface Morphology

Figure 6 shows the FESEM images of the docetaxel-loaded PLGA and PLGA-TPGS nanoparticles. Both PLGA and PLGA-TPGS nanoparticles were spherical in shape and appear smooth within the FESEM resolution level. Their size was observed to be around 250 nm, which further confirmed the results of particle size determined by DLS.

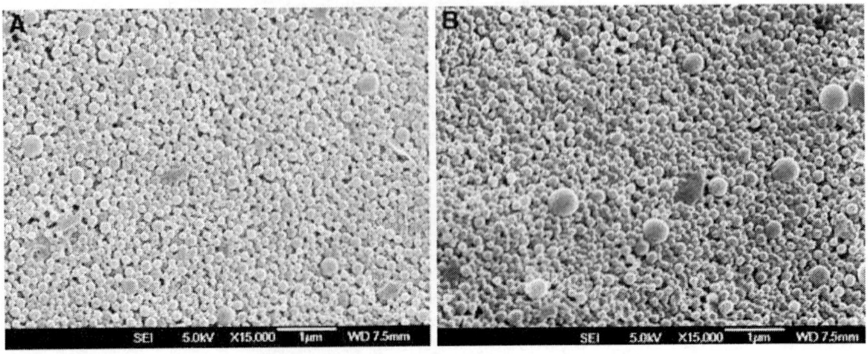

Figure 6. FESEM images of docetaxel-loaded nanoparticles with 0.03% TPGS as emulsifier and 10% drug loading. **a**, Docetaxel-loaded PLGA nanoparticles; **b**, docetaxel-loaded PLGA-TPGS nanoparticles

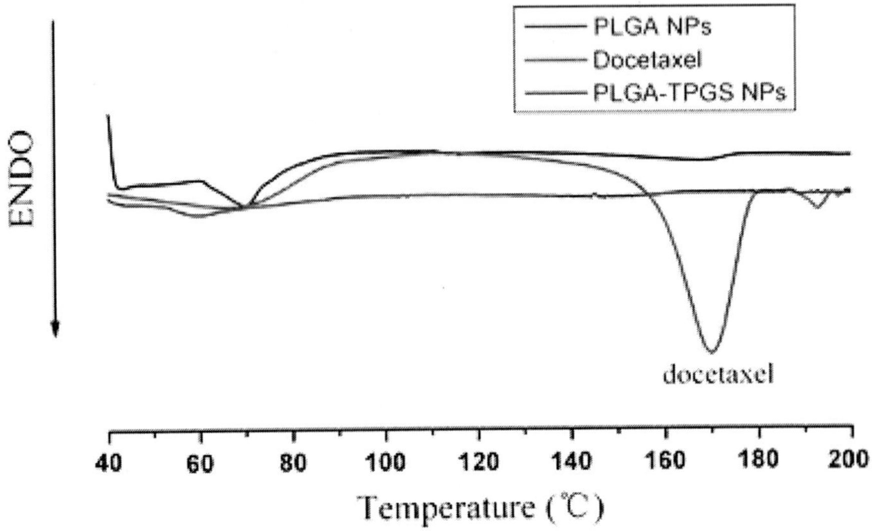

Figure 7. DSC thermograms of pure docetaxel, docetaxel-loaded PLGA-TPGS nanoparticles and docetaxel-loaded PLGA nanoparticles

Differential Scanning Calorimetry (DSC)

The physical state of docetaxel in the nanoparticles that could influence the in vitro and in vivo release of the drug from the systems was investigated by differential scanning calorimetry (DSC). Figure 7 shows the DSC thermograms of pure docetaxel powder, docetaxel-loaded PLGA-TPGS nanoparticles and docetaxel-loaded PLGA nanoparticles. The melting endothermic peak of pure docetaxel appeared at 173°C. However, no melting peak was detected for both nanoparticle formulations. Thus, it can be concluded that docetaxel inside the nanoparticles was either in an amorphous, disordered crystalline phase or in the solid solution state.

In Vitro Drug Release

As shown by Fig. 8, the in vitro drug release profiles of the docetaxel-loaded PLGA-TPGS nanoparticles and PLGA nanoparticles showed biphasic release pattern with an initial burst followed by a sustained release. The drug release from the PLGA-TPGS nanoparticles was found to be 22.83 and 58.61% of the encapsulated drug in the first three days and after 28 days, respectively, which was much faster than the docetaxel-loaded PLGA nanoparticles in the same periods. The faster drug release of the PLGA-TPGS nanoparticles may be caused by the lower molecular weight and the higher hydrophilicity of PLGA-TPGS random copolymer in comparison with the PLGA nanoparticles. This is also another advantage of the PLGA-TPGS nanoparticles versus the traditional PLGA nanoparticles, which were found to release the drug too slowly to meet the therapeutic needs.

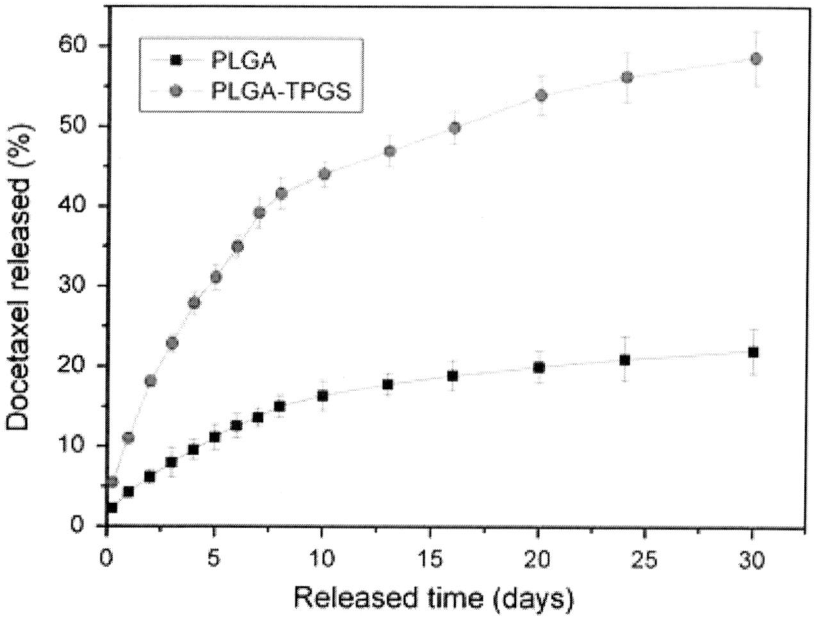

Figure 8. In vitro drug release profiles of docetaxel-loaded PLGA and PLGA-TPGS nanoparticles

Cellular Uptake of Coumarin-6–Loaded PLGA-TPGS Nanoparticles

Confocal laser scanning microscopy (CLSM) images (Fig. 9) showed that the fluorescence of the coumarin-6–loaded PLGA-TPGS nanoparticles (green) was closely located around the nuclei (blue, stained by DAPI), which indicated that the coumarin-6–loaded PLGA-TPGS nanoparticles had been internalized into the cells.

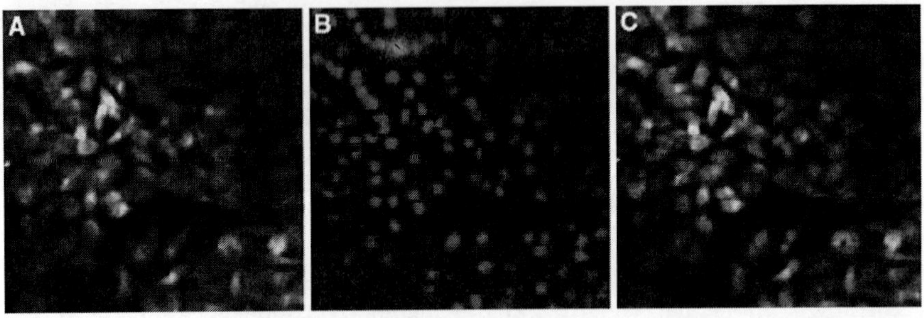

Figure 9. Confocal laser scanning microscopy (CLSM) images of HeLa cells after 4-h incubation with coumarin-6–loaded PLGA-TPGS nanoparticles at 37.0°C. The cells were stained by DAPI (*blue*) and the coumarin-6–loaded nanoparticles are*green*. The cellular uptake was visualized by overlaying images obtained by EGFP filter and DAPI filter: *left* image from EGFP channel (**a**); *center* image from DAPI channel (**b**); *right* image from combined EGFP channel and DAPI channel (**c**)

In Vitro Cytotoxicity of PLGA-TPGS Nanoparticles

The in vitro cytotoxicity of drug-free PLGA-TPGS nanoparticles and docetaxel-loaded PLGA-TPGS nanoparticles in HeLa cell line was assessed by the MTT assay. The range of concentrations of docetaxel (0.25–25 μg/ml) corresponds to plasma levels of the drug achievable in humans [24]. From Fig. 10, we can draw some general conclusions: (1) no obvious cytotoxicity was observed for the drug-free nanoparticles at various nanoparticle concentrations. The synthesized PLGA-TPGS copolymer was considered biocompatible since the drug-free PLGA-TPGS nanoparticles show little decrease in cellular viability for Hela cells; (2) the docetaxel-loaded PLGA-TPGS nanoparticles showed significant cytotoxicity against Hela cells. Hela cell viability decreased from 91.37% for drug-loaded PLGA-TPGS nanoparticles containing 0.25 μg/ml docetaxel to 82.65% for drug-loaded PLGA-TPGS nanoparticles containing 25 μg/ml docetaxel after 24-h cell culture (8.62% more effective in vitro therapeutic effect,$p < 0.05$). After 48-h cell culture, the cell viability decreased from 65% for drug-loaded PLGA-TPGS nanoparticles containing 0.25 μg/ml docetaxel to 47.21% for drug-loaded PLGA-TPGS nanoparticles containing 25 μg/ml docetaxel (17.79% more effective in vitro therapeutic effect, $p < 0.05$). Other concentrations of drug-loaded PLGA-TPGS nanoparticles showed similar in vitro therapeutic effects; (3) the cellular viability decreased with the incubation period in all cases. For example, Hela cell viability decreased from 88% for drug-loaded PLGA-TPGS nanoparticles containing 2.5 μg/ml docetaxel after 24-h cell culture to 60% after 48-h cell culture (28% more effective in vitro therapeutic effect, $p < 0.01$) and achieved 22.98% cell viability after 72-h cell culture (38.02% more effective in vitro therapeutic effect than that of 48-h treatment, $p < 0.01$). With the increase in docetaxel concentration, more effective in vitro therapeutic effects could be observed. The strongest in vitro therapeutic effect could be found in 25 μg/ml docetaxel concentration, which achieved 19.61% cell viability after 72-h cell culture, because the nanoparticles released the most amounts of drugs and the degradation of PLGA-TPGS random copolymer may release the most amounts of TPGS components that have synergistic anticancer activity in the presence of anticancer agent [14, 15, 16] after 72-h incubation.

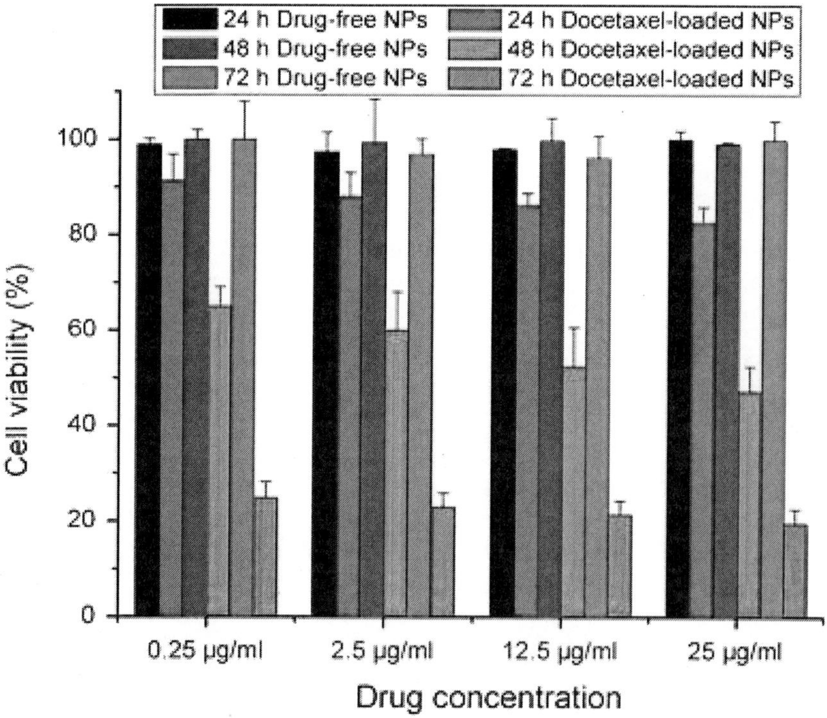

Figure 10. Cytotoxicity of Hela cells cultured with drug-free nanoparticles and docetaxel-loaded PLGA-TPGS nanoparticles containing 0.25, 2.5, 12.5 or 25 μg/ml docetaxel concentrations after 24-, 48- and 72-h cell culture. ($n = 3$)

CONCLUSION

For the first time, the poly(lactide-co-glycolide)-d-a-tocopheryl polyethylene glycol 1000 succinate (PLGA-TPGS) random copolymers were successfully synthesized as nanoparticle carrier of small molecular anticancer drugs with docetaxel as a model drug. The docetaxel-loaded PLGA-TPGS nanoparticles were prepared by a modified solvent extraction/evaporation method. The size of such nanoparticles was found to be around 250 nm. The docetaxel-loaded PLGA-TPGS nanoparticles could achieve much faster drug release in comparison with PLGA nanoparticles. In vitro cellular uptakes of such nanoparticles were investigated by CLSM, demonstrating the fluorescence PLGA-TPGS nanoparticles could be internalized by human cervix carcinoma cells (HeLa). The results showed that PLGA-TPGS–based nanoparticles were biocompatible, and the docetaxel-loaded PLGA-TPGS nanoparticles had significant cytotoxicity against Hela cells. The cytotoxicity against HeLa cells for PLGA-TPGS nanoparticles was in time- and concentration-dependent manner. In conclusion, PLGA-TPGS random copolymer could be acted as a novel and potential biocompatible polymeric matrix material applicable to nanoparticle-based drug delivery system for cancer chemotherapy.

MISC

Yuandong Ma and Yi Zheng contributed equally to this work.

ACKNOWLEDGMENTS

The authors are grateful for financial support from the National Natural Science Foundation of China (Grant No 30900291), China Postdoctoral Science Foundation (No. 20090450030), Shenzhen Bureau of Science, Technology & Information (No. JC200903180531A) and Shenzhen Nanshan Science and Technology Program (KJ02S0210900000109). The author owes an especial debt of gratitude to Prof. Feng Si-shen for his advice and assistance.

REFERENCES

1. Kawasaki ES, Player A: **Nanotechnology, nanomedicine, and the development of new, effective therapies for cancer.** *Nanomedicine* 2005,

2. Kim KY: **Nanotechnology platforms and physiological challenges for cancer therapeutics.** *Nanomedicine* 2007, **3:**103–110.

3. Sahoo SK, Parveen S, Panda JJ: **The present and future of nanotechnology in human health care.** *Nanomedicine*2007, **3:** 20–31.

4. Zhou S, Xu J, Yang H, Deng X: **Synthesis and characterization of biodegradable poly(ε-caprolactone)-polyglycolide-poly(ethylene glycol) monomethyl ether random copolymer.** *Macromol. Mater. Eng.* 2004, **289:** 576–580.

5. Duan Y, Sun X, Gong T, Wang Q, Zhang Z: **Preparation of DHAQ-loaded mPEG-PLGA-mPEG nanoparticles and evaluation of drug release behaviors in vitro/in vivo.** *J. Mater. Sci. Mater. Med.* 2006, **17:** 509–516.

6. Zhang Z, Feng SS: **Nanoparticles of poly(lactide)/vitamin E TPGS copolymer for cancer chemotherapy: synthesis, formulation, characterization and in vitro drug release.** *Biomaterials* 2006, **27:** 262–270.

7. Ravi Kumar MN: **Nano and microparticles as controlled drug delivery devices.** *J. Pharm. Pharm. Sci.* 2000, **3:** 234–258.

8. Traber MG, Schiano TD, Steephen AC, Kayden HJ, Shike M: **Efficacy of water-soluble vitamin E in the treatment of vitamin-E malabsorption in short-bowel syndrome.** *Am. J. Clin. Nutr.* 1994, **59:** 1270–1274.

9. Mu L, Feng SS: **A novel controlled release formulation for the anticancer drug paclitaxel (Taxol®): PLGA nanoparticles containing vitamin E TPGS.** *J. Control. Release* 2003, **86:** 33–48

10. Ling Y, Huang YS: **Preparation and release efficiency of poly (lactic-co-glycolic) acid nanoparticles for drug loaded paclitaxel.** In *7th Asian-Pacific Conference on Medical and Biological Engineering APCMBE, IFMBE Proceedings.* Edited by: Peng Y, Wen X. Springer, Berlin, Heidelberg; 2008:514–517.

11. Fischer JR, Harkin KR, Freeman LC: **Concurrent administration of water-soluble vitamin E can increase the oral bioavailability of cyclosporine A in healthy dogs.** *Vet. Ther.* 2002, **3:** 465–473.

12. Dintaman JM, Silverman JA: **Inhibition of P-glycoprotein by Dalpha-tocopheryl polyethylene glycol 1000 succinate (TPGS).** *Pharm. Res.* 1999, **16:** 1550–1556.

13. Yu L, Bridgers A, Polli J, Vicker A, Long S, Roy A, Winnike R, Coffin M: **Vitamin E-TPGS increases absorption flux of an HIV protease inhibitor by enhancing its solubility and permeability.** *Pharm. Res.* 1999, **16:** 1812–1817.

14. Youk HJ, Lee E, Choi MK, Lee YJ, Chung JH, Kim SH, Lee CH, Lin SJ: **Enhanced anticancer efficacy of alpha-tocopheryl succinate by conjugation with polyethylene glycol.** *J. Control. Release* 2005, **107:** 43–52.

15. Constantinou C, Papas A, Constantinou AI: **Vitamin E and cancer: an insight into the anticancer activities of vitamin E isomers and analogs.** *Int. J. Cancer* 2008, **123:** 739–752.

16. Neuzil J, Tomasetti M, Zhao Y, Dong LF, Birringer M, Wang XF, Low P, Wu K, Salvatore BA, Ralph SJ: **Vitamin E analogs, a novel group of "mitocans," as anticancer agents: the importance of being redox-silent.** *Mol. Pharmacol.* 2007, **71:**1185–1199.

17. Mei L, Sun H, Jin X, Zhu D, Sun R, Zhang M, Song C: **Modified paclitaxel-loaded nanoparticles for inhibition of hyperplasia in a rabbit arterial balloon injury model.** *Pharm. Res.* 2007, **24:** 955–962.

18. Mei L, Zhang Y, Zheng Y, Tian G, Song C, Yang D, Chen H, Sun H, Tian Y, Liu K, Li Z, Huang L: **A novel docetaxel-loaded poly (ε-caprolactone)/pluronic F68 nanoparticle overcoming multidrug resistance for breast cancer treatment.** *Nanoscale Res. Lett.* 2009, **4:** 1530–1539.

19. Yan F, Zhang C, Zheng Y, Mei L, Tang L, Song C, Sun H, Huang L: **The effect of poloxamer 188 on nanoparticle morphology, size, cancer cell uptake, and cytotoxicity.** *Nanomedicine* 2010,**6**(1):170–178.

20. Liu K, Kiran E: **High-pressure solution blending of poly(ε-caprolactone) with poly(methyl methacrylate) in acetone plus carbon dioxide.** *Polymer* 2008, **49:** 1555–1561.

21. Gu SY, Wang ZM, Zhang CY, Ren J: **Synthesis and evaluation of a biodegradable material with cell recognition motives.** *Carbohydr. Polym.* 2008, **74:** 572–578.

22. Liggins RT, Burt HM: **Polyether-polyester diblock copolymers for the preparation of paclitaxel loaded polymeric micelle formulations.** *Adv. Drug Deliv. Rev.* 2002, **54:** 191–202.

23. Feng SS, Huang GF: **Effects of emulsifiers on the controlled release of paclitaxel (Taxol (R)) from nanospheres of biodegradable polymers.** *J. Control. Release* 2001, **71:** 53–69.

24. Raymond E, Hanauske A, Faivre S: **Effects of prolonged versus short-term exposure paclitaxel (Taxol) on human tumor colony-forming units.** *Anticancer Drugs* 1997, **8:** 379–385.

Index